COMPLETE IN THREE VOLUMES

Radio REPLIES

First Volume

Given from the Catholic Broadcasting Station 2SM
Sydney, Australia

by

THE REV. DR. LESLIE RUMBLE, M.S.C.

Edited in Collaboration with

REV. CHARLES MORTIMER CARTY
Diocesan Missionary

With a Preface by

RT. REV. MSGR. FULTON J. SHEEN, D.D.

•

1588 QUESTIONS and ANSWERS
on
CATHOLICISM AND PROTESTANTISM

These books are now widely used as texts and reference
books in Study Clubs, High Schools, Colleges, Universities, Newman Clubs, Novitiates and Seminaries.

Invaluable for the uninformed Catholic—the educated
and uneducated lapsed Catholic and
Prospective Convert.

WIDE CIRCULATION AT MISSIONS AND RETREATS

•

*For paper or cloth bound copies of Volumes I, II & III address
your order directly to*

FATHERS RUMBLE and CARTY
**Radio Replies Press Society
St. Paul 1, Minn., U. S. A.**

TAN BOOKS AND PUBLISHERS, INC.
Rockford, Illinois 61105

IMPRIMATUR:

John Gregory Murray
Archbishop of St. Paul, Minnesota
February 11, 1938

Copyright © 1938 by Radio Replies Press Society.

Copyright © 1979 by TAN Books and Publishers, Inc.

Originally published in 1938 by Radio Replies Press Society,
St. Paul, Minnesota.

Library of Congress Catalog Card Number: 79-51938

ISBN: 0-89555-089-X

Complete and unabridged.

Printed and bound in the United States of America

uli

TAN BOOKS AND PUBLISHERS, INC.
P.O. Box 424
Rockford, Illinois 61105

1979

TABLE OF CONTENTS

ANALYTICAL INDEX

(Numbers refer to paragraphs)

CHAPTER TEN—THE CHURCH AND HER DOGMAS

CHAPTER ELEVEN—THE CHURCH IN HER MORAL TEACHINGS

CHAPTER TWELVE—THE CHURCH IN HER WORSHIP

CHAPTER THIRTEEN—THE CHURCH AND SOCIAL WELFARE

INTRODUCTION TO THE AMERICAN EDITION
OF "RADIO REPLIES"

"Radio Replies" by Rev. Dr. Rumble, M.S.C., is the result of five years of answering questions during a one-hour Question Box Program over Radio Station 2SM Sydney, N.S.W. The revision of "Radio Replies" for American readers was prompted by the widespread interest the Australian edition created among Protestants and Catholics during the summer of 1937, when I was carrying on as a Catholic Campaigner for Christ, the Apostolate to the man in the street through the medium of my trailer and loud-speaking system. In the distribution of pamphlets and books on Catholicism "Radio Replies" proved the most talked of book carried in my trailer display of Catholic literature. The clergy and laymen engaged in Street Preaching agree that it is not so much what you say over the microphone in answer to questions from open air listeners but what you GET INTO THEIR HANDS TO READ.

My many converts of the highways and parks throughout the Archdiocese of St. Paul have embraced the faith as a result of studying this book. Whole families have come into the Church through reading the book by this renowned convert from Anglicanism. The delay in getting copies from Sydney and the prohibitive cost of the book on this side of the universe led me to petition the author to have published a CHEAP AMERICAN EDITION in order to get this encyclopedia of Catholic Doctrine into the hands of fellow citizens. Because of the author's genius for brevity, preciseness, fearlessness and keen logic that avoids the usually long Scriptural and Traditional arguments of the average question and answer book, which is beyond the capacity of the man in the street, this manual of 1,588 questions and replies has already attracted readers throughout Australia, New Zealand, Africa, India, England, Ireland, Canada and now the United States.

The questions he answers are the questions I had to answer before friendly and hostile audiences throughout my summer campaign. The piquant and provocative subject matter of this book makes it a fascinating assembly of 300 or more worth-while pamphlet tracts, a dictionary of doctrine for the desk of the FAMILY, the STUDENT, the SHOP HAND, the OFFICE WORKER, the ATTORNEY, the DOCTOR, the TEACHER, and the PREACHER. It is a handy standard reference book of excellence for popular questions which are more than ever being asked by restless and bewildered multitudes. It is a textbook for the Confraternities of Christian Doctrine Classes and Study Clubs.

A non-Catholic Professor after reading the book stated that, "If the Catholic Church could defend herself so logically as 'Radio Replies' demonstrates, then I do not see why you don't get more converts." Members of the Knights of Columbus, the Holy Name Societies and numerous women's societies have written in that they no longer have to apologetically say, "I can't answer that one." Catholic students in non-sectarian colleges and universities write in that they now walk the campus with this book under their arms, ready for all challenges and that this manual of ready reference has cured their INFERIORITY COMPLEX ON EXPOSITION OF CATHOLIC CLAIMS. Lapsed Catholics have come into my trailer-office to confess that the reading of "Radio Replies" has brought them back to the Church.

I am grateful to His Excellency Archbishop John G. Murray, D.D. for his approval of this compendium of dogmatic and moral theology for readers of the American Commonwealth and I am deeply appreciative to Rt. Rev. Msgr. Fulton J. Sheen, D.D. for writing the Preface to this American edition.

From my experience on the Catholic Radio Hour, on the lecture platform, and in the pulpit, I do not hesitate to say that HERE AT LAST is the book that has something for everybody, the book for the UNINFORMED CATHOLIC, THE UNEDUCATED AND EDUCATED LAPSED CATHOLIC, and the PROSPECTIVE CONVERT.

REV. CHARLES MORTIMER CARTY

PREFACE

There are not over a hundred people in the United States who hate the Catholic Church. There are millions, however, who hate what they wrongly believe to be the Catholic Church—which is, of course, quite a different thing. These millions can hardly be blamed for hating Catholics because Catholics "adore statues"; because they "put the Blessed Mother on the same level with God"; because they say "indulgence is a permission to commit sin"; because the Pope "is a Fascist"; because the "Church is the defender of Capitalism." If the Church taught or believed any one of these things it should be hated, but the fact is that the Church does not believe nor teach any one of them. It follows then that the hatred of the millions is directed against *error* and not against *truth*. As a matter of fact, if we Catholics believed all of the untruths and lies which were said against the Church, we probably would hate the Church a thousand times more than they do.

If I were not a Catholic, and were looking for the true Church in the world today, I would look for the one Church which did not get along well with the world; in other words, I would look for the Church which the world hates. My reason for doing this would be, that if Christ is in any one of the churches of the world today, He must still be hated as He was when He was on earth in the flesh. If you would find Christ today, then find the Church that does not get along with the world. Look for the Church that is hated by the world, as Christ was hated by the world. Look for the Church which is accused of being behind the times, as Our Lord was accused of being ignorant and never having learned. Look for the Church which men sneer at as socially inferior, as they sneered at Our Lord because He came from Nazareth. Look for the Church which is accused of having a devil, as Our Lord was accused of being possessed by Beelzebub, the Prince of Devils. Look for the Church which, in seasons of bigotry, men say must be destroyed in the name of God as men crucified Christ and thought they had done a service to God. Look for the Church which the world rejects because it claims it is infallible, as Pilate rejected Christ because He called Himself the Truth. Look for the Church which is rejected by the world as Our Lord was rejected by men. Look for the Church which amid the confusion of conflicting opinions, its members love as they love Christ, and respect its Voice as the very voice of its Founder, and the suspicion will grow, that if the Church is unpopular with the spirit of the world, then it is unworldly, and if it is unworldly, it is other-worldly. Since it is other-worldly it is infinitely loved and infinitely hated as was Christ Himself. But only that which is Divine can be infinitely hated and infinitely loved. Therefore the Church is Divine.

If then, the hatred of the Church is founded on erroneous beliefs, it follows that basic need of the day is instruction. Love depends on knowledge for we cannot aspire nor desire the unknown. Our great country is filled with what might be called *marginal Christians,* i. e., those who live on the fringe of religion and who are descendants of Christian living parents, but who now are Christians only in name. They retain a few of its ideals out of indolence and force of habit; they know the glorious history of Christianity only through certain emasculated forms of it, which have married the spirit of the age and are now dying with it. Of Catholicism and its sacraments, its pardon, its grace, its certitude and its peace, they know nothing except a few inherited prejudices. And yet they are good people who want to do the right thing, but who have no definite philosophy concerning it. They educate their children without religion, and yet they resent the compromising morals of their children. They would be angry if you told them they were not Christian, and yet they do not believe that Christ is God. They resent being called pagans and yet they never take a practical cognizance of the existence of God. There is only one thing of which they are certain and that is that things are not right as they are. It is just that single certitude which makes them what might be called the great "potentials," for they are ready to be pulled in either of two directions. Within a short time they must take sides; they must either gather with Christ or they must scatter; they must either be with Him or against Him; they must either be on the cross as other Christs, or under it as other executioners. Which way will these *marginal Christians* tend? The answer depends upon those who have the faith. Like the multitudes who followed Our Lord into the desert, they are as sheep without a shepherd. They are waiting to be shepherded either with the sheep or goats. Only this much is certain. Being human and having hearts they want more than class struggle and economics; they want Life, they want Truth, and they want Love. In a word, they want Christ.

It is to these millions who believe wrong things about the Church and to these *marginal Christians*, that this little book is sent. It is not to prove that they are "wrong"; it is not to prove that we are "right"; it is merely to present the truth in order that the truth may conquer through the grace of God. When men are starving, one need not go to them and tell them to avoid poison; nor to eat bread because there are vitamins in bread. One need only go to them and tell them that they are starving and here is bread, and the laws of nature will do the rest. This book of "Radio Replies" with 1,588 questions and answers goes out on a similar mission. Its primary task is not to humble the erroneous; not to glorify the Catholic Church as intellectual and self-righteous, but to present the truth in a calm, clear manner in order that with the grace of God souls may come to the blessed embrace of Christ.

It is not only the point of "Radio Replies" to prove that the Church is the only completely soul-satisfying Church in existence at the present day; it is also to suggest that the Catholic Church is the only Church existing today which goes back to the time of Christ. History is so very clear on this point, it is curious how many minds miss its obviousness. When therefore you, the readers of "Radio Replies" in the twentieth century, wish to know about Christ and about His early Church, and about His mysteries, we ask you to go not only to the written records but to the living Church which began with Christ Himself. That Church or that Mystical Person which has been living all these centuries is the basis of our faith and to us Catholics it speaks this way: "I live with Christ. I saw His Mother and I know her to be a Virgin and the loveliest and purest of all women in heaven or on earth; I saw Christ at Caesarea-Philippi, when after changing Simon's name to Rock He told him he was the rock upon which the Church would be built and that it would endure unto the consummation of the world. I saw Christ hanging on a cross and I saw Him rise from His tomb; I saw Magdalene rush to His feet; I saw the angels clad in white beside the great stone; I was in the Cenacle room when doubting Thomas put fingers into His hands; I was on Olivet when He ascended into heaven and promised to send His Spirit to the apostles to make them the foundation of His new Mystical Body on earth. I was at the stoning of Stephen, saw Saul hold the garments of those who slew him, and later I heard Saul, as Paul, preach Christ and Him crucified; I witnessed the beheading of Peter and Paul in Rome, and with my very eyes saw tens of thousands of martyrs crimson the sands with their blood, rather than deny the faith Peter and Paul had preached unto them; I was living when Boniface was sent to Germany, when Augustine when to England, Cyril and Methodius to the Poles, and Patrick to Ireland; at the beginning of the ninth century I recall seeing Charlemagne crowned as king in matters temporal as Peter's vicar was recognized as supreme in matters spiritual; in the thirteenth century I saw the great stones cry out in tribute to me, and burst into Gothic Cathedrals; in the shadows of those same walls I saw great Cathedrals of thought arise in the prose of Aquinas and Bonaventure, and in the poetry of Dante; in the sixteenth century I saw my children softened by the spirit of the world leave the Father's house and reform the faith instead of reforming discipline which would have brought them back again into my embrace; in the last century and at the beginning of this I heard the world say it could not accept me because I was behind the times. I am not behind the times, I am only behind the scenes. I have adapted myself to every form of government the world has ever known; I have lived with Caesars and kings, tyrants and dictators, parliaments and presidents, monarchies and republics. I have welcomed every advance of science, and were it not for me the great records of the pagan world would not have been preserved. It is true I have not changed my doctrine, but that is because the 'doctrine is not mine but His who sent Me.' I change my garments which belong to time, but not my Spirit which belongs to eternity. In the course of my long life I have seen so many modern ideas become unmodern, that I know I shall live to chant a requiem over the modern ideas of this day, as I chanted it over the modern ideas of the last century. I celebrated the nineteen-hundredth anniversary of the death of my Redeemer and yet I am no older now than then, for my Spirit is Eternal, and the Eternal never ages. I am the abiding Personage of the centuries. I am the contemporary of all civilizations. I am never out of date, because the dateless; never out of time, because the timeless. I have four great marks: I am One, because I have the same Soul I had in the beginning; I am Holy, because that Soul is the Spirit of Holiness; I am Catholic, because that Spirit pervades every living cell of my Body; I am Apostolic, because my origin is identical with Nazareth, Galilee and Jerusalem. I shall grow weak when my members become rich and cease to pray, but *I shall never die*. I shall be persecuted as I am persecuted now in Mexico and Russia; I shall be crucified as I was on Calvary, but I shall rise again, and finally when time shall be no more, and I shall have grown to my full stature, then shall I be taken into heaven as the bride of my Head, Christ, where the celestial nuptials shall be celebrated, and God shall be all in all, because His Spirit is Love and Love is Heaven."

RT. REV. MSGR. FULTON J. SHEEN, D.D.

AUTHOR'S FOREWORD

THE matter contained in this book is the result of a "Question and Answer" Session conducted by the writer during a continuous period of five years by Radio in Sydney, N.S.W. The Session, given from the Catholic Station 2SM on Sunday evenings, averages one hour in duration, from 7 to 8 p.m., and so great has been the interest awakened that letters have poured in from all the States of Australia, as well as from New Zealand. The work still continues with unabated appeal, apparently because, even though the same difficulties recur at times, they are proposed from so many varying aspects by different inquirers that no sense of sameness is experienced. Certainly no questions have ever had to be improvised to keep the Session fully occupied. The results of the work have more than justified the labor it has entailed. Constant expressions of gratitude are received from Catholics, who appreciate the deeper instruction in their faith the Sessions have afforded them; from careless Catholics who have returned to the fervent practice of their religion; and, above all, from non-Catholics, whether to acknowledge the dispelling of their prejudices, or to announce their actual conversion to the Catholic Church. As many as thirty notifications of conversion have been received from distant places in a month. And by no means all, of course, think to write in of God's goodness to them.

That a personal element has been unavoidable will be evident from these few typical questions and answers due to people who found it utterly incredible that anyone in his senses could become a Catholic. Such questions varied through all the grades of suspicion, grudging concession, accusation, prediction, and compassion.

Q. *Are you a Catholic born, or were you converted to the Catholic Church in later life?*

A. I was born of Protestant parents and brought up as a Protestant, joining the Catholic Church in later life.

Q. *It is so unbelievable that one who has tasted the open, free, and sincere worship of a Protestant Church could change to the Catholic religion.*

A. If it be a fact, and it is a fact, it is not unbelievable. You face so many things that are not facts, that you ought to feel no difficulty in facing things that are facts. As for the open, free, and sincere worship of a Protestant Church, I did taste it, but for me it proved in the end to be not only open, but empty; it was altogether too free from God's prescriptions; and whilst I admit that many Protestants are quite sincere, I would not have been sincere had I remained a Protestant against my convictions. So I followed the grace God gave me, and became a Catholic. In doing so, not for a moment have I lost my respect for good Protestants.

As for your finding it unbelievable that I should change to the *Catholic* religion, that is inevitable when you entertain such notions of that Catholic religion. Whilst I entertained similar notions I was as opposed to it as you are. But I can assure you that you have not a true idea of the Catholic Church, your notions being based upon lack of information, or even upon wrong information.

Q. *Your answers seem to show culture and refinement.*

A. That is a very candid admission. Apparently you never dreamed that a Catholic could be cultured or refined. The dispelling of this prejudice is one good result of these talks.

Q. You are a Catholic with a Protestant broad mind, fashioned at home when your mind was plastic, before you became subservient to the Catholic Church.

A. I am a Catholic, I hope with a broad mind, though I hope still more, not with a Protestant mind. As for the plastic period, my broad-minded Protestant teachers taught me to dislike the Catholic Church intensely, whilst my subserviency to the Church is but submission to the Will of God, Whom only "Thou shalt serve."

Q. You have a good knowledge of the Bible, but you must have acquired it when you were a Protestant, not since you became a Catholic and a Priest.

A. I have constantly read the Bible since the age of ten. In my Protestant days I knew the Authorized Version fairly well, and if the moment a man begins to read the Bible it leads him out of the Catholic Church, you will find it difficult to explain how this did not keep me out. Yet I can assure you that not until I did become a Catholic did my real study and understanding of the Bible begin. Before becoming a Priest I had to study Sacred Scripture daily for many years, and far from shaking my faith, this has but confirmed my decision to live and die a member of the Catholic Church.

Q. If you really knew Catholicism, you would not advocate it.

A. You are convinced that you have a right idea of Catholicism, and cannot see how I could accept it, if *that* be Catholicism. But *that* is not Catholicism. And since our ideas conflict as to what Catholicism really is like, the only thing to do is to ask whose ideas are more likely to be correct. I have given many years to the study of Catholicism, and am, at present, professor of theology in a Catholic Seminary. The authorities of the Catholic Church at least give me credit for knowing the Catholicism that must be taught to future Priests. How much time have you devoted to the study of Catholicism?

Q. You can be mistaken, even though sincere.

A. That is quite true, and I have often been mistaken, as most men at times. And it is precisely to make sure that I will not be mistaken in the supremely important matter of religion that I cling to a Church which cannot be mistaken, but must be right where I might be wrong. God knew that so many sincere men would make mistakes that He deliberately established an infallible Church to preserve them from error where it was most important that they should not go wrong.

Q. You once quoted an Anglican clergyman, who said that ex-Catholics in Anglicanism were weeds thrown out of the Catholic Church by the Pope. Are you not a weed thrown out of Protestantism and taking root in the Catholic garden?

A. No. I was not thrown out of Protestantism. A Priest, ex-communicated because he will not live up to Catholic ideals, can often find a home in some Protestant Church. He has gone lower, and he knows it. I was attracted by the higher ideals of the Catholic Church, and begged as a favor to be allowed to share in Catholic privileges. After twenty years of Catholic life, that is still my happiest memory, notwithstanding the fact that the Catholic Church demands a far higher standard than any other Church.

Q. What do you hope to gain by deserting, and then publicly denouncing, the faith of your forefathers?

A. By deserting the faith of my immediate forefathers, I went back to the faith of their forefathers, and to the true religion they should never have deserted. They deserted truth for error; I deserted error for truth. That was what I hoped to gain, and I have gained it.

As for publicly denouncing the faith of my forefathers, that is not the object of these talks. My purpose is to explain the Catholic position to those who desire such information, for I know that a clear explanation of the truth will carry its own weight with unprejudiced people. If inquirers ask me why the Catholic Church condemns their religion, I tell them sincerely and frankly, and I presume that this is what they wish.

Q. You questioned what you were taught and changed, though you did not change entirely. You will further question the doctrines of the Catholic Church, and perhaps change your religion again.

A. It is true that I changed, and that I did not change entirely. I changed to Catholicism, but still preserve traces of my original lineaments, am still the son of the same human father and mother, and still have a tendency to some of the same faults which grew up with me from my youth.

Also I shall certainly ask further questions about Catholic teaching, since its depths are almost inexhaustible, even though I am too sure that God speaks through the Catholic Church to dream of questioning those teachings. It is one thing to ask questions about a doctrine revealed by God; quite another thing to question it.

Q. You are a Protestant tool used by the Catholic Church, but you have not been made to realize that yet.

A. I have long ago realized that I am but an instrument in God's work. I did not redeem the world. But I am not a Protestant tool, for I renounced Protestantism long ago.

Q. When you have done your all for Rome in public, you will be put into a Monastery to learn the beauty of humiliation and starvation.

A. I am already a member of a Religious Order, and live in a Monastery, although I have never been invited to starve myself. As for the beauty of humility, I hope to learn that some day, being invited to do so by the Christ who said, "Learn of Me, because I am meek and humble of heart."

Q. Then you will be sent to the Confessional to hear secret sins of women which will appal your senses, weakened already by your so-called purifications.

A. I have been in the Confessional very, very often, and have heard thousands of confessions. You have never been there, and conclude that what you imagine to be true must be true. Also, you seem to have a shockingly low estimate of your own sex. Let me tell you a few things from experience. A Priest in the Confessional does not want material descriptions, but facts, and he is in a far happier position than the average medical man. As for being appalled, I have never heard confessions without being edified by the wonderful dispositions of sorrow in the penitents, and without a deeper sympathy for the frailties of human nature, whether through mental darkness or weakness of will.

Q. When you realize it all, mental torment will be your lot, and your soul will be plunged in gloom.

A. Not a bit of it. I do not believe in gloom-religions, and am the sworn enemy of mental torment. I fully realize everything, and am bubbling over with happiness all the day long. You will at least allow me to be the judge of my own interior dispositions.

Q. *I shall pray for you that you may become free, and not tied down by the doctrines of a Church.*

A. If God hears your prayers, I shall become even a better Catholic. I shall be set free more and more from all error by the teachings of the Catholic Church, and liberated from my faults and defects by her wonderful Sacraments and other means of grace.

The foregoing Questions and Answers are already an indication of the spirit in which these Sessions have been conducted. But perhaps I could not do better than reproduce the general opening talk itself, setting out the objects of the undertaking. In substance, it was as follows:

"Good-evening, listeners all. For some time I have been promising to give a Session dealing with questions of religion and morality, in which the listeners themselves should decide what is of interest to them. Such a Session will commence next Sunday evening, and I invite you to send in any questions you wish on these subjects. To-night, however, let us see what I can promise you in regard to this Session.

"Will it be of interest? Why, religion has ever been one of the most interesting things under the sun. Men get excited about few other things as they do about religion. Something or other is likely to upset a man sometimes, but religion alone seems to be able to do so almost always. Dispute with him about ordinary events, he is quite undisturbed; dispute his policies, and more often than not he will laugh; but start on religion, and you find it a very different matter. This is because religion is fundamentally one of the deepest things in man. He is a religious animal. It is part of his human nature which finds a religion of some sort as natural to it as breathing.

"Now by listening-in to other people's difficulties, you will find many of your own problems solved, apart from your interest in what fellow men are actually thinking themselves. We are curious beings. We would not turn up the last pages of a novel as soon as we begin it if we were not. And we like novels because they deal with human life. We are so interested in other people's experiences that we have to invent them. But the truth that is stranger than fiction is usually a bit shy. It is in such a Session as this that you will hear it. And many of the questions will express just your own difficulties, for it is a fact that if you set twenty men thinking you can be sure that they will more or less think along much the same lines, according to the information at their disposal.

"So now I invite you, non-Catholics above all, to send in any questions you wish on religion, or morality, or the Catholic Church, and I shall explain exactly the Catholic position, and give the reasons for it. In fact, I almost demand those questions. Many hard things have been said, and are still being said, about the Catholic Church, and too often she has been condemned without a hearing. She has the right to ask a fair trial, and to be allowed to state her case. We insist that even the worst criminal should have the chance to say what he can for himself. And the Catholic Church, though no criminal, has been so abused, that she has a right to be heard. I do not ask that you give your name and address. A *nom de plume* will do. Call yourself Voltaire, Confucius, X.Y.Z., what you like, so long as you give indication enough to recognize your answer.

"My own promises are legion. Every letter sent in will be certainly acknowledged. If it is worth writing and mailing, it is worth answering. I will evade no serious question on the subject of religion. All credit will be given for sincerity. No matter what others may think of it, I will take it for granted that it is your own personal difficulty, the result of much thought, perhaps the voice of years of distress and doubt. Or the question may be the result of a talk with others, or of things you have heard at work, or that you have read in the papers. All I ask is that you submit it for explanation. That some hard things are bound to be implied I know quite well. If I had the idea some people have of the Catholic Church, I would be far more indignant than they are, and would do all possible to force it out of the country. But I have not that idea, because I happen to know the Catholic Church as she really is. 'Oh,' you may reply, 'but you do not know any other Church.' I do. I became a Catholic only after having tried Protestantism in various forms. So at least the replies will come from one who has seen both sides.

"At times you will find yourself in complete agreement with things which you thought Catholics rejected. With all good faith, a lot of people misunderstand the Catholic Church, basing their ideas upon what other non-Catholics say of her. But there's nothing like asking a Catholic himself, and if you are shy of meeting a Priest personally, here is your opportunity. Send in your inquiry to this Session.

"At other times, even after the explanation given, you will find yourself only in partial agreement with Catholic teaching. Well, the information will be of value, and you will at least appreciate the fact that we prefer to say what we know to be true, rather than consult your feelings. To say what one believes to be false for the sake of pleasing others is sheer hypocrisy, and it appeals to no one with a spark of manhood in him.

"Finally, some Catholic doctrines will be a flat contradiction of what you have hitherto believed. Then I can but ask you to weigh the force of the reasons for the Catholic doctrine. And even if you are not convinced, it is good to know not only that other people do think differently, but in what way they differ from you. At the same time remember that one can dislike another man's doctrines without disliking the man. If a reply seems rather hard on your pet beliefs, do not regard it as being hard upon you. It is not meant to be. Not one word is intended to hurt anybody personally.

"In conclusion, then, I predict that you will all find this a fascinating Session, whether you are hearing replies to your own questions, or noticing what other listeners think on the subject, or simply listening to the actual teachings of the Catholic Church."

Since the broadcasting of that first invitation, as I have remarked, questions have never been lacking from all the Australian States and New Zealand. And from the thousands of questions sent in, a selection is given in this book, space being allotted to each subject relatively to the interest shown in it by inquirers. The replies appear just as they were given over the air, though not with any semblance of the order in which they were received. The necessity of classification in book form is evident. Each question is numbered, so that, with the help of the full index to be found at the end of the volume, readers may find the book useful as a manual of ready reference concerning the various topics with which it deals.

One final duty confronts the author which it is most pleasant to fulfill. I wish to acknowledge my great debt to the Rt. Rev. Monsignor James Meany, P.P., Director of Station 2SM. I owe very much to his sympathy and encouragement from the very inception of the Question Box Sessions. And now he has not only granted my request by contributing the preface to this work, but has generously attended to all the technical details involved in the printing and publishing of the book. Any attractive qualities in presentation and appearance are due to his taste and discernment, and I gladly express my gratitude to him for his valued co-operation in its production.

CHAPTER ONE

GOD

1. *Please give me evidence that God exists. I have never had any such evidence, for I do not accept the Bible.*

What do you mean by evidence? Some people think that evidence must be seen and touched, as an animal sees a patch of grass and eats it. But men are not mere animals. They have reason, and can appreciate intellectual evidence. For example, the evidence of beauty in music or in painting is perceived by man's mind, not by his senses. An animal could hear the same sounds, or see the same colors, without being impressed by their harmony and proportion. Apart from the Bible altogether, reason can detect sufficient evidence to guarantee the existence of God.

2. *What is this evidence for God's existence, apart from the Bible?*

There are many indications, the chief of which I shall give you very briefly:

The first is from causality. The universe, limited in all its details, could not be its own cause. It could no more come together with all its regulating laws than the San Francisco Harbor Bridge could just happen, or a clock could assemble itself and keep perfect time without a clock-maker. On the same principle, if there were no God, there would be no you to dispute His existence. A second indication is drawn from the universal reasoning, or if you wish, intuition of men. The universal judgment of mankind can no more be wrong on this vital point than the intuition of an infant that food must be conveyed to the mouth. The stamp of God's handiwork is so clearly impressed upon creation, and, above all, upon man, that all nations instinctively believe that there is a God. The truth is in possession. Men do not have to persuade themselves that there is a God. They have to try to persuade themselves that there is no God. And no one yet, who has attained to such a temporary persuasion, has been able to find a valid reason for it. Men do not grow into the idea of a God; they endeavor to grow out of it.

The sense of moral obligation confirms these reasons. In every man there is a sense of right and wrong. A man knows interiorly when he is doing wrong. Something rebukes his conduct. He knows that he is going against an inward voice. It is the voice of conscience, dictating to us a law we did not make, and which no man could have made, for this voice protests whether other men know our conduct or not. This voice is often quite against what we wish to do, warning us beforehand, condemning us after its violation. The law dictated by this voice of conscience supposes a lawgiver who has written his law in our hearts. And as God alone could do this, it is certain that He exists.

Finally, justice demands that there be a God. The very sense of justice among men, resulting in law-courts, supposes a just God. We did not give ourselves our sense of justice. It comes from whoever made us, and no one can give what he does not possess himself. Yet justice cannot always be done by men in this world. Here the good often suffer, and the wicked prosper. And, even though human justice does not always succeed in balancing the scales, they will be balanced some day by a just God, who most certainly must exist.

3. You, as a Priest, argue to a clock-maker. I, as a rationalist, ask, "Who created your uncreated clock-maker?"

That is not a rational question. I say that the universe is obviously created, and that what is created supposes a Creator who is uncreated, or the problem goes on forever, the whole endless chain of dependent beings as unable to explain itself as each of its links. It is rational to argue to an uncreated clock-maker. It is not rational to ask, "Who created this uncreated clock-maker?" God was not created. If He were, He would be a creature and would have a creator. His creator would then be God, and not He Himself. God always existed. He never began, and will never cease to be. He is eternal.

4. You talk of universal persuasion. Men used to believe that the world was flat!

A sufficient reason for that error is evident, *viz.*, lack of data, and the fact that men followed their senses, which seemed to say that the earth was flat. That was not a judgment of the pure reason. The senses supplied no immediate manifestations that there might be a God as they indicated that the world might be flat. The cases are not parallel, and the transition from a judgment based upon the senses to one based upon pure reason is not valid. In any case, the scientific and metaphysical proofs justify belief in God quite independently of this psychological reason. They would be valid supposing that only one man in a million believed in God's existence. This latter supposition, however, will never be verified, for the common rational judgment of the vast majority will always intuitively perceive this truth.

5. There is no need to talk of future balancing of the Scales. Virtue is its own reward in this life, even as the wicked endure remorse.

That will not do. Consciousness of virtue is not much good to a man about to be wrongfully hanged and who cannot live to enjoy it. Nor does vice always bring proportionate remorse. Many are too hardened to experience deep remorse. There will be a levelling-up some day, after this life, and by God.

6. Joseph McCabe believed in God, but he renounced bigotry and became an Agnostic.

There are many men such as Joseph McCabe who have given up their profession of a belief in God. But, they do not give up that belief because Agnosticism offers them a higher and holier life. They find Agnosticism less irksome, whether it be by emancipation from moral laws, or from the restraints of truth and logic. Nor should you talk of bigotry. Many Agnostics have a far worse bias than that which they attribute to believers, garbling facts and distorting evidence without any of the scruples which one who really believes in God would certainly experience.

7. If I sincerely believe that there is no God, and there be a God, would not invincible ignorance save me?

Such ignorance is not invincible. You can overcome it. You violated your reason in suppressing its spontaneous concept of God, and by persuading yourself that religion is false. If you took the pressure off your reason and let it swing back to the Supreme Cause of its very being, it would do so as the needle to the pole. Pascal rightly says that there are two types of men, those who are afraid to lose God, and those who are afraid that they might find Him.

8. What do you mean by the term God?

God is a spiritual, substantial, personal being, infinite in intelligence, in will, and in all perfection, absolutely simple or lacking composition, immutable, happy in Himself and by Himself, and infinitely superior to all that is or can be conceived apart from Himself. He is incomprehensible in His infinite perfection by all lesser intelligences, although knowable as to the fact of His existence as Living Creator and Lord of heaven and earth, almighty, eternal, immense, and distinct from all that He has created. That is what I mean by God.

9. How do you know that God is eternal, or always was, is, and will be?

Because if God ever had a beginning, then before He began there was nothing. Now nothing, with nothing to work upon, and no faculties with which to work, could never turn its non-existent self into something. But there is obviously something, and there can never have been a time when there was nothing. God at least must always have existed, and if no one is responsible for His beginning, there is no one who could possibly bring His existence to an end. He always will be. God rightly declared Himself the eternally existent Being when He said to Moses, "I am Who am."

10. Spinoza said that if God created the world for an object, He desires something He lacks, which denies His infinite perfection.

Spinoza's objection is not valid. He fails to distinguish between God's essential constitution, which is necessary to His being, and His free operations resulting in created things. If God's creating operations were necessary, Spinoza would be right. But God did not create in order to acquire perfection necessary to Himself. He created to bestow perfections upon others. If I am laboring to acquire, I lack something I want. If I give to others, that proves not my lack, but my superabundance.

11. Can men whilst earth-bound understand the working of the Divine Mind?

The Divine Mind does not "work." God does not have to reason slowly and painfully to conclusions, as do men. His Divine Intelligence is a permanent and simultaneous act of perfect knowledge embracing all things, past, present, and future. We cannot fully understand God's being, knowledge, and plans. However, St. Paul rightly said that the pagan Romans were inexcusable for not noting the power and divinity of the true God in visible things, and for not having glorified Him, nor given Him thanks. If it were beyond the power of man to know this much of God, they would not have been inexcusable.

12. Have we attained to a full knowledge of God, or are we advancing towards the fulness of truth?

The fullest revelation of those things of God which man is intended to know has been made as far as this life goes. It has been given by Christ, as we shall see later on. No man yet has sounded the full depths of the truth revealed by Christ, and as we progress in the knowledge of His doctrines we get nearer and nearer to that fulness of truth which is possible on this earth. I am speaking of the knowledge to be attained by individuals. The fulness of truth is contained in the deposit of faith confided to the Catholic Church. The perfect fulness of knowledge is possible only in the heavenly vision of God.

13. What becomes of God when you think of the misery and starvation in the world?

We have already seen that there is a God. Inability to comprehend every detail in the universe does not prove that there is no God, but merely the limited capacity of the finite human mind. However, the human mind can propose certain principles which go a long way towards the removal of difficulties.

Firstly, evil is really the negation or privation of good, and if there is evil in the world, there is also much good which can be accounted for only by the existence of God.

Secondly, the fluctuations of this mutable life cannot affect God's existence. I mean that you cannot have God when things seem to be all right, and annihilate Him when things seem to go wrong. If God exists before things go wrong, He still exists despite the unhappiness of an individual. And note that word individual. Viewing the race as a whole, we find that life is a mixture of comfortable and uncomfortable things. When we are happy, others are suffering. When we are suffering, others are happy. And we cannot say that God is existing for the happy ones, and simultaneously not existing for the unhappy ones. We must not take local and individual views only, but a universal outlook.

Thirdly, and particularly as regards the uneven distribution of this world's goods with consequent starvation for some, God's providence has not failed. Man's administration is at fault. Whilst individuals suffer want, we know that the world has produced enough wheat, fruit, meat, and wool to feed and clothe everyone. God has not failed to provide enough to fill every mouth. But He has given this world over to the administration of men, and it is their bad management they must correct rather than blame God. At least their incapable administration should teach them the saving grace of humility.

14. Where is the justice of God, in permitting this uneven distribution?

A satisfactory explanation could scarcely be given, were this life all. But it is not. God permits these things only because He knows that there is a future life where He will rectify and compensate all inequalities. In the meantime He draws good out of these miseries, for they teach men not to set their hopes entirely upon this world as if there were no other, and help to expiate the sins of mankind. If we cannot be entirely happy here, let us at least make sure of being happy in the next life.

15. If God is almighty He could prevent volcanoes, earthquakes, etc., which kill innocent and wicked people alike.

If He were not almighty there would be no volcanoes to erupt, and no human beings to be injured or killed. These physical events happen according to natural laws established by God, with the operations of which He is not obliged to interfere because the finite minds of men are surprised by them. Nor does the death of such people terminate their real existence. The transition from earthly conditions to our future state is as normal as the transition from infancy to adolescence. Death is a natural law for all, and God permits it to come in various ways to various people.

16. If God is loving, just, and all-powerful, why does He permit moral evil, or sin?

Because God is Love, He asks the freely given love of man, and not a compelled love. Because He is just, He will not deprive man of the free will which is in accordance with his rational nature. Nor is this against the omnipotence of God, for even His power does not extend to contradictory things. Man cannot be free to love and serve God, without being free to reject Him and rebel against Him. We cannot have it both ways. Even God, if He wants men to be free, cannot take from them the power to choose evil. If He enforces goodness, He takes away freedom. If He leaves freedom, He must permit evil, even though He forbids it. It is man's dignity that he is master of his own destiny instead of having to develop just like a tree which necessarily obeys natural law. Men, as a matter of fact, misused their freedom, and sin and brutality resulted. But it was impossible to give man the gift of freedom and the dignity of being master of his own destiny without risking the permission of such failures.

17. *At least, being all-powerful, just, and loving, He ought to give everyone a fair chance of obtaining the good things of this world.*

Being all-powerful, there is no reason why He ought to do our bidding as if we were all-powerful.

Being just, He is not going to give us a tin trumpet and let us think that to be our real good when it is not.

Being loving, He will not usually allow man to have those riches which may cause difficulties in the way of salvation. I do not want Him to say to me, "Amen, I say to you, you have had your reward." We are Christians, and Christians are disciples of a crucified Master. We have no right to complain if we also must tread the path of suffering.

18. *Do you tell me that a good God permits deformed children, with a lifetime of misery before them?*

God is certainly good, and if He permits evil of any kind it is only because He knows that He can draw greater good from it in the end. The human race misused its freedom, abandoned God, and found not happiness but misery. It is good to be just, and God's justice permitted this misery. Also, in His wisdom, He may permit a child to be born deformed who with health and strength would fling itself into pleasures which would end in eternal loss. Again, an imbecile is incapable of sin, and it would often seem to us a mercy had some apparently sane people been born imbeciles. Poor people, whether mentally or bodily deformed, do not spend the whole of their lives in misery and suffering. We must not judge them by our own experiences. Likewise, we must remember that what we call "the whole of their lives" is not confined to this earth. There is a continuance of existence in eternity, where all will be rectified.

We might say, "If God be good, why did He allow His Son to go through excruciating torture?" Sin is the real evil, not suffering. Christ found happiness in proving His love by suffering, a greater good than mere health. And the miseries of this world have driven thousands to God who would have been self-sufficient and independent only for the naturally insoluble problem of suffering. If only for this reason we can discern an indication of God's goodness in it.

19. *Is it, then, God's will that people should suffer from such terrible diseases as Cancer or Consumption?*

We must distinguish between God's positive will, and His permissive will. He positively wills all the good that happens. Suffering He permits to occur, and this only when he foresees that good can result from it. He positively wills that I should be holy. If He foresees that I will make use of good health to sin and to lose my soul, He may mercifully permit my health to be ruined, and thus lead me to Him where He would otherwise lose me. There would have been no diseases had men not sinned. God did not will sin, but having made men free, He permitted it and its consequences. This permission was a less serious thing than would have been the depriving us of our freedom.

20. *My poverty is due to the oppression of capitalism, not to the loving will of God.*

God has permitted it, but it has come about firstly, by mistaken conduct, with all good will, on the part of man; secondly, by faults both on the side of some capitalists and of some workers; thirdly, through mere force of circumstances. It is not against God's positive will to try to remedy these things. But, meantime, the present state of affairs would not exist, were it not for His permissive will.

21. Could not God at least have made life much easier, instead of making everything hard?

Everything is not hard. Some things are. The things that are difficult are made easier by the grace of which so many people deliberately deprive themselves. *All* difficulty cannot be removed, for God has a right to ask us to overcome at personal cost our self-inflicted bad habits, sins, and other injuries. Men's complaints are often about as reasonable as those of a man who cuts his throat, and then blames the doctor because it hurts to have it stitched up again.

22. But life seems to be becoming harder and more painful.

There has been a succession of world depressions and world recoveries through history. In any case temporal trials do not mean that life is becoming worse. It may be a means of great good. It is easy to follow all our lower instincts; difficult to battle against them. If your policy is to do only that which is easy and pleasant in life, you will never be much of a man. Christ came to make men better, and offers His grace and assistance whenever virtue demands what is difficult and painful to our lower nature and sensitiveness. He offers His special grace to those who have the good sense to pray for it.

23. Why does He permit those who do serve Him to live in poverty, whilst the godless have a smooth path through life?

This is not always the case. However, when this does occur, it is not difficult to understand. The godless do not deserve to be invited to share with Christ in a life of suffering. Also, all men do some good in life sometimes. No one is entirely evil. God's justice rewards natural good, therefore, by natural prosperity, and that may be all that such men will receive. "You have had the reward of such good as you did," may be said at their judgment, "and now answer for the evil of your irreligious lives." On the other hand, those who love God are not given worthless and perishable rewards, but will receive a full return of supernatural happiness, the only kind that really matters. If Christ promised us happiness in this world, then let us murmur when we see the infidel prosper. But what did He promise? He promised what He Himself received, suffering here, and happiness hereafter. The disciple is not above his Master.

24. In all these replies to difficulties you are postulating free will, the sinful state of man, redemption by Christ, grace, and the eternal destiny of man!

That is so. These things are facts, and no problem can be fully solved except in the light of all the facts. I am quite prepared to justify these facts. Meantime, without them, no reasonable solution of the problems of God's providence can be found at all; with them, the solution, even though inadequate, is at least rational and intelligible. The world with its miseries may be a problem difficult to reconcile with the existence of God; but that same world without God is a far greater problem, leaving exactly the same miseries to be endured in hopeless despair. Christianity does not deny the existence of suffering, but it can give happiness in the midst of suffering, and this practical solution is the true solution God gives to men of good will.

CHAPTER TWO

MAN

25. *What is a man?*

Man is a living being, endowed with a sensitive material body, and a spiritual soul which is immortal of its very nature, and which rejoices in the two spiritual faculties of intelligence and freewill.

26. *May we say that man has a soul?*

We may speak that way. Strictly speaking, however, man is a composite being consisting of both body and soul, the soul, of course, being the nobler component element.

27. *Prove that a soul does exist in man.*

A living human body is not the same thing as a corpse. Now the soul is the difference between a corpse and a living being. A dead body cannot move, eat, think, express itself, enjoy, or be miserable. It can but fall to pieces and go back to dust. There is something that stops your body from doing that now. It is your soul. For every activity you must find a principle of operation behind it. The principle in a man which thinks and loves, and is happy or miserable, is a very real thing. It is not nothing, less than the very body it animates. Nor is it a chemical. No doctor, examining a corpse, can tell you what chemical is missing that it should not live. If there be nothing else save chemical substances, let doctors and scientists gather together the requisite chemicals and say, "Live!" They can effect nothing like this. There is something that chemistry cannot reach; it is the soul or spirit. Look anyone in the face, and behind those animated features, those changing expressions, in the very eyes, you will read the soul.

28. *If a soul is the difference between a living being and a corpse, then an animal, or even a vegetable, must have a soul.*

That is so. Sane philosophy admits a vegetative soul, a sensitive animal soul, and an immortal, spiritual, and intelligent human soul.

29. *Man does not possess a soul. He is a soul. The Bible says that God breathed the breath of life into the body, and it became a living soul.*

That breath of life was either a definite something, or it was nothing. But you cannot tell me that nothing vitalized that body. It was a definite something, and that something was a created human intelligent soul.

Again, if man has not got a soul, then instead of being composed of body and soul, he is a body. And if that body is a soul, then a soul wears boots! However you quote the Bible, the authority of which we shall consider later. Meantime, since you accept it, you will notice that Christ clearly shows the difference between the material body and a spiritual soul when He said, "Handle and see, for a spirit hath not flesh and bones, as you see me to have." Lk. XXIV., 39. A body, of flesh and bone, could never become a living soul. Man was but named after the superior element of his being.

30. *Do the words spirit and soul mean the same thing?*

The word spirit can have a very wide meaning. It is derived from the Latin word *spiritus*, meaning a breath. Then because the soul of man is as invisible to bodily eyes as a breath, and also because its presence is manifested by the breathing of a living body, the word spirit acquired a transferred sense, becoming a substitute for the word soul. If then we intend by the word spirit the principle of life in a man, that principle which enables him to live, to know and to love, to be happy or to be sorrowful, then the spirit is the soul.

And in a further sense, because a man's dispositions depend upon his soul, we use the word spirit for character, and thus speak of a man's spirit. But this is only the soul, manifesting itself in a man's external conduct. The soul, therefore, is the living principle which makes the difference between a living man and a corpse, and spirit and soul in this sense mean the same thing.

31. *Is not the soul the breath of God?*

No, for God is a spirit, a purely spiritual substance, and does not breathe. The expression is only a human way of putting things. The soul is a spirit, and is called the breath of God merely because caused or created by God in its spiritual or breath-like nature.

32. *Did the soul exist before conception?*

No. God creates each soul as each body is generated. It is difficult to fix the exact moment, but the more general opinion is as soon as the embryo begins to exist.

33. *You spoke of the soul as being immortal?*

Yes. The body is naturally mortal; the soul by its very nature immortal.

34. *What indications have you that the soul is immortal?*

That the soul will, and indeed must, survive the death of the body is demonstrable from many points of view.

Firstly, its essential structure forbids dissolution by death. Death is the disintegration of parts. Only composite things can die. Yet the soul is not composite. Its power of pure immaterial thought proves its independence of matter. It is endowed with spiritual faculties, and is as spiritual as the faculties it possesses, which will enable it to live and operate when separated from the body. Not being material, it can never be destroyed or fall to pieces like matter. Nor would God endow it with a nature essentially fitted to live on just for an idle freak, and with the intention of annihilating it after all.

Secondly, every individual experiences a sense of moral obligation, and every obligation demands a sufficient sanction. If the State said, "This is the law," and I replied, "What if I do not observe it," it would be ludicrous were the State to reply, "Oh, nothing will happen. I say only that it is the law. If you break it, you break it, I suppose." That would be a joke, not a law. I know that I shall have to answer some day for my attitude towards the interior sense of moral obligation. I can go right through this life without encountering anyone capable of judging me concerning it. The real answer must be given at the judgment seat of God, and my soul will have to be there. Consequently it must survive.

Thirdly, a more universal view of human life shows us the many inequalities which offend against the sense of justice. We know that justice will be done some day, and as it is not always done in this life, it will be done in the next. This implies our presence, and therefore our living on after death.

Fourthly, every soul naturally has an insatiable natural desire for happiness, and for lasting happiness. No earthly or temporal good can satisfy this hunger. Yet this innate natural tendency cannot lack its rightful object. As well try to conceive the existence of the human eye, perfectly adapted to sight, yet without the possibility of light anywhere to enable it to see.

Reflection, then, upon the simple structure of the soul, upon the future administration of the sanctions attached to the moral law, upon the rectification of worldwide inequalities, and upon the teleological inclinations to a lasting and perfect good, makes it a violation of reason to deny the survival of the soul.

35. *The idea of a sanction proportioned to the individual's sense of moral obligation has much less influence upon men than you religious people think.*

I admit that it has much less influence than it should have, but their not thinking of it does not alter the fact.

36. *It has no real bearing on morality, and if anything would have a bad influence, making men cowards.*

Since there is a future life, it has a lot to do with morality. Man is endowed with reason and is bound to exercise foresight. The future as such, whether here or hereafter, is a reasonable motive for present conduct. I refrain from eating certain foods now, because reason tells me that future indigestion will result. That is reasonable conduct. I try to refrain from morally wrong conduct because it is wrong; offends God; is a personal disgrace; and will wreck my whole future existence if I persist in it, dying without repentance. All these motives are good. If the nobler motives fail to impress me in a given temptation, the thought of hell at least will tend to stop me.

You will say, "So you are afraid of hell?" I reply, "Of course I am!" Knowing that hell is a reality, any sane man will live so as to avoid going there. It is not cowardice, but ordinary prudence. If a man leaps for his life off a railway line as an express tears past the spot where he was standing, you would not go up to him, tap him on the shoulder, and say, "You coward, you jumped for your life through sheer fear of that train!" God gave us our reason that we might use it for our well-being, and it is quite reasonable to weigh both advantages and penalties attached to moral law.

Nor is this influence probably to the bad. The knowledge that retribution will follow violations of the moral law makes that law a real law. Could we say that all the penalties attached to the laws of the State are to the bad? Thousands of temptations to crime are resisted by citizens because of the thought of the future penalties. Nor does it matter much whether the penalty be future by a few weeks and in this life, or by some years, and in the next life. The principle is the same.

37. *Right is right, and wrong is wrong, whether we are mortal or immortal.*

That is true. But the difficulty is to make people do right because it is right, and avoid wrong because it is wrong. We have to be trained to right conduct from childhood, and that very training demands commendation or punishment. Spare the rod and spoil the child is a truism. We must take a sound psychological view of man's nature, and realize that right because it is right does not always appeal as the best thing to be done in practice. The advantage to be gained from evil conduct often seems better to many men.

38. *Our code of morality must be founded upon the only life of which we have any knowledge—this one.*

This life is not the only one of which we have knowledge. We can have knowledge in two ways, experimental knowledge, or knowledge based upon reason and authority. I have experimental knowledge of America for I have been in America, but I have no experimental knowledge of Africa. Yet you cannot say that I have no knowledge whatever of Africa. I certainly know that it exists. Now we have experimental knowledge of this earthly life. But we know by principles of reason and by the authority of God that we shall continue to exist when this earthly life shall have come to an end. We cannot expect to have experimental knowledge now of a state which is essentially future. The code of morality, moreover, should regulate your personal character throughout the whole of its existence, building up a moral perfection as a permanent attribute of your character as long as it shall exist. If your code is as extensive as your complete life, it cannot be limited to this brief section of it.

39. *Your argument from justice weakens morality. If there were to be no rectification of things in the next life, all the more reason for men to remedy injustices in this world.*

That might seem to you a reason why it would be better if there were no future life and reparation of justice. But we know that there is such a future life, and *a priori* possibilities cannot avail against fact. Also it is a fact that men who give up their belief in a future life are not consumed with a passion for the rectifying of injustice in this world. On the contrary, those who lead evil lives have every reason to persuade themselves that there is no future life. There are honorable exceptions of naturally good men who have not had all the data necessary for the formation of a right judgment, or who have not adverted to the force of the reasons for immortality. But they are the few. Men do not have to persuade themselves that there is a future life, but try to persuade themselves that there is no future life, just as the Christian Scientist has to persuade herself that pain and suffering do not exist.

40. *Why bother about justice here, if all injustice is to be rectified and compensated in the next world?*

You are forgetting your own principles. We must do right always because right is right. If we do not, we shall be punished by God precisely because the right was right and we should have done it. It belongs to God to adjust all seeming inequalities in the next world, but that in no way exempts man from his present duties. Men must acknowledge the benefits they have received from God, and discharge their obligations towards God, even as they discharge their obligations towards fellow men. This is a strict duty. Not all men will fulfill this duty in practice, and God will deal with them sooner or later, compensating those who have suffered from the injustice of their fellow men.

41. *Can we say that there will be justice in another world because it is conspicuously absent in this?*

Yes, because you would not advert to the absence of justice unless you had a sense of justice. The relative and inferior sense of justice possessed by men supposes an absolute justice, and that absolute justice will secure the absolute balance it demands—some day. The fact that absolute justice does not prevail in this life is indication enough that it will do so in a future life.

42. *The injustices of this life demand another life, but I believe in re-incarnation.*

Justice does say that this life cannot be all. But your idea of re-incarnation is a mistaken notion based upon your notion that life is impossible unless on this earth. But there is no need for another life on this earth, which would involve further inequalities. There is a better life than this, afterwards and elsewhere. Re-incarnation is a myth.

43. *Your doctrine of immortality supposes consciousness after death. I do not believe it, otherwise the soul would be conscious under chloroform, or when the body is knocked senseless in an accident.*

This fact does not invalidate the reasons given already, and is also easily explained. The soul whilst in a state of union with the body operates by using the faculties of that body. If the sense instruments are incapacitated, the soul can no longer operate adequately whilst united to the body. But once released from the body, its intelligence and will and power to love at once assert themselves. Hydrogen and oxygen unite to form a drop of water. They can operate as water only whilst united. Hydrogen is there, but it cannot operate as hydrogen until released from the union. Soul and body make one human being. And both elements must be fit to co-operate in the activities of a bodily human being. The soul cannot operate separately as a distinct unit whilst still united. But once released, it can operate independently every bit as much as hydrogen when released from its essential union with oxygen to form water.

44. *Are the souls of animals also immortal?*

They are not immortal. Animals are not capable of any operations which transcend the conditions of matter, and do not rise above the sensitive to the intelligible order. Also they are devoid of the moral intuition. Animal souls are therefore dependent upon matter both for their being and their operations, and cease to exist with death.

45. *Why should the fact of our being born give us the right to exist forever?*

It is not the mere fact of being born, but of being born with such a *nature*. The soul is fitted by its very nature to live on forever, for a spiritual entity cannot disintegrate and die. Why should we have been endowed with such a nature? Because He who made us chose to give us such a nature. Since we did not make ourselves we did not give ourselves our rights. They came from the One who is responsible for our being. If an artist painted an image of a girl on canvas, and the image were endowed with the power of speech, the girl might say, "What right have you to give me brown hair?" The artist would rightly reply, "Since I made you, I have the right to give you whatever colored hair I wish." God had the right to create indestructible souls if He wished. He did so. And our right to live on is vested in His will to endow us with an immortal nature.

46. *What is the purpose of life on this earth?*

Man is created to praise, love, and serve God in this life, and by doing so to attain eternal life with God hereafter. This is not our only life. It is but an infinitesimal part of it.

47. *I can't imagine what this future life can possibly be like.*

There is a vast difference between imagining a future life and conceiving it. This is the difference between imagination and thought. I cannot imagine or picture the future life any more than you are able to do so. The only images we could form would be derived from this life, and would fit this life, not the next. Yet although we cannot imagine what the next life will be like, we can conceive the fact that it will be, and also the intelligible principles by which it will be regulated.

48. *Is the future spiritual world an educational one?*

Not in the sense you probably intend. We are now progressing towards our final destination. There we shall have attained it. The one exception is in the case of a soul that goes to Purgatory, where it undergoes a progressive purification fitting it for the Vision of God. This cannot strictly be called educational, but it is a spiritual evolution towards perfect holiness.

49. Do these doctrines of moral obligation, sanctions, and a future life imply the freedom of man's will?

They do, for if man were not free he could not be responsible for his conduct, and could neither merit commendation by good actions nor condemnation by evil actions.

50. Prove to me that man is endowed with freewill.

It is a necessary corollary from all that has been said already. If man be not free, he cannot be expected to keep laws, and should not be punished for breaking them. There can be no obligation to observe a law when it is not possible to keep it. This is the judgment of every normal mind. The judicial and punitive application of human legislation is outrageous if men are not responsible for their conduct. The theorists who talk of determinism never dream of applying their doctrine in practice.

Again consciousness affords sufficient proof for every normal man. We are not only conscious before acting that there are various courses open to us, but we are conscious that we may desist from a course of action already adopted, and after acting, are conscious of self-approbation or self-reproach, realizing that we were not compelled to act that way.

Finally, the possession of reason or intelligence cannot be without freedom of will. Granted a reasoning faculty which can apprehend finite things under different aspects, freewill follows. For example, the acquiring of another man's money may be considered as involving the moral evil of obtaining it by theft, or as yielding one's own goods in exchange for the sake of possessing cash. The object itself allows a man to concentrate upon one aspect or the other, proposing motives to himself for a good or an evil choice.

51. Even granting freedom, man is not entirely free, but only within certain limits.

We admit that environment and heredity can weaken will power, and that lunacy can deprive a man of self-control altogether. But these are not normal cases, and God will make every allowance as regards salvation. He will blame men only for those things for which they are actually responsible, and in the degree in which they are responsible. Granted weakening factors, God knows that responsibility is lessened. A born imbecile will never be punished for sins which he is incapable of committing. But the question of how everything will be adjusted does not affect the fact that the human will is normally and of its very nature endowed with freedom.

52. If God knows all things beforehand, is not that the end of our freedom?

No. God's knowledge does not make us so act. An astronomer may be able to say, "There will be an eclipse of the sun." When the eclipse comes, no one says that it had to come because the astronomer said it would. The astronomer's knowledge was caused by the fact that it would come; the eclipse was not caused by the fact that he foresaw it.

53. If I am free, why was I given no choice as to whether I should exist or not?

One has to exist before one can be consulted, and then it is rather late to consult us concerning that which has already occurred. We therefore had no choice in this particular matter. Nor could we reasonably wish to have a choice. If a thing will necessarily be to my harm, I would reasonably wish to have an opportunity of declining it. But if you wish to send me $1,000, you need not consult me. You may say that life entails a great risk. It does. But there is no danger if we take certain means which are within the power of all. God has placed us all upon this earth, and we know that if we obey our conscience we cannot go wrong. And no one can force us not to obey our conscience. If men force us against our will to do things which conscience forbids, we are not guilty as long as we sincerely refrain from willing that the thing should happen.

54. It is necessary, then, that we should be on earth?

It is necessary in so far as God has decided that we should be here. It is not absolutely necessary for any being to exist except God. All other beings depend upon God's will. But God has willed that we should have our opportunity to praise, love, and serve Him in this life, and be happy with Him forever in the next. Surely a great destiny. The secret of life is summed up in three words—I come from God; I must live for God; and I shall go back to God.

55. You constantly speak of some kind of a relationship between God and man.

I do. A personal God exists. Intelligent human beings exist. Those human beings owe all they have to the personal God who made them, and, being intelligent, are able to recognize the fact. Reason demands that they do so, and render a suitable, practical acknowledgment of the fact to God.

56. What form will that practical acknowledgment take?

It must be expressed in the duties of religion, which will imply reverence for God's Person, and obedience to such instructions as He pleases to issue in our regard.

CHAPTER THREE

RELIGION

57. *What do you mean by religion?*

By religion I mean that act of justice by which we render to God, both privately as individuals, and publicly as social beings, the honor, gratitude, and obedience due to Him, and in the way prescribed by Him.

58. *Is the practice of religion necessary?*

Yes. God has definite rights which no man is justified in ignoring. Moreover God definitely commands you to adore and serve Him. "Thou shalt love the Lord thy God . . . this is the first and greatest commandment." A man with no religion, who never worships God, never says a prayer to Him, is far from fulfilling this commandment of love. It is not enough to admit off-hand that God exists, and then ignore His definite claims.

59. *You suppose that He has made definite claims.*

I do, and shall justify that postulate as a definite fact in due course.

60. *I don't see that a man should kneel and pray to anyone.*

Do you see that there must be a God? Do you see that you are one of His creatures? Prayer is conversation with God, and an act of religion. To ignore prayer is to ignore God and deny His rights. Being an adult male does not exempt from this duty. Men are not less the creatures of God than women and children. Nor will heaven be less worth having for men, or hell more tolerable.

Or do you mean that you are above this sort of thing? Before God you are a child. There are no privileged classes in the presence of Infinite Wisdom; no exemptions before an Eternal God; no strength before Omnipotence. We are all children before God.

Or is it that you are ashamed to kneel? Instead of being ashamed to kneel, you should be ashamed not to do so, for it is the only fitting attitude of a creature and a sinner before Almighty God. Men often pray almost frantically at the hour of death, fear making them do then what love and generosity will not make them do now. Is God less worth serving because He gives health and strength now than He will be then?

61. *If there be a good God, He must wish us to try to make this world beautiful.*

There is a good God, and He does wish that. But He does not wish our attention to be wholly given to creatures, and the Creator to be ignored. We must acknowledge and love Him. He can no more dispense us from this than He could dispense children from their privilege and duty of honoring and respecting their parents.

62. *We want a religion, not of sanctifying piety, but of pity.*

You seem to think that it must be one or the other. Both are necessary. There is no real sanctifying piety unless it inspires a religion of pity. If there is no pity, there is no piety and no sanctity, but self-deception and hypocrisy. At the same time, banish sanctifying piety, and mere pity or kindness is not religion. It may be philanthropy or humanitarianism, but it is not religion. Religion essentially means that we must love God, and that our love for God must overflow upon other children of God.

63. Will religion get us our bread and butter?

I might just as well ask you whether we can get milk out of a locomotive. However religion does inspire the supplying of bread and butter to innumerable people through thousands of charitable societies.

64. I don't miss much by not having a religion.

Religion is the virtue of justice which renders to God the honor and worship due to Him. Your remark is like saying, "I do not miss much in refusing to acknowledge my debts." However you do miss more than you think.

65. I am well known and respected.

You may be well known and respected by fellow men; but, though you are well known by God, He does not respect you for your neglect of your obvious religious duties.

66. The giving up of religion has made no change in me for good or evil, sorrow or happiness.

If you ever had a religion and it did not have any influence upon you, then you would not experience any change in being without it. You would perceive a difference in favor of the good and happiness if you became a really practical Catholic. You would then know the peace of Christ—a peace the world cannot give.

67. The laws of nature regulate all and I worship only at her altars.

Laws don't float round without a lawgiver. If nature has laws they have been imposed by a lawgiver. All legislation supposes a legislator. And who authorized you to specify that particular form of religion? Surely the one who is to be worshipped has the right to specify how he shall be worshipped.

68. You say that religion is necessary. I say that it is positively evil and degrading. It restrains our freedom.

Sincere religion spells freedom—freedom from vice, from all injustice and want of charity. There is no absolute freedom. You must be free from vice and subject to virtue, or free from virtue and subject to vice.

69. Nevertheless, religion degrades man, giving a God-complex or an inferiority complex, with a subconscious reference to a supernatural authority in all actions.

Not subconscious, but conscious reverence for the authority of God certainly guides the conduct of a religious man. Your terminology is based upon a false idea that the notion of God is a kind of psychological abnormality due to natural causes. It is true that one with a right idea of God is fully aware that he personally is inferior to God, and therefore possesses the saving grace of humility.

70. Where are a man's ideals who cannot do right for right's sake, but needs a heavenly policeman to keep him straight?

To do right for right's sake implies that right ought to be done. Why ought it to be done? Ought or must supposes some kind of law. All law derives its force from the right of the lawgiver. To do right for right's sake pushes us back to doing right for the sake of the Supreme Author of all right. No one can do right for right's sake if he ignores God, for without God he cannot prove that what he thinks to be right is right or has any binding force at all. Also in the state we have laws and policemen. But it is absurd to say that no citizen is good except through dread of the law, and that the police are necessary to keep every single one of us on the path of duty. A religious man knows that God is his Father, and he serves as a child of God from a motive of love, a love which casts out servile fear without diminishing filial respect.

71. You cannot face life unaided, and reliance on God saps self-reliance and initiative, and must develop the weakling.

The religious man knows that he cannot face life unaided, but that is not to his detriment. We do not ridicule a child at school who cannot face the problem of mathematics without the help of a master. If God needed help He would be imperfect. But man is not God. He is very conscious of limitation, and if he wishes to behave as if he were God, quite self-sufficient and capable of all things, he denies the truth of his limitation. The man who realizes that he did not make the universe, which anyway he cannot stop or rearrange, is nearer the truth, and behaves reasonably in asking the perfect Being who made him to preserve him from the mistakes and frailties of his own imperfection. An imperfect being should behave as if limited, not as if supremely perfect. Nor does religion sap man's self-reliance and initiative. These he uses to the full, and then asks additional help from God. If a man employs extra help in his business, is he sapping his self-reliance? Must he do everything himself? No man can do everything. God helps those who help themselves, but He expects men to turn to Him where they cannot help themselves. This secures full personal initiative, and the help of God to supply for one's essential deficiencies. As for the developing of weaklings, read the history of the early Christians in the days of Nero and the Roman persecutions. For the love of God and with the help of God, children faced the reality of torture and suffering before which strong men quailed. The irreligious man is the weakling, shirking the duty of rendering to God what is due to God; shirking the humility of admitting that he is not infinitely perfect; shirking the greatest reality of life.

72. I have no religion and am well off; the poor wretches who practice religion do not seem to gain much by it.

Religion is not supposed to be an easy road to temporal prosperity in things which death takes from those who have them. It is the road, not always comfortable, to never-ending and eternal happiness. We do not expect religion to result in earthly advancement. If it did men would rush it as a good business proposition, and offer to God a devotion quite without value. Temporal things are subject to the natural course of events. You are not materially well off because you have no religion. There are thousands who have no religion and are not well off. So, too, the poor are not poor because they practice religion. There are well-to-do people who also practice their religion. And if the poor gave up their religion they would not suddenly become rich. Meantime, you prosper because of natural circumstances or natural ability, or because God is giving you temporal rewards for such good as you do. Everyone does some good sometimes. For the poor, God often reserves their compensation for the next life.

73. I am perfectly happy. Your kill-joy religion will leave you feeling a dreadful fool when you find that death ends all.

If you are perfectly happy you are the only one on earth who is. Is there absolutely nothing further you would like to have but which you do not yet possess? Anyway, religion is not a kill-joy. One of the really happiest men who ever lived was St. Francis of Assisi, born and bred in the Catholic spirit. The simplest Priest finds more joy in saying one Mass, and the least of our Catholic people in one

Communion, than you have experienced in your whole life. Then, too, I have already shown that death cannot end all. If it did, the religious man would hardly be able to feel a fool. But if it does not, as it cannot, you will scarcely enjoy meeting a God whom you have consistently ignored. The idea that death ends all is not the result of thought. It is the result of refusing to think.

74. Religion gives a dread of death which I do not experience.

If a religious man dreads death it is not because he is religious, but because he is not trying sincerely to live up to his religion. Then he has need to dread death. No one is asked to dread death in the name of religion, but one is taught to be ready for it.

75. If religion is such a wonderful thing, even though it does not advance a man's temporal welfare, it should make him better. But it does not. No one honestly believes that a religious man is less likely to embezzle or be brutal than a non-religious man.

Even were that true it would not justify irreligious men in their crime of ignoring the public acknowledgment of God. But it is not true. If one who professes to be religious is guilty of such things men experience a special indignation, and it is made much of precisely because the unexpected has news value. The majority of men know that they are less likely to find evil in a God-fearing man than in others.

76. All know that creed has nothing to do with conduct. Religious people sin, and are hypocrites.

All do not know that creed has nothing to do with conduct. In fact no man knows precisely what motive has moved men to do given things. God alone can read the heart. We have no experience save of our own interior dispositions. Religious people may sin. But they do not call vice virtue. They know they sin. Nor do their sins dispense them from the duty of continuing to pay due honor to God. I know tax-payers who are drunkards, but that does not exempt them from paying their taxes. If some are hypocrites, that is not due to the teachings of their religion. Blame them, not their religion. They must give up what is evil, their hypocrisy; not what is good, their religion.

77. I am honest without being religious. But I know many people who are religious without being honest.

Now you take your own virtue as a standard, and proceed to find other people wanting when measured by it. It often happens that those who practice no religion canonize themselves as the models of perfection, and regard religious people as sinners and hypocrites. But those who go to church are constantly told of their own failings, and that they must not judge others. It would be better for you to take up your religious duties. As a matter of fact, it is impossible to be really honest without being religious. Religion is the highest form of honesty, a strict duty to God. Take this case: Jones owes one man $100, and to another $1. He pays the $1, but not the $100. Smith also owes $100 and to another $1, but pays the $100, neglecting to pay the $1. Whose is the greater dishonesty? Now each man owes a tremendous debt to God and a lesser one to his neighbor. You may pay the lesser, but you neglect the greater. Your neighbor, who fulfills his religious duties, at least tries to pay the greater, though he may seem to you to neglect the lesser. But he is the better man at least in so far as he attempts to pay the greater. The man who is just to his neighbor, but does not bother about his duty of religion, is the kind of man who pays the baker for the bread he puts into his body, but nothing to God for the body he puts the bread into. Religion is a strict duty of justice to God, acknowledging our indebtedness to Him. If religious people sometimes fail in honesty towards their fellow men, I do not justify it. But their creditors are insignificant compared with the Creditor who supplied you with all you have and receives no acknowledgment from you. You are both in the wrong, but I would rather be in the position of those you condemn, if a choice had to be made, which of course has not to be made. Their religion may save them despite their faults. Your honesty will not save you.

78. Well, I believe in God, but practice no religion.

Thus charges give way to excuses. It is something to believe in God. But what notice do you take of God? You believed in the existence of your own parents, but I am sure you paid them more attention than you have ever paid to God, in whom you say you also believe.

79. I not only believe in God. I lead a clean life. Is not that enough?

On one condition—that you honestly believe no more to be necessary, and have never had an opportunity of discovering the real truth. But if, for example, you have ever heard of the claims of the Catholic Church and have refused to inquire into them, I could not answer for you. If you did inquire, realized that you should become a Catholic, and refused, you would have less chance still, for you would obviously be insincere.

80. What is your idea of a good man?

One who is firstly just to all others, including God. His first duty is to render to God what is due to Him. Secondly, and for the love of God, he renders all that is due to his fellow men. In addition he must manage himself in his own personal life, overcoming with fortitude the difficulties in the way of right conduct, and practicing temperance by restraining sensuality and other lower appetites.

81. But surely I can do that without adopting a particular form of religion. If I adopt a particular Church I antagonize my fellow men, so I keep neutral and bear ill-will to none.

Once you find that God has revealed a particular form of religion you must accept it. You will not assume any obligation to bear any ill-will towards others. Rather you will have an additional obligation to avoid it. But you are not justified in refusing to adopt that particular form of religion because you will thus antagonize your fellow men. If thus you secure the ill-will of others, that is not your fault, and it is their loss. We may never let what men think of us matter more than what God thinks of us. And after all, it is God who will judge us, not our fellow men.

82. I call myself religious, follow truth wherever it leads, and am not afraid of gods, devils, or clergymen. Is that sin?

You may follow what you think to be the truth, but how do you know that it is the truth? If because you think so, is there no possibility of mistake? If you accept ideas because wise men have uttered them, remember that equally wise men have denied them. You need not be afraid of gods, devils, or clergymen, if you are sincerely looking for the truth. But you need to be afraid of your own mental limitations. The wisest philosophers have fallen into the most absurd errors at times, above all in questions of religion. Meantime you owe a debt to God you do not pay in the way He rightly demands. If you refuse to pay earthly bills, you are arrested and have to answer in court. God is not foolish. He does not give commandments for nothing. He cannot be escaped. Death arrests every man, and he who neglects God's just demands for religious worship and acknowledgment will have to answer for his conduct.

83. *There are many intelligent people who do not bother about religion.*

In what way are they intelligent and clever? Some are clever in mathematics; others in law, but they may be very ignorant in the science of religion. A Catholic school-child could teach many of them quite a lot in this matter. Your argument might have some value if they were well instructed in the truths of religion. But it is little use saying, "I know a very clever doctor, and he has never studied music, so I do not see the use of music." The doctor's medical knowledge is no argument against music, and not all the learning of your friends in mathematics, science, physics, or astronomy, can be an argument against religion. Their knowledge of these things does not make heaven the least bit less worth having, nor hell one jot more comfortable. Let us serve the God before whom all the wisdom of men is childish prattle, and who in His infinite wisdom declares that religion is necessary not only in addition to honesty and goodness, but in order to be honest and good.

84. *You keep hinting that God not only demands religious worship, but that He has actually specified the way in which men must offer such homage. Do you mean that God has actually told men of His demand, explaining its conditions?*

Yes. God has told mankind very clearly why He created man, what is the destiny of man, and what man must do in order to attain that destiny. He sent the Prophets to teach men His will; after that He sent His own Divine Son, Jesus Christ; and Christ sent the Catholic Church—a Church still teaching with the infallible authority of God in our very midst.

CHAPTER FOUR

THE RELIGION OF THE BIBLE

85. *What is meant by natural religion, and why is it not sufficient?*

Natural religion is simply the religion a man would be obliged to practise, even if he never received a revelation from God. Man could know by reason alone that there is a God and that He must be acknowledged by a worship dictated by reason as to its form, and by obedience to the natural moral law as manifested by conscience. But this natural religion is not sufficient in the present condition of the human race. God has given to mankind a supernatural destiny higher than any merely natural destiny, and this requires the revelation of a knowledge higher than that which could be attained by the merely natural reason.

86. *Granted immortality and the need of natural religion, could we prove that more would have to be revealed?*

Even where natural religion is concerned, the lack of ability and of time for study amongst the masses of men, and the differences of opinion and absurd errors even of philosophers where the natural principles of religion and of morality are in question, would argue to the need of some help by revelation. But we could not prove that truths beyond the natural order would have to be revealed, because such revelation supposes a supernatural destiny for man, a destiny dependent entirely upon the good pleasure of God. We simply have to accept the fact that God has revealed supernatural truths beyond the requirements of merely natural religion. Once we have an historical fact, there is no longer room for speculation as to what should or should not be. God has revealed very definite doctrines and moral obligations. It is for us to accept and fulfill them if we have any idea of pleasing God and saving our souls.

87. *Do you maintain that your mysterious Bible contains the revelation of God?*

I maintain that it contains part of God's full revelation. All that is contained in the Bible has been revealed by God, although further information is given us in other ways. That the Bible contains very mysterious doctrines I admit.

88. *These mysteries make me feel that there is nothing authentic about religion.*

We attain truth by our intelligence, not by our feelings. You feel that religion is unreal. That notion must be tested by evidence. To hold it you must say that the proofs for the unreality of revealed religion are stronger than the proofs in its favor. This means that you must be able to prove that God did not reveal, or that He did, but does not know what He says; or else that He does know, but deliberately deceived us. You cannot prove any of these things. Your only argument is that you cannot fully understand some of the things He has revealed. That argument would be valid if the human reason had infinite capacity, and could expect to understand everything. But facts prove that reason is limited in capacity, and that many truths, even natural truths baffle it. "I do not understand, therefore I do not believe it," is an argument which no reasonable man would utter. "I can disprove it, therefore I do not believe it," is lawful argument.

89. We are material beings, and cannot believe in spiritual things which our minds cannot conceive.

That is a most extravagant assertion. It is true that we are material beings as regards our bodily frame. But we are not merely material. Our flesh and blood cannot think. But we have intelligence also, and we believe things with our mind, not with our flesh and blood. We cannot be expected to believe in things which our minds cannot conceive, but when you suggest that we cannot conceive things spiritual you hopelessly confuse your imagination which you possess in common with brute animals, and your reason which is proper to man. If you stood side by side with a horse, both sets of eyes could see chalk-marks on a blackboard. But in addition you would see an intelligible meaning in the writing which the animal could never discern. You have a higher and nobler faculty which is not merely material. As a matter of fact, you have disproved your assertion in writing it down. You have conceived ideas which you have committed to writing. Ideas are not material things. You cannot saw them up and burn them as so many logs of wood.

90. Anyway we cannot fully understand mysteries. How can God expect us to believe them?

The fact that you cannot fully understand mysteries is due to the limited powers of the human intelligence. You accept many natural things as facts, though their nature is most mysterious. That is not unreasonable. If we know a mysterious fact by revelation it is just as reasonable to believe it. Moreover, if God does reveal that a certain thing is true, He has every right to demand that you believe it. No finite mind has the right to call God ignorant or untruthful.

91. Is your God interested in propounding conundrums?

He is interested in telling men the truth, and in asking them to pay Him the homage of their reason by the acceptance of that truth, thus acknowledging His infinite wisdom and veracity. Reasonable men know that the truth concerning the nature and operations of an infinite Being will baffle a finite mind to some extent. But they are not so foolish as to deny a truth declared by God merely because they do not fully grasp it.

92. Homage of our reason! Blind unreasoning obedience would be a better phrase.

It is wideawake reasonable obedience. Instead of being blind, a man must know that God has spoken. He must prove this by examining the evidence. Once he knows that God has spoken, reason demands the obedient acceptance of God's teaching, even though it be as mysterious as radium, instead of pitting fallible human guesswork against such teaching.

93. You priests make the mysteries and pretend to be acquainted with the unknown, in order to boost your superior position.

God has definitely given His revelation. It involves mystery because the human mind is finite. Are there no mysteries for you, who do not acknowledge the authority of priests? Would you tell me exactly how much radium there is in Arcturus per cubic yard? You are wrong, too, in your talk of pretence. No Catholic priest pretends anything in this matter. He admits that the mysteries revealed by God are as much mysteries for him as for the people he teaches. I am a Catholic priest, and I can assure you that if I found part of my equipment as a priest was to be the art of pretence I would have left the Catholic Church more quickly than I joined it. Nor has any priest the idea of boosting himself. He fulfills his obligation to teach the truths he was sent to teach by God.

94. Is it not the function of priests of all religions to pretend to explain mysteries?

It is not the function of Catholic priests. Some so-called priests of humanly manufactured religions have been professional dealers in the occult. The Catholic priest is a very different being. He does not pretend to fully comprehend mysteries himself. He rather explains that there are mysteries in God, and in God's work.

95. Among other mysterious things, belief in the Bible demands a belief in miracles.

It demands a belief in certain historical events which cannot be accounted for save by the intervention of God.

96. I am a mechanic, you a theologian. There are no mysterious happenings in my trade. I want facts, not phantoms.

God's revelation is for all men, and clear enough in itself for all men whether mechanics or theologians. And all who have been confronted by it will answer to God for their acceptance or rejection of it. Religion is not within the scope of your trade and should not be judged by the standards of your trade. In any case there are many mysterious things involved in your trade, if you were but aware of them. And miracles are facts, not phantoms.

97. I am a materialist and cannot admit miracles, alleged or otherwise.

You are not really a materialist. Neither thought nor love are material things, yet you believe in them. Your statement, too, conflicts with reason. When you say "alleged or otherwise" you can only mean "alleged or not merely alleged but historically true." The miracles in favor of revelation are historically certain.

98. I am glad my religion rests upon its own intrinsic good, not upon foolish miracles.

Whence came your religion? Did you invent it for yourself? And are you sure that because it is pleasing to you it is therefore pleasing to God? Did He tell you so? And how can you say that you are glad that your religion ignores facts? That does not seem to be an intrinsically good position. Remember, also, that the revelation given by God is not only guaranteed by miracles, but really does rest also upon the firm foundation of its own intrinsic good. Your religion, including the denial of facts, does not.

99. Why did God perform incomprehensible miracles for the Jews, before the period known as historical?

Men cannot be expected to believe in a doctrine as of God unless they have manifest signs that God is really speaking. But what do you mean by incomprehensible? If you mean that we cannot believe that they occurred, then the whole of historical science is useless. If you mean that they really happened, but that no man can comprehend the laws accounting for them, you are right. A miracle is a fact that occurs in a naturally incomprehensible way. If we could fully account for it apart from God, it would be because we could account for it by the ordinary laws of nature, and then it would not be a miracle. Finally, if God performed miracles before a period known as historical, we would know nothing of them. We know of them through history.

100. Must I believe the miracles recorded in the Gospels? Believe a thing which cannot be substantiated in order to be saved?

You are not asked to believe anything which cannot be substantiated in order to be saved. By what rule of evidence, then, can the miracles of the Gospel be substantiated? By sworn affidavit, or in other words, by written declaration on oath. If, in a modern court, I offered documentary evidence given by my friend Jones, the court would wish to be satisfied concerning five things. (1) Did Jones write this statement, or is it a forgery? (2) Is it just as Jones wrote it, or has it been altered or tampered with by interested parties? (3) Did Jones have reliable knowledge, or could he have been misinformed? (4) Granted his knowledge, was he telling the truth or lying? (5) Does he make this statement under oath before God? Now when I offer the Gospels as documentary evidence I am prepared to prove that the assigned authors wrote the books, that the books have not been tampered with, that the writers had first-hand knowledge, that they did not lie, and that they gave their testimony under oath before God.

101. If miracles were necessary to convince men 2,000 years ago, why not to-day?

Miracles were necessary during the preparatory stages of religion, and, above all, during the earliest years of Christianity that the final perfection of that religion might be rapidly and firmly established. Once that true religion was solidly established under the form of the Catholic Church, there was no longer the same need. The Catholic Church is evidence enough in herself, if any man will study the facts without prejudice. However, miracles still occur in the world, and a study of the happenings, say, at Lourdes, will provide any man with sufficient evidence if he approach the matter with a fair and open mind.

102. It is always the same. Miracles happened last week, last century; they will happen some day in the future. They never happen to-day.

That is a sophism of the purest ray serene. Don't you realize that time is essentially in constant succession? Do you want to-day to stay fixed? Never to yield to to-morrow? If a miracle did happen to-day, you would only have to wait twenty-four hours and then say with a sigh, "Ah, yes! It happened yesterday—never to-day!" All the miracles which have happened, occurred on definite days. It was "to-day" when they happened, but the "to-day" on which they happened cannot remain static. And if it is an historical fact that a miracle occurred a century ago, or a week ago, the fact that our "to-day" does not happen to be a week ago in no way disproves the fact. Is all this too deep? Let me give you a simple argument based upon your principles. "They say that Kings of England have died in the past. It is thought that they will die in the future. But I have searched the papers in vain to learn that one died to-day. The truth is, I don't think Kings of England ever die at all!"

103. Will you prove the reliability of the Gospels according to the five requirements outlined by yourself to a previous inquirer?

By all means, although I cannot go very deeply into the matter in the brief time at my disposal. However I shall do my best to give the main elements.

Firstly, the authors assigned wrote the books attributed to them. A knowledge of Hebrew shows that the authors were certainly Jews. Historical and political references show that they were Jews of the first century, for Palestine is shown under conditions before and not after the Fall of Jerusalem in the year 70 A.D. Also had they been written after that date, the writers would not have omitted to make the point that Christ's prophecy had been fulfilled. They do not mention it. All the descriptions, also, are so vivid that they could only have been written by eye-witnesses. And in addition to this internal evidence, we have solid external evidence. Thus Papias, who was the disciple of St. John the Apostle, and who certainly lived in the first century, has left it in writing that one named Matthew first wrote in Hebrew, and that one named Mark wrote what he had heard of Peter. Papias could not have written this had not these two Evangelists already written their Gospels. The Muratorian Fragment, dating from at least the year 170, tells us that the third Gospel was written by Luke; the fourth by John. And there is no evidence at all to the contrary. We have not as much evidence for the authorship of many classical books, of which no one doubts. Also the Apostles and immediate disciples would not have allowed forgeries to be palmed off as genuine. Heretics and pagans would have found their strongest argument in showing the basic documents to be falsely attributed to immediate disciples of Christ. And all regions accepted these four Gospels. If they were not genuine, and one region began the fraud, the rest would have risen up in violent protest. No critic of any value denies the fourfold authorship to-day.

Secondly, the Gospels have never been tampered with or substantially altered. The Gospels had been multiplied by copyists and were quite familiar to the early Christians. Not all could be falsified simultaneously, and changes could easily be detected by comparison. And the early Christians were most vigilant, holding the Gospels in great veneration. Marcion the heretic fabricated a Gospel in the year 110 to suit his heresy, and there was a universal protest at once. All existing manuscripts, back as far as the fourth century, quote the Gospels as they are now. No substantial alterations can have occurred since the fourth century, and they were far less likely to occur during the times nearer to the Apostles. Sincere critics to-day admit the substantial integrity of the Gospels, and those opposed to Christianity concentrate upon other lines of attack.

Thirdly, the Evangelists were reliably informed. Rationalists take refuge in the thought that they were sincere, but laboring under some strange delusion or hallucination. They have no evidence to support the contention, but stake all on a preconceived improbability. They practically say, "We do not see how such things *could* happen, therefore it's no use telling us that they *did* happen." This is prejudice. A few years ago men said, "A man *could* not speak to Australia from England by telephone, and therefore we do not believe that he ever will." The fact has disproved them. A man with a theory can see almost anything, provided it supports his theory, and be blind to the most evident facts if they seem to upset his theory. Rationalists do not like the Gospel facts, and therefore deny them. Forced to admit authorship, integrity, and sincerity, they say, "The writers *must* have been the victims of some hallucination." But if you wish to deny a man's right to the property next door, you must prove something, if only that his title-deeds are false. But it is no use saying, "I do not like the man!" Meantime, all the evidence is against the position of these Rationalists. They have to admit exactness as regards geographical, political, and religious conditions of Palestine. Why should they be less accurate when they describe the sayings and doings of Christ? They are perfectly sane in all their other statements. And are all *four* to have the *same* hallucination, and *all* their lives? There is no trace of fanaticism in their sober accounts; Christ had to accuse them of being "slow to believe"; enemies then and there could not deny the miracles, and must have been suffering from the same hallucination; and the Jews never attempted to deny the facts. The Evangelists were quite reliably informed.

Fourthly, they were sincere. They not only knew the facts, but they told the truth. They gained martyrdom in this life, and on their own principles, stood to gain only hell in the next, if they were lying in so important a matter. If they intended to lie, they could have painted themselves as heroes, instead of depicting their own faults; and above all should not have described a mocked, humiliated, and crucified Master in order to win the veneration of men. On the Jewish material at their disposal they could not have invented the type represented by Christ as the Messiah, and if they did want to invent, might just as well have painted the portrait of a far more glorious Leader from a worldly point of view. No thinker to-day brings the old charge that the Evangelists lied. Finally, that the statements were made under oath before God is abundantly clear. The writers call upon God to witness to the truth of what they write. St. John says, "I testify to everyone that heareth these words"; "He that saw it hath given testimony, and his testimony is true, and he knoweth that he saith true, that you also may believe." St. Paul, also: "I speak the truth. I lie not—my conscience bearing me witness in the Holy Spirit." No modern law-court would reject evidence as clearly given as that for the events and utterances attributed to Christ.

104. Where are the original records?

The original documents have long since perished. The earliest copy is about fourth century, but 1600 years have had their effect even upon that copy. Even parchment perishes with time.

105. You admit no original documents in existence, and therefore no real evidence. Where are your claims?

I have never admitted that there is no real evidence, nor that there are *no* original documents in existence. There are thousands of original documents in existence. The particular original documents, the copies of which we now possess in the Gospels, have perished. But the copies are perfectly reliable, as has been established by comparison of hundreds of independent transcriptions reaching back to the times when the originals were certainly in existence.

106. Why did not God preserve the originals by a miracle?

That was not necessary that we might know their contents. We have true copies. Also that would not have bettered things. Christ did not base His religion upon the reading of Scripture. He established the infallible Catholic Church to teach in His Name. That Church He has miraculously preserved.

107. Why does no reputable historian mention Christ, and His wonderful works?

I have just shown that five reputable historians record the events, the four Evangelists and St. Paul. Their books are as historical as any others. Tacitus, the Roman historian, writing about 70 years after the death of Christ, mentions Him. Also Josephus, the Jewish historian. Also Roman historians were not much concerned with Palestine, an outpost of the empire, and moreover had a supreme contempt for the Jews, discounting all their doings. It is obvious also that the Jewish writers would not be bent on recording an event they would very much like to forget. Finally, absence of evidence in other writers who do not deal *ex professo* with a given subject weighs nothing against positive evidence recorded by reliable historians.

108. I do not mind admitting that the Gospels are historical. But you claim much more than that. You wish us to accept those books as the inspired Word of God. And if we accept the Gospels, we must accept the whole Bible as being the Word of God, for the New Testament quotes the Old Testament again and again as having the authority of God.

All that you say is true. The Bible is the inspired Word of God. There may be difficulties in the interpretation of the Bible, but the fact of its inspiration is certain.

109. *What proof is there that the Bible is the Word of God? Is it any more true than the sacred books of other religions?*

Various texts in the Bible say that they are spoken or written with the authority of God. But that is rather a vicious circle, arguing from the inspiration of the book to its authority, and from the authority back to its inspiration. However, a book that is the inspired Word of God would be expected to say so, and the Catholic Church supplies the further evidence required, as I shall show in a moment.

The fact that the Jews always accepted the Old Testament as inspired, and that Christians have also accepted both Old and New Testaments for so many centuries, also argues to the truth of their inspiration. Such a conviction indicates more than human influence. But still, men may point to a somewhat similar phenomenon among the Mahometans in regard to their Koran, and really sufficient proof is found only in the authority of the Catholic Church in our own times. Let us take the four Gospels first.

We ask you to consider them for the moment as if they were not inspired. We do not deny their inspiration, but for the moment we abstract from it, and make no use of it.

Let us subject the Gospels as books to all the laws of historical criticism—the same laws that we apply to other books. They prove to be reliable historical documents—indeed, there is no genuine historical document in existence, if these are not so. Now these historical documents tell us of a certain historical person who declared that He was God, justified that claim by works which no ordinary man could do, and said that He would establish an infallible church—a church still in this world.

Thus we prove Christ's life and works from historical documents. We prove His divinity from His life and works. We prove the infallible Church from the promise of this divine Person. But we do not yet say that Scripture is inspired, though of course we know that it is. But our rational grounds for that belief come from the fact that the infallible Church of Christ teaches with her authority that the Bible is inspired and the Word of God, and also tells us what books comprise the Bible.

That the Bible is infinitely superior to the sacred books of other religions becomes at once apparent. The most rigid criticism shows the strictly historical character of the Bible. Fabulous narratives cannot stand this test. The supernatural character of the Bible stands out in vivid contrast when compared with the teaching of other religious documents. The Catholic Church, whose very existence in the world to-day cannot be explained by natural forces, guarantees the Bible as the Word of God.

110. *We Protestants know that the Bible is inspired without having to accept the authority of the Catholic Church. We feel that it is the Word of God, and know from the lofty doctrines it contains.*

Your belief is right, though many Protestants are rapidly giving up that belief. For the grounds you allege for your belief scarcely provide a sufficiently rational foundation. You may feel that it is inspired, but nothing can be proved from feelings, and in any case there are others who do not feel that it is inspired. Again, whilst many passages contain lofty doctrines, many other passages are not lofty, and this argument cannot justify the Bible as a whole.

111. *I, for one, do not believe in the Bible. Your own proof is a vicious circle, the Church proving her own infallibility from Scripture, and the inspiration of Scripture from her infallibility.*

It is not a vicious circle, but a lawful spiral argument of which the ends do not meet. Taking the Scriptures as historical documents only, the Church proves the historical fact that Christ endowed her with infallibility. Then using that infallibility she throws new light on the historical books by assuring me that they are inspired. I begin with merely historical books. I finish with inspired historical books. But I did not use inspiration as the basis of my first premise. So, too, I could prove that the present King is the rightful ruler from history only, and after that view him under the aspect of his authority, obeying his legitimate commands. Thus St. Augustine rightly said, even in the fourth century, "I would not accept the Gospels unless the authority of the Catholic Church impelled me."

112. *You think the infallible authority of the Catholic Church grounds enough for your belief?*

Yes. You have only your fallible human opinion as proof that Scripture is not inspired. I uphold the infallible and consistent teaching of the Catholic Church. Disprove her authority to decide which books are inspired and which are not inspired, and you will have made some headway. But until you have done so, your idea is nothing more than an opinion with a value proportionate only to your limited knowledge and mental capacity. That the Catholic Church has the authority I attribute to her I shall show on another occasion.

113. *Ingersoll says that the moment we admit that a book is too sacred to be doubted, we are mental serfs.*

So Ingersoll said that! But the point is, what if he did say it? Is Ingersoll infallible? Has he any more authority than other men, that you should attach such talismanic value to his words? Or do you regard this as a solemn *ex cathedra* utterance binding all irrational men throughout the world?

114. *If God is the Author of the Bible, why did He select words with several meanings, knowing this would ultimately cause confusion and scepticism?*

The progress and mutation of an essentially variable human language is unavoidable. And God did know that the changing mentalities of subsequent generations would lead to confusion. To obviate the danger He could do one of two things. He could stabilize human reason and prevent each human being from mistaking the original sense, or else He could establish certain men to teach in His Name, and finally, if necessary, an infallible tribunal which men could consult in matters of religion. He chose the latter course, and thus never intended Scripture to be the ultimate guide in religious belief. Men who will not accept the Catholic Church, but insist on puzzling out the sense for themselves, have only themselves to blame if they end in scepticism. If the government establishes an inquiry office as a guide to the city and a complete stranger refuses to use its services, he is to blame if he gets lost.

115. *Read the Bible, and you will soon admit that God could not possibly be the author of such a book.*

I have read it many times. But nothing in the Bible disproves the fact of its inspiration. It may be difficult to secure the right interpretation of certain passages, or to grasp the principles involved, but our difficulty in comprehending everything, a difficulty to be expected, avails nothing against the known fact that the Bible is the Word of God.

116. *I believe in the New Testament, but not in the Old Testament.*

There are things in the New Testament just as hard to believe as many things in the Old Testament, and on your principle you should reject much of the New Testament itself. Yet let us act on your admission that you do accept the New Testament. Christ and the Apostles had the same Old Testament as we have to-day. They treat it always as the inspired Word of God in its totality. Christ, the Son of God, would have been the first to declare that it was a fraudulent invention claiming to be the Word of God as people believed, if it were not really the Word of God. Instead, Christ quoted it, giving it full authority. "Do not think that I am come to destroy the law or the prophets. I am not come to destroy, but to fulfill . . . not one jot or one tittle shall pass of the law, till all be fulfilled."—Matt. V., 17. In Luke XXIV., 27, we read, "And beginning at Moses and all the prophets, he expounded to them in all the scriptures the things that were concerning him." Yet you, beginning at Moses, would reject all the scriptures Christ sanctioned! In John V., 39, Christ says, "Search the scriptures for you think in them to have life everlasting; and the same are they which give testimony of me." But Christ did not add, "Yet whilst searching the scriptures, watch out for the parts not inspired!" Not to believe in the Old Testament gives the lie direct to the New Testament; insults the wisdom of God and of Christ; and makes shipwreck of the faith.

117. *Can a Christian believe everything in the Old Testament?*

A Christian must believe that the Old Testament, with all its canonical books, is the inspired Word of God. But one has only to believe in the correct interpretation of what is there written, as is evident. If you reject any genuine part of the Old Testament as not inspired, you violate the Christian faith. It is strange that Protestantism began by charging the Catholic Church with not giving the Scriptures to the laity, and now the Catholic Church has to defend those same Scriptures from the efforts of Protestants to tear them to pieces.

118. *Old Testament teaching is barbaric in parts; not in keeping with the New Testament; nor would God inspire such a record of outrageous crimes.*

Things were permitted in the Old Law not in keeping with the more perfect New Law. But the change is in the Law. There is nothing in the Old Testament which violates any attribute of God, save, of course, the sins of men described in the Old Testament. These latter are recorded, not with approval, but as evil to be reprehended, and as motives of repentance. It is a fallacy to measure the simple blunt standards of more primitive times by modern standards. Also, these accounts prove the trustworthiness of the reports. They are not out to say only the best of Jewish heroes, but narrate exploits far from flattering to the vanity of the Jews, though written by members of the race, not by enemies.

In your readings you have either understood the correct sense, or you have not. If you have, you had better change your ideas. Is the Bible, the inspired Word of God, going to be true when it suits your ideas, or are your ideas going to be true when they are adjusted to God's revealed truth? If God says a thing not quite in accordance with your notions, then you can be sure that your notions are wrong, and you had better renounce them, as you have had to renounce so many other mistakes during your life. Men can be so easily mistaken; God cannot be mistaken.

119. *Is the Book of Genesis to be taken literally or allegorically?*

Each and every word of Genesis need not be taken literally. But the substance of all facts which are fundamental in Christianity are to be taken as literally true.

120. *Colonel Ingersoll has pointed out the mistakes of Moses. He says, "I am probably the only man who has read the Bible through this year in the United States. Everybody talks about the Bible and nobody reads it. That is why it is so generally believed. I have wasted this time, but I had a purpose in view." Ingersoll was a man of great intellectual powers, and had he lived earlier he would have been put to death, as thousands of others, by the Church when they dared to challenge priestcraft.*

What was the basis for the probable opinion of Ingersoll that he alone had read the Bible through that year? An opinion, to be probable, must have good reasons. A guess won't do. Ingersoll's only reason was that other men did not come to his own conclusions. Therefore they could not have read the Bible! If he can get a probable opinion out of that, he is not a fit guide for other men's thought.

Again, it is certain that not everybody talks about the Bible, whilst it is nonsense to say that nobody reads it. Many do believe in the Bible without knowing why, but their reason is not because they have not read it.

That Ingersoll had a purpose in view supplies the key to almost all his writings. Where others read to learn to know and love God, he read with one idea—to destroy religious belief. This purpose colored all his views and rendered him about as fit to interpret religion as a Russian Bolshevic on the British Constitution. Let me assure you that, despite his "great intellectual powers," Ingersoll is one of the easiest of adversaries to refute. No one has been put to death by the Catholic Church, and had Ingersoll been put to death, it would not have been for challenging priestcraft. For such action he would have been commended. But he would have been ordered to cease reviling the Christian Priesthood, though he would have been free to denounce any genuine abuses to the proper authorities.

121. *Is the story of creation, and of Adam and Eve true, despite Evolution?*

The account of creation in Genesis is certainly true, though men have not fully perceived the true interpretation of every detail given in that account. There is nothing in favor of evolution to justify doubting the direct formation of Adam and Eve by God, as we shall see on another occasion.

122. *Ingersoll paints the pretty picture! God made all the animals walk before Adam that he might name them. And the animals came like a menagerie into town, and as Adam looked at all the crawlers and jumpers and creepers, this God stood by to see what he would call them!*

The appeal to the gallery in the mention of a menagerie and town, and then the omission of all names except crawlers, jumpers, and creepers, is evident. "This God *stood* by," is another little lapse. Ingersoll falls down on the simplest Hebraism. The whole passage means that God gave Adam a knowledge suitable to man's estate, and that Adam gave names in human language to the animals of which God gave him intellectual vision. Ingersoll was out of his depth, and had not the intelligence to know it.

123. *Must we believe the account of the fall of man?*

Yes. And facts confirm it. I shall deal with this topic later.

124. *Why did God forbid the Tree of Knowledge? Having endowed man with reason He should encourage man to advance in knowledge. And how I would have liked to have spoken to that serpent! What language did it speak?*

God forbade that tree which could lead man to a knowledge of evil. He gave man reason that he might know what is right and good. It is not advancing in knowledge to acquire erroneous and evil notions. As for the serpent, if you knew what you were talking about, you would not like to have spoken to him. The language he spoke was the language of pride, sensuality, and rebellion.

125. *Is it not absurd to say that Methuselah could live 900 years?*

No. Insects, animals, and men have lives of varying length. Why? It is dependent entirely upon the will of the Omnipotent God who made them. And could He not will 900 years for man just as easily as 90? Is there any reason why He should not will 900 then, merely because He happens to will 90 now? And which is the greater wonder, to make man, or to make him live 900 years? Surely to make man at all. He who can do the greater could quite easily do the lesser. The special reason why God should will such long lives for the patriarchs of old was that they might generate many children and thus set the human race upon its feet. That necessity is no longer in existence.

126. *Angels fell in love with the daughters of men and begat giants. What a legend!*

Genesis VI., 2, says that the sons of God took wives from the daughters of men. These sons of God were not Angels, but the descendants of Seth, whilst carnal and fleshly men were the descendants of Cain. God was rightly angry with these mixed marriages between those who knew the true religion and those who had forgotten and abandoned it. As for the giants, the children of these unions were monsters rather in violence and wickedness than in size, though they were probably big men, and independent in their self-sufficient strength.

127. *The ridiculous story of the flood offends against my common sense.*

Any ridiculous element is supplied by your own imagination. It would be better to find out what the narrative involves, and then put your difficulties. Archæological research justifies the fact. The flood need not have covered the whole world, but could have been local. We have to admit, however, that it destroyed all human beings then living except Noah and those with him in the Ark.

128. *That Ark surely is a fable or symbol. Even on the measurements given it could never have contained all said to be in it.*

It is not a fable, although it does symbolize the Catholic Church in which souls are saved from the moral flood of sin. It was over 400 feet long, 70 wide, and 40 deep. The flood was most probably local, and the animals were of various types from the region only of its occurrence. We are not obliged to believe that all living animals were represented, nor that all animals outside the Ark were destroyed. Men themselves had not spread so far afield at that time, so that Noah and his family were the sole human survivors. The flood happened; the Ark was a fact; all men were drowned save Noah and those with him in the Ark; that much must be accepted in the literal sense. But many subsidiary details need not be, whilst the wholesale imaginative exaggeration of those details is to be entirely rejected. A thing is credible when a sufficiently capable cause is assigned; incredible if the cause I allege could not do it. But if the cause alleged could do it, then it becomes a question of fact. Did it occur? God says that He caused the flood and its consequences. We cannot say that He is mistaken or deliberately deceiving us. I accept it. You must make your choice. But you have given no sufficient reason for unbelief in your letter.

129. *What right had God to drown the animals? They did no harm!*

The question of right does not enter into this question. God has a perfect right to do as He pleases with the work of His own hands. He did not have to create, nor has He any obligation to creatures that He should continue to confer existence upon them. The drowning of the animals is no more difficult than the destruction of vegetation, and what God makes, He is free to unmake. Nor is the vegetative and animal world to be regarded as entirely independent of man who, as a rational animal, is the representative of all material creation. He sums up in himself the mineral, vegetable, and sensitive kingdoms, and is in fact the intelligent voice of creation, alone capable of responsibility. Mysterious though it be, there is a law of solidarity in this world which cannot altogether be overlooked. However, inability to comprehend the full significance of this event is proof only that the human mind is limited, and in no way affects the historical fact.

130. *Do you believe that reflection and refraction caused no rainbows before the flood?*

No. I do not believe that. Nor does Scripture say that there were no rainbows before the flood. If God said, "Look at the sun. As surely as it is there in the heavens I shall not do this thing again," that would not suggest that the sun had not existed before that moment.

131. *God sent the flood to wipe out sin. But in vain. Sin began again. Did God make a mistake, or is it all a fable?*

You are making the mistake. God sent the flood as a just punishment for previous sins and as a lesson to future generations. He did not send it to wipe out the gift of freewill, nor to prevent the possibility of future sin.

132. *Lot was blessed by God. Yet can you imagine a lower moral code than that of a man who would sacrifice his own daughters?*

Lot was blessed by God in some things—not in others. He ended his days in miserable poverty. Not every man who is approved for some good points is therefore an example of all that men should be in everything. God did not approve of Lot's action in this particular case. Yet let us analyze it. Lot was in a sudden and grave difficulty, with little time to weigh things. He was obsessed by the notion of a duty to his guest greater than that to himself and his household. The law of hospitality was very strict, and is still very strict in the East. Absorbed by this ideal, he did not advert to the full gravity of the alternative he hypothetically suggested, an alternative which he probably felt would not be acceptable. It was the act of a man distracted by anxiety, much as a mother might cry, "Kill me rather than my child," in the hope of moving hardened hearts to spare the child she loves rather than with any deliberate intention of being killed herself.

Can I imagine a lower moral code than this code of Lot? Yes. That of the man who is ever ready to take the worst possible view of other people's conduct, with no allowance for interior states of mind, circumstances, or environment, is a far lower code than that of Lot, with his ideals of charity and hospitality, even though they were excessive ideals. Lot did not lack a moral sense. He wished to prevent what he considered the greater of two evils.

133. Can the infallible Catholic Church give me the chemical equation of the reaction which took place when Lot's wife was turned into a pillar of salt?

The Church does not exist to dispense chemical equations. But your question is not based upon reason. Probably Sodom and Gomorrah were destroyed by natural agencies set in movement by God, with earthquakes and volcanic eruptions. Rock-salt abounds in that region, and an upheaval of that material could easily have over-whelmed and embedded Lot's wife because of her delay, leaving a standing hillock of salt as her memorial.

134. Deut. XIII. says that a husband should stone his own wife to death if she try to persuade him to join her in idolatry. "Well now," says Ingersoll, "I hate a god of that kind, and I would not do it." Did God make a mistake, or is Deut. wrong?

Ingersoll, as usual, makes many mistakes.

Firstly, he forgot the theocratic nature of the nation of the Jews at that time. God was the direct ruler of the Jews, and idolatry was going over to the king's enemies, and an act of treason, even in the temporal order. And God has full rights over life and death.

Secondly, if Ingersoll were a judge administering the law of the land, and his own relatives were the criminals brought before him, he would have to act according to the law with impartial justice. He could not condemn others and exempt relatives because they were relatives.

Thirdly, Almighty God took necessary precautions to bring home to the Jews the full malice of a blasphemous idolatry. Ingersoll, with childish imagination, concentrates upon material details, ignoring the vital reason behind them.

Ingersoll's mistakes are nearly as great as those of the man who takes him as a mental and religious guide, regarding his every utterance as infallible.

135. Ingersoll says, "God taught polygamy. I denounce it as the infamy of infamies."

God did not teach polygamy. He permitted it because of men's weakness and frailty without the helps of Christianity, and because it was not opposed to the primary end of the natural law. Ingersoll may constitute himself the supreme dictator of moral law, and give his irrevocable decisions. But the fact remains that his deliberate distortions of the truth are a far more guilty thing than the frailty of men, owing to their bodily passions.

136. God blessed Jacob, who robbed his brother Esau, and lied to his father.

Jacob did not rob Esau. Esau sold his birthright to Jacob, and Jacob obtained blessings which belonged, not to Esau, but to himself. When Isaac asked, "Are you my son Esau?" he really wished to know whether he was speaking to the son to whom he should give his blessing. Jacob, knowing that he was the son who should receive it, replied in the affirmative. Even if we accuse Jacob of a lie, that sin would not destroy his right to the blessing. In this case, God did not inspire the lie, which was Jacob's sin. God did inspire the writer of the Sacred Book to describe the event just as it happened. Of course, God ratified Jacob's right to the blessing.

137. How could Jacob wrestle with an Angel?

An Angel received power from God to employ physical force, as did the Angel who rolled away the stone from the sepulchre of Christ. Jacob was detained against his will in a given place, and naturally described his vain efforts as struggling with an Angel. St. Paul, too, speaks of an Angel to buffet him when alluding to physical trials.

138. *Ingersoll says, "I cannot imagine the Infinite Creator giving a recipe for hair-oil for Aaron's beard!"*

That is just what he did imagine. He cannot describe even his own mental processes. It is patent dishonesty to imply that modern notions of hair-oil are in any way equivalent to the anointing and consecrating of a Priest to God in the ancient Jewish rites.

139. *Could there not have been a hidden spring in the rock struck by Moses?*

There could have been. That would not affect the question. There was no water flowing when Moses struck the barren rock. And to strike a barren rock with a rod is not the normal way of opening up a spring of whose existence one is unaware. If there were no spring, then God also created the water which flowed forth. He who created the oceans could quite easily create a flowing spring of water, for it is certain that God's infinite power was not exhausted by the creating of the oceans.

140. *How could God harden Pharaoh's heart and then punish him for not letting the Jews go?*

The sense is that God permitted Pharaoh to harden his own heart. It is but a Jewish mode of speaking. Exod. VIII., 15, says, "And Pharaoh hardened his own heart." God sent Moses to ask Pharaoh to let the Jews go, and that means that He meant Pharaoh to do so. God would not, therefore, have deliberately prevented Pharaoh from doing so. God permitted Pharaoh to harden his own heart, just as He permits men to sin even in our own days, if they are determined to do so.

141. *The crossing of the Red Sea by Moses and the Jews must surely be a fable.*

No man on earth can prove that this thing did not happen. The only argument is, "It seems to us unlikely." I reply, "Most unlikely, if anyone less than God were responsible for such a happening." But to say that God could not do it, is to misunderstand the difference between the finite and Infinite, between impotence and Omnipotence.

142. *Why did they not cross over by the dry land where the Suez Canal now exists?*

It is not certain that the contour of the country was the same then as now. Some authorities say that the Red Sea swept much farther inland in earlier times, including even the bitter lakes. In any case, under God's direction, the Jews were led away from the dry sections we now know, as described in Numbers ch. 33, that He might show His power and protection, and that the Egyptians might be justly punished, as shown by Exod. XIV., 2.

143. *Will present scientific knowledge let us admit that the sun stood still for Joshua?*

Present scientific knowledge has nothing to say on the subject. With all our present knowledge we still say that the sun rises. We know that it is due to the earth's rotation, but speak of things as they appear to our senses. Joshua would have more right to laugh at us for speaking of the sun as rising, despite our boasted knowledge, than we have to ridicule his expression that the sun stood still. He experienced the phenomenon of light for a period longer than usual, and he describes it by the phrase, "The sun stood still." The phenomenon could have occurred by the cessation of the earth's rotation at God's bidding, or simply by His willing the light to be continued despite the ordinary movements of the earth. However, the Church has not defined the literal truth of each and every event described in Scripture. She teaches that the Bible is the Word of God, whatever be its correct interpretation. Miraculous events are to be accepted, until the opposite is proved true. Exactly what God did in such cases is not certain, but presumption is for the literal fact in default of contrary evidence. The general lesson of God's Providence is to be accepted without reserve.

144. God did this to enable Joshua to kill a few more innocent people fighting for their homes and families!

That was not the reason. You do not advert to a great principle. God owns the earth, and can allot any particular portion of it to any particular people. And if He, the Owner of all does so, then the tenants for the time being lose their right to the appropriated land. Joshua warned the Gabaonites beforehand, "If you dwell in the land that falls to our lot we can make no league with you." Jos. IX., 7. The Gabaonites knew this to be the will of God. "It was told us thy servants," they said, "that the Lord thy God had promised his servant to give you all the land." Jos. IX., 24. Realizing their obligation, they determined not to go, thinking themselves strong enough to rebel against God's decree. God taught them a lesson, and the Jews had as much right to put them out by force as I would have to evict you from a house occupied by you without definite lease, should the house suddenly come to me by sale or gift, and I wished to live in it. This objection of Ingersoll overlooks the question of just title, but his end in view made the lawyer ignore his legal brains whenever his irreligious complex affected him.

145. Are we to believe that the story of Jonah and the whale is true?

When Christ told the story of the prodigal son, the characters of the story were not really historical persons. But the story was a true description of types and of God's mercy. Now some authors say that the Book of Jonah narrates a kind of parable somewhat akin to the parables of Christ. Others, and more probably, say that it is actual history, and that a real Jonah was really swallowed by a real fish, though not necessarily by a whale as we understand that word. The Church leaves us free to accept either view. The purpose of the Book is worthy indeed of God, teaching as it does that God much prefers to show mercy to a repentant people rather than vindicate His justice by the infliction of punishment. Nor is the story incredible even as actual fact. A thing is credible or incredible according to the presence or absence of a sufficient cause. I grant that the events in the Book of Jonah can be explained only by a miraculous intervention on the part of Almighty God. But once I say that God was the Agent at work, then the cause alleged could account for it, and the question is not, "Could it happen?" but, "Did it happen?" The main reason why people doubt the fact is because they cannot see *how* it could happen; a thing which does not necessarily prove more than that they cannot comprehend everything. The life of a human embryo during the period of its gestation is as much a mystery according to God's natural laws as would be the life of Jonah for three days inside a large fish according to God's extraordinary intervention. And who will say that God is never free to act outside the ordinary laws He Himself has established? In reality there is no more difficulty in accepting the miracle of Jonah than there is in accepting the undoubted miraculous fact of Christ's resurrection.

146. *There is nothing in heathendom more pagan or cruel than the story of Job.*

I grant the apparent cruelty in the sufferings of Job taken in themselves. How the circumstances justified them I shall show in a moment.

You cannot say you know of nothing more pagan, for pagan means without the true God, and this story is very much one of the true God. If you know of nothing more cruel in heathendom, you also know of nothing in heathendom approaching the sublime moral lessons and lofty principles inculcated by this Book.

147. *Satan wagers with God that he can make Job curse his Maker!*

It is certain that Satan and God did not meet and make a wager. That is but a literary expression, driving home the truth that Satan is opposed to God and resents that others should serve Him. Job was a good man, devoted to God. Satan wished to rob God of the honor and glory given by such an adherent, if necessary by special and extraordinary efforts. Even Satan could not do so without God's permission, and God, who knows all things, permitted his efforts.

148. *God takes the wager, and delivers His servant to all the fiendish cruelty the devil can devise!*

Firstly, God's allowing Satan to afflict Job is no more difficult than His permission of other temporal afflictions, such as the sufferings of an individual from cancer, or of thousands from an earthquake. It is the ordinary problem of suffering, the difficulty of reconciling a merciful God, who certainly does exist, with the fact of physical and moral evil, which also certainly does exist. The answer to the problem of suffering in general is also the answer to the story of Job, to a great extent.

Secondly, in this world there are certain things better than bodily health and worldly goods. Many a man has thought more of his honor than of his life before to-day. The asset of a noble character is better than the asset of a prosperous earthly career, and God gave Job the opportunity of a supreme nobility, to be attained only by way of the cross similar to that of Christ. A brave man feels honored when selected for some noble duty fraught with danger, and is grateful for the trust reposed in him by his leader.

Thirdly, Job was enabled to glorify God far more by fidelity when things went wrong than by fidelity when things were going right. And God more than compensated Job for his temporal trials by eternal happiness. Job would not have been without his experience for any earthly good, once it had been accomplished.

149. *Do you maintain that Job really existed?*

Yes. He was chosen as a type, and really did serve God in the midst of great trials. But the incident has been described in poetical form, allowing for the use of literary description and amplification. I could tell the same facts in dry technical language, or in glowing prose, or in highly polished verse, and the literary form would not affect the objective historical value of the event described.

150. *Wherein did God show Himself kinder or more reliable than Satan?*

All through, God permitted affliction for the greater good of Job. Satan inflicted suffering for the greater misery of Job. God intended the justification of right principles, Satan their destruction. God was more reliable than Satan, for He was ever prepared to assist Job by His grace as often as Job demanded it, whilst Satan intended only the degradation of Job and the insulting of God. God is always reliable, Satan never. And above all when we view the lasting results of their influence.

151. *Are there not difficulties in the New Testament as well as in the Old Testament?*

Yes. But there are no real contradictions. To prove a contradiction you must show that the texts are undoubtedly authentic, and that they admit of no possible conciliation. When supposed contradictions have been urged by adversaries, expert defending scholars have advanced various quite probable theories by which the difficulties would be solved. They are not obliged to prove one or other of their theories certainly true. The one who asserts contradiction declares that there is no sense in which both accounts *could* be true. The moment competent scholars offer a reasonable and probable explanation by which difficulties would be reconciled, necessary contradiction is excluded. Even if rationalist critics proved every suggested explanation to be unreasonable and certainly false, they would not necessarily have proved a contradiction in Scripture. At most they would have proved that interpreters had not yet discerned the correct method of reconciling an apparent divergence.

152. *If the Gospels are inspired, why the inconsistencies on all important matters?*

There are no inconsistencies in any single important matter. Each Gospel is a fragmentary account, and each writer gives complementary, not contradictory details. Supposing that I went from London to Rome for a three months' holiday, but on the way broke my journey for a week in Paris. Later on I might write to a friend, "I spent my holidays in Rome." Yet to another friend I could say, "During my holidays I stayed in Paris." There is no real inconsistency, although the friends, on comparing notes, might find an apparent inconsistency. But almost at once they would say, "He might have done both. The one does not exclude the other. He omitted to mention Paris in the one account, Rome in the other." So, too, with the Gospels. One Gospel will mention details which others pass over in their brief accounts.

153. *Do you maintain that mistakes and interpolations by copyists were not possible in transcriptions of the Bible?*

Mistakes and interpolations were certainly possible, but by comparison of independent copies these are discoverable. Yet remember that the Catholic Church does not say that copyists were inspired. Inspiration is claimed for the original Evangelists. In so far as later copies or versions exactly correspond with their original writings they give the inspired Word of God. In so far as they are not exact, they do not.

154. *The genealogies of Christ as given by the Gospel afford one much difficulty. If Jesus was not the son of Joseph, why is His genealogy traced through Joseph?*

Jesus was not the natural son of Joseph. But Mary, who was the Mother of Jesus, was related to Joseph, whose genealogy was also her own. It was a Jewish custom to record descent only through the male line.

155. *St. Matt. gives 42 generations; St. Luke gives 72. Why?*

Neither intended to give all the generations. The present Prince of Wales could say, "I was born of George V., who was descended from Queen Victoria." Another writer could say, "The Prince of Wales was born of George V., who was born of Edward VII., who was born of Queen Victoria." Both accounts would be right, although one would be inadequate.

Why did St. Matt. choose to give 42 generations only? Because he wrote for the Jews, and wished to show that Christ was the Messiah, the Son of David. In Hebrew David's name consists of three letters, and those letters numerically signify 14. Thus D-V-D have the numerical signifiance of 4-6-4. Following a Jewish custom, St. Matt. gives three times 14, *i. e.*, 42 generations, or the Davidic generation.

St. Luke, on the other hand, chose 72, because, having been the companion of St. Paul, the Apostle of the Gentiles, he wrote for the Gentiles. Jewish tradition held that there were 72 races of men throughout the world, and St. Luke wished to show that Christ would call all nations to His religion. This may seem complicated to us, but it was not to the Jews of those times.

156. But even granted no real inconsistency in the numbers, there seems to be a great inconsistency as regards the names. Also, how could Jacob be the father of Joseph, as St. Matt. says; yet Heli be his father, according to St. Luke's account?

Many scholars have replied that Jacob and Heli were half-brothers. Upon Heli's death without issue, Jacob married his widow in accordance with the Levitical law to provide children to Heli. Joseph would thus be the natural son of Jacob, and the legal son of Heli. In this case, since St. Matt. gives the natural genealogy, and St. Luke the legal genealogy, we have two different yet correct lines of ancestry.

157. Can you prove this solution correct?

The obligation to do so does not rest with me. An adversary has failed to prove contradiction until he has succeeded in proving it incorrect. It would be very difficult to do so. Meantime, the theory certainly has its own probability in accordance with the Levitical law.

158. You say that many scholars thus reply. Do you suggest that others propose a more satisfactory explanation?

Others believe that they have a more satisfactory solution of the difficulty. The Jews disputed among themselves whether the Messiah was to come from David through Solomon or through Nathan. St. Matt. abstracts from the notion of consanguinity and deals only with the juridical rights of Davidic succession. A successor is not necessarily a son, and St. Matt. shows how the Davidic rights descended to Joseph and his legal son Jesus through Solomon. The genealogy given by St. Matt. has thus only a conventional value, and necessarily differs from the real and legal genealogy according to consanguinity given by St. Luke. Many modern scholars claim that this theory has greater probability than the preceding explanation, and would reply by denying the existence of the problem when asked to solve "the problem of reconciling the divergent genealogies." On their principles there would have to be divergence.

159. How could Augustus order a census of the "whole world" at that time?

The expression meant *everybody*, whether in a given province or locality.

160. Antiquarians say that there never was a census of the Roman Empire.

If men say that, ask them to prove it. If they could mention a thousand books which do not mention such a census that would not prove that a census did not take place, but merely that those books do not mention it. Josephus, in his Jewish Antiquities, describes a census of Judea; a census to which St. Luke refers in Acts V., 37. An ounce of positive evidence is worth a thousand omissions.

161. *But the census mentioned by Josephus took place A.D. 6, not at the time of Christ's birth!*

There was a previous census at the time of Christ's birth, of which Josephus makes no mention. St. Luke is a perfectly reliable historian. Both in his Gospel and in the Acts he proves his exact knowledge of Graeco-Roman affairs, and begins his Gospel with a reference to his diligence in verifying the facts he narrates. He would not at once proceed to make serious and easily avoidable errors. The census did not necessarily take place simultaneously in all parts, and the distinct census St. Luke mentions in his Gospel c. II., V., I could easily refer to a preliminary census according to Jewish customs. His very expression "In those days" suggests a long drawn-out process.

162. *At least St. Luke says that Cyrinus, governor of Syria, published the decree of enrollment. But Quintilius Varus was governor at the time of Christ's birth.*

The English version has the words, "This enrolling was first made by Cyrinus, the governor of Syria." But a better translation of the Greek would be, "The first enrolling was made by Cyrinus, the procurator, or quaestor, of Syria." St. Luke knew of two distinct enrollings under Cyrinus, the first when he was procurator under Varus, and which he mentions in his second chapter of the Gospel; the second under Cyrinus as governor; an enrolling which he mentions in the Acts. It is not mere hypothesis that Cyrinus twice exercised authority in Syria; the first time under Varus, the second time in charge. It is the conclusion of the studies of Mommsen, and also of Zumpt, after his study of inscriptions dealing with this matter at Tivoli, outside Rome.

163. *Matt. II., 14 says that the Holy Family went to Egypt until the death of Herod. Lk. II., 39, says that they waited 40 days for the Purification, and went thence to Nazareth! Which is correct?*

Both are equally correct. After the child was born Joseph and Mary waited 40 days for the Purification; then came the flight to Egypt, followed by the return to Nazareth, as mentioned by St. Matt. II., 23. St. Luke omits to mention the flight to Egypt, and mentions only the Purification, and the return to Nazareth. In II., 39, St. Luke says, "*After* they had performed all things according to the law, they returned to Nazareth." He does not say *immediately* after, and it is evident that he intends to stress the faithful observance of the law, not to fix the time of their return. Some people are only too ready to take an inconsistency for granted, and then to use their assumption as sufficient grounds for the denial of inspiration. This attitude is most unscientific. Also it must be noted that the argument from silence is very much abused. Remember that it has no value unless the author, according to his scope, be strictly bound to state what we find omitted. None of the Evangelists sets out to give every detail of Our Lord's life, and it is absurd to say, "This writer should have given what we desire, if it be true; but he does not give it; therefore he knew nothing of it, and it must be false." On such a principle, any historian who gives what another historian chooses to omit, could be accused of falsehood.

164. *Can we believe that the devil would promise things to God in order to secure His worship?*

No. But he could quite well tempt an apparently human being whom his finite intelligence did not know for certain to be God, and in order to test his conjecture that he might be.

165. How could the devil carry off God and set Him on a hill in Galilee from which he could see all the kingdoms of the earth?

God cannot be carried anywhere. He is a Spirit, and not subject to local transportation. Nor is it honest to attribute to God, making no mention of his incarnate human nature, that which happened to that human nature. The Son of God in His assumed human nature was subjected to this temptation. There is nothing repugnant in the devil being allowed to carry a material object to a height. The devil is a spiritual being, and if God, a spiritual being, can create a material universe, a spiritual being can certainly receive the power to make displacements in the universe. As for seeing all the kingdoms of the earth, we can see in two ways—by eyesight, or by intellectual vision. In this case, mental vision was sufficient.

166. Have not critics proposed hundreds of difficulties such as the foregoing?

Yes. But the mere fact of their having proposed them is not very disturbing. Catholic scholars have in every case provided possible and probable explanations, according to which apparent divergencies are reconciled. Nor can any number of difficulties in interpretation destroy the value of the positive proofs of the authentic and inspired character of Sacred Scripture as briefly outlined under Nos. 103 and 109 above. Further difficulties will be encountered when we come to deal with particular phases of the Christian religion, but in the meantime the fact stands that as human beings we owe certain duties to God which involve the practice of a religion, and that we are obliged to accept from among all the religions in the history of mankind the religion of the Bible.

CHAPTER FIVE

THE CHRISTIAN FAITH

167. *Are not the Jews the chosen people of God?*

They were God's chosen people until the coming of Christ, and they could have been among His chosen people now, had they remained true to God. God did not change in His attitude to them; rather they changed in their attitude to Him. They had been taught to look forward to the Redeemer. But when He came they rejected Him because they wished Him to bring them temporal, not spiritual gifts.

168. *What was the religion of Noah?*

Man has always had a religion taught by God. But this religion falls into four great divisions:—

1.—The religion of Adam, who was instructed immediately by God. This was the first stage, and is known as the religion of innocent man.

2.—After Adam's fall, Adam handed on to his children the truth about God, and the duty of worshipping Him. Thus Abel offered sacrifice. The traditions were transmitted by Adam's posterity, but memories faded. Still, conscience always dictated what was naturally right, and this period could be called the period of natural law. However, God gave occasional revelations to various individuals, such as the Patriarchs, over and above the natural law, and this stage is often called the period of the Patriarchal religion, or the period of pre-Mosaic unwritten law.

3.—The third stage came with Moses. After the re-multiplication of the human race from Noah, men again began to forget God, and God gave to Moses a clearer exposition of religious duties to be put into writing. This is known as the stage of the written law, or that of the Mosaic religion.

4.—Finally God sent His own Son to give the more perfect law—the Christian law—which the Catholic Church teaches to-day in its fullness, and will teach till the end of time.

Noah belonged to the second of these four stages, that of the Patriarchal unwritten law.

169. *Why did God delay the sending of His Son with the perfection of the law?*

The delay was adapted to mankind's natural methods of progress from the less perfect to the more perfect. It taught the human race its need of God from sad experience. It brought out the real dignity of Christ which could thus be heralded by a long series of prophets. God is not so impatient as man. He is quite content to wait for an acorn to become an oak tree, rather than create all oak trees immediately.

170. *Christ was a Jew, and practiced the Jewish religion. Why would He establish another religion when the religion of God was already in existence?*

As stated above, God gave the true religion to mankind gradually, so that men would be prepared by more simple doctrines for still more noble truths. Thus He sent Moses the lawgiver, and after him a series of prophets to explain the law and to predict the coming of the Messiah. Christ fulfilled these predictions and taught the perfect law of God. The religion known by the Jews before Christ was therefore but imperfect and preparatory. The religion of Christ was its perfect fulfill-ment, and the Jews should have recognized and accepted it. They did not, and then Christ sent his Apostles to preach it to the Gentiles. Christ did not therefore es-tablish another religion. Christianity is the perfect development of the Jewish re-ligion, just as the perfect tree is the perfect development of the seed from which it grew.

171. Can you show from Scripture that Christ intended this perfect de-velopment of the Mosaic religion to be distinct from the religion of the Synagogue?

Yes. Referring to the future, Christ said, "I will build my Church." The Synagogue was already established. Christ prescribed new doctrines, new modes of worship, and a new form of authority. He even predicted to His Apostles, "In the Synagogue you shall be beaten." Mk. XIII., 9. The intended distinction of His Church from the prefigurative Synagogue is most clear.

172. In what did the religion of Christ differ from that taught by Moses?

Christ retained all the basic laws of religion and morality contained in the progressively revealed Jewish preparation, abolishing only the particular rites and ceremonies which were purely figurative, and also the imperfections of the initial religion.

173. If Christianity is the true development of the Jewish religion, why is it not the religion of the Jews to-day? Why did not the Jews accept Christ?

Many individuals did. As a race the Jews did not. This was not because Christ did not sufficiently prove His mission, but because the leaders of religious thought, and the teachers of the people had lost the true religious spirit, had self-ishly transferred their affections to a love of their own high places, and had sub-stituted the idea of a magnificent temporal ruler for the idea of a spiritual Saviour. They wanted deliverance from the tyranny of the Romans, and help to trample upon them in turn. Since Christ did not fit in with their earthly notions and ambitions, the leaders rejected Him. The majority of the people, dependent upon the Scribes and Pharisees for religious direction, obeyed these leaders, their own fears, and their national pride. The first members of the Christian Church were individual Jews chosen by Christ to spread His doctrines among the Gentiles; and this, in accordance with Christ's own prediction in the parable of the great supper, where those first invited would not come. Indeed an earlier warning had been given to the Jews that their birthright would pass to the Gentiles if they did not overcome their attachment to earthly ideals in the incident of Esau's selling his birthright to Jacob. Although Christianity should be the religion of the Jews, therefore, it is not, through their own fault as a race. The modern Jew takes his religion for granted, without inquiring deeply into the question.

174. God treated the Jews unfairly. It must have been difficult to com-prehend the teachings of Christ, and He offered them no material ben-efits.

God did not treat the Jews unfairly. They had every opportunity given them to recognize the truth. Christ offered them the evidence of many miracles in the material order and before their eyes. They could not deny these miracles, but in their bad will ascribed them to the devil. Christ, as promised, came to offer eternal spiritual benefits, the only lasting ones and the only ones which the grave cannot take from us. Had He not offered such benefits, the Jews would have been justified in rejecting Him. But that He did not offer the material benefits He did not come to give, can never justify the Jews in their rejection of Him.

175. If the miracles were so evident, I don't see how the Jews could refuse to accept Christianity?

Many a man knows what he ought to do, but to do it is another thing altogether. The Jews could not honestly deny that Christ was of God, and that His religious teaching should be accepted. Some did accept it; others did not. Even God would not compel these to accept the true religion, and Christ warned them of the guilt in their bad will when He said, "He who does not believe shall be condemned."

176. Most people who are Christians cannot give a valid reason for their faith. Will you give me a valid reason for your faith?

Yes.

Historically, it is certain that Christ really lived, really claimed to be God, proved that claim by His supreme command over the laws of nature established by God, taught the Christian religion, and obliged man to accept that religion.

Philosophically, Christianity alone gives an adequate solution and explanation of the origin, condition, and purpose of the human race.

Religiously, it infinitely surpasses all other forms of religion, and alone completely responds to the innate religious tendencies of man.

Theologically, I am a Christian because God has given me the grace to perceive the truth of Christianity, and to embrace it.

Morally, I am obliged in strict justice to accept a religion specified and imposed by Almighty God.

177. Christ did not intend His religion for you. He intended it for the Jews only.

Christ was fully aware of the prophecy of Isaiah II., 2, that all nations would be called to His Church. He *did* intend that His doctrines should be preached to the Jews first, and only afterwards to the Gentiles, and for this reason He told His disciples not to preach it to the Gentiles during the period reserved to the Jews. But in St. Matt. XVIII., 19, Christ Himself tells the Apostles to "Go, teach all nations."

178. If acceptance of Christianity be necessary for salvation, what of those who lived before Christ?

The merits and grace of Christ were applied by God to men of goodwill in anticipation of His death on the Cross. God, in His eternity, is not conditioned by time, and men could benefit by the death of Christ just as they can make use of an inheritance which is absolutely certain to be given to them in due time. The merits of Christ were applied to Jews of goodwill in virtue of their faith in a Redeemer to come. Those who through no fault of their own did not know of a Redeemer to come were saved if they obeyed the natural dictates of their conscience, and repented of their failings. Every single human being has the moral standard that what is apprehended to be morally good must be done, whilst moral evil must be avoided.

179. If Christianity taught people to be so good, why did the early Christians meet with nothing but persecution?

The more evil a man is, the more he resents the goodness of others. Every good man is a living condemnation of the conduct of evil men. The Jews could not point to a single sin in Christ, yet they crucified Him. And Christ said, "The servant is not above his master. As they have persecuted Me, they will persecute you." The quickest road to unpopularity is to refuse to do evil with the majority. The world has no hatred of its own, but the enemies of worldliness it hates. The early Jews and Romans hated Christianity, for both peoples feared that it would interfere with their comfort. To-day the Catholic Church enjoys this inheritance of antagonism as does no other religion.

180. *Does not Christianity to-day differ vastly from the religion Christ preached?*

Outside the Catholic Church, yes. But in the Catholic Church the exact religion of Christ has come down to us in virtue of Christ's promise to be with His Church all days till the end of the world. This assertion will be justified in a later section.

181. *Have not downright absurdities been tagged on to the teachings of Jesus?*

They have—but not by the Catholic Church. And remember that greater absurdities still have been put forward by pretended human reasoning.

182. *Early Christianity boasted many miracles; Christianity can boast none to-day!*

God has never ceased to perform miracles in favor of true Christianity, but it is not necessary that so many should occur to-day. More frequent miracles were necessary in the early Church to secure its rapid propagation. But the Catholic Church is now firmly established. Read a little history, note all the forces employed against the Church during the centuries, and then tell me whether it is not a standing miracle to find that Church still existing with undiminished vitality and able to claim over 400 million adherents. On this subject of miracles, also, consult Nos. 95-103.

183. *Would you say that the world has benefited by Christianity?*

Yes. It has benefited in a thousand different ways. Christianity has elevated men's thoughts to a higher level, directed men's wills to a greater good, and has indirectly affected their well-being even in this world in almost every department of life. If the world is less happy to-day than in years past, it is because, whilst men still profess to be Christian, they are less willing to behave as Christians and to put their principles into practice. Christianity does not force men to be good in spite of themselves. But if men can be really miserable only by forsaking Christian principles, it shows that Christianity practiced is very likely the one true remedy. Let all men live up to Christian principles, and then if the world is not better, you can blame Christianity.

184. *Christian Churches are everywhere, yet misery and distress get worse all over the world!*

The growth of misery and distress is not due to the multiplication of Churches. Many professing Christian Churches, of course, do not stand firmly for the true principles of Christ. And even the growth of the Catholic Church cannot influence much those who will not submit to her laws. As the Church grows, so does population, and with population, evil practices. Man is endowed with intelligence, and this gives him an uncanny power of inventing new modes of iniquity which animals could not suspect. Thus we have a rotten Press, the propagation of birth-control, Godless education, and what-not. The mystery is, not that we have so many troubles, but that the distress is not greater than it is. We can account for it only by God's mercy, and by the fact that the Church does make some reparation to Him in the name of mankind. If mankind got all it really deserves, you would have something to write about!

Another little matter to remember is that Christianity is not to rid the world of trouble and distress, but to save souls from having to endure these things in the next life. Christianity enables people to bear gladly those sufferings which are permitted by God for their greater sanctification, or as an expiation of their past sins. Also many have been brought to God by suffering who have believed in their self-sufficient health and strength that they could manage quite well without Him. Consider once more the principles given in the replies 13-24.

185. There are millions belonging to other religions. Are we Christians superior to them?

At least, Christianity is the superior religion in historical foundation, reasonableness, and in loftiness of teaching and destiny.

186. They think we are wrong as we think they are. May not Christianity be wrong, and some other religion right?

There is no possibility of that. There is a chance that a man who has not studied the solid evidence for Christianity might become flurried and doubtful in the presence of rival and confident claims. But his doubts would be due to defective information. Again, the fact that a man believes a religion true does not prove it right. It only proves that he thinks it right. He is right who can prove his belief to be solidly grounded. A comparative study of religions proves that Christianity alone has demonstrative evidence of its divine origin. However lofty the doctrines of other religions, they prove to be man-made doctrines, or else they are traced to the influence of primitive or later revelations of God, revelations which legitimately end in the Catholic Church, and not in any other religion.

187. The more I learn, the more I wonder!

The more you learn about diverse opinions, the more you will wonder at such diversity. The more you learn about the foundations of Christianity, the more you will wonder that men do not advert to its solidity.

188. Is it not likely that the worship of the sun-gods and earth-gods was replaced by the milder form of the sacrifice of Christ-god, and that Christianity will also yield place to a more ethical system?

It is absurd and quite unhistorical to maintain the derivation of the divinely revealed worship of the true and Infinite God, given precisely to correct the errors of men, from the humanly invented worship of sun-gods and earth-gods. Also human reason will never invent a more ethical system than that prescribed for all men by the Author of all justice. It is a little bit early to talk of a more ethical system when men cannot even live up to the ethics of present Catholicity. The Catholic Church tells her children to avoid sin as a very plague; to be strictly temperate, chaste, and pure; to practice humility, yet to possess the courage of the Saints in resisting all evil inclinations and overcoming obstacles to their sanctification; to be strictly just and truthful in their relations both with God and their fellow men; to be faithful for life in the duties of marriage; to love and worship God because He is God, and not merely because, and as long as they feel like doing it. Catholic ethics perfect all that is noblest in man, and culminates in that supreme charity which thinks no evil and much less utters it. When men have come to this standard, then it will be time to speak of a more ethical system. But when they do attain it, their intelligence will be so unclouded by the influence of lower passions that they will see clearly that they have attained the full truth. To Catholics, of course, all this is clear by the very gift of faith.

189. You speak of faith. But faith is an emotion, an involuntary action of the senses.

If that is your idea of faith, no wonder you find difficulty. But that is not faith at all, and certainly not the faith required by the Catholic Church. By faith we believe things. Now people do not believe with their feelings and emotions. They believe with their minds. Belief is a mental conviction. If I tell a woman that her son has been killed, her faith in my knowledge and veracity will make her believe the truth that her son has actually been killed. From this knowledge emotion may follow as an effect. But an effect is not its cause. Faith, then, is not an emotion, nor is it of the senses. Faith is the intellectual admission that a certain thing is true because although we have not seen the reality ourselves, we reasonably admit that the one who has told us must be reliably informed and not intending to deceive us. Nor is faith involuntary. If I see an accident, I know that it occurred, and it is useless to tell myself that it did not occur. But if you tell me of an accident, and I did not see it myself, then I have no direct evidence. All my evidence is indirect, and I can choose to believe you, or not to do so. I can put my faith in what you tell me, or refuse. It should console you to know that the Catholic Church is just as opposed to the idea of faith you condemn as you yourself are opposed to it. In fact she has solemnly defined such a type of assent to be no faith at all, and forbids any priest to receive into the Church one who believes that such a caricature can do duty for the intellectual conviction known as faith.

190. Your faith may be right, but may it not be wrong?

True Christian faith cannot lead one into error. We prove that God has said a thing, and believe because He has said it. Doubt would be possible only could God be deceived, or deceive mankind. But He could not. He knows all things, and is Truth itself. Also He has given abundant external signs to confirm His revelation. We are certainly right because He must be right.

191. I cannot understand how highly intellectual men can accept obvious legends and fairy tales as historical facts without question or doubt!

Highly intellectual men do accept the doctrines of Christianity as certain. Being highly intellectual, they have not done so without profound investigation of the reasonable grounds for their position. And knowing that such men are convinced, it is not highly intellectual conduct to reject as legends and fairy tales the doctrines they accept, without making a similar investigation.

192. I myself refuse to accept anything which will not stand the acid test of reason. Faith may be a virtue, but it is no use burying one's head in the sand!

I fully agree. Faith is a virtue, and a great gift of God. But it does not imply the burying of one's head in the sand. It teaches us a number of things which are above reason, for the revealed truths known only to God must be a little above ordinary human thought. But whilst faith teaches some truths so profound as to be above natural reason, it never teaches any single doctrine which is opposed to sound and rational principles. Prove any given doctrine to violate correct principles of reason, and I shall cease to believe in it at once.

193. Do you not maintain that faith in Christianity is necessary for one's eternal salvation?

Those who do not know the facts are not required to believe doctrines of which they are unaware. Those who do know the facts cannot be saved unless they believe, for refusal is to insult the God who has deigned to reveal the truth to men.

194. Ingersoll says that it is monstrous that future happiness should depend upon belief.

Is that so! Then even if you prove to demonstration that God has said a thing, you need not believe it! You may call God a liar, and if your doing so interferes with your happiness it is monstrous! Ingersoll was a wise man!

195. He says that the notion of faith in Christ being rewarded, whilst dependence upon reason, observation, and experience merits eternal punishment is too absurd to need refutation.

No one ever said that dependence upon reason, observation, and experience merits eternal punishment. Such an assertion proves that Ingersoll did not use reason, observation, or experience to find out the exact teachings of Christianity. He just wrote on, his prejudice supplying for reason in the construction of his nonsensical arguments.

196. If a man does not accept the Bible, can you convince him of your supernatural doctrines by reason alone?

We can prove historically that God certainly gave the Christian revelation, and right reason cannot refute the evidence. It has to admit the value of the Gospels as documentary sources. But reason alone cannot make a man accept the contents of that revelation as having binding value. Only the grace of God can do that, and the preparation best suited to the reception of the gift of faith is a good moral life, and earnest prayer for the help of God.

197. Then without the grace of God one cannot have this faith?

By reason alone any ordinary man can know that God exists, that He has given a revelation to man, and any ordinary man is capable of learning the fundamental teachings of Christianity. Yet the perception of the vital force and the sheer reality of the truths God has revealed, with consequent belief in them, requires grace from God. But one who has the goodwill to submit to God's authority, and to pray earnestly for the light to know God's will, can be certain that the necessary supernatural help will be offered to him.

198. I do not see that I am responsible for my position. I applied my reason to the Bible just as I would to anything else, and I doubt Christianity.

You have ignored the element of grace, and have not implored the help of God. Merely human reasoning is not enough. Brains cannot be the condition of salvation. If so, the intellectual would have a better chance of salvation than the less intelligent. You must look round for another method of approach to the religious problem. Whilst no one asks you to go against right reason, yet you must be prepared to rise above it. St. Paul rightly says that the natural man does not perceive those things which are of the spirit of God.

199. But I cannot believe in the Divinity of Christ.

Since God does not deny any man of really goodwill sufficient grace, the fault lies in your own will. You can believe, if you wish. If you have not examined the evidence for His divinity, you can do so. Until you have done so, your belief that He is not God is mere credulity. You should say, "I have no opinion on the subject. I have not studied the evidence." When you have studied the evidence carefully, you will have found at least three things:

(1) The documentary evidence concerning Christ is perfectly sound.

(2) Christ certainly claimed to be God.

(3) He certainly did things for which God alone could be responsible.

Whether, after this, you will accept what Christ taught or reject it will be a matter for your own choice.

200. Then men can believe or disbelieve in Christianity as they please?

They can, although they may not, once it has been sufficiently brought to their notice. You see, Christ taught certain doctrines, but did not offer any intrinsic demonstration of their truth. He demands that we accept them as a tribute to His knowledge and veracity. As, therefore, He did not do more than merely tell us these truths we are physically free to accept them because of our faith in Him, or to refuse them. To believe is to pay a tribute of confidence, and thus to merit His friendship and the rewards He promised. To refuse to believe deserves punishment because it insults so good and wise a being as Christ.

201. I have studied Christianity, and it is my honest opinion that it is not true. Yet you tell me that I am to believe that it is true!

With the help of God's grace, which will not be refused if you desire it, you are able to believe that it is true. A classification of possible states of mind will clarify things for you.

(1) After due study of a certain proposition, a man might see that its truth is intrinsically evident, as one knows for example that two and two make four. By intrinsic analysis the opposite is evidently false. In this case a man has not an opinion, nor a belief. He has knowledge by intrinsic evidence, and is not free to think differently. He does not merely incline to think so.

(2) Another state of mind, however, is that of the willfully ignorant. One who adverts to the fact that there is a certain problem can refuse to study it, and freely choose to have no opinion on the subject.

(3) Another stage is that of the willful doubter. He studies the question to a certain extent. After thinking it over somewhat inadequately he says, "I do not know. There seems to me to be six for, and half a dozen against. I am not inclined to accept one position rather than another. I am in doubt about the whole matter." Such a man can choose to let it go at that, or to continue his investigations until he solves his doubts one way or the other.

(4) After due reflection, a man can come to the conclusion that there is intrinsic evidence neither for nor against a given doctrine. As far as he knows, it could be true, or it could be false. But he knows that some authoritative person has said it is true. There is nothing in the proposition itself to prevent his acceptance of it. All is a question of the credentials of his informant. He diverts his attention to the qualities of this authority. If he is satisfied that his authority must know and is truthful, he is free to accept the doctrine because of faith in his teacher, or he is free to disbelieve it on the score that it has not been intrinsically demonstrated to his personal satisfaction.

Now you have studied Christian doctrine, seeking always intrinsic evidence of its truth. You have chosen to adopt the position that it will be false unless you find such intrinsic evidence. You are quite unable to prove it intrinsically false. In the circumstances you are perfectly free to divert your attention from the aspect you prescribe, study the credentials of Christ as a divine teacher, and, once convinced of their value, accept the doctrine upon His authority. If you do not do so, it will be because you do not choose to do so.

202. If God did not give me sufficient intelligence to be able to believe, surely no blame attaches to me?

That is true, if God failed to do so. But He did not. Your reason tells you that Christianity teaches certain mysterious things. You ask on what authority it so teaches. You are told that Almighty God has revealed those doctrines. At once the fact that the doctrines are extraordinary becomes of no account. God must know, and is certainly supremely truthful. The only point is, did He reveal such doctrines. You are shown that they are contained in the Bible, and that the Catholic Church teaches them. Your duty is to make sure that the Bible is a reliable source of such information, and that the Catholic Church is an institution guaranteed by God as a safe and authentic teacher of men in religious matters. If these things have been reasonably verified, as they certainly can be, you reasonably and freely accept the doctrines thus guaranteed as being of God. Now God has not failed to endow you with sufficient reason to do this. If you refuse to use your reason, or if you misuse it, or if you refuse to believe all that you do not fully comprehend for yourself, despite your knowledge that God has revealed such doctrines, you are to blame. Remember that to refuse to believe because reason does not entirely comprehend a doctrine, is to say that human reason is the ultimate test of all truth. That is not true which human reason cannot demonstrate to its own satisfaction! In the light of the obvious limitation of human reason, and the history of human aberrations in thought, this is clearly an irrational position. The conclusion remains that Christ justified His claims to be the divinely sent Teacher of men; that He sent His Apostles and their legitimate successors to teach all nations; that He thereby laid upon all nations the obligation of being taught; and that, once His teaching has been sufficiently put before them, men are guilty if they presume to reject it. In the case of such men, acceptance of the Christian religion is necessary if they are to be saved.

CHAPTER SIX

A DEFINITE CHRISTIAN FAITH

203. *I cannot adopt any definite profession of faith because the heads of all the different Churches disagree.*

If they disagree, that shows at most that you cannot take their word on behalf of their own churches. But it does not follow that there is not a right church amongst them all. Your duty is to inquire, and find the church Christ actually established.

204. *But if the clergy themselves are in deadly opposition, and cannot tell me for certain what Christianity means!*

There is no confusion amongst the clergy of the Catholic Church, which alone was established by Christ. And the Catholic Church alone can lawfully claim your allegiance. If you insist upon including all the man-made variations, then you are right about the conflicting views of the clergy. But that would not give you a true view of Christianity. As an Agnostic friend of mine wisely remarked to me, "If there be any true Christian church, it can only be the Catholic Church." He was right in his assertion, if not in his personal choice of unbelief. The logical choice does lie between Catholicism and Agnosticism.

205. *Why is there such enmity between the Churches?*

There should never be enmity between the adherents of various churches. Nor should there be separation between the churches themselves, and the best thing the children of the Reformers could do would be to return to the Catholic Church their forefathers should never have left. Yet, granted the existence of separated churches, Catholics who belong to the true Church, whilst esteeming members of other churches, are obliged to condemn the principles which led to such a separation. Esteeming Protestants, they must try to separate the Protestants they esteem from the Protestantism they deplore.

206. *How is it possible to believe all the religions that claim to be true?*

It is not possible. If any one of them is right, then the others are all wrong. No one asks you to take our word, however, for the truth of the Catholic Church. It can be proved historically that Christ lived, that He was God, and that He founded an imperishable Church, which was to be one, holy, catholic, and aspostolic. Find that Church and you will have the true religion of Christ.

207. *Can any one Church claim to have all the truth, which has so many angles?*

The Catholic Church can and does claim to have all the truth. For you must not confuse false ideas which are opposed to the truth with merely different angles of the truth. If, for example, it be true that Confession is a Sacrament instituted by Christ, then denial of Confession is not a different angle of the truth, but its negation.

208. *Your preceding replies are based upon a misapprehension. There is no real lack of essential unity in the Christian Churches at all. All together form the one true Church.*

However nice that looks on paper, it is impossible. We cannot hold that hundreds of conflicting churches, even those disowning each other, are all one united church. The good Wesleyan who says that Rome is idolatrous would have to admit that the idolatrous Catholic belongs to the same church as himself, and is equally a Christian. The notion demands not a little suppression of reason. Again, if the Catholic Church ex-communicates a man, almost any Protestant Church will promptly receive him. If the Catholic Church and the Protestant Church which receives him are one and the same, you will have the same Christ accepting and rejecting the same man at one and the same time!

The Son of God, who knew that a kingdom divided against itself cannot stand, took precautions precisely to avoid such internal divisions. He declared that there would be absolute unity in both doctrine and government, and He has preserved His Church from doctrinal and disciplinary dissension. In the fourth century there was the same Catholic Church as to-day, and almost as many cut-off sects, Montanists, Manicheans, Arians, Donatists, Nestorians, Pelagians, and Eutychians, were solemnly telling men that they were part of the one true Church. Sincere men like yourself were deceived, and maintained many sections. But the cut-off sections died, lacking the promise of Christ. To-day we have the same Catholic Church, but a new host of cut-off sects, Anglicans, Wesleyans, Presbyterians, Baptists, Adventists, Christadelphians, etc., and they have not yet lasted as long as many of the earlier heresies. They too will die, and a new lot will arise in the ages to come. But you are making the same mistake as many sincere men in the earlier centuries, thinking these man-made substitutes to be part of the one indivisible Church of Christ.

209. Did not St. Paul acknowledge the various individual churches of his time?

The churches to which St. Paul wrote were as much united as Catholics in London to-day are united in one Church with the Catholics in New York, Berlin, Italy, and Australia. Non-Catholics, however, are not united, have not held fast to the traditions, believe practically as they please, and have made shipwreck of the faith as well as of disciplinary unity.

210. Tertullian says that, as in the ocean there are many seas and ports, so in the Catholic Church there are many churches. How can the Roman branch exclude the other branches?

Tertullian had in mind the expansion of the one Catholic Church to many centres, each branch remaining united to the same legitimate authority.

211. To my mind the whole of Christianity is like a wheel. Christ is the centre, whilst the various churches are the spokes.

Christ forms the complete wheel, and as He identifies the Church with Himself as his mystical body, the Catholic Church is the complete wheel, hub, spokes, and all, of Christianity in this world. And Christ prayed to His Father that the Church might be one as He and His Father are one. All non-Catholic forms of professing Christianity are broken and discarded spokes, no longer in the wheel at all as churches, whilst most of the members of these churches disown all connection with the wheel which they abandoned at the Reformation.

212. Could we not call Christ's Church a garden? The Roman Catholic Church is the original tree—the others slips cut off, and growing in the same garden, and producing the same fruit, but with a slightly different flavor?

That is not possible. These analogies may be suitable to wrong ideas, but they do not prove those wrong ideas correct. Christ said that His Church would be one Church, not a garden of churches. As for the same fruit, the Catholic Church forbids divorce—non-Catholic churches allow it. There is more than a difference of flavor here! One fruit of the tree is unity and obedience, a fruit which the Catholic Church alone produces. That the non-Catholic churches bear some fruit I admit, but they do not produce all the fruit Christ intended. The explanation of such fruit as they seem to produce we shall see later on. Meantime your attempts to maintain the unity of all the conflicting churches are opposed both to revelation and to reason. Christ said, "If a man will not hear the Church, let him be as the heathen." Your system would leave him baffled. "Hear which Church?" he would cry. If you replied, "Any Church, for all churches constitute the one Church of Christ," he would complain, "But the Catholic Church forbids this, and the Anglican Church permits it!" Again, you say that the Catholic Church is as much part of the true Church as any others. But she solemnly declares that the others do not belong to the true Church. If she is truly speaking with the authority of Christ, they do not. If she is wrong, she forfeits any claims to be part of the true teaching Church. No, they cannot all be true, and the Catholic Church is the only one that is really certain that she is right.

213. *I admit that it is impossible to maintain that all the churches are really united into one Church; but I deny that lack of unity really matters. After all, go into any Christian church, and you will hear Christ preached, and the Word of God spoken.*

On that score, the Seventh Day Adventists who teach that the Pope is Anti-Christ, and the Catholic Church which teaches that he is the very Vicar of Christ would both be teaching doctrines equally pleasing to God! As a matter of fact you will not hear Christ preached in *any* Christian church, for in all non-Catholic churches you will hear now one, now another distorted aspect of Christian doctrine. Even did you hear the uncorrupted Word of God in some non-Catholic church, that would not make you a member of Christ's true Church.

214. *But our intentions at least are all good. We are all striving for the one end.*

The Jews could have made a similar remark to Christ when He tried to convert them to Christianity. If we are Christians, we must deny that good intentions will suffice. And if Christianity is better than the Jewish religion—as Christ knew it was—then if the Catholic Church has the complete doctrine, and every form of Protestantism is incomplete and erroneous, it follows that Catholicism is better than Protestantism, and should be embraced.

215. *If there were twelve roads leading to the one goal, would it matter which you took?*

Since God has distinctly said that He wishes us to take one particular road—the Catholic road—it does matter. Any doctrine which begins with the fundamental notion that one religion is as good as another soon ends in the conclusion that one religion is as useless as another. And the children of those who insist upon proclaiming that principle end up, as a rule, with no religion at all.

216. *We Protestants worship the same God as you Catholics—how can we be wrong?*

You are not wrong in worshipping the same God. You are wrong in so far as you do not do so in the right way. If I were your employer, and ordered you to go to London via Suez, and you went via Panama, you would do the right thing in going to London, but you would do the wrong thing in pleasing yourself as to the choice of route. God wants all men to serve Him, and to serve Him in the Catholic Church. The Catholic way is completely right; the Protestant way is more than half wrong.

217. I am a Protestant who leads a good life. That is enough.

That you lead a good life is to be commended. But it would be better to do it in the way God wishes, rather than in your own way. Your leading a good life cannot prove your religion true. If it did, then the fact that a Catholic lives a good life also proves the Catholic Church true. Yet if your religion is true, the Catholic Church is not. You cannot appeal to your own life as proof, but must find out how Christ described His Church, and then look for that Church.

218. But we Protestants believe that if a man lives a good life, no matter what Church he accepts, he will save his soul.

Some Protestants believe that. Many do not. Good Protestants can be saved, but if they are good they are Protestants in good faith who have the will to do God's will, and are not Catholics merely because they do not realize their obligation to join the true Church.

219. Yet surely the only thing wrong is to do wrong.

And is not one doing wrong when he refuses to bother about doctrinal belief? Why did Christ say, "He that believes shall be saved?" Why did He send the Apostles to teach doctrine? Not only are good works required, but also the true faith.

220. Christianity is not a thing to be proved; it is a life to be lived.

That is taking refuge in credulity. Every rational man, if he does a thing, should know why he does it. Moreover, Christianity is a set of truths to be believed as well as a life to be lived. It imposes obligations upon the intelligence as well as upon the will and the passions. Jesus said, "Repent and believe the Gospel." But before a reasonable man believes, he must either prove the doctrine true in itself, or at least that God has revealed it, then he knows that it must be true even though he himself does not fully comprehend it. To say that God is indifferent as to whether a man is a Protestant or a Catholic goes very close to blasphemy. If he revealed the doctrines of Protestantism, He could not possibly be pleased with one who would deliberately accept the opposite by embracing Catholicism.

221. There is good and bad in all the churches.

If you mean that there are good men and bad men in all religions, you are right. But if you mean that the teachings of all churches, including the Catholic Church, are partly true and partly false, you are wrong. The teachings of all non-Catholic churches are partly true and partly false. Partly true, for a religion consisting wholly of error could not exist. Partly false, because all non-Catholic churches are a denial that Christ made sufficient provision for the Church He established. But not a single false doctrine is to be found in the official teaching of the Catholic Church, which is the work, not of man, but of God. If a man is obliged to accept the truth in its entirety, and not a fragment of the truth, he is obliged to accept the Catholic Church as his guide.

222. Protestants know that no more is needed than prayer in their own hearts.

Few Protestants would thank you for such a dreadful description of their religion. Nothing more is necessary? Do what you like, but say that prayer in your heart! Also, had Christ but one doctrine to give, namely, "Say a prayer in your own hearts," He went a very strange way about teaching that doctrine.

223. You must admit that spiritually I am your brother.

In so far as you are sincere, Our Lord overlooks your mistaken notions and accepts your love for Him. But the fact remains that you serve Him in your way, and not in His, and that He does not obtain from you all that He desires. Also what He overlooks in you He would not overlook in a Catholic who has known the truth.

224. Have not the disciples of Jesus, even outside the Catholic Church, power and authority given them by the Holy Spirit?

No. Not all the sincerity in the world can be a sufficient substitute for authentic credentials in this matter. An immense power and authority over the souls of men requires solid proof that it is really possessed. Christ proved that He had it. The Catholic Church can prove that He entrusted that power to Her. Founders of other churches had no more than their own personal conviction that they possessed such authority—a persuasion as insufficient as would be my own personal belief that I had the authority of the Chief Justice in the land.

225. But I feel that I am right. I have the witness in myself.

Witness in oneself may easily be purely subjective persuasion, and is no sure test of truth. Men holding totally divergent views claim to experience this witness within themselves, yet they cannot all have the exact truth revealed by Christ. Thank God, intellectual mistakes do not always mean evil dispositions. But remember that Christ allowed the Jews to go because they knowingly refused to accept His teaching on the Eucharist—a teaching you also reject, as we shall see. If you knew what you were doing, He would reject you also.

226. The Kingdom of God is within you.

The Kingdom of God as established by Christ is at once a visible Church in this world, and an invisible spiritual Kingdom of grace within the soul. External adherence to the visible Kingdom demands also that Christ reign by grace within the soul. But this interior grace does not dispense a man from accepting the will of Christ once he is aware of it, nor from the obligation to join the visible Kingdom established by Him in this world. Christ distinctly said, "I will build my Church"; and again, "If a man will not hear the Church, let him be as the heathen." He was obviously referring to the authority of a visible Church. He also likened His Church to a net holding good and bad fish. This cannot refer to a Kingdom of spiritual and invisible grace only, for bad fish are not in a state of grace.

227. Christ died for all, and does not say that He did so for members of any particular Church. He does not mention either Catholicism or Protestantism.

The teaching of Christ clearly condemns Protestant principles, and insists upon the acceptance of Catholic principles. He did die for all who would accept Him, but one does not accept Him who rejects knowingly the very definite and particular religion He gave to the world. And He predicted that that religion would be characterized by unity of doctrine, holiness of moral precepts, catholicity or universality, and continuous succession from the Apostles.

228. The denominations are necessary to save us from the dictation of priests.

The authority of the priesthood will be the subject of our consideration in due time. Meantime the denominations were not necessary according to the mind of Christ. He prayed that all might be one, as He and His Father are one. St. Paul said that even though an Angel from heaven were to preach a gospel differing from that already given, he should be regarded as accursed. No one had any right to establish the denominations, with their varying doctrines.

229. I admit that it is a pity that there is so much conflict.

It is ten thousand times a pity. But remember that the Catholic Church did not start the conflict. She cannot be blamed for the domestic troubles of Protestantism. All Catholics at least are in doctrinal unity.

230. But why keep insisting that the Catholic Church is the only Church?

Because Christ said, "If a man will not hear the Church, let him be as the heathen." He did not say, "If a man will not hear a portion of the Gospel in manmade substitute churches."

231. You cannot deny that you are bigoted in your exclusive claims.

Bigotry is blind zeal. It is not bigotry to say that a thing cannot be true if its opposite is proved to be correct. Truth must exclude error.

232. We are as entitled to our opinions as you are to yours.

You are. And you might be able to think out ideas just as valuable as ourselves. But here it is not a question of human opinions. It is a question of God's teaching, and neither your opinions nor our opinions have any value if they contradict that. Catholic doctrine is not our opinion, but His doctrine who sent the Church to teach in His name.

233. But are you not obliged by the law of charity? Christ said, "Do unto others as you would have them do to you."

We are obliged by the law of charity. But charity does not forbid one to tell the truth. It forbids blaming people who, through no fault of their own, do not know the truth. Nor would the Catholic Church wish Protestants to admit that she is right if she were not right. And since she can prove that they are not right, she is not doing to them what she would not have them do to her in denying the correctness of their religion.

234. All the same, your claims are insulting to Protestants, and they are human beings just as Catholics.

The Catholic Church has to condemn Protestantism as a system. But she desires to insult no single Protestant. That Protestants are human beings does not prove their religion true. Otherwise the fact that Catholics are human beings also would prove *their* religion true. As a matter of fact, in so far as Protestants are human beings we Catholics love them, and it is our very interest in them which makes us want to give them the best religion in the world—Catholicism. Protestantism is not good enough for them.

235. Your Church is doing more to prevent reunion than any other Church.

That is a great compliment to the Catholic Church, when we consider the conditions others lay down as the basis of reunion. For it means that she is doing more than any other church to keep intact the religion entrusted to her by Christ, and that she steadily refuses to let her heart run away with her head by admitting that whatever sincere but mistaken men would like to be true is good enough, and that what Christ exactly taught does not really matter.

236. *Anyway, only one in a hundred thousand ever changes from the religion of his parents.*

One instance is enough to refute that statement. Your proportion would be about four hundred in forty millions. Now the population of England is about forty millions, and in England alone the average number of converts to the Catholic Church is over twelve thousand yearly. The number is even greater in America, and a steady stream of converts is the experience of most other countries also. However, the one instance of England is a sufficient reply to your extravagant assertion.

237. *At least Protestantism is more tolerant than Catholicism. I am an Anglican, but I do not say that I am right. I believe in everyone believing as he thinks best, and not criticizing others?*

You take up an extraordinary position. If you do not say that you are right, you cannot have definite grounds for your belief, and such belief is credulity.

And do you really believe in everyone believing in his own belief? Whether that belief be right or wrong? If so, you believe in people believing in error. But Christ came precisely to stop people from believing in error. Far from allowing people to believe in their own beliefs, He commanded them to give up their previous beliefs, and believe in what He taught, if they wished to save their souls. I believe with you in not criticizing others. I give them credit for sincerity and goodness. But it is quite lawful to criticize their theories.

238. *But in the end, is not religion a matter of opinion?*

If you except the Catholic Church, I'm afraid it is. That other churches think so is shown by the amazing exchanges of pulpits and attendances. But the Catholic Church is a different thing altogether. Until we prove a thing it is a matter of opinion. Thus before Australia was discovered, it was a matter of opinion as to whether a southern continent existed or not. But once discovered, it was no longer a matter of opinion. So, too, if God had never given a revelation about religion, it might be a matter of opinion. But once God speaks in a definite way, it is no longer a matter of opinion. When the Creator speaks, the creature must simply accept. Now God sent His Son, Jesus Christ, who established one definite Church, to which He gave His teaching authority. This does not look like religion being a matter of opinion. Here we have God's decision, and we must accept it. If our human opinions suggest anything against the teaching of Christ, or against the teaching of His Church, we just renounce our own fallible ideas as being the foolish notions of untaught children. The Protestant clings to his own opinions whether they are in harmony with God's explicit teachings or not. Nor does he make much effort to find out what those teachings are. But God would no more admit that the religion revealed by Him is a mere matter of opinion than your grocer would admit that the amount owing to him is a mere matter of opinion.

239. *Would it not be better to say that religion is a matter of conscience?*

No. If the individual conscience is to be the guide, there will be as many religions as consciences. There are right consciences and wrong consciences. Conscience is right if it squares with the laws of God. It is warped if it be at variance with the will of God. However, if conscience alone matters, why did not Christ leave us all to our consciences, instead of carefully teaching His Apostles a definite set of doctrines to be preached and to be believed? Conscience must accept the teachings of Christ, who could neither be deceived, nor deceive us.

240. *Why try to convert people to the Catholic Church?*

Why did Christ try to convert people to His special doctrines? And why did He send His Church to teach all nations? If God gives the truth to man by sending

His Son, is it not better to have that truth to guide one's conduct? Or is it better to be in partial or total ignorance, omitting much that ought to be done, and being forgiven by God only because not knowing any better? To know the truth and live exactly as God intends is much better than asking to be excused from it on the plea of ignorance.

241. I know that Protestants are ignorant of Catholicity, but are not Catholics ignorant of Protestantism?

Very often. But there is this difference. The Catholic who does not understand Protestantism does not know the wrong thing. The Protestant who does not know Catholicism does not know the right thing. I personally know both, having been brought up in Protestantism, which I renounced in favor of Catholicism.

242. Have Catholics any advantages not possessed by good Protestants?

All things else being equal, and strictly from the viewpoint of the religions, Catholics have many advantages. They have the full truth contained in Sacred Scripture and in the teaching Church. The Protestant accepts only part of Scripture, and has no God-appointed guide. Certainly a man with full information as to the road leading to a given destination has greater advantages than one with defective information. Again, Catholics have more means of grace than non-Catholics. They have the sacrifice of the Mass, and seven Sacraments. You may say that Christ gives grace at times independently of the Sacraments instituted by Him for this purpose. But why should He, when He definitely institutes seven Sacraments for the purpose? And even granting that He does give certain graces to those in good faith, those graces are not so plentiful, nor of the same nature as the special Sacramental graces.

243. You insist, then, that not any form of Christianity will do, but that we ought to join the Catholic Church?

Yes. As a matter of fact, a close study of other forms will suggest only reasons for abandoning them, whilst an equally close study of Catholicism intensifies the conviction that in the Catholic Church, and in her alone, can the full truth be found.

CHAPTER SEVEN

THE FAILURE OF PROTESTANTISM

244. *Do you say that the Protestant faith is false?*

There is no such thing as the Protestant faith. There are hundreds of varieties of Protestantism, each variety containing some true things mixed up with its own particular errors. As religious systems I say that all Protestant sects are wrong.

245. *How does Protestantism in general disobey Christ?*

In general it says that Scripture is a sufficient guide to salvation, although Scripture says that it is not; it denies the authority of the Church established by Christ; it has no sacrifice of the Mass; it does not believe in confession; it denies Christian teaching on marriage; it rejects Purgatory, and very often its advocates refuse to believe in Hell. But I could go on almost forever. Meantime, if you give me any doctrine taught by one Protestant Church, I will produce another Protestant Church which denies it, save perhaps the one doctrine that there is a God of some sort.

246. *Would you call Protestants heathens?*

Christ said, "If a man will not hear the Church, let him be as the heathen." Matt. XVIII., 17. He referred, of course, to a deliberate and willful refusal of a known obligation. If a man knows that the Catholic Church is the true Church, yet refuses to obey it, he will certainly be as the heathen before God. But Protestants who are ignorant of the truth of the Catholic claims, and who believe in Christ, trying to serve Him as best they can, would not be regarded as heathens. An exception is made in their case because of their lack of knowledge and because of their good dispositions.

247. *Protestantism is not a protest against Christ, but against the Roman Church.*

Christ promised that His Church would not fail. The Protestant Reformers said that it did fail. Instead of protesting merely against the bad lives of some Catholics, and even of some Priests, they went too far, and protested against the Church as such, asserting that Christ had failed to keep His promise concerning it. This was a protest against Christ, who had promised to be with His Church till the end of the world. Protest as much as you like against individual abuses in the Church, but no man has the right to set up a new Church.

248. *But a re-formed Church is not a new Church.*

Protestantism was not a true reformation of the Church. The identity of the Church is indissolubly linked with a continuous identity of doctrine, worship, and discipline. The so-called Reformation involved the abolition of essential doctrines, worship, and discipline, substituting completely different and humanly invented alternatives.

249. *The Protestant Churches have as much right to say they have the truth as the Churches of the Corinthians, Ephesians, Colossians, etc., in early times.*

You are supposing that the Protestant Churches have the same doctrine, worship, and discipline as those early Churches. But this is an unwarranted supposition. Those early branch foundations of the one true Church had the true doctrine, and were in communion with St. Peter, Bishop of Rome, who addressed his first Epistle to the Galatians and several other Churches. Protestant Churches do not hold the same doctrine as those early Churches, nor do they acknowledge the same obedience. Also, in all the countries where Protestant Churches exist, there exists also the Catholic Church which corresponds exactly with the Churches of the Corinthians, Ephesians, Colossians, etc.

250. *According to you, Christ was a Catholic. All followers of Christ, therefore, belong to the Catholic Church.*

Christ, as the Founder of the Catholic Church, was of course a Catholic. But your conclusion does not follow. Many profess to believe in Christ, but do not accept the whole of His teaching. They are mistaken. Certainly the Anglican does not believe in the correct doctrines of Christ if the Baptist does. The Catholic Church alone teaches the complete doctrine of Christ, and the only way to become a Catholic is to submit to her teaching authority and disciplinary directions.

251. *Since Christ forbade divisions in the Church, you must admit that every Christian Church is a branch of the true Church. The Protestant Churches are but offshoots from the Roman Catholic Church.*

The Protestant sects constitute a breakaway from the Catholic Church. That is their condemnation, for there could never have been a valid reason for leaving the Church established and guaranteed by Christ. In any case, branches of the Church must be living branches still retaining their union with the parent tree. The Catholic Church as established in England, or in America, or in Australia, fits in with the idea of living branches. But at best, the Protestant sects are branches sawn off, and without the true life of the tree. Protestant Churches are divisions from the Church, not co-ordinated parts within the Church, and making up one complete body.

252. *You have no right to deny our claims. Christ meant Protestantism to be, or it would not exist.*

On the same reasoning you would argue that because sin exists Christ meant it to be! Christ predicted that heresies would arise, but distinctly forbade men to abandon the Church and originate them.

253. *God sends all for our good, and it is our fault if we do not make good use of Protestantism.*

Not everything is sent by God. He permits some things which the perverse will of men causes, and He permitted the evil of heresy. However, He never permits any evil without drawing some good from it. There are many good Protestants despite the sin of those who began Protestantism. And it is undeniable that Protestantism occasioned the reform of many abuses among the members of the Catholic Church.

254. *What right has the Catholic Church to arrogate to herself powers given by Christ, rather than any other body of believers?*

None whatever. No body of believers has any right to arrogate to itself any powers at all in this matter, just as no ordinary citizen has the right to enter a court and declare himself to be judge. Yet a lawfully appointed judge has the right to act in virtue of his commission. The Catholic Church takes nothing upon herself, but she does endeavor to fulfill the commission given her by Christ. Historically she alone can possibly inherit the jurisdiction given by Christ to the Apostles, and handed down through the ages. All other Churches exist because men arrogated to themselves the right to coin new doctrines and set up Churches of their own.

255. We have the Creeds, Saints' Days, Baptism, Confirmation, and Holy Communion. These things guarantee that we are true Christians.

Some Protestants have those things, at least theoretically. Others have some of them. Others have none of them. But in any case they would not prove Protestants to be true Christians. At most they prove that some Protestants are attempting to do some Christian things. But a true Christian accepts the complete teaching of Christ, and does all that He commands. And all is accepted on the authority of Christ, not on the authority of one's own human judgment. A self-made religion built upon a personally approved selection from the teaching of Christ does not give us the Christian religion.

256. Anyway, there are Protestants as good as Catholics, and the Protestant Church is as good as the Catholic Church.

The idea that there are Protestants as good as Catholics has no bearing on the question. There are very good and sincere Mahometans, but that does not make Mahometanism true. And again, there is not a Protestant Church, there are dozens of different brands of Protestantism. Tell me which brand of Protestantism is as good as the Catholic Church, and I shall tell you when it started and who started it. Christ certainly did not begin it.

257. Protestants at least are allowed to think for themselves.

And when they do they end in chaos, or with no religion at all! However, the chief characteristic of the majority of Protestants is absence of thinking on matters of religion.

258. If Protestantism continues because Protestants do not think, is not the same true of Catholicism?

No. There is no really rational foundation for Protestantism, and if Protestants did reflect soundly upon the subject they would discover this. But there is a rational foundation for Catholicism. All Catholics at least know that their Church would not be so vast and united, not to speak of its mere existence, after centuries of misrepresentation, hatred, and attack, were it not for the protection of God. And if they give deeper thought to the matter they find many other solid reasons for their conviction. Impartial study leads a man out of Protestantism. It never leads a man out of Catholicism.

259. Just the opposite is true. Catholics remain Catholics because they have never developed any reasoning powers on the subject of religion.

You show complete ignorance of Catholic theological works, written by the cleverest men of the centuries. St. Thomas Aquinas had the Catholic Faith very deeply, yet wrote probably the greatest masterpiece of religious thinking the world has ever seen.

260. You are most ungrateful, for your own change from Protestantism to Catholicism was due to the very freedom of thinking given you by Protestantism.

You are in a quandary. Catholics remain Catholics because they do not think, yet thinking led me to become a Catholic! However, Catholics are free to think as much as they like about religion, and the more the better. The Catholic Church merely keeps them from thinking wrongly. Protestants are free to think whatever they like, apparently, with no safeguard against error at all.

261. *If all that you say is true, why is the British Empire Protestant?*

Because the ancestors of its present members rejected and left the Catholic Church, setting up Churches of their own. But must the religion of the British Empire be the true religion? Is that the infallible test? If Anglicanism is true because it is British, we may as well add, "and because it is not French, or Spanish, or Italian, or German, or Austrian, etc." In other words, because it is not the religion for all nations established by Christ.

262. *But surely the majority of the millions of Protestants would realize their mistake, if indeed they are mistaken. They would on any other important subject.*

It is not certain that men would realize their mistakes on other subjects. In political and national affairs men differ hopelessly, and absurd political policies seem ever to find followers. Yet, even granted that men would realize their mistakes in other matters, they would not therefore realize the falsity of Protestantism. In the first place, religion is very different from other matters. It is not here a question of a merely intellectual admission. The acceptance of Catholicism is a complex matter demanding adherence of mind, heart, and will, under the influence of God's grace. The absence of one or other necessary condition can mean a dimming of one's powers of comprehension. And until a man sees the truth of Catholicism, he is liable to rest more or less content with the religion he has. Again, Protestant prejudice is a real, if unrealized, force in those educated under the influence of Protestantism, a force blinding people to the defects of Protestantism, and to the merits of Catholicism. I remember a man who went through many forms of Protestantism, ending in Agnosticism, and who replied to my question as to whether he had ever studied Catholicism, "No. But Catholicism can't be right!" Protestantism had ceased to grip him positively, yet still left the negative poison in his system, "Rome must be wrong—I would not even consider it." Finally, and especially with Englishmen, the Protestant religion has been so blended with nationalism that it has become a matter of sentiment and patriotism. Its adherents go far more by feeling and emotion than by reason and true faith. Indeed it has been said strongly, yet not without a degree of truth, that when an Englishman enters his Church, he leaves his brains on the doormat. In other words, the average Protestant gives little real thought to his religious position at all.

263. *That Protestantism commends itself more to men is evident from the fact that it is not attacked as is Catholicism.*

The world is not afraid of Protestantism, which has always been ready to water down Christian obligations to suit it. But instinctively the world hates and fears the Catholic Church, which will make no compromise, but insists upon the fullness of Christian doctrine, comfortable or uncomfortable. She insists upon the intellectual obedience of faith; disciplinary submission of the will; the impossibility of divorce and re-marriage; the iniquity of birth-control by evil means; the inadequacy of a merely secular education. Her repetition of Christ's axiom, "Deny thyself; take up thy cross; and follow Me," interferes too much with the comfort of men. If Christianity demanded merely the admission of a few religious doctrines, men would not object to it. But since it imposes moral obligations difficult for human nature, I am not surprised that men refuse it in its original and austere form when they are offered a less exacting substitute with the assurance that it is just as good.

264. *Are not the Protestant Churches at least working for reunion?*

Not for reunion with the Catholic Church. Meantime, if they were to unite among themselves, the union would not last a generation. As long as men refuse to submit to the Catholic Church, they will insist upon the right to think for themselves and build up systems accordingly. If Protestantism grants the right of private judgment, it may secure the cry, "Good. I think Catholicism wrong." But it must be prepared to hear the words, "And I think Protestantism wrong also." Already-established Protestantism can say nothing, and the man sets up for himself. So it will go on. The Catholic Church alone can preserve true unity. Every year finds Protestantism splitting up into still further sects, and in the end it will fall, as must every house divided against itself.

265. Did not Luther give ninety reasons for leaving the Catholic Church?

He gave many excuses, but no real reasons. Before he left the Church, he was a member of a religious order, vowed for the love of Christ to poverty, chastity, and obedience. He broke all three vows. Vices, whether intellectual or moral, are excuses, not reasons, for leaving the Church.

266. Was not Luther a brave man to follow his convictions despite the opposition of the Catholic Church?

He had a certain natural courage. But that was no more a virtue than the courage often found in evil-doers. I do not maintain that merely human courage is the monopoly of good Christian men. However, I deny that Luther was following his sincere convictions. Rather he followed his passions.

267. Luther knew that his love for God did not forbid his entering the state of matrimony which Jesus had blessed at Cana.

Luther knew that it was certainly contrary to his duty to God to violate the solemn vows he had made to God, and still more so, to take a Nun from her Convent as his wife. As for love of God, Jesus invited His Apostles to love Him so much as to leave aside all attachment to father, mother, wife, or children, in order the more closely to follow Him. He blessed marriage for such as are called to that state. But He Himself did not marry, nor did His Apostles after they were called to the ministry.

268. Luther believed that he is happy whose conscience alloweth the thing that he doth.

The only lawful sense of such a saying is, "Happy is he whose conduct never goes against what a right conscience allows." With Luther it meant, "Happy is he whose conscience is twisted and distorted until it allows whatever one wishes to do." If a Catholic Priest to-day did what Luther did then, the Protestant world would hold up its hands in horror, and the newspapers would broadcast it as yet another scandal in the Catholic Church. Picture the heading, *"Priest runs away with Nun!"* Yet you pretend that it is edifying in Luther. No one who has an elementary knowledge of the life of Christ and of that of Luther could possibly reconcile them. The majority of those who glorify Luther know little or nothing about him save his name. They believe in a legendary Luther, accepting it on trust that he tried to follow the pure Gospel. Sincere Protestants to-day do wish to follow Christ, but the more they do so, the less like Luther they become.

269. Do you know of any good in Luther?

Intellectually, not much. He declared that reason was of the devil, and that the Christian must regard it as his greatest enemy. Morally, less still. St. Paul says that those who are Christ's have crucified their flesh with its vices and concupiscences. Gal. V., 24. That Luther indulged his vices and concupiscences is clear from his writings, where he gives disgraceful descriptions of his own indulgence in everything passionate. His diaries record shocking excesses of sensuality, which could not be printed in any decent book to-day. A true Apostle of Christ does not give vent to such expressions as, "To be continent and chaste is not in me," or, "Why do I sit soaked in wine." I do not say these things merely to detract from the memory of Luther. But it is not right that people should be duped by the thought that Luther was a well-balanced and saintly reformer. He was not entirely devoid of good qualities. He was endowed with a certain kindness and generosity. But this does not compensate for his vices. He should have controlled his sentimentality and emotional nature in the light of Christian principles. He did not, but gave free rein to his lower passions, calmly saying that a man has to do so, and will not be responsible for such conduct.

270. Was the Diet of Spires held under Catholic or Protestant auspices?

Under Catholic auspices. It was convened by Charles V., a Catholic sovereign, chiefly to secure temporal peace. In 1517 Luther had broken into open revolt against the Catholic Church, preaching new and heretical doctrines. Charles V. became Emperor in 1520. Many German states, anxious to revolt politically against Charles, followed the new religious revolt of Luther. Chaos reigned in Germany. The Emperor was anxious for political peace; the Pope was anxious to stop the corruption of Catholicism by the preaching of these new doctrines. Charles, therefore, called a Diet or general assembly of all the lesser German princes at Spires in 1529. Pope Clement VII. urged Charles to take up the cause of the Catholic religion at the same time, and in reference to religion, the Diet made three main propositions. The celebration of Mass was to be permitted in those states where Protestants had forbidden it. The reformers were to be free to practice their new religion in those states where it had already been accepted, but it was not to be propagated beyond those states. No sect which denied the Real Presence of Christ in the Eucharist could be tolerated. The vast majority of Protestants at the Diet approved these laws, but the evangelical minority, whilst accepting the third law, refused to permit Mass, and to refrain from preaching Protestantism to still Catholic peoples. They formally protested that the religion of the people in a given place must be the religion of the temporal ruler of the country, and it is from this protest at the Diet of Spires in 1529 that the word Protestant is derived. It was a protest against freedom of conscience, and against the spiritual authority of the Catholic Church, as well as against the temporal authority of Charles V.

271. Did not the Diet of Spires profoundly affect the history of human thought?

It did, but rather for evil than for good. It led to dire results and the wrecking of the Catholic faith in many unthinking people. I am speaking, of course, of those delegates at the Diet who protested against its decisions, and am dealing with *religious* thought. Scientific thought would have gone on in any case. It is not to Protestantism that we owe the scientific and mechanical progress of modern times. That would have come just the same. But in religion Protestantism has given us only chaos, dreary contradictions, and several millions of would-be infallible individual authorities on religious questions. It was a regression from the authority of God to that of erratic man. And where Protestantism began by pretending to defend the rights of the Bible, it has ended by practically declaring the Bible to be worthless.

272. Did the Anglican Church have anything to do with the Diet of Spires?

The Anglican Church did not exist then. But when later established it gradually adopted Protestant principles, and is a Protestant Church.

273. *The Church of England repudiates the term Protestant, and, as far as I am aware, has never used it.*

I myself was brought up as an Anglican, and in the firm belief that I was a Protestant. An Anglican paper, *The English Churchman* is subtitled *A Protestant Family Journal.* The King of England is an Anglican, and in his coronation oath uses the words, "I solemnly and sincerely profess, etc., that I am a faithful Protestant."

274. *We Anglicans strongly claim to be part of the Catholic Church.*

Some Anglicans do; some do not. In any case, if a stray child wandered into some home and declared that it was a member of the family, it would not avail much if the whole family declared that it was no relative at all. And despite the claims of a few Anglicans, not only Catholics, but practically everyone knows that the Church of England is not a part of the Catholic Church, and that it is as Protestant as the Plymouth Brethren. Catch an Anglican off his guard, whoever he may be, and his own Church never enters his head when asked to direct someone to a Catholic Church. The oath taken by the King of England is as un-Catholic a formula as could well be conceived, and it definitely declares Anglicanism to be a Protestant sect cut off from, and distinct from, the Catholic Church.

275. *We Protestants look upon the King, not as head of the Anglican Church, but as the representative of the British Empire.*

If you have any respect for the law of England you must regard the King as head of the Anglican Church. The law says that he is, and to deny it is disloyal. As an Anglican I always accepted the King as head of the Anglican Church. As a Catholic, I still look upon him as head of that Church. Every loyal subject must do so. In the Book of Common Prayer, prior to the Articles, you will read the profession of the King, "Being supreme governor of the Church which is committed to our care." By law the very Bishops of the Anglican Church are subject to him in things spiritual as well as in things temporal. A man is loyal if he respects the laws of his country. We Catholics admit that the King is head of the Church of England, and we are loyal in doing so. But whether the Anglican Church is the true Church of Christ is another question. That we deny, and no law asks us to admit it. Nor could any valid law demand such an admission.

276. *But your Church is the Roman Catholic Church.*

It is the Catholic Church, a Church which has its headquarters at Rome, subjection to the Bishop of Rome being the test of true Catholicity. Anglicans, or at least some of them, would like to pretend that we have the Roman form of Catholicity, and that they have the English form. But this is mere pretense. The Catholic Church is international. The Church of England is national, its authority being vested, not in a successor of the Apostles, but in a successor of Henry VIII.

277. *What is the difference between the Church of England and the Catholic Church?*

The differences are legion. Firstly, there is all the difference between a Church established by Henry VIII., King of England, and that established so carefully by Christ. Secondly, the Anglican Church is still subject to parliament; is national in character; is chaotic in doctrine and discipline; has no valid orders; rejects the Mass, and the obligation of Confession. But why continue! All is summed up in the fundamental difference that the Catholic Church is the true Church, whilst the Church of England is a man-made substitute Church.

278. *I want to know the difference between the English Catholic Church and the Roman Catholic Church?*

If you mean by the English Catholic Church that Catholic Church in England which is under the jurisdiction of the Cardinal Archbishop of Westminster, there is no difference. But if you mean the Church of England I can only reply that that Church is not Catholic at all.

279. *The Church of England is Catholic, because she is sending missionaries throughout the whole world as far as possible.*

Other Protestant Churches are doing as much as the Church of England in this matter, yet you will not admit that they are Catholic because of that. But apart from that, what does the word *Catholic* really mean in its technical Christian sense? It does not refer to area alone. To be really Catholic a Church must have originated with Christ; must have existed in all ages since Christ; must be suitable for all nations and be ever expanding amongst them; must possess all the doctrine of Christ; and must ever retain all its members within the same unity of authoritative discipline. The Church of England fails in all these requirements. In origin, it was by British law established, and remains subject to the crown of England. In time, it dates from the 16th century, and therefore has certainly not existed in all ages since Christ. Nor is the Church of England adapted to all peoples. If a man seriously accepts the Church of England Prayer Book, he has to accept the King of England as the supreme head and governor of the Anglican Church. How could you ask a Frenchman to accept the President of France as his civil ruler, yet the decisions of the British parliament as his rule of faith? If we turn to facts, we find no trace of a truly Catholic expansive principle in Anglicanism. In spite of its belated and isolated missionary efforts since the 18th century, some hundreds of years after its establishment, it is not even attempting to convert all peoples. I have never met any body of Italian Anglicans, or Spanish, or German, or French, or Austrian Anglicans. No European nation accepts your Church except the British. Why does the Church of England make no effort for these peoples? Have they not the right to the truth taught by Christ? Or is it because the Catholic Church is quite all right for them? Yet if this be the case, why does the Church of England plant missions in newer lands where the Catholic Church already exists? The fact that it neglects other European countries shows that it has not a truly Catholic spirit, whilst the fact that it does set up isolated missions in opposition to already existing Catholic missions shows that it is not really conscious of being part of the Catholic Church at all. But let us turn from origin, time, and extent, to doctrine. Catholic doctrine demands that all members of the Church accept the same truths. Otherwise it cannot be a question of the same religion everywhere. Now the Church of England does not accept all the doctrines of Christ. It terms many of them fables and blasphemies. Nor only that. In such part of Christian doctrine as it does accept, Anglicanism is a house of confusion. Bishop Barnes and Lord Halifax claim to belong to the same Church, yet would cheerfully excommunicate each other as heretics. A low-church missionary will establish a Church in Papua which can scarcely be recognized as being of the same religion as that established by a high-church man in Fiji. Finally, I need scarcely speak of unity in discipline. There is hardly any such unity within the Anglican Church in practice, and whilst some Anglicans claim unity with the Catholic Church, that Church denies any such bond. So great is the difference between the Church of England and the Catholic Church that we can safely say that, if the Anglican Church be the true Church, then the Catholic Church is certainly wrong, and *vice-versa.*

280. You have said that Henry VIII. started the Church of England in the sixteenth century. But history shows that the Church was in England long before Henry VIII.

History shows that the Catholic Church was in England before the time of Henry VIII. To-day we have the Catholic Church and the Anglican Church, in addition, of course, to many others. The Anglican Church was unheard of, until Henry VIII. determined to establish it. Previously, he had been as subject to the Pope as I am. The Church which history records as being in England before Henry corresponds exactly with the Catholic Church in England to-day under the Archbishop of Westminster. Anglicanism is the intruder.

281. Henry reformed the Church, giving back to England a purified Church. If you remove foreign matter from the eye, the eye is not destroyed.

Henry gave no Church back to England. To give back is to restore what was possessed before. But nothing like the Anglican Church had previously existed in England. You cannot term Henry's action the removing of foreign matter from an eye. Rather he removed the eye, and filled up the cavity with foreign matter. The Catholic Church was suppressed, and a new Church of England was created.

282. But the very word reformation supposes a continuously existing body.

Historians use the word reformation to designate the religious changes of the 16th century, but the radical change cannot be called reform. The Church of England began with a new constitution altogether, with Cæsar as supreme in the things which should belong to God. Before the Reformation the Mass was the very centre and essence of religion, yet before very long it was banished and ridiculed. The new religion meant a change in both worship and discipline.

283. The Roman Church has often changed its constitution.

Never. The Catholic Church, subject to the Bishop of Rome, has the same constitution as that given her by Christ when He said to St. Peter, "Thou art Peter, and upon this rock I shall build my Church." She has the same foundation as the one and only Church *in* England until the substitution of himself by Henry VIII. as the foundation stone of the Church *of* England. The Anglican Church came into existence by a complete change of constitution which every previous Archbishop of Canterbury from the time of Augustine would have rejected with horror.

284. The constitution was changed by that very Augustine. The Church in England before him was not in communion with Rome.

Your statement is erroneous, and in any case you cannot claim that the present Church of England has any connection with the Church which was in England prior to the coming of St. Augustine. Let us put it this way. There are two sets of Bishops in England to-day. There are the Bishops of the Church of England, and the Bishops of the Roman Catholic Church—if you like such a phrase. The Anglican Bishops are not subject to the Pope—the Catholic Bishops are. Now in the year 1500—we need not go back to the pre-Augustine Church, though the same thing was true then—there was but one set of Bishops in England. Which of the two sets of Bishops *now* corresponds with the one set of Bishops *then?* If we can solve that, we shall be able to find the intruder.

Without dwelling upon probable traditions concerning the sending of missionaries by Pope Eleutherius about the year 170 A.D., it is certain that the very first elements of Christianity came to England from the Continent, where all true Christians were subject to the Pope. In 314 A.D., English Bishops were present at the Council of Arles, in Gaul. This was over 200 years before St. Augustine set foot in England. Now every Bishop of the Council of Arles was in communion with Rome. The Council was held under authority from Pope Sylvester, who sent his legates, and who received from the assembled Bishops this greeting, "In the unity of our mother the Catholic Church, we salute thee, most glorious Pope, with the reverence due." No Anglican Bishops to-day would be invited to sit in Council with the Bishops of Italy, Spain, France, Africa, Germany, and other regions, as those early English Bishops did at the Council of Arles. Something has gone wrong somewhere!

In 596 Pope Gregory sent St. Augustine to England, giving him authority over all the Bishops already in England. They must all have been *Roman* Catholics for the Bishop of Rome to use such words as these: "We give you no authority over the Bishops of Gaul. But as for all the Bishops of Britain, we commit them to your care, that the unlearned may be taught, the weak strengthened by persuasion, the perverse corrected by authority."

In 735 the Venerable Bede wrote, "The Pope bears pontifical power over the whole world." St. Anselm of Canterbury wrote, in the 11th century, "It is certain that he who does not obey the Roman Pontiff is disobedient to the Apostle Peter, nor is he of that flock given to Peter by God." In 1154 a member of the Church *in* England at that time was elected Pope. His name was Nicholas Breakspeare. You cannot imagine a member of the Anglican Hierarchy to-day being elected Pope! In 1170 St. Thomas, Archbishop of Canterbury, wrote, "Who doubts that the Roman Church is the head of all Churches, and the source of doctrine." In 1208, Stephen Langton, Archbishop of Canterbury, wrote, "Pope Alexander, possessing plenitude of power, gave back this Archbishopric to Thomas independently of the royal assent." This was the one set of Bishops in England before the reformation, and the Catholic Bishops in England to-day are their corresponding Bishops. Where were the Anglican Bishops before the reformation? They did not exist. Or take this simple reasoning. St. Thomas More was beheaded because he refused to give up the old religion. Then whatever religion he was clinging to, was the old religion. But he was clinging to what you would call the Roman Catholic religion, refusing the oath of supremacy which Henry VIII. claimed over the new Church of his own creation. If this new Church *of* England was the same as the old Church *in* England, St. Thomas More was a fool indeed to lose his life. Yet he was an exceedingly good and wise man.

285. Does the present Archbishop of Canterbury enjoy the jurisdiction granted to his pre-reformation predecessors by the Pope, or is he linked with them only by orders?

He has no link with them either by jurisdiction or by Holy Orders. He merely retains the name without the reality, and owes his position to the crown. All the privileges once granted to the Archbishops of Canterbury by Rome are now granted to the Cardinal Archbishop of Westminster. If the present Archbishop of Canterbury were converted to the Catholic Church, and wished to exercise priestly functions in that Church, he would have to be ordained as if he had never claimed to be a cleric of any description previously.

286. How can you deny the Orders of Anglican Bishops? They go back to the Bishops of the Reformation period.

There have been Anglican Bishops continuously since the Reformation, but valid Orders have not been continuously handed on. Henry VIII. began the Church of England in 1534. The Bishops who submitted to him were validly consecrated, and validity lasted until 1550. But in that year, under Edward VI., a great effort was made to protestantize still more the Church of England both in doctrine and in practice. The form of Ordination was deliberately changed, all reference to priest-hood in the true Christian sense of the word being eliminated. This defective form, utterly useless for the true ordination of priests, remained unchanged until 1662— 112 years later. Then the mistake was realized and the form was corrected. But the correction was too late, for those with correct Orders had died, and only those who had been invalidly consecrated remained to hand on their pretended Orders. Not a few Anglicans have tried to make sure of Orders by re-ordination at the hands of schismatical Bishops. The Anglican Bishop Knox, writing in the *National Review* for September, 1925, said correctly, "The Pope refused absolutely to recognize our Anglican Orders on the ground that our Church does not ordain priests to offer the Sacrifice of the Mass. In spite of attempts made by our Archbishop to conceal this defect, the Pope from his point of view was unquestionably right. It is true that certain priests of the Church of England offer so-called Masses, but as they were not ordained by the Church with the intention that they should offer the Body and Blood of Christ to the Father, the Sacrament of their Ordination is for this purpose a failure. The Prayer Book and Ordinal are simply un-Catholic, since they show no sign of fulfilling the most important of all Catholic functions."

287. Have not the Patriarchs of the Orthodox Church admitted our Orders?

Firstly, there is no such thing as a united Orthodox Church. Nor can the ad-missions of one or two sections of that Church be quoted as the universal judgment of the Greek Church.

Secondly, the Greek Bishops do not claim infallibility. They may say, "This is our opinion," but they cannot add, "And our opinion is certainly true." In other words, the admissions of some isolated Greek Patriarchs prove nothing.

Thirdly, such opinion as some Patriarchs may have expressed was based upon defective information. They could judge only upon the information given them. But the true facts were not put before them. High-Church men submitted an ex-position of the case against which Anglican newspapers in England protested strong-ly as being a most distorted view of Church of England principles. The verdict of a misinformed Greek Bishop cannot avail against the verdict of a well-informed Anglican Bishop, such as Bishop Knox.

288. Is the decision of Rome regarding Anglican Orders irrevocable?

Yes. It is an infallible decision concerning a secondary object connected with and necessary for the defence of revealed dogma. We have to accept the de-cision, not from a motive of divine faith, but because of the infallible authority of the Church. The question was submitted to a thorough and even sympathetic consideration, the Pope knowing that if Anglican Orders could be admitted as valid the road to re-union would be much easier. But the evidence compelled the Pope to declare them invalid. Pope Leo XIII. definitely adopted the decision of the appointed Commission, and published the condemnation with his own infallible authority to support it. No Anglican clergyman could officiate in the Catholic Church without being ordained by a Catholic Bishop.

289. At least you cannot quarrel with Anglican teaching.

I am afraid I would have to ask you to tell me what you believe to be the teaching of the Anglican Church. Anglicans hold all kinds of conflicting beliefs. Dr. Gore writes a book on Church of England doctrine, and Bishop Barnes flatly contradicts it. I have a dozen Anglican books on Church of England doctrine, and all explain it differently. Anglican teachings, however, do contradict those of Christ.

290. *Could you tell me how?*

All Anglicans at least accept an Erastian Church subject to political and parliamentary authority in England, and throughout the world they deny the necessity of submission to the lawful authority of the successor of St. Peter, the present Bishop of Rome. Again, half the members of the Anglican Church say that they believe in the real presence of Christ in the Eucharist, and half say that they do not. Now Christ said, "Hear the Church." If the Anglican Church were the true Church, which half must men hear? As a teaching Church Anglicanism fails, and is compelled to tolerate such men as Bishop Barnes, who openly deny the explicit doctrines of Christ.

291. *We Anglicans have the same Apostles' Creed as you Catholics.*

You recite the same Creed, but you do not believe in it in the true Catholic sense. Catholics recite and accept the Apostles' Creed in practice. Anglicans recite it. All Anglicans say, "I believe in Jesus Christ, His only Son, Our Lord." Many Anglicans do not believe that He is truly the Son of God. All Anglicans say, "Born of the Virgin Mary." Many deny the Virginity of Mary. All Anglicans say, "I believe in the Holy Catholic Church." But none of them joins it, or if he does, he ceases to be an Anglican. All Anglicans say, "I believe in the Communion of the Saints," but few dare enter into communication with the Saints. All say, "I believe in the forgiveness of sins," but the vast majority ignore the Sacrament of Confession. Anglicans may recite the Creed, but most Anglicans certainly do not realize what the words imply.

292. *Would you say that the Archbishop of Canterbury is preaching an anti-Christian doctrine?*

He preaches the doctrine of the Church of England as he understands it, and being in good faith, no fault probably attaches to him. But the real question is, "Are the doctrines of the Church of England anti-Christian?" The reply is, "Not in every single matter. Various groups within the Anglican Church have kept some parts of Christ's teaching intact. But in many things all Anglicans reject certain doctrines without warrant. The present Anglican Archbishop of Canterbury is, of course, a heretic and a schismatic objectively. Catholic Bishops throughout the world will enter into no official relations whatever with those Anglican Bishops who have appeared on the scene only since the 16th century."

293. *Are not Anglo-Catholics passing slowly to Catholic ways?*

Why should they have to do so, if the Anglican Church is right, and has ever been right? But, even so, Anglo-Catholics are not passing to Catholic ways. The Catholic way is obedience to the God-given authority of the Catholic Church, and Anglo-Catholics are as far off from that as ever.

294. *They are practically the same in their services.*

They imitate many of our external practices. But even this attempt is in defiance of their own Bishops. Nor does their imitation of Catholic worship make them Catholics. If some stranger were my double in appearance, that would not make him my blood brother. The only way to be a Catholic is to be one. We went from God by disobedience, and the one way back is by obedience. Obedience is the very essence of religion, and it is obedience to the Catholic Church in belief and practice which makes a man a Catholic.

295. I am an Anglican, and I was present in the Anglican Church of St. James in Sydney where a Requiem Mass was celebrated for the repose of the soul of one of our deceased priests. This occurred in 1930.

The Clergy of that Church wish to adopt the titles and ceremonies of the Catholic Church, but not the obligations of Catholics. No Requiem Mass was really celebrated. A service was held, and called a Requiem Mass. At the Synod held shortly after this event Bishop D'Arcy Irvine protested most strongly against the whole affair. Here are his words, as reported in the *Daily Guardian*, October 13th, 1930, "Requiem Masses are in direct contrariety to the plain and emphatic statements both of the Articles and also of the devotional language of the Book of Common Prayer. They are repugnant to Anglican theology; they are repugnant to Anglican authority; they are repugnant to the Anglican Liturgy and worship. From the fable, or deceit, or folly—from the practice and doctrine of Requiem Masses may God preserve the Church of England. From cover to cover the Book of Common Prayer has no place for Requiem Masses."

296. I belong to the High Church party, but I think it is wrong to criticize other parties.

I presume you are High Church because you think it right, and not Low Church because you think that wrong. If you think them equally right there is no reason why you should insist that you are High Church rather than Low Church. You could not defend your own position without criticizing the position you cannot accept.

297. In spite of all that you say, I still believe that Henry VIII. was justified in establishing the Church of England. He purified English religion.

Had he left the Catholic Church in order to become a better man himself, and in order to make his people better, you *might* have a case. But he did not.

298. He left the Church merely because he was not going to be told by the Pope what to do.

You have said it. Henry was not going to be told even by the Pope to keep God's law, so he rebelled, and his rebellion was the genesis of Anglicanism. It began in disobedience, even as all the world's troubles began in the cry of Satan, "I will not serve." When men refused to obey God, they found everything else refusing to obey them, even their own passions. And when Anglicanism refused to obey the Catholic Church, it lost the power to secure obedience even from its own clergy.

299. Old England still stands under the Protestant flag of liberty!

The Protestant flag of what liberty? You are dealing with a very dangerous word. There is no absolute liberty. Liberty always implies relative restriction. If I am free from truth, I am subject to error; if free from virtue, subject to vice. When science proved the world round, it took away my liberty to believe it to be flat. But I do not want to be free to believe it flat. When God revealed His law, that revelation took away my liberty to do what that law forbade. When He revealed a definite religion, He took away my liberty to belong to any religion I might wish. His law takes away the liberty of divorce and re-marriage. Good old England gives her subjects the liberty to have it. But that is the liberty of the devil and refusal of submission to God. A man can be free from God and be the servant of Satan, or be free from Satan and be the servant of God. Choose which liberty you will have. But quite a lot of England's liberty is liberty from the law of God.

I am of purely English descent, and there is no national prejudice in what I say. But if my own mother commits murder, I refuse to be so blinded by my love for her as to deny that it is a crime.

300. *Since the opening of the Bible to her people, God has favored England as no other nation since Israel.*

England has progressed materially, but no argument can be deduced from that. God gives temporal benefits to good and bad alike. Spiritual blessings are the real blessings. England is rapidly drifting to irreligion altogether, and the Book you say she has opened to her people is being torn to shreds and ridiculed by Englishmen in a way which Catholic reverence for the Word of God could never tolerate.

301. *Christian conditions came to England with Protestantism.*

Christian conditions are rapidly fading in England as a result of Protestantism. Protestantism gave men so-called liberty to think for themselves, and men have interpreted it as license to think whatever they please.

302. *England would still be Catholic had not men taken to thinking.*

Englishmen left the Catholic Church originally through fear for their property and their lives. Not many desired to share the fate of St. Thomas More, and dear old Henry VIII. had the delightful habit of confiscating all the possessions of those who would not transfer their allegiance from the Pope to himself. Four hundred years have dimmed the memory of these things, and no real thought is given to the matter by the average Englishman. But those who can and do think are rapidly giving up Protestantism, and becoming either Agnostics or Catholics. Unfortunately there is no particular prejudice against becoming an Agnostic, whilst there is still a strong lingering prejudice against becoming a Catholic. Also to become a Catholic requires more thinking than to become an Agnostic, and thinking is too much like hard work on such an unimportant matter as the rights of God over mankind.

303. *Could you give me six short reasons why you left Anglicanism?*

Certainly. (1) It is a national Church. (2) It has no Apostolic succession. (3) It has no spiritual authority. (4) It omits much Biblical teaching. (5) It is chaotic and contradictory in so much as it does retain. (6) It has produced no Saints of its own. There are many other reasons, but you ask for six.

304. *The Roman Church is built upon one interpretation of Scripture, the Anglican Church upon another. The latter may be as equally right as the former, for all we know.*

Since the Anglican Church is a contradiction of the Catholic Church, it could not possibly be equally as right. If one of the two is right, the other must be wrong. Meantime, the Anglican Church is not based upon Scripture. It is based upon the revolt of Henry VIII. from the Catholic Church. Later on interpretations were read into Scripture to suit the Church he founded. That is a matter of history. Many other non-Catholic churches have been originally based upon peculiar misinterpretations of Scripture, and it would be possible to build up hundreds of other churches upon further such misinterpretations. The Catholic Church, however, whilst in full accord with the true sense of Scripture, is not built upon it. She existed before a line of the New Testament was written. Her members wrote the New Testament, and she tells us what they really meant when they wrote them. She is built upon the historical Person of Christ, and proves her divine commission by her continued possession of the attributes Christ conferred upon her. Now that the Gospels are written they confirm her claims when rightly interpreted—but that is all. If not a line of the New Testament had ever been written, the Catholic Church would still be here.

305. *Anglican ministers are just as good and intelligent as you are, and have studied the Bible just as deeply.*

For the sake of argument, let us suppose that to be true. But that does not make the Anglican Church true. If they are just as learned as Catholic priests, so also Catholic priests are just as learned as they. So too, they are just as good. And if the learning and character of Anglican ministers make the Anglican Church true, so the learning and character of Catholic priests would make the Catholic Church true. You are forced to the conclusion that the Anglican Church is the only true Church, and that the Catholic Church is also the only true Church. But you cannot have two only true churches.

306. *Does the Catholic Church recognize the Greek Orthodox Church as part of itself?*

No. As a matter of fact there is no one Greek Orthodox Church. There are many independent Greek Churches. They originated by rebellion against the Catholic Church in the ninth century, and have split up into many different allegiances. As long as they refuse to submit to the authority of the Catholic Church they are as much outside the Catholic Church as the Protestant variations.

307. *How does the Greek Church differ from the Catholic Church?*

The Greek Churches are both schismatical and heretical. They are separated from the obedience due to the authority of Christ in His true Church. They acknowledge no infallible head. They may retain valid orders and the Mass—things which Protestantism lost—but they have fallen into errors concerning the Holy Trinity, the Immaculate Conception, Purgatory, and various other points of Christian doctrine.

308. *What is your attitude towards John Wesley?*

Wesley was a good and sincere man, but he was mistaken in his notion of Christianity. It was evil that he should have created a further sect. Yet because he and his followers were sincere God blessed their goodwill in many things, drawing good from their work in spite of the undoubted evil of preaching erroneous doctrines as if they were indeed the true doctrines of Christ. Meantime God wills for Wesleyans the greater good still of a return to the Catholic Church.

309. *The Baptist Church is the true Church. It really acts as did the first Christians, whilst the Catholic Church is not mentioned in Scripture as the true Church.*

The Baptist Church is certainly not mentioned in Scripture. The Catholic Church is most clearly described there. Meantime, do Baptists act as did the first Christians? Do they go to Confession? Have they the sacrifice of the Mass? Baptists, like other Protestants, insist upon one thing not commanded by Christ, and neglect most of the things insisted upon by Him. Also, Christ said that His Church would be in the world all days from His time until the end of the world. But where was the Baptist Church before the 15th century? Christ certainly was not the Founder of the Baptist Church. It is subject to all the defects common to other forms of Protestantism.

310. *Whatever you say of other churches, you will never be able to prove that we Seventh Day Adventists are wrong whilst we remain true to the Bible.*

If you were true to the Bible, no one could prove you wrong. But you are most unbiblical. Your very system leaves you without any real proof that the Bible is the inspired Word of God. It cannot say what is the real sense of all that is contained in the Bible. It concentrates upon a few misinterpreted texts, and ignores the whole trend of Scripture, although all Scripture is of equal value as God's Word. The Catholic Church alone can guarantee Scripture as the Word of God, and alone can guarantee its correct meaning.

311. *Why not be charitable and admit that the Salvation Army with their good works are God's people?*

I charitably say that their good works are often very pleasing to God, and they themselves also, for many of them have the utmost goodwill and devotion. But charity does not oblige me to say that the true Church of Jesus Christ was founded by General Booth. However well-intentioned these good people may be, they are mistaken. Christ gave us a definite set of truths to be believed and of precepts to be fulfilled. He is a true Christian who believes all that Christ taught, and does all that He commands. Members of the Salvation Army reject much of Christ's doctrine. Some say that Baptism is not really necessary. All reject Christ's teaching on the Eucharist, although Christ allowed the Jews to go their own way when they refused to accept this teaching. The Army says, "Believe in the Name of Christ and that you are saved by Him." The Catholic Church rightly says that that is not enough, and gives the advice, "Believe in Christ. Believe every single doctrine He taught, and believe that you can be saved by Him provided you try to obey sincerely His moral teachings." I admit that many members of the Salvation Army try just as sincerely to live up to their inadequate knowledge of Christianity as Catholics try to live up to the full truth. In that sense they are good people. But they are not true Christians in so far as they do not accept the full truth revealed by Christ.

312. *Have you any reason for the rejection of the "Witnesses of Jehovah"?*

The "Witnesses of Jehovah" merely constitute a form of that sect known as the Russellites. They have no evidence whatever that Jehovah ever asked them to be His witnesses. The Russellites were named after Pastor Charles T. Russell, an American who started a new form of Protestantism. Their religion is based upon the conjecture that Christ's second coming is imminent. They pay little or no attention to the obvious things in Scripture, but concentrate upon one point in particular which Christ purposely left obscure, saying, "It is not given to man to know these things." They regard all organized churches and their clergy as agents of Satan, but entertain a special hatred of the Catholic Church, regarding the Pope as the Beast predicted by Daniel and St. John. Their exegetical gymnastics in the interpretation of mystical texts is astonishing. Meantime they claim to have originated in 1874, which is just 1874 years too late for one who seeks the Church actually established by Christ.

313. *What of Christian Science?*

Christian Science was founded by Mary Baker Eddy in 1875. Mary Baker was born in 1821. She married a Mr. Asa Gilbert Eddy, after securing a divorce from Mr. Patterson, whom she had married after the death of her first husband, Colonel Glover. Despite its title, her religion is really but an unscientific heresy. It denies the existence of suffering, matter, human beings, sin, death, and a whole lot of other things which we know quite well to exist.

314. Does not Christian Science rely upon prayer through belief in Christ's words, "Whatever you ask in My name, it shall be granted"?

I am afraid that it requires more belief in Mrs. Eddy than in Christ. It relies also far more upon auto-suggestion and self-persuasion than upon prayer. After all, favors must be asked in the Name of Christ, and therefore in conformity with the Will of God. But God expects us to use the natural means He has put at our disposal. His ordinary law for our health is the use of natural remedies and medical aid. It is absurd to say that He provided these things uselessly, and does not intend us to use them. If we deliberately neglect God's ordinary means we cannot expect Him to help us in some extraordinary way of our own devising.

315. Do not Christian Scientists produce miracles just as at Lourdes?

No. They exploit the natural powers of auto-suggestion, but no cure at Lourdes which could be due to auto-suggestion is ever accepted and registered officially as a miracle. Auto-suggestion will not mend a broken leg. Also it will not avail for infants who have not attained the age of reason. Yet Lourdes has seen the cure of broken and deformed bones, and the recovery of little children who could not possibly have suggested themselves back to health. Christian Science cannot produce any really authenticated miracles.

316. The higher synthesis known as Theosophy at least does not exclude Catholics.

Theosophy is not a higher synthesis. It is an anti-Christian confusion of philosophical remnants. And whether it excludes Catholic adherents or not, the Catholic Church excludes Theosophy, prohibiting its doctrines as being utterly irreconcilable with the teachings of Christ. The doctrines were well weighed before the Church issued the decree of 1919, and that decree will never be withdrawn. By it the Catholic Church showed once more how conscious she is of her duty to preserve the exact doctrine of Christ just as He gave it to mankind.

317. May Catholics assist at Spiritistic Seances?

No. In 1917, the Church decreed as follows: "It is not lawful to assist at Spiritistic Seances or manifestations whether with or without a medium, even though such meetings seem to be honest and religious." Spiritualism claims to be a new religion, and therefore meets with the same fate as all other religions invented by men since the time of Christ. The only true religion is that established by Christ, and in the form in which He established it. It is little use to call oneself a Christian, and reject the Church as Christ built it, accepting any form of religion men would like to substitute for it.

318. Is there any truth in the claims of Spiritualism?

There is truth in the claim that the soul is distinct from, and can survive the body. All men instinctively know this, and as they lose faith in Protestantism, this fundamental truth of reason remains. Many of them therefore turn to Spiritualism. Thus this new phase gains ground among non-Catholics. As a religious system Spiritualism is the outcome of human effort, and is in vogue among certain men for a time. But it is valueless as a religion in the sight of God. It will die out in due course, possibly to give place to some other extravagant form of religious excitement. Man is constitutionally religious, and if deprived of Catholic truth will grasp at anything for a time. But substitutes are bound to disappoint in the end.

319. *Why precisely does your Church condemn Spiritualism?*

The Catholic Church certainly believes in the existence of the spiritual world, of God, of good and evil created spirits, and in the continued existence of the souls of men. But the phenomena of Spiritualism are due at best to natural causes; at times to imposture; very often to evil spirits. Certainly any effects due to the influence of spirits are not due to the intervention of good spirits. The medium acts under uncanny and feverish excitement; the effects are evil only too often; and messages received, as well as the methods adopted, are openly blasphemous and immoral, and quite unworthy of God. God Himself says, "Neither let there be found among you . . . one that seeketh the truth from the dead." Deut. XVIII., 10-11.

320. *Has the Catholic Church ever been in communication with spirit beings from the next world?*

In the history of the Catholic Church there are many accounts of messages received from the souls of the departed. The truth of these accounts is subject to the ordinary laws of historical criticism, and some accounts have certainly been proved doubtful. Others leave no room for prudent doubt. As a rule, God permits a soul only occasionally to communicate momentarily a warning, or a request for prayers, but nothing fantastical. Likewise, the messages are spontaneous, and not due to the curious efforts of people seeking the truth from the dead. The Church tests the messages received, or claimed as received, in order to discern whether good or evil spirits are responsible for the communication. (1) The message must in no way conflict with Catholic teaching or moral principles. Gal. I., 9. (2) The person who claims to have received such a communication must be characterized by sound common sense, and even be undesirous of such occurrences. (3) The effects of the message must be good, the recipient being moved to a holier life, and to nothing indecent, shameful, or contrary to Christian standards.

321. *Spirits have told Spiritualists that we shall not see God face to face, and that we shall have only natural happiness in Heaven. Is there any truth in this?*

The idea of merely natural happiness in Heaven is nonsense. The supreme happiness of Heaven is totally different from any happiness we know on earth. "Eye hath not seen, nor ear heard . . . what things God hath prepared for them that love Him." I. Cor. II., 9. An eternity of the things we know here, and of life as we experience it would soon become blank misery, and not Heaven at all. God Himself tells us that we shall see Him face to face, and it is better to believe the God who made us than the Spiritualist who would only unmake us as regards our rational nature.

322. *It is most unkind of you to speak so sarcastically of other religions.*

Inquirers put their religious theories before me, and if they are illogical I say so, giving my reasons for saying so. This is not sarcasm, above all since I respect the sincerity of those whose theories are mistaken. Nor is it unkind. If you saw a sick man taking, not the medicine prescribed by the doctor, but some other drink by mistake, would it be kindness to keep quiet just to spare him the confusion of realizing his mistake?

323. *God is love.*

Right. But whilst love may excuse the man who makes a mistake, it cannot say that the mistake is not a mistake. I deny that truth is error, or that error is truth. But I make every allowance for those who mistake error for truth.

324. *We are all going to the same place, and there will be no distinction there.*

We all wish, perhaps, to go to the same place. But the difficulty is as to the right road to that place. One man says one way; another maintains that another way is the correct path. All sick men wish to get better. But you do not argue, "After all, they all hope to attain the same health, therefore let this sick man drink anything, even the wrong medicine altogether." Is it immaterial as to the means one takes merely because all hope to attain the same health? There will be a distinction in Heaven, at least in degrees of happiness and glory. But we shall all be united in the same charity as I hope we are now, and also in the same truth as we are not now. For when you get to Heaven you will change your ideas, and accept all that Catholics now believe on earth. Thus you will be in perfect harmony with them throughout eternity. That is, of course, unless you become a Catholic still earlier in this life, as I hope and pray you will, for the sake of all that it would mean to you, both in time and in eternity.

CHAPTER EIGHT

THE TRUTH OF CATHOLICISM

325. What is the Catholic idea of the Church?

The Church is that visible society of men upon earth which was founded by Jesus Christ, guaranteed by Him to exist all days until the end of the world, and sent by Him to teach all nations with His own authority. It is one definite society for man's spiritual good, and its members are bound together by the profession of the same and complete Christian faith, by the same Sacraments and worship, and by submission to the same spiritual authority vested in the successors of St. Peter—the present successor being the Bishop of Rome.

326. The Church means an assembly of men united in prayer, not a building.

The word Church has a twofold sense. Its proper meaning is a union or assembly of men united not only in prayer, but also in a definite creed, worship, and obedience. In that sense I speak of *the* Catholic Church. Or again, it can refer to a building erected for purposes of worship by members of the Catholic Church, and in that sense I speak of *a* Catholic Church.

327. What positive proof have you that the Catholic Church is the only true Church?

The proof lies in the fact that the Catholic Church alone corresponds exactly to the exact religion established by Christ. Now the Christian religion is that religion which—

(a) Was founded by Christ personally;

(b) Has existed continuously since the time of Christ;

(c) Is Catholic or universal, in accordance with Christ's command to go to all the world and teach all nations;

(d) Demands that all her members admit the same doctrine;

(e) Exercises divine authority over her subjects, since Christ said that if a man would not hear the Church he would be as the heathen.

Now the Catholic Church alone can claim—

(a) To have been founded by Christ personally. All other Churches disappear as you go back through history. Christ said, "Thou art Peter, and upon this rock I will build my Church." There are many claimants to the honor of being Christ's Church. But among all non-Catholic Churches, we find one built on a John Wesley; another on a Martin Luther; another on a Mrs. Eddy, etc. But the Catholic Church alone can possibly claim to have been built on Peter, the chief of the Apostles, and one-time Bishop of Rome.

(b) To have existed in all the centuries since Christ.

(c) That every one of her members admits exactly the same essential doctrines.

(d) To be Catholic or universal.

(e) To speak with a voice of true authority in the name of God.

328. *You have given those tests from Christ's predictions and intentions. What of the test given by Mark XVI., 17?* "*These signs shall follow those who believe; they shall take up serpents; and if they shall drink any deadly thing it shall not hurt them.*"

The passage you quote was never meant to indicate a permanent test of the true Church. Christ predicted that certain signs would occur to justify the preaching of His followers. He did not say that they would occur continuously, nor that every individual follower would be endowed with such miraculous powers. The signs did occur in the case of some followers of Christ in the early Church, and thus Christ's prophecy was fulfilled. Thus St. Paul himself was bitten by a deadly viper and suffered no harm, to the astonishment of the people around him. Acts XXVIII., 3. But the miracle was for the sake of the unbelievers who had no other external sign. But now that the Church has been solidly established and propagated, such extraordinary signs are not necessary. You have plenty of external evidence, now that the Church exists throughout the world and stares you in the face.

329. *Let me have you bitten by a poisonous serpent, and if nothing happens to you, I will believe!*

You are asking me to do that which is sinful in order to prove God's religion true! Satan said to Christ, "Throw thyself down," and Christ replied, "It is written, thou shalt not tempt the Lord thy God." It is wrong to try to force God to do even things we believe that He has promised—for Satan quoted a promise of God. Above all, it is wrong when you want God to do always what He has promised to do on some particular occasions only. The Jews cried, "Come down from the cross, and we shall believe." You would have watched Him die for your salvation, and then refused to believe because He did so! You have sufficient evidence, and if you refuse to look at that, you would not believe even if one rose from the dead before your very eyes. I do not fear death. I do fear sin. But your logic in promising to believe that I am a true successor of the Apostles provided I indulge in sinful conduct is baffling.

330. *I admit your tests of a Church founded by Christ, continuously existing, united, universal, and authoritative. But I cannot admit the machine-made organization with its hard and fast rules, which you call the Catholic Church, to be that Church.*

If the Catholic Church is not it, no other can be it. However, the Catholic Church is not a machine-made organization. It is just as established by Christ. Were the Catholic Church a man-made system, it would have gone the way of all man-made kingdoms and empires which have come and gone, whereas it has serenely kept going with a humanly inexplicable vitality.

331. *Where in Scripture does it mention that Christ founded any such system?*

In general, Christ terms His Church a kingdom, which supposes some organized authority. However the explicit steps in the establishing of an authoritative hierarchy are clear. Christ chose certain special men. "You have not chosen me: but I have chosen you." Jn. XV., 16. He gave them His own mission. "As the Father hath sent me, I also send you." Jn. XX., 21. This commission included His teaching authority: "Teach all nations . . . whatsoever I have commanded you." Matt. XXVIII., 19; His power to sanctify—"Baptising them," Matt. XXVIII., 19—forgiving sin, "Whose sins you shall forgive, they are forgiven," Jn. XX., 23—offering sacrifice, "Do this for a commemoration of me," I. Cor. XI., 24; His legislative or disciplinary power—"He who hears you, hears me, and he who despises you despises me," Lk.

X., 16; "Whatsoever you shall bind on earth, shall be bound also in Heaven," Matt. XVIII., 18. "If a man will not hear the Church, let him be to thee as the heathen," Matt. XVIII., 17. The Apostles certainly exercised these powers from the beginning. Thus we read in the Acts of the Apostles, "They were all persevering in the doctrine of the Apostles," II., 42. St. Paul himself did not hesitate to excommunicate the incestuous Corinthian. I. Cor. V., 4. And he wrote to the Hebrews, "Obey your prelates, and be subject to them," Heb. XIII., 17.

332. Cannot the Congregationalist make out an equally strong case for a universal spiritual brotherhood, but with local independence of churches?

There is no evidence of independent local churches in Scripture, nor in primitive documents. There is evidence that there were distinct groups of Christians in various places, just as there are Catholics in London under one Bishop, and Catholics in New York under another. All true Christians certainly formed a universal spiritual brotherhood, as Catholics do to-day; but local autonomy existed only in the sense that there were Bishops in charge of various localities, the Bishops themselves being subject to St. Peter, and after his death, to the successor of St. Peter.

333. I am loyal to Christ, not to any supposed representatives on earth.

No one wants you to be loyal to any supposed representatives on earth. But loyalty to Christ demands loyalty to those commissioned by Him to teach and guide in His name. Test the claims before you reject them on prejudice only.

334. Whilst I walk in the spirit, I do not think it necessary to be subject to any visible organization.

You may say that you believe it unnecessary. But pay attention to the words of Christ I have just quoted. He thought it necessary, and He has the right to map out the kind of religion we are to accept. If Christians had to accept such disciplinary authority in the time of the Apostles, they must accept it now. Christianity is Christianity. It does not change with the ages. If it did, it would lose its character, and not remain the religion of Christ, to which religion alone He attached His promises. And remember His prediction that His flock would be one fold with one shepherd. Jn. X., 14. You would have sheep, not gathered into one fold, but straying anywhere and everywhere, having no shepherd with any real authority over them.

335. I admit that the way Catholics are taught by their hierarchy is a most successful policy.

The Catholic method is not a method of human policy. We accept it because Christ imposed it. Yet the mere fact that Christ chose such a method is a guarantee of its wisdom. And the scepticism and irreligion which are the fruits of non-Catholic systems are but a further tribute to the wisdom of Christ.

336. Why do you reserve the hierarchical authority to men? Why not give women a chance?

Nowhere did Christ ever commission women to teach in His name and with His authority. St. Paul explicitly forbids women to attempt to exercise such functions. I. Tim. II., 11-12; I. Cor. XIV., 34. People who would ordain women in the Church seem to believe that they know more about Christianity than St. Paul.

337. *I don't agree with any of these priestly claims. Anyway, the search-light of modern science is gradually breaking them up.*

The searchlight of science is doing good work in destroying superstition, and showing the fallacies of false religions which are due to the natural instinct of religion in all men, and the ignorance of the true religion revealed by God. But sound science is doing a great work for the Catholic Church and helping many towards her. What is called modern science and thought keeps men away from the Catholic Church only when what is modern but not scientific is falsely supposed to be scientific, or when men, in their attempts at thinking mistake sophisms and fallacies for legitimate conclusions.

338. *Are not your priests a great army of drones who neither toil, nor spin?*

That idea may arise in the minds of those who do not personally ask their services. But you cannot argue that, because they do nothing according to your specifications, they do nothing at all. Earth worms might similarly argue that men do nothing because they don't burrow in the mud as they. Priests are regularly occupied in their own duties and studies. They would have less hours of employment in a worldly career. And if the Church allowed them to engage in secular business, our Catholic people would be uncared for, and religion would become a mockery. The man who slaves at some mechanical trade or in a commercial office, with little opportunity for regular prayer or continuous study, is not the man to teach religion to others and devote himself to the sanctification of their souls.

339. *Do you think society will allow them to continue in existence, despite their place in economics?*

Society has no say in the matter. For two thousand years society—the world—has hated the Catholic Church and her Priests. But society has not made much progress against the Catholic Church. Nor have economics anything to do with it. The omnipotent power of God guarantees that the Church will last till the end of time, and as long as the Church lasts, the Sacrifice of the Mass will be offered, which means that there will be Priests to offer that Sacrifice.

340. *You claim, of course, that the Pope is supreme head of this organized hierarchy. Yet was it not the Emperor Phocas who first gave the Pope his title and universal jurisdiction? History records this as having happened in 607 A.D.*

It does not. It records that, at the request of the Pope, the Emperor made it illegal for any other Bishop to usurp the title which had always belonged to the Bishop of Rome. To forbid others to take a title which has ever been the rightful possession of one is not to confer the title upon that one. And if the Pope did not possess universal jurisdiction until 607, how could St. Clement, third successor of St. Peter as Bishop of Rome, write to the Christians at Corinth, "If any disobey the words spoken by God through us, let them know that they will entangle themselves in transgression and no small danger, but we shall be clear of this sin." Thus the fourth Pope demanded obedience under pain of sin from Christians living abroad. Again, how could St. Irenaeus, Bishop of Lyons in Gaul, and who died in the year 202, say that all churches were subject to, and must agree with the Church at Rome, because St. Peter had founded the Church there, and the Bishops of that city were his lawful successors, beginning with Linus? Irenaeus died over 400 years before the date you give. The Council of Ephesus in 431, embracing all Bishops and not even held at Rome, decreed, "No one can doubt, indeed it is known to all ages, that Peter, Prince and Head of the Apostles and Foundation of the Catholic Church, received the keys of the kingdom from Christ our Redeemer, and that to this day and always he lives in his successors exercising judgment." This was 176 years earlier than the date you give.

341. Was not the title of Universal Bishop much sought after, the Bishop of Rome winning it because he had the largest number of adherents?

No. Whatever abuses arose in later times, the early saintly Popes, nearly all of them martyrs for Christ, were not the men to seek after office, and dignities which they knew to be spurious.

342. Who gives the Pope his jurisdiction, if he is elected by men and not by God?

God ratifies the choice of those who elect him. When Matthias was elected as an Apostle by the other Apostles he was elected by men, and not directly by God, but God ratified their choice and granted to him also apostolic power.

343. Did not Christ say, "Neither be ye masters, for one is your master, Christ." Matt. XXIII., 10.

The Pope is the servant of the servants of God. He himself tells us that one is our master—Christ, whom he and all are bound to serve. He claims no authority independently of Christ. The text you quote forbids selfish tyranny in one's own name over members of the Church. It does not forbid the exercise of legitimate power. "Obey your prelates, and be subject to them," says St. Paul. Heb. XIII., 17.

344. The servant of the servants of God! Is not the Pope rather the Beast predicted by Dan. VII?

Certainly not. He would be a very peculiar representative of the Beast, so given to the love of God and man, and to prayer. I have met the present Pope (Pius XI.) several times, and he is one of the gentlest men I have ever met. He scarcely opens his lips save to bless and praise God in the Name of Jesus Christ.

345. I have heard that he is Anti-Christ, and that he was described by St. John as 666, the numerical equivalent of the Latin words of the Pope's title, Vicarius Filii Dei.

That interpretation is absurd, and rejected by all reputable scholars, Catholic and non-Catholic alike. In any case, St. John wrote in Greek, and there is no warrant whatever for the transition to the Latin language. Moreover, whatever be the true interpretation of this mystical number, it certainly refers to some one individual being. If it referred to one particular Pope, it could refer to none of the others. To which Pope will people refer it? To a past Pope? Then he is dead and gone, and we need not worry about him. To the present Pope? He is the very antithesis of all the conditions of the Beast as described by St. John. However, the number does not refer to any of the Popes at all.

346. Who is 666, if not the Pope?

Many fantastic interpretations have been given, but none have been proved. The vast majority of interpreters regard the number as a mystical symbol, designating some man who will be the chief agent of Satan towards the end of the world. Some people thought it was Mahomet, saying that he died in 666 A.D. But he died in 630 A.D. Calvin wished to attribute it to Pope Boniface III., or to the Popes in general. His only foundation was prejudice, and his theory is utterly rejected to-day. Martin Luther's name, and dozens of others have been made to signify the number in various languages, but in all these cases the wish was father to the thought, and was made to supply for the lack of reason. The true solution of this question cannot be given.

347. Why was St. John so obscure? Was it merely to give us a conundrum?

No. He desired to show us that he knew the future by revelation, but that he was not free to manifest all that he knew to us. He explicitly says, "Let him that hath understanding count the number." The understanding required is not merely human wisdom, but an understanding on the same high plane as was the very revelation given to St. John. Undeterred by this warning, those who are so confident that it refers to the Pope modestly rank themselves with St. John. But no special wisdom is shown in any answer yet given. When a man has practiced all the other good advice in the New Testament, more practical and more clear, he will be making some progress towards the wisdom necessary to understand such references. Possibly the text is intended for those who will be living in the times when it shall be clear from events themselves.

348. Anyway Scripture does not mention a Pope.

Do not be misled by mere words. Later designations of an office do not alter the office, and the office of the one whom we now call the Pope is clearly taught by Scripture. After all, the word Pope simply means father, or one with paternal authority over a household. And certainly, Scripture often likens the Church to the "Household of the Faith," and indicates one as being in supreme charge of that household.

349. Gregory the Great, Bishop of Rome, refused the title of universal Bishop himself, and blamed John the Faster of Constantinople for his presumption in claiming such a title!

Gregory was Pope, and knew that he was Pope. Far from refusing the title, he showed that he was universal Bishop by excommunicating John the Faster, over whom he could not have had such jurisdiction had he not the privilege of being universal Bishop. In his 21st Epistle Gregory writes, "As to what they say of the Church of Christ, who doubts that it is subject to the Apostolic See?"

350. That was in the 7th century. Who was head of the Church for the first three hundred years?

The various Bishops of Rome who succeeded St. Peter—St. Peter having been head of the Apostles, and having died as Bishop of Rome.

351. St. Peter was not head of the Apostles. All the Apostles acted as having the same authority.

The Apostles, as having been sent by Christ to all nations, had universal jurisdiction. But this universality of jurisdiction was extraordinary, and did not pass to those successors whom they consecrated for particular localities. Also, whilst the Apostles each rejoiced in jurisdiction over all regions, St. Peter had all authority centred in him. Hence St. Paul went to consult him at Jerusalem.

352. Why did the Apostles ask Christ who was the greater among them, if they knew that Peter was the greater?

They were disputing as to who should be the greater in Heaven, not concerning their office on earth. The fact that Christ replied by teaching a lesson of interior humility shows that He knew them to be referring to their personal standing in God's esteem.

353. Why did not Christ say that St. Peter was the greater, taking advantage of this occasion?

You must remember the sense of the discussion. Peter was not necessarily the greater from an aspect of grace and holiness. Eternal rewards depend rather upon Christian virtue than upon earthly office. St. Peter was chief in earthly office, although we know that St. John was called the beloved disciple.

354. Christ forbade any attempt to exercise authority when He said, "Do not lord it over others as do the Gentiles." Matt. XX., 25.

Christ warned the Apostles against exercising authority in unjust and domineering ways such as those of worldlings, who delight to be thought great, and who love tyranny. He forbade the evil method, but He deliberately gave His authority to the Apostles, and chiefly to St. Peter.

355. Does Scripture show that Peter was even aware of, or openly claimed supreme power?

Since none of the Apostles disputed it, St. Peter had no need to insist upon it. All knew that Christ had said to him, "Thou art Peter, and upon this rock I will build my Church." Matt. XVI., 18. And again, "I have prayed for thee, that thy faith fail not: and do thou, being once converted, confirm thy brethren." Lk. XXII., 32. They knew, too, that Christ's commission to St. Peter to feed both the lambs and the sheep of the flock included themselves. Jn. XXI., 15-17. Implicitly St. Peter claimed his right by being the first to announce the Gospel after Pentecost, by conducting the election of Matthias as an Apostle in place of Judas, by presiding at the Council of Jerusalem, etc. St. Paul wrote to the Galatians I., 18, that he went to Jerusalem to see Peter, and stayed there fifteen days with him. Why to Peter rather than to any other of the Apostles? And why does he add that, having gone to Jerusalem, he also saw James? He does not say that he went to see such Apostles as were at Jerusalem, or that he went to see James, and also happened to see Peter whilst there.

356. Yet did not James preside at the Council of Jerusalem, although Peter was present?

He did not. St. Peter presided. Acts XV., 7, says, "After much disputing Peter rose up and said"; he then solved the question. Verse 12 tells us that after Peter had spoken all held their peace. James then spoke in support of Peter's decision, as much as to say, "Peter is right. I too think that the Gentiles should not be disquieted." St. Jerome remarks, concerning this incident, "The whole multitude held their peace, and James the Apostle together with all the priests passed over to the judgment of Peter. . . . Peter was the prime mover in issuing the decree." St. John Chrysostom wrote, "See the care of the teacher towards his subjects! He has the first authority in the discussion because to him all were committed."

357. But if all this be so, why did Paul boast that he resisted Peter to the face?

St. Peter was supreme head of the Church and infallible in his doctrinal teaching, but it does not follow that he would not be indiscreet in some act of administration. Now no doctrinal error was involved in this particular case. St. Peter indiscreetly ceased to eat with the Gentiles because of the presence of some Jews. But to cease from doing a lawful thing for fear lest others be scandalized is not a matter of doctrine. It is a question of prudence or imprudence. St. Paul did not act as if he were St. Peter's superior. Nor did he boast. To show the urgency of the matter, he practically said, "I had to resist even Peter—to whom chief authority belongs." And his words derive their full significance only from the fact that St. Peter was head of the Apostles. St. Cyprian, who lived in the third century, knew of this passage and certainly understood Christianity. Yet he did not perceive any objection against St. Peter's supremacy in this case. He writes, "Peter, whom the Lord chose to be first and upon whom He built His Church, did not proudly assert the primacy he possessed, nor despise Paul who had once been a persecutor of the Church; but he accepted meekly, giving us an example of patience." St. Hilary, in the fifth century, says, "Both Paul and Peter are to be admired; Paul because he did not fear to point out the right practice to his superior; Peter because, knowing that all acknowledged his primacy, he had too much humility to resent any reproach offered to himself."

358. Did not St. Paul say, "I have laid the foundation . . . but let every man take care how he buildeth thereon"? I. Cor. III., 10.

St. Paul declares that he personally laid the foundations of a particular branch of the Church at Corinth. But Christ had founded the whole Church upon Peter. Each must take care how he builds, and St. Paul took care that the Church at Corinth would be in full accordance with the universal Church founded upon St. Peter. Anyone who departs from the authority of St. Peter is not taking care, but going outside the constitution of the Church as established by Christ, and severing himself from that Church.

359. St. Paul was head of the Gentile Churches; St. Peter was head of the Jewish section only.

If so, you are in a great difficulty. If the Church was thus divided and St. Paul was head of the Gentile section, where is St. Paul's successor to-day? We have the successors of St. Peter in the Popes, and the present Pope is head of the Church with over 400 millions of subjects, the vast majority of them Gentiles. In any case, St. Paul again and again addressed the Jews in their Synagogues, and St. Peter certainly ministered to the Gentiles in his turn, above all as Bishop of Rome.

360. I cannot believe that the Church was founded upon Peter. It was built upon Christ, who is the true foundation stone.

No one claims that St. Peter was the principal foundation stone. But that Church which is in communion with St. Peter and his successors is the genuine Church built upon the foundation of Christ. Christ Himself said to Peter, "Thou art Peter, and upon this rock I will build my Church." Christ is the solid rock upon which the Church is built. But the first rock laid upon this foundation is Peter, Christ being the principal foundation stone, Peter being the secondary foundation chosen by Christ.

361. Christ said, "Upon this rock," meaning Himself, not Peter.

That is erroneous. In Jn. I., 42, we find Christ saying to Peter, "Thou art Simon . . . thou shalt be called Cephas, Which is interpreted Peter." Christ had a special purpose in thus changing his name to Cephas or rock, a purpose manifested later on as recorded by Matt. XVI., 18, "Thou art Peter, and upon this rock I will build my Church." Let us put it this way. Supposing that your name were Brown, and I said to you, "They call you Brown, but I am going to call you Stone. And upon this stone I shall build up a special society I have in mind to establish," would you believe that I was alluding to you, or to myself? Now Peter's name was Simon, and Christ changed it to Peter, or in the original Aramaic language, Kepha, which was the word for rock or stone, and which was never used as a proper name in that language. Thus He said, "Thou art Kepha, and upon this Kepha I will build my Church." In modern English it would sound thus, "Thou art Mr. Stone, and upon this stone I will build my Church." The word could not possibly refer to Christ in this text.

362. But in the Greek text the word for Peter is Petros, and for stone, petra. They are not the same.

There is no value in pointing out the differences of form in this word according to the Latin or Greek languages, in which they are accommodated to the masculine for Peter as a man, and to the feminine for stone. Our Lord spoke in Aramaic, in which the form is the same in both cases, simply Kepha.

363. You appeal to the Aramaic. I know nothing of that, nor of the Latin, nor of the Greek. I accept the Bible in its English form, in which the two words are Peter and rock, and nothing whatever alike.

How can you appeal to the English form, if the English translation does not adequately express what Christ meant? Surely you want the exact teaching of Christ! The English version is not an infallible rendering, nor does anyone versed in these matters claim that the English language fully expresses the sense of the originals. But apparently you are content to be without the truth, if it is not to be discovered superficially by the reading of your talismanic English version.

364. Have not many authorities held that Christ intended to build His Church not upon Peter, but upon Peter's confession of faith in His divinity?

That is an antiquated interpretation abandoned by all the best scholars, Protestants included. Christ did demand a profession of faith from Peter as a pre-required condition, after that, conferring the fundamental primacy upon him personally. But to say that the profession itself was the rock has not a single valid reason in its favor. Those who adopted such an interpretation did so from their desire to avoid the Catholic doctrine. Grammatically the Catholic interpretation is alone possible. Contextually the whole passage obviously refers to Peter's person. "Blessed art thou . . . I say to thee . . . thou art Peter . . . I will give to thee the keys, etc.," nor could the Church be built upon one article of faith. All the articles of faith are essential Christianity. The Protestant Scripture scholar Hastings says that the confession theory must undoubtedly be excluded. The German Protestant Kuinoel writes, "Those who wrongly interpret this passage as referring to the confession and not to Peter himself would never have taken refuge in this distorted interpretation if the Popes had not wrongly tried to claim for themselves the privilege that was given to Peter." You see, he does not believe that the Pope inherits Peter's privileges, but he does know that Peter was personally the foundation stone. Loisy, the French Rationalist, rejected the historical sense of the Gospels, but he says that it is absurd to accept that sense as do Protestants, and then violate that sense in order to avoid what they do not wish to admit.

365. If you became an Atheist would you still say that, if the New Testament were true, the words cannot mean anything else except the Catholic interpretation?

Yes.

366. Did the early Fathers interpret the text as you do?

They were morally unanimous in that interpretation. Loisy, whose rationalizing tendencies are well known, wrote, "The confession interpretation was proposed by some Fathers in view of the moral application, and has been resurrected by Protestant exegetes in polemical interests. But if one takes the historical sense of the Gospels it is only a subtle distinction doing violence to the text."

367. *Even were the office of head of the Church conferred in Matt. XVI., 18, surely it was withdrawn in Matt. XVI., 23, where Christ said to Peter, "Get thee behind me. Satan!"*

The fact that the office was not withdrawn is clear from the later words of Christ to Peter, "And do thou, being converted, confirm thy brethren." Lk. XXII., 32; and again, from the commission to feed the whole flock given to Peter after Our Lord's resurrection, as recorded in Jn. XXI., 15-18. Prompted by love and reverence for Christ, Peter had protested that Christ ought not to suffer. And Christ would have been the first to appreciate such motives. However harsh the English may seem to be, Christ really replied gently, as if to say, "Peter, you do not yet understand the plan of God. You are letting your human affection sway your judgment. But such thoughts are opposed to my vocation. Get thee behind me, Satan." The word Satan is not used personally here, as of the devil, but in the sense of adversary, Christ intending merely, "I cannot accept the natural promptings of your affection for me." No withdrawal of office is involved.

368. *I don't see how all this affects your claims for the Pope. Where is the connecting link between Christ's promise to Peter and the city of Rome?*

The connecting link is the fact that Peter journeyed to Rome, and died there as Bishop with universal jurisdiction over the whole Church.

369. *I have heard it said that St. Peter never was in Rome.*

You may have heard that stated, but you have never heard any proof advanced in its favor. It is simple history that St. Peter went to Rome about the year 43 A.D., went back to Jerusalem after a few years for a short time, and then returned to Rome until his death, save for very short absences. He died about the year 67, during the reign of Nero. Papias wrote, about 140 A.D., "Peter came and first by his salutary preaching of the Gospel and by his keys opened in the city of Rome the gates of the heavenly kingdom." Lanciani, the eminent archaeologist, wrote, "The presence of St. Peter in Rome is a fact demonstrated beyond a shadow of doubt by purely monumental evidence."

370. *I want proof outside your Catholic tradition. Does Scripture say that St. Peter was ever in Rome?*

Catholic tradition is not a mere matter of rumor and report. It is down in black and white in documents as historical as any other documents, beginning from the year 97 with the declaration of the fact by Clement. It would not matter if Scripture did not give any evidence on this point. However it does. St. Peter ends his first Epistle with the words, "The Church which is in Babylon salutes you, and so doth my son, Mark." All reputable scholars admit that the first Christians called pagan Rome Babylon on account of its vices. St. Peter, therefore, was writing from Rome. St. Paul wrote to the Colossians from Rome, sending the kind wishes of Mark, thus also indicating Mark's presence in Rome.

371. *Of course, as a Catholic, you have to try to prove it.*

The point is, have I succeeded in doing so? Anyway, not only Catholics admit the fact. No single writer ever denied it until the 13th century. Then it was denied by the Waldenses, heretics who had a purpose in view, yet who could produce no evidence that he died anywhere else. No other place has ever disputed this honor with Rome. Wycliffe, Luther, and other Protestants took up the Waldensian assertion, thinking it a good argument against Rome. But enlightened Protestant scholars to-day are ashamed that such an argument, with all the evidence against it, should ever have been used. Cave, a Protestant writer, says, "That Peter was at Rome we fearlessly affirm with the whole multitude of the ancients." Dean Milman admits the fact as incontestable. Dr. Lardner, in his history of the Apostles and Evangelists, says that it is the general uncontradicted and disinterested testimony of ancient writers. The Protestant Whiston, in his Memoirs, remarks, "It is a shame for any Protestant to have to confess that any Protestant ever denied it."

372. Does Scripture say that Peter was ever Bishop of Rome?

Scripture tells us that he was head of the Church, which implicitly demands that he was universal Bishop, and it also tells us, as I have said, that he was in Rome.

373. How can you prove that he was the first Pope?

The word Pope means Father or Head of the Church as an ordinary father is head of a family. St. Peter was certainly in Rome, and died there as Bishop. By legitimate succession the one who succeeded as Bishop of Rome after Peter's death inherited the office of Head of the Church, or if you wish, as Father of the whole Christian family he was Pope. All the Bishops of Rome right through the centuries have belonged to the Catholic Church. No one disputes that. They are known as the Popes, and as St. Peter was first of that long line, Catholics rightly regard him as the first Pope.

374. If St. Peter was Pope, who was his successor?

St. Irenaeus, writing in the second century, gives us the list of the Popes from St. Peter as follows:—Linus, Cletus, Clement, Anacletus, Evaristus, Alexander, Xystus, Telesphorus, Hyginus, Pius, Anicetus, Soter, Eleutherius. Eleutherius was reigning as Pope in the time of Irenaeus.

375. Was Peter told by Christ to establish a Roman Catholic Church?

He was not told to establish the Church. Christ established the Church, choosing Peter as the foundation stone. The Apostles were told to propagate the Church Christ had established, and of course according to the constitution given it by Himself. Wherever Peter went he remained Head of that Church, and as he went to Rome and died there whilst still exercising his office, that office is necessarily attached to the See of Rome. This was not by mere accident. We have to admit the guidance of the Holy Spirit in the choice made by St. Peter in a matter of such moment to the Church.

376. We Protestants can equally claim Peter with Catholics.

Protestants cannot make that claim. Protestantism is essentially a protest against the Catholic Church, and therefore supposes that Church as previously existing. If Peter had not consolidated and built up the Catholic Church there would be no Protestantism to oppose it. In any case, Protestantism was unheard of until over 1500 years after St. Peter's death.

377. Does your Pope perform miracles as did St. Peter?

As we do not claim that he succeeds to the power of working miracles such a criterion is quite irrelevant in this matter.

378. All that you have said seems reasonable in itself, but this monarchical hierarchy seems so dreadfully opposed to the spirit of the Gospel which proposes Christ as the only Mediator.

Christ is the one principal Mediator. But He Himself chooses to dispense His mediation through secondary agents. There is but one king of England, but that does not deny the existence of officials to whom the royal power is delegated. If fifty officials act in the name of the king, that does not make fifty kings. Now Christ delegated His power to Priests and, as the one Mediator, acts through many channels. St. Paul wrote to the Corinthians, "Let a man so account of us as of the ministers of Christ, and the dispensers of the mysteries of God." I. Cor. IV., 1. In the Epistle to the Hebrews we read that the Priest "ought, as for the people, so also for himself, to offer for sins." V., 3. This cannot refer to Christ, who certainly had not to offer for His own sins.

379. Christ said, "Come to Me all ye who are burdened." But Catholics cannot go directly to Him. They must approach through a complex hierarchy.

The Priesthood is a form of secondary mediation appointed by Christ. To ignore His provision for the Church is to ignore Christ. We do not say that Catholics cannot directly approach Christ. They may unite themselves to Him by private prayers whenever they wish. But in many matters they need also the other means appointed by Christ and committed officially to the administration of Priests. Remember, too, that Christ identifies Himself with His Church, and meant what He said when He declared of her, "He who hears you, hears Me." That implies the doctrine, "He who comes to you, comes to Me." In fact, when Saul was persecuting the Church, Christ appeared to him and said, not, "Saul, Saul, why persecutest thou the Church," but, "Saul, Saul, why persecutest thou Me."

380. Catholics call their Priest "Father," yet Christ said "Call no man your father upon earth." Matt. XXIII., 9.

Your rigid interpretation would forbid your calling an earthly parent father. Yet God Himself, in the commandments, terms one of your parents father, and tells you to honor him as such. Your text means simply, "Call no one your father as if you had no other father with rights over you." That is, you must realize that all paternity is of God, and that you owe your being, and all that you have, including your earthly father, to Him. Nor can any claims of an earthly father avail against our duties to God, our heavenly Father. Meantime, Catholics do not call a Priest "Father" in the same sense as that in which they call God their Father. A Priest, by God's Providence and by the authority of Christ, is a father in the spiritual sense, just as a natural parent is a father in an earthly sense. By administering Baptism he gives spiritual life to a soul; he nourishes that life by conferring the Sacraments; he warns, teaches, helps with his advice, corrects, and does all in the spiritual life that an earthly father does in the temporal order. So much so that St. Paul attributes a true paternity to himself, saying, "I admonish you as my dearest children . . . for in Christ Jesus, by the Gospel, I have begotten you." I. Cor. IV., 14.

381. Anyway I want no Pope or Priest.

Will you go to Christ on His conditions, or on your own conditions? Christ decided that Priests were necessary to His religion, gave to His Church the Sacrament of Orders, and authority to His Priests. You profess to believe in Christ, yet regard His appointments as a nonsensical farce.

382. Has not the fact of an organized visible hierarchy led to great troubles in the temporal sphere?

Even had it done so, that would not alter the fact that Christ willed its existence. But what precisely do you intend?

383. I allude to the fact that the Roman Church has ever striven for and possessed temporal power.

Remember that the Church has to exercise the authority of Christ in this world. To do this, she needs to be free to deal with Catholics of every nationality, and therefore to be free from the political interference of any particular nation. Now she can be free either by being independent of all rulers, or by being subject to a king who guarantees absolute liberty of action at least to the Pope. Kings, however, have ever been jealous of their authority, and prone to abuse it. If they grant freedom, they always regard it as being by privilege, and there is ever the danger that, if they happen to be displeased, they would try to interfere in Church administration. Hence God's Providence arranged that certain early kings legally donated territory to the Church, rendering her independent of earthly authority altogether. After hundreds of years these states were illegally taken from the Church, and she certainly protested.

384. Was Pius IX. just when he plotted to keep the Papal States and hinder a united Italy?

Pope Pius IX. was in just possession of the Papal States, and he was just in taking all ordinary precautions to preserve what lawfully belonged to the Church.

385. But you cannot escape the fact that the Catholic Church is a kingdom of this world, although Christ said that His Kingdom was not of this world.

The Catholic Church is not a kingdom of this world. It is the Kingdom of Christ in this world. And the Pope as Pope is not monarch of the Church in any national sense. No national considerations sway his rule over the millions of Catholics of every race and clime. He has temporal authority to-day in Vatican City, but that is merely that he may secure complete immunity from the interference of worldly powers.

386. Christ said, "Render to Caesar the things that are Caesar's and to God the things that are God's."

He did. And the Pope demands independence of any earthly king's authority precisely that Caesar, with his worldly power, may not interfere with the things that belong to God.

387. You say that the Pope is not swayed by national considerations. In a war between Italy and England, would not his sympathies be with Italy?

The Pope as Pope must forget his nationality. As a man his sympathies might be with Italy. But he could not favor Italy in his official capacity. Despite his national sympathies, the Pope has insisted upon being perfectly independent of Italian authority. If an English Pope had done this many would have ascribed it to anti-Italian prejudices. But when an Italian Pope insists upon it, whose national sympathies are all with Italy, there is no explanation except that in his official capacity the Pope refuses to be an Italian. If an unjust war broke out between Italy and England, and Italy was in the wrong, the Pope would condemn the unjust policy of Italy.

388. But in almost every country where she exists, the Catholic Church meddles with politics and causes trouble.

Catholics are human beings with souls devoted to the service of God according to their Catholic Faith, yet with bodies which link them with this world, and render them subject to social relations and duties. These duties are regulated to a great extent by civil law, and Catholics do their share as citizens in the making of those laws. But do not think that all their activities as citizens are necessarily to be attributed to them as Catholics, and to be regarded as due to the influence of the Catholic Church.

389. The Catholic Church controls Italy, Spain, Ireland, and Mexico, etc. I hope it never gains political control here in America!

The majority of the people in the countries you mention happen to be Catholics. But that does not mean that the Catholic Church as a Church has political control. Meantime the Church does not want political control here, and would absolutely refuse on principle to accept it, were it offered.

390. But you cannot deny that the Church exerts political influence, in the face of all the political diplomats at the Vatican.

The Church devotes her energies to the assisting of men in their spiritual needs. But since they are human beings in this world, these spiritual needs are often bound up with earthly cares. For men's bodily needs the Church has inspired the construction of institutions, homes, orphanages, and hospitals, throughout the world. In national and civic matters also she tries to sway the conduct of men by some degree of political influence, since the politicians of this world so often trespass against God's laws. But the Church does not interfere in lawful political matters which are of civic moment only, and which involve no violation of moral principles.

391. Are Catholics told in the confessional how to vote on political questions?

Not necessarily. If an anti-Christian law is proposed the Priest would probably warn his people publicly from the pulpit. In such a case he should do his best to persuade them to be true to God and vote against any law which God would forbid, repeating the words of Christ, "Render to Caesar the things that are Caesar's, and to God the things that are God's." If some individual wished for personal advice in the confessional, he could ask it there. But in ordinary matters Catholics are told neither in the confessional nor from the pulpit how to vote. They are told that they are free.

392. I know of many who have left the Church because Priests have used the pulpit for political ends.

I do not think you know of many. In any case, if some Priest did so offend, that would not justify anyone in giving up his religion. We have a duty to offer public worship to God. The faults of the clergy could not be a reason, they could at best be an excuse for another's neglect of duty. It is a foolish argument to say, "The Priest does not serve God as he should, therefore I shall not serve God as I should." Each must fulfill his duties to God no matter what others do. But, as a matter of fact, I deny that Priests as a body offend in this way.

393. Why does the Catholic Church favor only the Labor Party?

She does not. But the Catholic Church to-day is as it was in the time of the Apostles, "not many noble, not many of the worldly wise, not many powerful." Most of her children are drawn from the class Christ loved so much—the working class. And in civil life the majority of these workers happen to have Labor sympathies. But these men vote as workers, not precisely as Catholics.

394. But the great objection to your Church remains, in that it divides a man's loyalty from his country.

Loyalty to the Catholic Church does not divide a man's loyalty from his country. In religious matters a Catholic obeys his Church; in temporal affairs, the laws of his country. They are services in two different spheres.

395. Did not Christ say, "No man can serve two masters"?

He did. And we Catholics have but one Master—Christ. And we are serving Him even by the fulfillment of our lesser civic duties in so far as we do them for the love of Him. It is the man who gives himself up to worldly affairs in such a way as to separate them from the service of God who is attempting to serve two masters.

396. But does not your allegiance to the Pope conflict with your duty as a British subject? Remember that your Church is controlled by a foreign temporal king.

To British Catholics the Church is not controlled by a foreigner. She is controlled by the Vicar of Christ. It would be just the same if St. Peter were still there to-day, and he was a Palestinian Jew. If a Frenchman or an Englishman were elected, no Italian Catholic would regard the Pope as Pope in the light of any foreign nationality. I cannot be at once subject to two opposed monarchs as national sovereigns, but I can be subject to my earthly ruler in temporals and to the representative of Christ in spirituals. Until the Reformation all Englishmen were subject to the Pope, yet were filled with great love for their country. You would not presume to say that there was not a single loyal Englishman in the time of Henry V. Yet all England was Catholic then, and any Catholic can do to-day what Catholics could do then. The only Catholics in the world who owe temporal allegiance to the Pope are those who actually reside in Vatican City, over which, and over which only, he has the full rights of a temporal ruler. If, through unjust ambition, the Vatican City State were to despatch an immense army to invade Australia, it would be the duty of Australian Catholics to join the Australian army and defend their country. That ought to make it clear that spiritual allegiance to the Pope does not interfere with our citizenship.

397. I still maintain that you cannot be loyal. By law the king is head of the Anglican Church, a law you must ignore.

Catholics are perfectly loyal to the Protestant king. They admit that he is head of the Anglican Church as the law declares. Since by law he is head of that Church, every Catholic says, "Right. Then he is head of the Anglican Church." And loyalty demands no more. It certainly does not demand that I accept the Church of which he is the head. In religious matters my loyalty is concerned with God. In earthly matters I respect the laws of my nation. That law does not say, "And every citizen must belong to the Anglican Church." If it did, it would be an unjust law, at variance with God's laws, and not binding in conscience.

398. Still you are subject to Rome, yet content to remain under the protection of the British flag?

Catholics are subject to the Bishop of Rome on questions of religion. But they are not subject to him in national affairs. This distinction naturally flows from the doctrine that the religion of Christ is not an affair of the British Empire, but for all men. Britishers should be Christians, but Christianity is not necessarily British. We Catholics are not so foolish as to confuse these two things. As Catholics and as citizens we are content to remain under the British flag, and to shed our blood in defending it. Why should we not be? We are not Italians, or Frenchmen, or Germans. And we have as much right to love our country and die for it, if necessary, as any other citizen.

399. Why do you hate everything English?

I do not. I am of purely English descent, and I acknowledge no other loyalty than that to the British Empire. I do not like English faults, but then, love of my own mother does not demand that I call her faults virtues. I am opposed to unjust laws which inflict disabilities on Catholics just because they are Catholics. I do not like the law which deprives the king of freedom of conscience, insisting upon his being a Protestant. But that does not affect my loyalty.

400. *If you are not satisfied with the king, why accept him as your protector? Why not get out? Why continue to accept his hospitality?*

I am quite satisfied with the king, and wish to hear nothing to his discredit. I do not accept his hospitality. A child does not accept the hospitality of his own parents. I was born a British subject. I do my duty. The king does his. I admit that he is head of the Anglican Church, although I deny that he is head of the true Church of Christ. The question of the relative merits of the Anglican Church and the Catholic Church has nothing to do with national status and loyalty.

401. *You could not say the things in other countries that you say in this!*

In other countries I would not have to deny that the temporal ruler was head of the Church. That anomaly seems to be peculiar to the British Empire. Of course it is no fault of our present good king. I think he must feel very uncomfortable about it at times.

402. *Tell us plainly. Do you put Church first and country second?*

If there be a conflict between the two interests, I put Church first. God comes before Caesar. The Church, as the Kingdom of God, is more important than any earthly kingdom. No country has rights against God. And in our own case, if there be a question of soul and body, the soul is the more important, and the body must give way to its interests. It is better to die keeping God's laws than to live breaking them. If a man is faithful to God and to his conscience, there is some hope of his being faithful to lesser duties. But if a man will not be faithful to God, how can a thing so much less than God as one's country expect him to be faithful to it? Think it over.

403. *I see the Catholic viewpoint in this matter, but a far greater difficulty arises for me concerning your Church in so far as she claims within her spiritual sphere to be infallible.*

She makes that claim under certain conditions.

404. *It is a most remarkable claim.*

It is. But then, the Catholic Church is a very remarkable Church. She was not founded by a Martin Luther, or a Henry VIII., or a John Knox, but by Jesus Christ, who guaranteed her as His official representative in this world. Yet although the Catholic Church is a remarkable Church, it is not really remarkable that Christ should have kept His promises to her.

405. *Your Church is composed of human beings like any other.*

Not like any other. The Catholic Church is composed of human beings knit together by the authority of Christ, and rejoicing in His perpetual protection and assistance.

406. *I find the Catholic assumption of infallibility simply appalling!*

I should be appalled if a Church claiming to be established by Christ and to speak with His authority did not claim to be infallible. A fine sort of a guide to eternal destiny God would have given us, if that guide calmly admitted that she was not sure of the road herself.

407. Do you deny the claim to be arrogant, to say the least?

I do. It would be an arrogant claim if she pretended to confer the prerogative upon nerself. But Christ endowed her with this gift, and she humbly admits the fact that it is not of her own ability. A duly accredited judge is not arrogant. But one who orders you to gaol without a vestige of authority for doing so is certainly arrogant.

408. With their infallible Church, Catholics do not need God at all.

They do. In order to live up to their religion, Catholics need God's grace and help individually all along the line. Their infallible Church teaches them with certainty what they must believe and do, but even this infallibility of the Church would be a farce without God. She is infallible because, and only because, God preserves her from error in her official teaching. God, therefore, becomes more necessary than ever.

409. Upon what grounds does your Church claim infallibility?

Christ established His church upon a foundation as solid as a rock, and declared that the gates of hell, or forces of evil, would not prevail against it. This implies the perpetual retention of the truth taught by Christ, forbidding its corruption. He commanded her to teach all nations, "all things whatsoever I have commanded you; and behold I am with you all days even to the consummation of the world." Matt. XXVIII., 20. His presence guarantees that she will ever teach a doctrine identical with His own principles. He promised that the Holy Spirit would abide with the Church forever, undoubtedly a pledge of perpetual infallibility. Jn. XIV., 16. St. Paul clearly manifests this doctrine by his words, "Behave thyself in the house of God, which is the Church of the living God, the pillar and ground of truth." I. Tim. III., 15. The early Fathers insist upon the infallibility of the Church, and reason also tells us that the unity of the Church could not be maintained if she could fail in her teaching of the truth; her very holiness forbids heresy; her catholicity demands expansion without loss of the self-same teaching; whilst her apostolicity requires perpetual duration of an unchanged Apostolic doctrine. Finally, if the Catholic Church be not infallible, then there is no Church on earth which is such as Christ predicted.

410. It is all a matter of viewpoint. In my opinion your viewpoint is utterly wrong, and the foundations of your Church worm-eaten.

Worm-eaten as the foundations of the Catholic Church may seem to you, the fact remains that she keeps adding story after story to her skyscraper heights. The Arians told her that her foundations were worm-eaten in the 4th century; the Greeks in the 9th; the Protestant Reformers in the 16th; the Rationalists in the 18th, and a few still continue to do so, although mere Rationalism is rapidly going out of date. At present the Modernists are the chief people who worry about the worm-eaten foundations of the Catholic Church. The only one who is not worrying about them is the Church herself. She just keeps on her way, never dying, but ever increasing, despite the fact that in every age outsiders have been busy composing her epitaph.

411. We Protestants believe that Christian doctrine was kept pure as long as the Apostles lived, but after their deaths, errors crept in.

You err both in fact and in doctrine. In fact, for the Apostles complained of errors, not of the Church, but of individual professing Christians even in their own days. In doctrine, because you practically assert that Christ failed to preserve His Church; that the Holy Spirit did not remain with her; and that the gates of hell did prevail against her. In other words, your doctrine is that Christ could not do what He said He would do.   No.   Individuals in all ages have fallen into error in so far as they departed from the teachings of the Church. And in falling into error, they have fallen out of the Church, even as the Protestant Reformers themselves.

412. *It was the Catholic Church which early departed from the doctrines of Christ, and thus forfeited the claim to be the true Church.*

If you think that, by departing from the truth, the Catholic Church forfeited the claim to be the true Church, then you believe that the infallible retention of the teachings of Christ must be a mark of the true Church. Is your own Church, therefore, infallible? Does it even claim to be so? I admit that if the Catholic Church has failed in witnessing to the truth she is not true, and I would at once leave her. But as this would mean that Christ was unable to keep His promise, I would also abandon belief in Christ. Certainly, wherever else I might go, I would not return to a Protestant Church based upon the doctrine that Christ has failed to keep His promise.

413. *But you cannot tell me that the Catholic religion is carried out to-day in accordance with the quite simple teachings of Jesus!*

Catholicity does not differ from what you call the simple teachings of Jesus, although they were not so simple as you suppose. However, the Catholic Church teaches all that Christ taught, whether His teaching was explicit or implicit. Essentially she exists just as He would have her exist. There may have been many secondary developments during the ages, but they were all foreseen and approved by Christ. After all, Christ established a living Church, and a living Church grows. He likened it to a seed. Even as a boy grows into a man with exactly the same personality, yet with many secondary changes in size, knowledge, and manners, so too has the Church rightly developed.

414. *The constantly changing laws of the Catholic Church show that her principles are man-made.*

The principles of the Catholic Church are not man-made, nor can her constitution, given her by Christ, ever be changed. But just as many small by-laws can be made and repealed in a country without any essential constitutional change, so in the Catholic Church special disciplinary laws can be enacted at special times to meet special needs without any constitutional change of the religion. At the Reformation, however, men left the Catholic Church and set up new constitutions for themselves, and their sects can be called indeed man-made religions.

415. *The doctrines of the Immaculate Conception and the Infallibility of the Pope were not believed before 1854 and 1870 respectively, yet had to be believed after those dates.*

Both doctrines were believed in so far as Catholics believed in the revelation given by Christ, which contained these doctrines implicitly. When the Church defined them she merely made explicit and of faith what had been hitherto implicit. She gave, not a new truth, but simply made these matters clear by defining these doctrines to be part of the revelation brought us by Christ. The Church is here for that. Indeed, of what use is a teaching Church if she does not teach? All doubts concerning the correct interpretation of the original Christian doctrine on these two subjects were cleared away by these definitions, and to-day the 400 million Catholics in the world know the truth and accept it without hesitation.

416. The Catholic Church is described in I Tim. IV., 1-3. In the latter times some shall depart from the faith—teaching doctrines of devils— speaking lies in hypocrisy—forbidding to marry—commanding to abstain from meats. Where is her infallibility?

I am afraid this is a case of mistaken identity. The Catholic Church is not involved in this description. All through the ages men have departed from the faith in departing from the Catholic Church. Thus in the 16th century the Protestants departed from the original faith, and have been departing from each other ever since, going further and further into conflicting heresies. The Catholic Church does not teach doctrines of devils. No Church warns her children so earnestly against the devil as the Catholic Church. She clearly teaches that lies are never justified. The references to marriage and the eating of meats you simply do not understand. St. Paul warns the early Christians against those who would say that marriage of itself is evil, as also the eating of meat. But the Catholic Church does not forbid marriage. She certainly says to her young men, "You may marry, or if you feel that you are called to such a life, you may become a Priest. But if you become a Priest, you may not marry." That is a very different thing. Meantime, the fact that she forbids meat especially on Fridays shows that she permits it on other days.

417. Did the Church depart from the faith when she condemned Joan of Arc, a condemnation reversed 500 years later?

The Church did not condemn Joan, but was responsible for her canonization. Joan died a good Catholic, receiving Holy Communion the morning of her death. A renegade and recalcitrant French Bishop, in the pay of the English, condemned Joan, and violated the laws of the Catholic Church in doing so. Joan had appealed to the Pope as she had a right to do, but her appeal was illegally disallowed. Within 25 years of her death Pope Calixtus III. declared her mock trial to have been null and void and ordered a new examination of the evidence. Joan, who had been burned to death in violation of Church law in 1431, was re-habilitated in 1456, the Pope's tribunal declaring that she was innocent of all charges. This was the only official judgment of the Church at the time. And her canonization in our days is in full accordance with that judgment.

418. If a civil judge gave an unjust verdict because of a bribe, would you deny that the judiciary was part of the legal system?

I would deny that such a verdict had the true authority of the state behind it. And the state would disown the verdict if the facts were manifested, just as the Church disowned the verdict of the unjust ecclesiastical judges.

419. Was the Church right or wrong in condemning the theory of Galileo?

The Committee or Congregation appointed to consider his teachings declared that his theory was wrong. In doing so, the members of the Committee were mistaken. But as no infallible decision was given on the subject in the name of the Church, infallibility is not involved in this matter. Meantime Galileo had advanced no really satisfactory proofs of his theory, and the prudence of the prohibition forbidding its being taught is more than defensible, in the light of the circumstances of the times. But that is another question.

420. No one would guess from the lives of bad Catholics that their Church was infallible.

The Catholic Church is infallible in her official teaching on faith and morals. But she does not claim to be infallible in making people live up to those teachings. Her infallibility does not deprive her subjects of their freewill. After all, you yourself would admit that God is infallible, yet you would not account for people who violate the commandments by denying God's infallibility. You would account for it by the evil dispositions of the people concerned. And as the infallibility of God does not take away freewill from men, neither does the infallibility of the Catholic Church take it away from her subjects.

421. If your Church is infallible, why does she not impose peace upon earth, and banish poverty and suffering?

Because ability to do these things is not included in the gift of infallibility. The Church is infallible in teaching us what we must believe, and what we are morally obliged to do.

422. It is strange that there is so small a percentage of Catholics in Australia, if your Church alone has the accurate teachings of Christ!

It is far from strange. Australia was colonized chiefly by Protestants. And because 75 per cent. of the population happens to be derived from Protestant forbears you prove, not that the Catholic Church is wrong, but only that the majority in this country happens to be Protestant. Again, this Protestant majority has not become Catholic because the greater number of Protestants go contentedly on, taking things for granted, and not bestowing much thought at all upon the subject of religion. Or, if they start thinking, many stop abruptly when the Catholic Church looms on the horizon, because social, family, business, or personal interests stand in the way of their becoming Catholics. Many, too, labor under an almost invincible prejudice which prevents them from admitting that there can be anything good at all in the Catholic religion, and they would not dream of inquiring into the claims of the Catholic Church. Finally, if you base your position upon relative numbers, then you have but to take a broad and world-wide view to find that there is a larger percentage of Catholics in the world than all Protestants taken together, regardless of the kind of Protestantism they support. It is absurd to restrict your outlook to Australia alone.

423. It is intelligible that the whole Church would be preserved from error; but you go further, and claim that the Pope is personally infallible.

It is the Catholic doctrine that he is infallible when he speaks for the whole church in defining a question of faith or morals.

424. Do you mean that he is the mouthpiece of a General Council, or that he is infallible independently?

The Pope is not merely the mouthpiece of a Council. He may, and usually does, consult other Bishops before giving an infallible decision. But he need not do so, and in the ultimate analysis the infallibility of a definition is due to his own personal authority. The infallibility of the Pope simply means that in his official teachings or definitions, provided he speaks as supreme head of the Church in questions of faith or morals and with the intention of binding all the faithful, God would not allow him to define erroneous doctrine. The Pope, as successor of St. Peter, is Vicar of Christ, and the final court of appeal in the Church. But all the conditions I have enumerated must be present. The Pope's word is not infallible whenever he speaks, though his decisions are always to be received with respect. But if he speaks merely as a private theologian, expressing his own views his opinions could be mistaken. Infallibility attaches to his decisions only when he speaks in his supreme and official capacity as supreme teacher of all the faithful.

425. Was not this doctrine invented in 1870?

No. Papal Infallibility was promulgated as a dogma in 1870, but the doctrine was not invented then. The Vatican Council under Pope Pius IX. merely said definitely, "This is the Christian doctrine contained at least implicitly in the revelation originally given to mankind by Christ." This prerogative of infallibility was conferred upon St. Peter, and upon his successors, in virtue of Christ's choice of St. Peter as the rock-foundation of the Church, His prayer for St. Peter that his faith might not fail, His commission to him to confirm his brethren and to feed the whole flock, lambs and sheep. The Church does not say in her definitions, "I now reveal this doctrine," but, "I definitely declare this to be the doctrine revealed by Christ." If she never taught with such authority, men would say, "What is the good of the Church?" If she does teach with authority they say, "She is inventing new doctrines." After all, the Catholic Church defined the "Filioque" in 1439, and you accept that without complaining that she invented a new doctrine. Why complain when she exercises the same functions in 1870? She will define other doctrines more explicitly in future times as need arises, doctrines we already believe in believing all that has been revealed by Christ, though we do not advert to the fact that these particular doctrines are certainly included. For although the definitions will be new, they will not involve new truths of religion. Now that the personal infallibility of the Pope has been defined we know that it belongs essentially to the original teaching given by Christ.

426. There is only one who is infallible—God. Satan tried to be equal to God, and the Pope who makes a similar claim will meet with a similar fate.

God alone is infallible of His very nature. But God can certainly safeguard a particular man so that he will be also infallible in certain matters on certain occasions. Thus Christ guaranteed that Peter would not fail in his teachings of the Faith. And if an infallible God says that He will make a certain man infallible, then that man will infallibly be infallible. Again the claim of the Pope is nothing like the claim of Satan. Satan claimed to be independent of God; the Pope claims to depend very much upon God. Nor does the Pope make himself equal to God. An infallible Pope is capable of sinning and losing his soul. And should a Pope do so, he would meet with a fate similar to that of Satan because of his unrepented sins. But he would not meet with that fate because of his claim to an infallibility which God insists upon giving him for the good of the Church whether he likes it or not.

427. Do you say that God makes a man infallible who has to be voted for just like politicians?

God says He does. But the Pope is not infallible because voted for. He is elected by votes, and when elected he receives infallibility from God. The Pope does not derive his infallibility from those who elect him.

428. If God makes the Pope infallible, why does he need theologians to go into questions first and arrange what he is to define?

Infallibility is not inspiration. If God inspired the Pope in his official teachings there would be no need of human research. But infallibility means that the Pope acts according to all the laws of ordinary prudence, studying and comparing the doctrines of the Church before coming to a decision. When research has concluded, the Pope may decide simply that the matter does not warrant definition. But if he does decide to define a given doctrine, the Holy Spirit will certainly preserve him from any error in doing so. And the defined dogma will owe its infallibility, not to previous human research or ability, but precisely to the assisting influence of the Holy Spirit.

429. *The early Church did not admit that the Pope was infallible, nor did any Pope before Pius IX. claim such a privilege.*

The doctrine is contained in Christ's words to St. Peter, and the early Church was well aware of the fact. Tertullian, about the year 200 A.D. wrote concerning St. Paul's rebuke to St. Peter, "If Peter was rebuked by Paul, it was certainly for a fault in conduct, not in teaching." St. Cyprian, about 256, wrote of the See of Rome, "Would heretics dare to come to the very seat of Peter whence Apostolic faith is derived and whither no errors can come." St. Augustine in the 4th century gives us the famous expression, "Rome has spoken; the cause is finished." The early Popes had little need to insist often upon a doctrine which was denied by none of the faithful. The Council of Ephesus in 431 thus expressed its firm convictions, "No one doubts, nay it is known to all ages, that Peter, the chief and head of the Apostles, the pillar of the faith and foundation of the Catholic Church, received the keys of the kingdom from Our Lord Jesus Christ . . . . Peter, who even to these our own days, and always in his successors, lives and exercises his authority." In 451 Pope Leo wrote his decision to the Bishops of the Church assembled at Chalcedon, and when the letter was read all cried out, "Peter has spoken through Leo."

430. *A later infallible Pope condemned Pope Honorius for having taught heresy.*

Firstly, Honorius did not give an infallible decision concerning the matter in question. Secondly, his personal opinion was not heretical. Within a few years of the death of Honorius, Pope John IV. wrote, "Some men have distorted the meaning of Honorius to their own purposes and contrary to the truth." Thirdly, no later Pope condemned Honorius as a heretic, but for imprudence and neglecting to settle the controversy of the time and thus prevent the growth of further heresy. He was blamed rather for not using his infallibility than for misusing it.

431. *If the Popes are infallible, the laws of earlier Popes must be those of later Popes—yet the laws of the Catholic Church have varied.*

It is not necessary that all the laws of earlier Popes must be those of later Popes. Infallibility concerns doctrine, and morals, not necessarily discipline. Disciplinary laws adapted to particular times change with the times.

432. *Did not bad Popes do acts which their successors thought wrong?*

Yes. The conduct of some Popes in their personal lives it is impossible to justify. They ought to have been thoroughly ashamed of themselves.

433. *Then where was the protection of Christ?*

With His Church, preserving her as a Church, in spite of the personal iniquity of these men. I have never claimed that the Pope can do no wrong. As a man he will have temptations like other men, and he will be free to resist those temptations, or consent to them. After all, he must save his soul like anyone else. He is not going to be preserved from sin in spite of himself. Why should he be compelled to be good? Goodness results in Heaven, and Heaven must be earned. Every man, infallible or not, must have his own struggle to be good and to save his soul. The Pope is not, and has never claimed to be impeccable. But for our sake, not for his own, God endows him with infallibility that he may tell us with certainty what we must believe and do in order to save ourselves; whether he lives up to it himself is quite another matter and his own business. It is quite possible to give splendid advice and not live up to it oneself.

434. What an elastic system! The Pope can be evil, and your doctrine from a sink of iniquity will be good!

The Pope cannot be evil in the sense that he is free to be wicked. He is not morally free to do as he pleases. But if some rare and individual Pope did happen unfortunately to be wicked, then we say that God would infallibly preserve him from error in such *ex cathedra* definitions as he might be called upon to make for the good of the whole Church. After all, under God's providence, the false prophet Balaam and Caiphas the Jewish Priest, both men of evil dispositions, predicted and taught the truth in spite of themselves.

435. Have you to believe the Pope whether what he says is true or not?

If a thing be not true, it is not to be accepted as true, no matter who says it. But when the Pope defines infallibly, he cannot say what is not true, and Catholics accept his official teaching precisely because it is infallibly true. If, prior to a definition, a Catholic was of a diverse opinion, then once the Pope has given the definition, such a Catholic becomes aware that his conjecture was erroneous, and abandons it in order to have the truth.

436. If you are not obliged to believe all that the Pope says, how say that he is infallible?

Because he is not infallible in everything. He is infallible only when he speaks in virtue of his supreme office as head of the Church on matters of faith and morals. He notifies us when he intends to define in accordance with all the conditions required for infallibility. This restriction to set occasions is as reasonable as the restriction of the jurisdiction of a civil judge to his official decisions in court.

437. Why does not the Pope define the facts about evolution?

That is a question of science, not of faith or morals. The Pope is not infallible on every possible question, nor has the Church ever maintained him to be so. If you have difficulties because the Pope is not infallible when he is not supposed to be infallible you have only yourself to blame.

438. Many things show the utter futility of your infallible Pope's blessings. Sixtus V. blessed the Armada, yet it was destroyed as much by the wrath of Heaven as by the English leaders.

You mean by a storm. There is a great difference between the wrath of Heaven and the wrath of the heavens. On your principles every man who has ever suffered shipwreck or been drowned or struck by lightning is a wicked wretch and the victim of God's anger. I am as happy as you are that the Armada failed, but I do not admit that God gave no graces to the poor men on that ill-fated fleet in virtue of the Pope's blessing. Nor will I admit that God's curse was on the fleet as a whole any more than that God's curse rested on Englishmen when they lost the American war of Independence. We are too ready to distribute God's curses and blessings according to our own prejudices, regarding ourselves as the fitting object of the blessings only. In any case, blessings bestowed upon various enterprises by the Pope have no connection whatever with the prerogative of infallibility.

439. The Archbishop of Peru was blessed by the Pope, and died of poison forty-three days later.

You do not say which Archbishop; but even so, infallibility does not come into the question. Meantime, the blessing of the Pope, or even if you wish, of God, is not intended to ward off every possible temporal evil, including death. God blessed Job, yet it did not preserve him from temporal trials. If the Pope blessed me, and a few days afterwards you put arsenic in my tea, I fully expect that I should die. Nor would death within 43 days prove the futility of the Pope's blessing any more than death within 43 years. The Pope did not bless the Archbishop, if your facts be true, in order that poison would have no effect upon him. There are much more important things than that. But all such difficulties as these are beside the point where infallibility is concerned. First find out exactly what the Catholic Church teaches concerning infallibility, noting the limits within which her claims are confined, and then restrict your examination of the question to those limits.

440. You said that the unity of the Church could not be maintained unless the Church were infallible. But are not the different faiths to-day accounted for by the fact that the Apostles went different ways and preached according to their different views?

The Apostles held and taught the same doctrines. St. Paul denied the right of anyone to preach different faiths. Gal. I., 8-9. In any case, the differing Protestant sects cannot go back beyond the 16th century, and certainly have derived neither their being nor their specifically Protestant doctrines from any of the Apostles.

441. But where was unity even within the Catholic Church during the fourteenth century, when there were three Popes at once, each with his own section of adherents?

There has never been more than one true Pope. At times there have been rival claimants to the Papacy, but if several pretenders put forward to-day their claims to be King of England, their claims would not invalidate the right of the present king. Anti-Popes are not really Popes. But take the 14th century. In 1378 Urban VI. was lawfully elected Pope at Rome. Some French Cardinals, wrongly thinking or maintaining that he had not been rightly elected, elected another who called himself Clement VII. Good men on both sides believed in each Pope's right, but no one admitted that both could be Popes at once. All held that one only of the two could really be Pope. To settle the difficulty, another group of Cardinals later on went beyond their rights, declared the rival Popes deposed, and elected a second anti-Pope, Alexander V. This gave rise to three lines of claimants and thus complicated the position. A general Council was called. The legitimate successor in the Urban line, Gregory XII., resigned. The successors of the anti-Popes were declared to be unduly elected, and the difficulty was overcome by the election of Pope Martin V. in 1417. The true succession was never lost; nor was essential unity. All the time there was but one true Pope, and the mistake on the part of the faithful as to which was the true Pope was not an error in faith. The Church, under God's guidance, weathered this difficulty of internal dissension, once more showing the divine protection which the Catholic Church has ever enjoyed in virtue of Christ's promise to be with her all days till the end of the world.

442. You mention not only the unity but also the holiness of the Catholic Church. Here at least your position becomes impossible. Indeed, how much of the spirit of Christ is found in any Church to-day?

It is to be found whole and entire only in the Catholic Church, as a Church, for the Catholic Church is holy in her Founder, in her teachings, worship and discipline, and can alone inspire a completely Christian spirit in men of goodwill. This, however, does not imply that every member of the Catholic Church is holy. Many, to their own shame, do not live up to their faith.

443. All religions teach holiness, Protestantism and even Mahometanism are as moral and tolerant as the Catholic Church.

Protestantism was not holy in its original founders, cannot preserve Christian teaching intact, and dare not insist upon truly Christian moral principles. Even its leaders excuse and approve laxity in practice, tolerating divorce and re-marriage, birth-control, contempt of Scripture, indifference in religion, and rationalism and humanitarianism in place of faith and charity. And you term this renunciation of Christ's principles tolerance! Tolerance may spare evil individuals, but it never says that evil conduct is justified. As for Mahometanism, you know as little about that as you do about the Catholic Church. The Koran allows divorce, polygamy, the right of husbands to thrash their wives, the right to murder unbelievers, the sanction of impurity provided a man washes his hands in clean sand, and much other evil doctrine absolutely condemned by the Catholic Church, and indeed by every right conscience.

444. The holiness of the Catholic Church is no argument. Satan pretends to be an Angel of Light.

Satan is said to be an angel of light in so far as he makes evil appear to be good, not that he ever inspires real good. He never inspires people to hate sin and to love God as does the Catholic Church.

445. How would he win people if he did not mix a few good works with his errors?

He mixes no good works with his errors. He permits some good to continue side by side with the evil he inspires. And that is the secret of the continued existence of Protestantism. It speaks much of belief in Christ, of broadminded tolerance, of being good to one's fellow men, of owing no man anything. But it shuts its eyes to Satan's propaganda of divorce, birth-control, the flood of doubtful literature poured out by the Press, the banishing of religion from schools, and a hundred other dangers of the day. People can be good Protestants yet carry on with practices for which they would never get absolution from any Catholic Priest unless they promised to abstain from them. At times Protestantism does raise its voice in protest, but nearly always against the wrong things, avoiding current evils which it finds it too unpopular to face.

446. The Catholic Church is Satan's Organization.

Then she is a very poor agent indeed. She would be far more efficient if she cried out, "Sin does not matter—go ahead. Confession is nonsense. Eat anything you like on Fridays, the day on which Christ died. Marriage does not bind, divorce yourselves whenever you like. Continence is absurd. Artificial birth-control is progress. Don't believe in Christ, or God, or Heaven, or Hell. Away with religion in the schools. The chief thing is to be comfortable. Eat, drink, and be merry, for to-morrow you die. Then get cremated, and that ends everything." Don't you see how ridiculous your statement is? All these things are the exact opposite of Catholic teaching.

447. But does not St. John, in Revelations, call Rome the Babylon of sin?

No. He describes a city of abominations which he terms Babylon. The early Christians, therefore, regarded pagan Rome, with its idolatry and sensuality, as a very Babylon. Thus St. Peter, writing from Rome, called it by that name. But once the city had given up its paganism for Christianity it ceased to be called by that name which had been given it precisely because of its paganism. Some few people since the 16th century, blinded by anti-Catholic prejudice, have termed modern Rome Babylon because it happens to be the headquarters of the Catholic Church. But no sensible people support such a view. The fight of the Catholic Church for the rights of Christ, and her urgent recommendations of true holiness to her spiritual subjects, are too obviously opposed to the conduct of the Babylon described by St. John.

448. But history shows that the Roman Church has been a hot-bed of vice, murder, trickery, violence and oppression.

History shows no such facts. It does show that there have been wicked men in the Church, and Christ predicted that there would be bad fish in the net. But these evil men were wicked in spite of the teachings of their Church, not because of them. Meantime in every age there have been Saints, good precisely because they lived up to Catholic teaching. It is proof that the Church as a Church is good, if men have to violate her teachings in order to be wicked. And it is proof of her divinity that she has survived not only attacks from external enemies, but the still worse evil of corrupt members within.

449. Have not Priests left the Church, admitting that they have been telling lies for years?

Occasionally Priests have left the Church. Some have unfortunately lost the gift of faith altogether, but such men often speak with great respect for the Catholic Church. The majority, however, have gone rather because they have been unwilling to live up to the lofty standards of morality demanded of them. They have obviously adopted, not higher, but lower standards of living. In their attempts to justify themselves, these men have often pandered to Protestant prejudice by reviling the Church they once served. Their case would sound better if they contented themselves with the mere admission that they had been hitherto mistaken. But if they confess that they have been habitual liars over a period of many years, you can hardly take their word for anything. A witness who admits that lying has long been almost second nature to him for years is not much of a witness.

450. Have not political intrigues sapped the Catholic Church of all spirituality and holiness?

No. Some Catholic individuals have lost their own spirituality through political ambition, but this does not affect the Church. Christ promised that His Church would never go wrong, not that individuals in the Church would never go wrong. You cannot argue from bad fish in a net to the rottenness of the net. A very good net can hold some bad fish.

451. Do not Catholics adore the Pope?

If the Pope were to ask me to adore him, I would tell him to go to confession and ask forgiveness of so great a sin before attempting to celebrate Mass. For he would commit mortal sin did he accept adoration even as it would be mortal sin to offer it to him.

452. Yet Leo XIII. said, "We hold upon earth the place of God Almighty."

At least he did not say that he *was* God Almighty! He simply meant that, through no merits of his own, he had been promoted to a position which has annexed to it the promise of Christ, "Whatsoever you bind upon earth is bound also in Heaven." Pope Leo was speaking of his commission, not of himself. Gladstone said to Queen Victoria, not with pride but with simple truth, "Madam, I am the people of England."

453. Holiness demands humility, and that forbids such arrogance as the Pope's claim to be the Vice-regent of God.

The Pope's claim is not arrogant, even as Gladstone's claim was not arrogant. The Pope merely claims to be the occupant of a constitutional office established and endowed with certain privileges by Christ.

454. That same Christ said, "Whosoever shall be the greatest, let him be the servant of all."

That is verified in the Pope, whose official title is Servant of the servants of God. Being first, he is the servant of all Catholics. He ministers to our spiritual needs and gives his life to the work, renouncing a self-chosen career. But the words you quote do not dispense us from honoring the Pope as Vicar of Christ.

455. There is not much holiness in having an evil woman as Pope. How could she be the Vicar of Christ?

Some misguided writers have spoken of a female Pope named Joan, who was supposed to have reigned from 855 to 857 A.D. But never was a greater hoax put over a credulous public. Voltaire laughed at the gullibility of fools who believed this tale. The Encyclopaedia Brittanica says that she is a pure myth. Chambers Encyclopaedia calls her "a fabulous personage." Gibbons, in his Decline and Fall exploded the legend half a century ago, saying, "A most palpable forgery is the passage about Pope Joan, which has been foisted into some manuscripts." Her advocates bear testimony against themselves, producing echoes of the 14th, 15th, and 16th centuries—at least five centuries after her supposed death. She has been annihilated by two learned Protestants, Blondel and Bayle, but others still attempt to save this poor engine of controversy.

456. Do all Popes and Priests go to Heaven?

Not unless they live good lives, or at least die repentant of their sins. They must save their own souls just as others, and can lose their souls if they wish.

457. Was not Alexander VI. one of the most evil men the world has ever seen?

Not quite, although he certainly was a disgrace to his office. But it is just because his office demanded such holiness that his life was so utterly incongruous. Yet if you reject the Papal System because of Alexander, you must logically reject the College of the Apostles because of Judas. And remember that the life led by Alexander disgusts Catholics far more than it disgusts Protestants, for Catholics know what is really to be expected of a Pope in accordance with Catholic spiritual principles. Had Alexander lived up to Catholic teaching in its fullness he would have been a saint, even as many of the Popes were saints. But then, of course, he would never have been mentioned by Protestants.

458. Many Popes died violent deaths.

Not so many—a few, very few. But the assassination of the king would prove neither that he was never lawful head of the nation, nor that he was an evil man.

459. A large proportion of the Popes were men of whom any Church should be ashamed.

Not a large proportion. History records six or seven as having been really unworthy of their office. Out of 260 Popes, the proportion is about 1 in 40. One in 12 is the proportion of evil men among the Apostles chosen by Christ Himself. But this does not affect the question under discussion. It proves nothing more than that certain individuals failed to live up to the obligations of their state in life, and that some bad men were rulers of the Church. And they could be quite good rulers from many points of view, even though personally lax.

460. You call the Pope the servant of the people, yet he does not minister to them. He lives a life of seclusion, shut away from the world.

There are various ways of ministering to the needs of souls. The Pope administers, with the help of many officials, a Church of some 400 millions. Jesus predicted that the small seed would develop into a vast tree, and the looking after the vast tree is a very different matter from the initial care required. Any of the 400 millions may visit the Pope, but it is unreasonble to expect the Pope to visit the 400 millions, except of course by letter as he does whenever he issues his encyclicals.

461. Let us turn to the priesthood of the Catholic Church. Is not all priestcraft the product of man's fear?

Priestcraft is the product of man's imagination, superstition, and perhaps fear. But priestcraft has nothing to do with the Catholic Church. The Catholic priesthood, a very different thing, is of divine institution, as can be proved to the hilt.

462. Then why are Catholics so afraid of their Priests?

Why do you think they are? If I were to ask you suddenly, "Why are all people of English descent born cross-eyed?" you would be rather astonished for a moment, to say the least. When I was a small Protestant boy I used to fear the very sight of a Catholic Priest, and I used to think that Catholic children must be equally terrified. I am a Catholic Priest to-day, and I have never seen the faintest sign of fear on any Catholic face when I have appeared on the scene.

463. I have never heard any Protestant clergyman speak as severely to his people as do Catholic Priests.

That is because Catholic Priests alone are conscious of the authority to guide their people. But they do not speak severely. They speak earnestly, because they do not wish to see their people running the risk of eternal loss. They speak at times with just indignation, because they are charged with the protection of God's interests. No Catholic Priest has even spoken more strongly than the prophets Isaiah and Jeremiah.

464. Priests have rendered dying people unhappy with their insistent demands that they should receive the last Sacraments.

Those Priests would have been more comfortable at home reading some pleasant book. Why should they put themselves out like that? Look at things from a Catholic standpoint. A Priest is obliged to do all he can that not one soul be lost through his indifference. If he knows that a Catholic is dying, he must do all he can to bring that soul to a good frame of mind before actual death. And the more such a soul does not want to rectify things, the more that soul needs the help of a Priest. Uneasiness for a few moments before death is nothing to uneasiness for all eternity. And if, after a few moments of uneasiness, a man dies repentant and with the last rites of the Church, he will bless for all eternity the Priest who had the unselfish zeal to labor for his conversion.

465. Priests themselves are not holy. I knew a very bad Priest.

Would you condemn a whole family as criminal because one child went wrong? An unworthy Priest does not inspire you with half the indignation he inspires in Catholic hearts. But try to grasp this principle. I have never undertaken to defend the conduct of every individual Priest. Nor, for a moment, would I wish to defend the evil conduct of anybody. But I say that the Catholic Church is the true Church, even though not all her individual members are true to her ideals. No valid argument can be based upon the conduct of individuals. I might argue against the

Wesleyan Church from history, logic, or Scripture. But I would not condemn it because of the bad conduct of some Wesleyan minister.

466. Is the Church a mythical something apart from its individual components?

No. The Catholic Church is the body of all the faithful. But not each member of the faithful constitutes the whole Church. And the vast majority in every age has been sufficiently good morally, even though saints have necessarily been the minority.

467. My difficulty with the Catholic Church, as far as holiness is concerned, arises from her avarice. The wealth of the Church is a scandal, when one thinks of the poverty of Christ.

It may be that your notions of Christ's attitude towards wealth need rectifying, before we can proceed with this question.

468. Both in practice and in teaching Christ condemned wealth.

He did not.

469. In practice did He not live poorly, aiming at having no means of support?

He lived poorly Himself, but He never commanded others to follow His own example in this matter. Meantime He did not aim at having no means of support. St. Luke, VIII., 3, speaks of many who ministered to His needs and those of His Apostles out of their possessions. He accepted their offerings, and we know that Judas carried the common purse, which held enough to allow of almsgiving to the poor. Jn. XIV., 29.

470. He visited only the poorest homes.

That is not so. He was dining in the house of a wealthy man when the woman who was a sinner came in and washed His feet with her tears.

471. He had no magnificent edifice to preach in, but always spoke in the open air.

He did at times teach in the open air. But Scripture tells us that He often spoke in the Temple at Jerusalem, calling it His Father's House. And He had an immense respect for that edifice as dedicated to His Father.

472. He drove the money-changers from the Temple.

That proves my assertion of His respect for that religious edifice. But it does not prove that Christ condemned money. Christ condemned the abuses of these traffickers in the Temple. They were desecrating that holy place by usury, and also as we know from various sources by selling dried peas, raisins, grapes, and apples, which should have been sold in the market place.

473. Was not Christ poor, and did He not forbid the hoarding up of treasure on earth?

Christ Himself set the supreme example of poverty, although, as I have said, Judas carried the purse containing money for His use, and for the needs of His Apostles. But Christ never commanded that His followers should adopt actual and absolute poverty. God had sanctioned the right of private property when He gave the commandment, "Thou shalt not steal." The right to private property is therefore just and not sinful. Christ did forbid men to make earthly goods their only treasure to the exclusion of their spiritual welfare. In fact, He warned those who have mammon or wealth, not necessarily to give it up, but to make it their friend by giving alms to the poor.

474. He commanded the rich young man to sell all, and give it to the poor.

This was not a command, obliging in conscience. It was a special invitation which the young man was free to accept or reject. If the possession of goods as such were evil, Christ would have been recommending the young man to cause evil in the very ones who bought or accepted possession of his goods. But you have misunderstood the passage. The rich young man said to Christ, "What must I do to be saved?" Christ replied, "Keep the commandments." Thus He specified what was necessary for salvation. But hearing that the young man had kept them, He went further: "If you desire not only to be saved, but to be perfect, then do more than is of obligation. Sell all, and follow Me." The young man turned away sad, for he had not the generosity of character required. But the Gospel does not suggest that he was lost. No man is lost who loves God enough to keep all the commandments. Meantime, in the Catholic Church, thousands of Priests, Brothers, and Nuns have renounced all worldly possessions and have vowed poverty for the love of Christ, giving up the right to possess or administer anything in their own name. Thus the invitation of Christ is fulfilled in the Religious Orders of the Catholic Church.

475. Christ said that a rich man could not enter Heaven.

He did not. He said that the rich would encounter special difficulties in the matter of salvation. But this is not because they are rich. It is because rich people are in danger of being so attached to their earthly goods as to forget God. The same Christ said, "Blessed are the poor in spirit." A rich man can be poor in spirit by being at least sufficiently detached from his worldly goods that he would not for all of them offend God.

476. Whatever may be said of rich individuals, the extreme wealth of your Church is a scandal, with millions crying out for bodily and spiritual help.

A family is not wealthy if it has scarcely enough to meet all its essential needs, and the Catholic Church certainly has not enough for its necessary work. Meantime she spends millions on her many works for men's temporal welfare, and is very hard put to it to provide her thousands of missionaries, who are laboring for the spiritual welfare of pagans, with the bare necessities of life. If ever a Church has tried to feed her sheep spiritually it is the Catholic Church.

477. But look at the Vatican, and all the other property in land and buildings!

For the administration of a huge society like the Catholic Church, consisting of over 400 million members, offices and temporalities are necessary. But these properties are not the possession of any individual Catholic, not even of the Pope. Even the Pope can will none of it away when he dies, as if it were his own private property.

478. Is it in accordance with the spirit of Christ to spend a million dollars on a Cathedral?

Quite. Christ is God. Yet God ordered the Jews to build at Jerusalem a magnificent Temple. During His life on earth, the Son of God commended the poor widow for her contribution to the needs of the Temple. When Judas blamed the woman for wasting precious ointment in Christ's honor instead of giving it to the poor, Christ rebuked him.

479. Can you blame governments for confiscating the property of the Church and giving it back to the people?

Yes. The government has no claim whatever to private property, unless in extreme necessity it has to confiscate or appropriate from all citizens alike. Our Catholic people voluntarily erect permanent buildings for the needs of their religion. Others have just as much money, in fact more than Catholics. If the government confiscates the useful results of Catholic generosity with surplus earnings, then it has the right to confiscate the surplus money of everyone else, above all when it is not put to good use. As for giving it back to the people, there is no Church on earth which can compare with the Catholic Church for the number of charitable institutions. She has more hospitals for the sick, orphanages for destitute children, homes for the aged and dying, for the deaf and dumb, than all other churches put together.

480. The workers of the world do not admit that large edifices and tracts of land are necessary to do the Lord's work.

The opinion of the one doing the work is of more value than that of the on-looker. The Church knows that these temporal things are necessary. Anyway these properties have been honestly and laboriously acquired by charitably minded citizens, are held in their name, and are not actually theirs only, because they have freely resigned the ownership of them to God. They certainly do not belong to the clergy. And it is quite unjust for other citizens to talk of confiscating them. Remember also that, besides beautifying the cities of the world, the greater part of the expense of these churchs, cathedrals, and institutions, has gone in wages to the workers.

481. The rich belong to your Church because it is convenient.

The poor who belong to the Catholic Church far exceed in numbers the rich. As for convenience, the Catholic Church is the most inconvenient of all to live up to, although I admit that it is convenient to die in, since it fits one so well for one's meeting with God.

482. Each convert you make means more revenue, but where is the advantage to the convert?

If the new convert did contribute to the support of his religion that would already be an advantage to him, if Christ rightly commended the poor widow who gave her mite to the Temple. But even if a convert could give nothing he would be none the less welcome. The Catholic Church never wants anyone for what he will bring to her, but for what she can give to him—absolution for his sins, Christ as his Saviour and Guest of his heart in Holy Communion, relief after his death, and heaven in the end. It is all very much to the advantage of the convert.

483. There are thousands living on the gullibility of the poor.

There are thousands giving their lives to the service of God and of their fellow men, their fellow men making a return, not by giving their lives, but by giving a small percentage of their temporal goods. One's life is more precious, and a greater gift, than a portion of that life's earnings.

484. Everybody is after riches, including religious teachers.

That is not true. The thousands of Priests, Brothers, and Nuns who have vowed poverty in the Religious Orders of the Catholic Church never receive a penny personally in wages, they renounce the possession and administration of property, and are given merely such shelter, food, and clothing as are absolutely necessary.

Those Priests who do not undertake this obligation of poverty are entitled to such revenue as the people provide in return for a life-work on their behalf.

485. Jesus had nowhere to lay his head, yet the Pope lives in a great palace, owns immense wealth, enjoying luxury and ease.

The Pope lives in the Vatican without for a moment pretending to own it, for it is simply the headquarters of the largest single institution on earth, containing the central offices of administration of that Church which Christ said would grow from a mustard seed into a great tree. Such buildings as the Vatican are built to last for generations, and in them the Pope must live a simple and Christ-like life. It is absurd to say that the Pope owns fabulous wealth. You might as well accredit all the assets of the Bank of England to the manager of that bank. Nor does the Pope live on the fat of the land, enjoying luxury and ease. He keeps a frugal table, has few amusements, gives from twelve to sixteen hours a day to work, hard worrying work with a great responsibility, and scarcely knows the meaning of the word ease. The Pope must be able to meet kings on their own level, and the faithful insist upon providing him with quarters befitting his position and dignity. But these externals give no indication concerning the spiritual life of the Pope personally.

486. Palaces are not necessary to enable Popes to meet kings on their own level. All men are equal.

All men are equal in so far as each is a human soul before God, and must meet the same judge. And God will not be more lenient with the Pope than He will be with the simple layman. But all men are not equal in other ways. Christ certainly gave the Apostles a higher office than simple Christians possess, and they and their successors were to rule the faithful. Preference on this earth follows one's office, but the office does not necessarily make a man any better as a Christian. He may or may not be better, and he will answer for his life just as anyone else.

487. The Bishops of the Catholic Church have never produced an atom, yet go globe-trotting whilst other people starve.

Not all production is measured by bodily comforts. There is an intellectual world and a spiritual world. If you know nothing of these, at least suspend your judgment, and do not interpret all things in terms of food and clothing. Not by bread alone does man live. Meantime you will let Catholics estimate the usefulness of their Bishops to them, and not judge by your own personal lack of benefits which you will not let them confer upon you. The Bishops of the Catholic Church have to visit Rome at stated intervals, for the administration of the Church must be carried on. The poor we shall always have with us, whether the Bishops visit Rome or not. And no Church expends so much upon the poor as the Catholic Church, with her charitable institutions in every diocese, and benevolent societies in every parish.

488. Ought not Priests to follow as closely as possible the teachings of Jesus Christ?

We must note carefully the force of the teachings given. Christ taught some things as being absolutely necessary; others He recommended, without obliging His followers to adopt them. Every Priest is obliged to avoid all deliberate sin, and to fulfill all that Christ declared to be necessary. The Church also obliges every Priest to renounce marriage in order that he may give undivided attention to the service of Christ and the salvation of souls. But whilst it is good if he does so, there is no obligation that every Priest adopt absolute poverty, as do those who enter Religious Orders. If a Priest avoids the sin of avarice and does good with such possessions as he lawfully obtains, he is fulfilling the necessary teachings of Christ.

489. Priests adopt their profession for the fat income and consequent luxury.

Had they devoted the same number of years to the study of law or medicine they would be immeasurably better off, have more time to themselves, and would not have had to renounce wife, home, and children, and much else that men so love.

Christ promised that if they labored for the spiritual well-being of souls, giving their very lives to the work, the faithful would give a portion of their earnings towards their support. Lk. X., 7. I. Cor. IX., 13. St. Jerome wrote in the 4th century, "Priests have a right to be supported and there will always be those ready to support them, not as beggars, but as those more worthy than themselves, whom it is their honor and glory to support." The Priest keeps himself in a state in keeping with his position according to the general standard of living prevailing in the society around him. And if you despise him for that, there are hundreds who would despise him were he shabby and unkempt. This too would be the shame of Catholics, and no Priest has the right to cast a reflection upon the generosity of parishioners. Whatever is over from necessary expenses, the Priest usually devotes to the good of the Church or the relieving of the poor. And the poor know that the Priest is the most ready of all men to give to them. In any case the fat income and luxury are as a rule mere chimeras. The vast majority of Priests are saintly men, as poor and detached in spirit as many who have entered Religious Orders, actually taking the vow of poverty. I am not a secular Priest trying to justify myself. I am a member of a Religious Order who would like to be as holy as many a secular Priest I know.

490. Why do Priests have motor cars, when Christ always walked?

Christ did not always walk. Motor cars were not in existence then, and Christ used the ordinary means of locomotion at the time. Instead of walking round the lake, He went across it by boat. Motor cars are efficient means of transport, and if a car gets a Priest to a dying man in time to help him prepare to meet God, instead of his arriving too late by walking, it is a good thing. In America, country Priests have to travel up to two hundred miles in order to say Mass in some parts of their parishes. Meantime, despite his car, such a Priest can be as detached in spirit from worldly goods as anybody else.

491. What is the difference between what you call a Secular Priest and a Religious Priest?

In the Catholic Church there are two vocations open to a man who feels called by God to His service. Either he will feel called to be simply a Priest, or else, in addition, to enter a Religious Order. If called to be a Priest, he enters college and is prepared for parish work, in which he must provide for his own necessities. This involves the necessity of income from which he can save enough to provide for possible years of sickness, or later years of retirement. If called to a Religious Order, he takes a vow of poverty, renouncing all personal income, the Order providing his necessary food and clothing. Both types give their lives to God, but in different ways, according to their different vocations. The former are called Secular Priests, because they must live alone in the world; the latter are called Religious Priests, because they live in Religious Communities. Secular Priests are not worldly Priests, Order men only being religious Priests. A Secular Priest could be a far more religious man than an Order Priest, and many an Order Priest is greatly edified by the Secular Priests he meets. It is simply a question of different types of vocation.

492. I have known Secular Priests to leave large sums of money.

Priests who do not join Religious Orders may own and administer their own property. They have vows of chastity, and obedience to their Bishops, but they do not take the vow of poverty. If such a Priest inherits wealth from his family, he may reserve it to provide for himself in case of illness, old age, or incapacity. Such large legacies are very rare indeed, and not the result of one's priestly work. Nor does the leaving of large sums of money prove that such Priests have set their hearts upon money to the exclusion of God and works of charity.

493. Should they not have assisted the needy whilst they were alive?

How do you know that they did not? One Priest I know who left a large sum of money deliberately refused to give his capital to the poor and be finished with it, but left it safely invested, regularly distributing the income from it to the poor over a period of many years. The poor got far more that way than otherwise. When he died, he left the whole of the capital to charity, to the scandal of unintelligent critics. But even supposing that a Priest who had wealth did not use it in the relieving of the necessities of the poor, his omission of this good work should not blind us to his other good works. All the more credit to him that, possessing such means, he did not devote himself to a life of idle pleasure, but to the service of God, and of his fellow men in their spiritual needs.

494. Why should Priests have more latitude than Nuns?

The duties of a Priest are very different from those of Nuns. Priests have parochial obligations, necessitating the visitation of the people, sick calls, the organizing of parochial functions, etc. Also the Nun belongs to a Religious Order, her vocation involving necessarily a retired life and Community observance. A Secular Priest is not obliged to the rules of Community life.

495. There is no evidence of the holiness of your Church in the lives of the Catholic people. Catholics do not practice what they preach.

You may know of some individual Catholics who do not. Unfortunately, so do I. But would you say that all Englishmen are dishonest because you know of some individual dishonest Englishmen? Be sure that a Catholic can be evil only by breaking the laws of his Church, and you cannot blame the Church for the conduct of members who can be evil only by refusing to live up to her teachings. If a man lives right up to Catholic teaching and then is evil, blame the Church by all means, but not otherwise.

496. Why are Catholics responsible for most of the crimes committed?

Firstly, your implied assertion merits no more than mere denial. Secondly, close examination shows that such Catholics as happen to be criminals have, for the most part, never been in Catholic schools to receive a Catholic training, whilst many were once in a Catholic school only to be transferred to a state school later on, eventually dropping their religion, save in name only. Finally, granted that some Catholics are criminals, their conduct is in spite of, and not because of their religion, for they do just what their religion forbids. They are in no way an argument against the holiness of the Catholic Church. That Church is holy in her Founder, doctrines, worship, and those of her members who are faithful to her guidance. Above all is she holy in the numerous Saints of the ages who have been supremely faithful to her teachings. And no other Church can claim a holiness similar to that of the Catholic Church under all these aspects.

497. You claim that your Church has not only the marks of unity and holiness, but also of Catholicity. What does the word Catholic mean?

It is derived from the Greek language, and means universal and complete. And as Christ told His Apostles to go and teach all nations all His doctrines, the word Catholic is reserved to that Church which alone teaches all Christ's doctrines to all peoples—the Catholic Church. St. Ignatius of Antioch, about the year 110, first used the word to designate the true Church. He wrote, "Where the Bishop is, there is the Catholic Church." Donatism broke away from the Church in the 4th century, just as Protestantism in the 16th, and St. Augustine declared that this heresy was cut off from the Catholic Church. In the same 4th century Pacian used the word Catholic as a mark of identification, saying, "Christian is my name, Catholic my surname." He did not wish to be taken for one of those who protested against the Catholic Church, yet still continued to call themselves Christians.

498. Whence do you get the name Roman Catholic?

The word Roman is derived from the fact that St. Peter established the headquarters of the Church in Rome. I am not a Roman Catholic in any sense of Roman citizenship. I am an American Catholic in communion with that Church which has its centre in Rome.

499. What is the difference between a Catholic and a Roman Catholic?

The same as between a Britisher and an Englishman, or if you wish, as that between the Jewish and the Mosaic religions. There is no real difference. The words Roman Catholic do not mean that there are other kinds of Catholics, but oniy that all true Catholics belong to that one great Church which has its centre in Rome. There are no Catholics apart from that one great universal Church. Those who leave that Church cease to be Catholics. At the time of the Reformation Protestants left the Catholic Church. They cannot leave it and belong to it. The only way they can be Catholic is to return to the Church their forefathers should never have left.

500. Is not Catholic Church broader in meaning than Roman Catholic Church? Catholic means universal, not Roman Catholic.

Catholic and Roman Catholic are alternative expressions. The Roman Catholic Church is the Church universal on earth. All Catholics in Europe, America, Asia, Africa, and Australia, and in the rest of the world, are subject to the present Bishop of Rome. Were you to stop any man indiscriminately in the street and ask him to direct you to the nearest Catholic Church, he would unhesitatingly point out what you term a Roman Catholic Church. The average man makes no mistake in practice on this point.

501. If the word Roman identifies your Church as the only Catholic Church, where do the other Churches come in?

They are man-made substitutes which do not come in, but which went out. Modern Protestants do not advert to the fact that they have been robbed of membership in the true Church by their ancestors. Protestant Churches cannot claim to have been founded by Christ, yet they confuse many people. But the true Church may be discerned by finding out that one which goes back to St. Peter, and through him to Christ. And he who is subject to the Pope is in communion with the very successor of St. Peter.

502. Scripture mentions neither the word Roman nor Catholic in connection with Christ's Church.

It is not a question of a name, but of the thing. And the universal spiritual society now known as the Catholic Church is most clearly described in Scripture. Christ said clearly that His Church would be one fold under one shepherd, the fold embracing all nations, the shepherd being St. Peter, and his successors. Either the Catholic Church is the one Christ established, or His Church has altogether ceased to exist.

503. We Protestants say, "I believe in the Holy Catholic Church," when we recite the Creed.

The recitation of a formula does not make one a member of the true Church. A profession of belief in America would not make a man an American citizen. Citizenship in the Catholic Church involves actual reception into that Church and submission to her authority.

504. Would you say that Christ Himself was a Catholic?

Yes. The Founder of the Catholic Church was certainly a Catholic, and history proves that Christ founded the Catholic Church, and identified it with Himself. Thus St. Paul says, "God hath made Him head over all the church (not churches) which is His body, and the fullness of Him who is filled all in all." Eph. I., 22-23.

505. How could Christ be a Catholic when He existed before the Church?

His pre-existence did not prevent His founding a Church and identifying it with Himself. As the Son of God He existed before the Incarnation, but that did not prevent His being man from the moment of the Incarnation.

506. How could Christ be subject to the Bishop of Rome?

The Founder of the Church is not subject to the Church He founded. Rather the Church He founded is subject to Him. And the Church of which the Bishop of Rome is supreme head on earth is the only Church which is so subject to the authority of Christ that it can truly be called His. From our point of view the test of communion with Rome became valid as a mark of identification only from the day that St. Peter, under divine guidance, definitely established his See at Rome.

507. Christ was above sectarianism.

He was. And so is the Catholic Church. She is not a sect. Sect supposes section or cutting off. The Catholic Church has never been cut off from herself. The sects are those religious bodies which have cut themselves off from the Catholic Church, and the clippings from the tree are not the tree.

508. By their fruits ye shall know them. If your Church were truly Catholic she would long ago have preached to all nations!

The Church was just as Catholic in the time of the Apostles as it is to-day, by virtue of the divine commission to teach all nations. But you must give the mustard seed time to grow. You could hardly expect the Church to preach the Gospel in America or Australia prior to the discovery of these countries. But her missionaries have gone forth with the very explorers, and to-day she reaches practically all nations far more efficaciously than any other Christian body.

509. So the Catholic Church cannot claim to be the only missionary force?

She claims to be the only divinely accredited missionary force, the only one which has a truly innate and perpetual expansive power, and the only one which has actually gone to all nations. In fact, there would be no other Christian missionary bodies were it not for her own missionary expeditions to the ancestors of those sects which later broke away from her despite Christ's promise that He would never fail to protect her.

510. It is a well known fact that all real missionary enterprise is carried on by the Protestants of England and America.

That is untrue. For over three centuries Protestantism could not inspire the thought of foreign missions. The Catholic Church was missionary from the very beginning and has ever retained that characteristic. In any case where are the English and American Protestant missions in Italy, Spain, Germany, Austria, Russia, etc.? Do not these Europeans deserve the truth? The Catholic Church is in all these countries.

511. I don't agree with foreign missions at all. It is better to leave natives as they are. The missions do more harm than good, causing physical sufferings and mental distress.

Your opinion cannot avail against Christ's command to the Church that she must go to teach all nations. Christianity, in its true form of Catholicity, gives many helps to the attaining of eternal salvation, and it is certainly better to have those helps than not to have them. Any harm which seems to follow missionary enterprise is due to the vices of so-called Christian traders and adventurers, to the introduction of false forms of Christianity, or to the mistakes of well-meaning men. But it is never due to the spreading of Catholic doctrine as such. Pagan and even cannibal tribes, noting the beneficial effects of the coming of the Catholic missionaries, again and again send requests that they too may receive a Priest to teach them.

512. In the name of Catholicity you often point out that your Church exceeds all others numerically. But that only disproves your case. Christ said that He scarcely expected to find faith on earth.

Christ said that His Church would teach all nations, and go to the uttermost parts of the earth, the tiniest of seeds growing into a great tree. His words, "When the Son of man cometh, shall He find, think you, faith upon earth?" refer not so much to numbers as to quality of belief, as the context shows. And He is referring to special conditions which will prevail towards the end of time when the charity of many shall have grown cold. Matt. XXIV., 12. The text in no way suggests that the body of believers through all the ages will necessarily be small.

513. Christ said, "Fear not, little flock."

The Church was a little flock at the time Christ spoke, for it was in the seedling stage. But even the vast grown tree can be called a little flock. The Catholic Church is little and despised by worldly-minded men because she consists chiefly of the poor and of the despised. And it is always little in spirit, insisting upon humility in accordance with Christ's words, "Unless you become as little children you cannot enter the kingdom of heaven."

514. The Catholic Church preaches democracy. How many non-Italians become Pope?

The Catholic Church preaches, not democracy, but Christian doctrine. In any case, democracy has nothing to do with your question. Democracy suggests that the lower classes are as equally considered as the so-called higher classes. And as far as the Papacy is concerned, democratic principles are observed. Pope Leo XIII. was a Prince by blood, whilst his successor, Pius X., was the son of a poverty-stricken farmer.

515. *How can you call your Church Catholic when all your Popes are Italians?*

Catholicity is not measured by the nationality of a given Pope. The Church numbers some 400 millions. If all Italians in the world died to-morrow there would be 350 million Catholics left. If this vast Church becomes Italian because we happen to have an Italian Pope now, then it was Jewish when St. Peter was Pope, English when Hadrian IV. was Pope, French under the French Popes, etc.

516. *Must not the Pope always be an Italian?*

No. Hadrian IV. was an Englishman; Martin IV. a Frenchman; Zachary a Greek; Gregory III. a Syrian; Hadrian VI. a Dutchman. The present Pope happens to be an Italian, but the Cardinals could quite easily elect an Englishman next time, should they think fit.

517. *How many of the Cardinals with power to elect the Pope are non-Italians?*

As a rule, slightly more than half the College of Cardinals are non-Italian.

518. *Then, as a rule, will they not elect an Italian Pope?*

Not because so many of the Cardinals are themselves Italian. All the Cardinals, before the election, take an oath that they will vote for the one whom in conscience they believe to be the best fitted for the position, independently of all national considerations. Yet, although there is no law forbidding the election of a non-Italian, as a rule it is to be expected that an Italian will be elected, even by the choice of the non-Italian Cardinals. Why? Because the Pope is to be Bishop of Rome, an Italian diocese, and just as we usually wish an English-speaking Bishop for English-speaking peoples, so the Italians should normally have an Italian Bishop. There is a greater reason wanted why he should not be an Italian than why he should be. Again, the Pope must live in Italy, and if he has to make a stand against the encroachments of Italian civil power, a Pope of Italian nationality at least cannot be accused of anti-Italian national sympathies.

519. *Ought not the Catholic Church to elect a Britisher as Pope sometimes, just to prove to the world its Catholicity?*

There is no reason why the Church should elect a Britisher, and such an election would in no way prove the Catholicity of the Church. Once a Pope is elected he is the Vicar of Christ, and cannot behave as an Italian, or as an Englishman, or in virtue of any other nationality. The Pope must have an equal love for all his subjects, and the Catholics of any nation cannot benefit by having a Pope of their own nationality. To Catholics it does not matter of what nation the Pope may be. The Cardinals elect that man whom God wishes them to elect. You want them to elect a Britisher just to please the English nation. The Cardinals would elect an English Pope if they considered it for the good of the Church and the glory of God in the light of the circumstances prevailing at the time.

520. *During all the centuries only one Englishman has been considered as "best fitted." Is not that a reflection on the learning and ability of our nation?*

No. As I have said, all things else being equal, an Italian would be the more suitable for a position to be occupied in Italian territory. And as a rule Italian Cardinals are every bit as pious and learned as others. Being international, the Catholic Church abstracts from national considerations. All are equal on that score. For purely external reasons, in no way intrinsic to the office, and all things else being equal, account is taken of the people in whose midst the Pope must reside.

521. So the fact remains that you must submit to a foreigner?

You have entirely failed to grasp the Catholic position. There are no foreigners in the Catholic Church. A supernatural standard prevails, and natural standards are not valid. If you call the Pope a foreigner because he is an Italian by birth, whom would you put there? An Englishman? If so, on your principles, all other nations would have the right to call him a foreigner! It is absurd to speak of foreigners in the one universal spiritual family. In Christ, an Italian, who has been baptised, is my born brother. From an earthly national standpoint we may be foreign to one another. But Christ's kingdom is not of this world.

522. I cannot reconcile myself to the Irish element which prevails in your Church!

The Irish element does not prevail. If the ten million Irishmen in the world were to die to-morrow the Catholic Church would not be affected as a Church. In this country the majority of Catholics are of Irish descent. But to judge from these local conditions is as absurd as the conduct of an Italian who would regard the world as Italian because he had lived all his life in Italy. And if you cannot reconcile yourself to the fact that at least in this country the Irish element prevails, would you join the Church in some other country in which it does not prevail? Will you rather do without the truth because the majority of those who have it in this country are of Irish descent? Is your dislike of everything Irish stronger than your love for Christ? Or will you say, "O God, I will accept the gift of Catholic faith, provided You do not ask me to share it with the Irish"? Imagine some Gentile saying in the early Church, "Really I am strongly attracted by this Christian religion, but I cannot reconcile myself to the Jewish element which so prevails amongst its present adherents."

523. The Irish do not welcome converts.

They do. You are outside the Church. I am within it. I am of purely English origin, and was instructed and received into the Church by an Irish Priest, and found myself more than welcome among the children of the Catholic Church. Nor was I expected to become a militant Irish sympathizer from any national point of view. I retain my own national ideals. But the glory of the Catholic Church is that she unites people in one Catholic ideal, yet does not interfere with national ideals. The 400 million Catholics love very many different lands from a national point of view, but all love the one Catholic Church of Christ, that only true Catholic Church whose every member is in communion with the Bishop of Rome, successor to St. Peter himself.

524. What do you mean when you say that the true Church must be Apostolic?

I mean that the true Church must be able to exhibit as an historical fact that she possesses lawful and uninterrupted succession of her Bishops from the Apostles, her faith, worship and discipline remaining ever the same in all essential things. Briefly, this means the identity of the Church to-day with that of the Apostles.

525. Are not the Greek Churches Apostolic?

No. The mere fact that they are in schism involves secession from the Church of the Apostles, and a direct violation of the constitution of the Church. Prior to their secession the Greeks admitted the absolute necessity of union in the bond of Apostolic authority. The early Greek ecclesiastical writers afford sufficient evidence of this.

526. What of Protestantism?

Protestantism is in a still worse plight, involving a more far-reaching constitutional change. Most forms of Protestantism do not even claim to inherit Apostolic authority.

527. The Anglican Church has retained Bishops.

Omitting for the time being the question of the validity of their episcopal consecration, Anglican Bishops are not even conscious of Apostolic authority, nor can they claim uninterrupted legitimate succession. To rebel against the lawful authority of the Church, abandon it, and set up for oneself is no way to succeed by lawful title to transmitted jurisdiction.

528. The Old Catholics are as Apostolic as your Church.

The Old Catholics are really new Protestants dating from 1870. Even though their Orders be correct, they lost Apostolic jurisdiction by leaving the Catholic Church.

529. The very name of my Church is the "Catholic Apostolic Church."

Your difficulty would be to prove your right to that title. The name alone proves nothing. Your Church owes its origin to Rev. Edward Irving, an ex-Presbyterian minister, in the early part of the nineteenth century. It is neither Catholic nor Apostolic, despite its title and claims to be a revival of an Apostolic Church which had perished—an idea quite foreign to the true notion of Apostolicity. The Catholic Church alone is truly Apostolic, and she alone rejoices in all those notes, marks, or characteristics which Christ manifestly intended His true Church to possess. She alone, therefore, is the true Church.

530. You have often hinted that the Catholic Church is indefectible, and that she will last forever. Is she not rather in her death-throes?

No. She has scarcely ever been in a stronger position, and she will last till the end of the world. Even then, instead of going into oblivion, she will merge into the Church-Triumphant in Heaven.

531. You cannot know that the Church will last till the end of time!

If I relied solely upon my finite intelligence as you do, I would not know. But I know precisely because the Eternal and Omniscient God who made me, and the world, and the Church, tells us that that Church will indeed last till the end of time.

532. Your Church began in paganism, has lasted but 2000 years, and can claim but a mere fraction of the time this world has existed!

The Catholic Church did not begin in paganism. It is, and ever was, the most bitter opponent of paganism, and paganism does not intend its own destruction. The Catholic Church was established by Christ, the Son of God, when the greater part of the world happened to be pagan. But this merely chronological connection does not prove derivation. Again, the fact that the world is much older than the Catholic Church proves nothing concerning the future of that Church. Your soul has been in existence a mere fraction of the time that this world has existed, yet it will last forever. As a matter of fact, if the Church has not the power to last till the end of this world, she would not have lasted till now. There can scarcely be greater obstacles for her in the future than those she has already met.

533. *I don't see how the fact that your Church has stood for so long proves its truth. Other religions have stood longer, and have perished.*

The mere fact that the Catholic Church has stood for so long does not prove its truth. The fact considered in the light of her teachings, moral obligations, and obstacles does. Indefectibility can be claimed as a proof for the Catholic Church alone. She demands humility, mortification, rigid duty, and subjection to God—things human nature dislikes. Protestantism abolished most of the things difficult for human nature, and is content with a more or less sentimental religion. Nor has any pagan religion demanded the consistent virtue demanded by the Catholic Church. Finally, reasons can be found for the life of non-Catholic religions, and for their death. But no natural reasons can be found for the continued vitality of the Catholic Church despite her difficult doctrines, and her enemies within and without. The protection of God alone accounts for her persistence.

534. *How do you account for the perseverance of older pagan religions?*

Religion is natural to man, almost as natural as breathing. Men are therefore naturally inclined to cling to the religion they already possess, until the truth is put before them and clearly apprehended by them. But these old religions have gone through many changes, and are essentially vague and imperfect. Nor can they be compared with Catholicity, which is so definite, and which makes such concrete demands upon the whole man.

535. *Will not the Catholic Church have to part with many of its doctrines in deference to modern thought, if it is to last till the end of time?*

No. The Catholic Church is living to-day precisely because she has ever refused to part with her doctrines, which are the doctrines of Christ. The heresies of the centuries parted with doctrines of Christian faith in deference to human opinions, and they died in turn through the ages. Protestantism is dying visibly to-day. Any attempt to adjust Christianity to men's fallible speculations is suicidal. The Catholic Church adjusts men's ideas to Christian doctrine, and she stands, and will stand. Catholic doctrines are offensive to modern thought only because modern thought has ceased to be Christian, and the Catholic Church refuses to cease to be Christian. If men insist upon walking along the wrong track, the only way the Catholic Church could keep in their company would be to take the wrong track with them. But she prefers the right track. If modern thought does not harmonize with the Catholic Church, so much the worse for modern thought. However, modern thought, as you call it, is chiefly the result of not thinking. Its authors are only too prone to ignore evidence and take that to be true which they would like to be true.

536. *Do you maintain that one is obliged to join your infallible, one, holy, catholic, apostolic, and indefectible Church, if he wishes to be saved?*

If a man realizes that the Catholic Church is the true Church, he must join it if he wishes to save his soul. That is the normal law. But if he does not realize this obligation, is true to his conscience, even though it be erroneous, and dies repenting of any violations of his conscience, he will get to Heaven. In such a case, it would not have been his fault that he was a non-Catholic and God makes every allowance for good faith.

537. *So I deserve Hell because I am a non-Catholic?*

If you say, "I know quite well that the Catholic Church is the true Church, which God obliges me to join, but what of that!" then you deserve Hell. That would be a serious sin. But apparently you do not realize this obligation. Your position is based upon insufficient or false information, and this leads you to a wrong if sincere conclusion.

538. *If one has to be a Catholic to get to Heaven I shall be glad to stay out-side.*

That is an absurd statement, for there is no eternal happiness outside Heaven. But I understand what you mean. You believe the Catholic Church to be wrong, and you will not do what you believe to be evil that good may come. But God does not want you to do that. Nor do I. As long as you believe the Catholic Church to be wrong, you are obliged not to join it. Yet if ever God gives you the grace to perceive its truth, you will be obliged to join it, no matter what the cost in renouncing your previous attachments.

539. *If a Catholic leaves his Church, and outside that Church lives a good and devout life, could he be saved?*

You give an impossible case. To live a devout life is to live a life devoted to God. Now no Catholic can have a really sufficient reason to doubt the truth of his Church. If doubts do come, he owes it to God to make sure of his position before he acts, and inquiry will show such doubts to be unfounded. If he leaves without such inquiry, he is to blame for throwing away the best of God's gifts. If he inquires sincerely, he stays.

540. *But what if he be fully convinced that the Catholic Church is wrong, even though his conscience be erroneous, would you blame him for leaving rather than violate his conscience by remaining?*

I would blame him for allowing his conscience to become so convinced by insufficient reasons, and for not studying the grounds which absolutely guarantee the Catholic Church as the only completely Christian Church. His first difficulties should have led him to seek advice from competent guides.

541. *So if a Catholic becomes a Protestant, he has no hope?*

Whilst there is life there is always hope. Such a man may return to the Catholic Church, or at least die sincerely repenting of ever having left it.

542. *Are Protestants free to leave the Protestant Church, yet Catholics not free to leave the Catholic Church?*

One may always renounce error for truth; but no one is free to forsake truth for error.

543. *Christ died for all. He did not say that we must all be Catholics.*

Since Christ died for all, it follows that He wants all to belong to the one Church He established and endowed with His authority.

544. *Many clever men have examined the Roman claims and have rejected them. They do not think it necessary to join the Catholic Church.*

Equally clever men are convinced of its necessity. After all, there are clever men who reject Christianity itself, but that does not make the truth of Christianity uncertain. We cannot argue from the degrees of intelligence in those who accept or reject the Catholic claim. Such differences of human thought prove nothing except that men differ. The real question is not affected. We must study carefully the value of the foundations upon which the claim rests.

545. You said that a Protestant in good faith could be saved. Does not that admit that his religion is sufficiently true?

No. Such Protestants are saved not because of, but in spite of their erroneous religion. They have simply been true to a conscience which was erroneous through no fault of their own.

546. What are the conditions for the salvation of such a good Protestant?

He must have Baptism at least of desire; he must be ignorant of the fact that the Catholic Church is the only true Church; he must not be responsible for that ignorance by deliberately neglecting to inquire when doubts have perhaps come to him about his position; and he must die with perfect contrition for his sins, and with sincere love of God. But such good dispositions are an implicit will to be a Catholic. For the will to do God's will is the will to fulfill all that He commands. Such a man would join the Catholic Church did he realize that that was part of God's will. In this sense the Catholic Church is the only road to Heaven, all who are saved belonging to her either actually or implicitly.

547. Since Protestants can be saved, and it is ever so much easier to be a Protestant, where is the advantage in being a Catholic?

Firstly, remember the conditions of salvation for a Protestant. If he has never suspected his obligation to join the Catholic Church, it is possible for him to be saved. But it is necessary to become a Catholic or be lost if one has the claims of the Catholic Church sufficiently put before him. I myself could not attain salvation did I leave the Catholic Church, unless, of course, I repented sincerely of so sinful a step before I died.

Secondly, it is easier to live up to Protestant requirements than to live up to Catholic requirements. Non-Catholic Churches do not exact so high a standard of their followers as does the Catholic Church of hers. But that is not the question. It is much easier to be a really good Christian in the full sense of the word as a Catholic than as a Protestant, and surely that is what we wish. What advantages contribute to this? They are really too many to enumerate in a brief reply. The Catholic is a member of the one true Church established by Christ. He has the glorious certainty of the true Faith, and complete knowledge of the whole of Christian truth is much better than partial information, if not erroneous information. By submission to the authority of Christ in His Church he has the advantage of doing God's will just as God desires. If he fails at times by sin, he has the certainty of forgiveness by sacramental absolution in the Confessional. He has the privilege of attending Holy Mass Sunday after Sunday, and the immense help of Holy Communion by which he may receive Our Lord Himself as the very food of his soul. He has the privilege of sharing in the sufferings of Christ, by observing the precepts of fasting and mortification. He receives innumerable graces from Sacramentals and from the special blessings of the Church. He may gain very useful indulgences, cancelling much of the expiation of his sins which would otherwise have to be endured in Purgatory. And he is more loved by God in virtue of his being a Catholic even as God loves the Catholic Church more than any other institution on the face of the earth. In short, even as there is an advantage in being a Christian rather than a pagan, so there is an immense advantage in being a true Christian and belonging to the one true Church rather than to some false form of Christianity. Thus a good Catholic has many advantages over and above those possessed by a good and sincere Protestant. But, as I have remarked, if a Protestant begins to suspect his own Church to be defective, inquires into the matter, and becomes convinced that the Catholic Church is the true Church, he has no option but to join that Church if he desires to avoid the risk of eternal loss.

CHAPTER NINE

THE CHURCH AND THE BIBLE

548. Why is the Catholic Church antagonistic to the Bible?

She is not. She protects and defends it. But she does teach that the private reading of the Bible with reliance solely upon one's own powers of comprehension is no sure way to arrive at the truth taught by Christ. And experience bears out her teaching.

549. Was not the Bible unknown to the people before the Reformation?

No. Beautifully illuminated copies of the Scriptures, wrought by the Monks, were in the charge of the Clergy and the Churches, and from these the Word of God was carefully preached to the people. Before the invention of the printing press, a wider diffusion was impossible.

550. Did not the Catholic Church burn all Bibles, and punish those who had copies?

No. The Catholic Church would have been very foolish to have copies multiplied only to destroy them. When the printing press was invented by the German Catholic Gutenberg in 1445, the first book printed was a Bible, before Protestantism had come into existence.

551. Yet does not the Catholic Church regard the work of the Bible Society as dangerous to Christianity?

She condemns the principle that Bibles should be distributed indiscriminately to people on the understanding that they will be able to attain the truth without the guidance of the Church, and by their own unaided efforts. The wildest absurdities have resulted from the theory of private interpretation of Scripture, and if it is not dangerous to Christianity to have a new pretended Christian Church arising every ten years from some mad-cap reading of an isolated text, I would like to know your idea of what is really dangerous to Christianity.

552. Does she herself forbid the reading of Scripture in the vernacular?

No. There are various Catholic societies for the diffusion of the Holy Gospels in the vernacular, such as the Society of St. Jerome, approved by the Church. Pope Pius X. granted special blessings to those who would read Scripture daily and recommend others to do so. But it is essential that the teachings of the living Church be kept in mind as a key to the true sense of the Bible.

553. Then why did Pope Clement XI. in 1713 condemn the doctrine that the Bible is for all to read?

He did not condemn the doctrine that it is good to read Scripture. He condemned the theory that it is necessary to do so in order to attain Christian knowledge. Christ's method was to establish a teaching Church, it being necessary to be taught by that Church. He did not order the Apostles to multiply and scatter copies of the Scriptures. If the reading of Scripture were necessary to salvation, what of the immense number of Christians through all the centuries prior to the invention of printing, when it was impossible to transcribe by hand sufficient copies for the multitudes? Could Christ make the possibility of His religion dependent upon the invention of the printing machine? And did He intend His religon to remain forever impossible as far as the illiterate are concerned? It is absurd to say that His religion essentially depends upon a printed book. The Pope wisely condemned the proposition that the reading of Scripture is necessary to all. Every reasonable man would condemn so unreasonable a proposition.

554. May a Catholic read the correct Word of God, or only the Bible as written to suit the Catholic Church?

He may read the correct Word of God in those translations which are approved by the Church. He is forbidden to read the Protestant versions in which there are many mistranslations, and in which the text is often distorted to suit the enemies of the Catholic Church. But then, distorted texts are no longer the Word of God.

555. You seem afraid that Catholics will be harmed by the reading of Scripture.

Even granted a correct version, thousands of people have been harmed by the reading of Scripture, thinking themselves capable of interpreting it aright. The Pharisees read Scripture, yet managed to use, or misuse, quotations from the Bible as an argument against Christ, just as men to-day quote Scripture as an argument against the true Church of Christ, the Catholic Church.

556. You say that Catholics may read the Bible. But do they do so?

Some do. Some do not. All are free to do so, but it is not absolutely necessary that they should give themselves to the private reading of Scripture.

557. Why do not Catholics have a Bible in the house?

Catholics are quite free to possess and read approved versions of the Bible. As you cannot have searched every Catholic home in the country I can but wonder at your credulity in thinking that Catholics do not have Bibles in their homes.

558. I have known Catholics to admit that they have never read the Bible. Why does not the Catholic Church teach it to them?

The doctrines of the Bible are taught to her people by the Catholic Church more faithfully than by any other Church. The Gospel is read to them, and explained every Sunday morning at Mass, and far more people are there to hear it than you will find in the Protestant Churches. Some Catholics do not read the Bible privately very much, but they know the doctrines taught by the Bible more clearly than any other people on earth. Non-Catholic Bible-readers may know many texts of Scripture, but they know very little doctrine. A Catholic may be at a loss when you quote some particular text, but he knows clearly what must be done to save one's soul—the true conditions required for this being simply unknown to hosts of non-Catholic Bible-readers.

559. In any case you have to admit that Protestants have more love for Scripture than Catholics. We owe the re-discovery of the Bible chiefly to the early Protestants.

I deny absolutely that Protestants love Scripture more than Catholics. Nor was the Bible ever re-discovered. Through all the centuries it had been carefully transcribed and preserved in Catholic monasteries, and was there already for Luther and others to broadcast.

560. To whom am I indebted for my English Bible?

You are indebted to many collaborators. Between 1525 and 1536 William Tindale translated into English various Greek and Latin copies of the Bible which had been made by Catholic monks, copies which could be traced back to the original Scriptures. Cromwell was not satisfied with Tindale's translation, so commissioned

Miles Coverdale to make a new one. Coverdale used and perfected to some extent Tindale's version, and published the "Great Bible" in 1539. Not satisfied with this, a committee of Anglican Bishops revised it, and in 1568 published what is known as the "Bishops' Bible." This was also faulty, and King James 1st of England ordered a new revision. Taking as their basis the Bishops' Bible, a committee of 47 revisers whose names are not known produced what is known as the "Authorized Version" in 1611. In 1881 a new revised version was published, correcting some 5,000 mistakes in the Authorized Version. Further revision of this "Revised Version" is being demanded. Thus you owe your English Bible to many unknown revisers, the Bishops of 1568, Miles Coverdale 1539, Tindale 1525, Monastic copyists through the ages, and thence to the originals.

561. Have Catholics a true copy of the Bible as used by Protestants?

Protestants have not a true copy. Their copy contains many mistranslations and omits complete Books. The Catholic Church provides a substantially true copy or version in English for her own subjects.

562. You speak of mistranslations. Do you accuse the Protestant translators of grossly infamous conduct in tampering with the text?

I do. Dixon, in his Introduction to Scripture says, "That the early Protestant translations were full of gross errors no unprejudiced Protestant will now deny, and that these errors were willful, Ward, in his Errata, satisfactorily proves." Bishop Ellicott, in his book, "Considerations on the Revision of the English Version," says that the translation "yields erroneous doctrinal inferences not to be drawn from the original." Blunt, in his "Key to the Knowledge and Use of the Bible," says, "The characters of the translators were not such as to command the respect of men." Robert Gell, chaplain to Archbishop Abbott, one of the revising committee, wrote of the discussions, "Truth was often outvoted. Dogmatic interests were in some cases allowed to bias the translation. The Calvinism of one party, the prelatic views of another, were both represented at the expense of accuracy."

563. What books are omitted from the Protestant Version?

Tobias, Judith, Wisdom, Ecclesiasticus, Baruch, the two Books of Machabees, and the various sections of other Books.

564. Is not the Douay Version a poorer rendering into English than the Protestant Version, apart from its Romish viewpoint?

The Douay Version has not a "Romish" viewpoint in the sense of having been deliberately accommodated to Catholic teaching. It is a substantially true Version which, because true, necessarily indicates the Catholic Church as the true Church. For that is the truth of Scripture. From a literary point of view, it is a less beautiful translation than that of the Authorized Version. But why? Merely because it is a more exact translation. When a foreign language, classical or modern, is translated into English, the more one clings to the text, the less purely literary beauty one attains in the new language. To obtain a more beautiful rendering one must translate more freely, thus more or less forfeiting the exact sense of the original. But in the matter of God's Word, we want, not so much literary beauty, but just what God intended. And for that, the Douay Version far surpasses the Authorized Version, despite its rather awkward literary structure at times.

565. The Gospel of Christ is simplicity itself.

In one way it is. It tells us clearly that Christ established a definite Church which He commissioned to teach all nations. It is very simple from this point of view, for men have but to accept the Catholic Church, and be taught by that Church.

But the Gospel is not simplicity itself in the way you intend. Men have devoted their lives to the study of the Gospels, preparing themselves for the task by profound research in the Hebrew, Syrian, Arabic, Greek, and Latin languages. And even then, many passages are most difficult to understand.

566. But at least the plan of salvation can be understood by the simplest person. We Protestants even tell our children to read their Bibles in order to discern it.

According to the findings of your simple readers there must be hundreds of conflicting plans of salvation, all revealed by the one Christ! As for the capacity of your children, you might as well give them the article in the Encyclopaedia Brittanica on Spectroscopic Analysis as the subject matter of their studies. But the Bible itself is against your theory. Thus St. Peter says that in Scripture there are certain things "hard to be understood, which the unlearned and unstable wrest, as they do also the other Scriptures, to their own destruction." II. Pet. III., 16. To his mind the private interpretation of Scripture can be most dangerous.

567. God has given us brains to think for ourselves. We do not need help to understand Scripture.

God had given men brains before He came to teach them Himself, and He came to teach them precisely because their brains could not succeed in finding out the things which were to their peace. If you say that His revealed teachings in the Scriptures together with our brains are enough, those very revealed teachings tell you that they are not. Even in the Old Law God said, "The lips of the Priest shall keep knowledge, and they shall seek the law at his mouth." Mal. II., 7. In the New Law Christ sent His Church to teach men, transferring to His Church that authority of God once possessed by the Priests of the Old Law. In the New Testament itself we find Philip the Deacon saying to the Ethiopian, who was reading the Scriptures, "Thinkest thou that thou understandest what thou readest?" and the Ethiopian replying, "And how can I unless some man show me?" Act VIII., 30. St. Peter, too, explicitly refutes your ideas. "No prophecy of Scripture," he writes, "is of any private interpretation." II. Pet. I., 20.

568. St. Peter means that the Prophets did not prophesy by their own will, but by the Holy Spirit. He does not refer to interpretation by us.

Your own Protestant Bishop Ellicott says of these verses, "The words private interpretation might seem to mean that the sacred writers did not get their prophecies by private interpretation, but by divine inspiration. But this is certainly not the meaning. The real meaning is that the reader must not presume to interpret privately that which is far more than ordinary human thought."

569. Any man who can think has the moral right to interpret anything.

He has not. The very laws of the state are not subject to the interpretation of each and every citizen. There is such a thing as thinking erroneously. In difficulties of civil law a man consults a lawyer who knows legal practice and parallel statutes. Who gives you the right to take greater liberties with divine legislation? A man who knows nothing of Hebrew or Greek, and is quite untrained in Scriptural exegesis, would misapprehend the sense of Scripture in hundreds of places.

570. Did not Christ promise that He would send the Holy Spirit to teach us all truth?

He did not promise that the Holy Spirit would teach each individual separately. If every individual were under the guidance of the Holy Spirit, all who read Scripture sincerely should come to the same conclusion. But they do not. The frightful chaos as to the meaning of Scripture is proof positive that the Holy Spirit has not chosen this way of leading men to the truth.   It is blasphemy to say that the Holy Spirit does not know His own mind, and that He deliberately leads men into contradictory notions.   Christ promised to preserve His Church as a Church by the guidance of the Holy Spirit, and the only Church which shows signs of having been preserved is the consistent Catholic Church.   The individual is guided by the Holy Spirit to a certain extent in the ways of holiness, but in the knowledge of revealed truth he is to be guided by the Catholic Church which Christ sent to teach all nations.

571. I don't see the need of learning to understand a simple story for simple people.

The Bible is not a simple story for simple people. We live thousands of years after the Bible was written, and our language and customs are very different now. No book written at one age is easy for another age. The study of antiquities demands a knowledge of primitive languages of which few are capable, and for which still fewer have the time. Anyway God never intended the Bible to be the sole guide to religion for all time. Christ taught orally and with authority, and He sent His Church to teach in the same way and with the same authority.

572. How does it help to know Hebrew or Greek?

Because one must know what the original words meant in the language in which Scripture was written. A knowledge of Hebrew and Greek soon shows that the translators do not always find an English word to express the exact sense of the original. God inspired the thoughts of the original writers, not the work of the translators. And if you read a sense into Scripture which God did not intend at all, you no longer have God's Word.

573. Christ chose poor fishermen, not learned men.

He trained them personally, and infused into their minds an exact knowledge of His doctrine. We cannot claim to have received a similar revelation, that we should rank ourselves with them.

574. Then Catholics have to believe just what the Priest likes to tell them?

The Priest cannot tell the people just what he likes. He is obliged to teach just what Christ taught, and which has been taught him in the Name of Christ by the infallible Catholic Church.

575. Is your Church afraid that people will form opinions for themselves?

If we consider some of the opinions people have formed for themselves from their private reading of Scripture there is need to be afraid. Christ's method was to establish a teaching Church. Protestants have a peculiar method of their own, but you cannot blame the Catholic Church for not using the Protestant method, a method which has led to nothing but uncertainty and widespread unbelief.

576. Admitting the necessity of guidance, are not our Protestant ministers as capable as Catholic Priests in telling us what Scripture means?

They might be, if Priests had not an infallible Catholic Church to guide them. The Catholic Church rejoices in the special assistance of the Holy Spirit, and the Priest has the help of her defined doctrines and the constant Catholic tradition as a safeguard. But your Protestant ministers do not claim to be spokesmen of an infallible Church. On their own principles they have to admit that they are possibly wrong. And as a matter of fact, where all Priests are agreed in the essential teachings of Scripture, your ministers come to all kinds of contradictory conclusions. The unity of teaching among Catholic Priests is a greater indication of capability than the chaos which prevails outside the Catholic Church. But the capability of Catholic Priests has little to do with relative personal attainments. It is derived from the authority of the infallible Catholic Church.

577. You speak of the authority of the Church and the weight of tradition. But I have been taught that Scripture is the only rule of faith.

You have been taught wrongly. Scripture itself denies that it is the only rule of faith. The last verse of St. John's Gospel tells us that not all concerning Our Lord's work is contained in Scripture. St. Paul tells us over and over again that much of Christian teaching is to be found in tradition. One who clings to the reading of the Bible only might be able to cite hundreds of texts yet not know Christian doctrine by any means. In fact, the adoption of the Bible only has led to as many opinions as there are men amongst non-Catholics. Finally, Scripture tells us most clearly that the Catholic Church is the rule of faith, that Church which Christ sent to teach all nations and which He commanded men to hear and obey. He who believes in Scripture as his only guide ends by believing in his own mistaken interpretations of the Bible, and that means that he ends by believing in himself.

578. Is not the Church built on the knowledge it gets from the Bible?

No. The Catholic Church was built by Christ and upon Christ before a line of the New Testament was written. She received her doctrine immediately from the lips of Christ, and is safeguarded from error in her teaching by the Holy Spirit. Between 40 and 80 years after her foundation, some of her members wrote the Books of the New Testament. If the Gospels were the only rule of faith, then before they were written there could have been no Christian rule of faith at all!

579. Christ gave us the command to search the Scriptures. Jn. V., 39.

That was a retort, not a command, and you cannot turn a particular rebuke into a universal law. Were it a universal law, it would have been impossible of fulfillment by the vast majority during the fourteen centuries prior to the invention of the printing press! But take the context. The Jews, who boasted of their fidelity to the Mosaic Law, would not believe in Christ. He challenged them: "(You) search the Scriptures, for you think in them to have life everlasting; and the same are they that give testimony of me." The Catholic Church could say in the same way to Protestants: "You are ever speaking of searching the Scriptures as opposed to my methods, and think in them to have everlasting life independently of me; yet the same are they that give testimony of me."

580. Do we not read that the early Christians searched the Scriptures daily? Act. XVII., 11.

They first received the true doctrine from the teaching Church, and then merely checked it in the Scriptures. That is the right procedure, and Catholics to-day do the same. But your way is not first to be taught by the Church, and then verify, but to try to make out your own religion from the Bible with an untrained mind and by that private interpretation which Scripture itself forbids.

581. Well, I am afraid of nothing as long as I have the pure Word of God to fall back upon.

Without the Catholic Church you cannot prove it to be the pure Word of God. Nor need anyone be afraid of the pure Word of God. What we must fear is the Word of God adulterated by people who read into it whatever they like.

582. *I object to the way you put human traditions on the same level as Scripture.*

As a source of doctrine the Catholic Church relies upon divinely guaranteed tradition, not upon merely human tradition. This divine tradition is the teaching of Christ, given orally to the Apostles and handed down in the Church, although not written in the pages of the New Testament.

583. *Then you appeal to tradition in addition to Scripture?*

Yes, and I am quite Biblical in doing so. Christ sent the Apostles to teach all things that He had taught them. In the last verse of his Gospel St. John tells us that not all is written in Scripture. If all is to be taught, and all is not set down in Scripture, part of Christian doctrine must be elsewhere. Where? St. Paul tells us clearly. "Brethren, stand fast; and hold the traditions which you have learned, whether by word, or by our Epistle." II. Thess. II., 14. "Hold the form of sound words which you have heard of me in faith." II. Tim. I., 13. "The things thou hast heard of me by many witnesses, the same commend to faithful men, who shall be fit to teach others also." II. Tim. II., 2. All Christians from the very beginning believed that Christian revelation was contained not only in Scripture, but also in tradition. Acts II., 42, tells us that "they were persevering in the doctrine of the Apostles," that is, in the oral teaching of the Apostles which they taught to one another, and handed on to their children. Those who repudiate tradition have lost the complete doctrine of Christ.

584. *I do not question traditions contained in Scripture. I object to the Roman traditions which are not in Scripture and which are against Scripture.*

The Catholic Church rejects all traditions which are against Scripture. She accepts divine traditions which are complementary to Scripture, and which are in perfect harmony with the principles taught in Scripture. The traditions themselves cannot be in Scripture for the traditional Word of God cannot be the written Word of God. But Scripture itself says that tradition exists, and that it is of equal authority with that written Word of God.

585. *Did not Christ blame the Pharisees, saying, "Why do you transgress the commandment of God for your tradition"? Matt. XV., 3.*

He did, but he called it their tradition, condemning their erroneous and merely human tradition, not the right traditions to which, according to St. Paul, we must hold fast. You quote this text merely because it happens to contain the word tradition, and without any appreciation of its true sense.

586. *St. Paul himself warns us, "Beware lest any man cheat you by philosophy and vain deceit; according to the tradition of men, according to the elements of the world, and not according to Christ." Coloss. II., 8.*

The text warns us against wrong traditions, but in no way condemns traditions which are not merely of human invention, but which are according to Christ. St. Paul does not contradict his own teaching.

587. *St. Peter condemns tradition, saying, "You were not redeemed by your vain conversation of the tradition of your fathers." I. Pet. I., 18.*

This is not a condemnation of Christian traditions, but of doctrines held by those to whom St. Peter wrote, and handed on to them by human tradition from their fathers. These were the traditions Our Lord condemned in Matt. XV., 3.

588. *I admit the force of Apostolic traditions for the early Christians. But they could be sure of them as we cannot to-day.*

That is a dreadful statement. Were the Apostolic traditions part of the Christian faith then? Is it therefore impossible to know the full Christian truth now? Did Christ mean it when He said that He would be with His Church all days till the very end of the world? Or would you suggest that He meant it, but could not accomplish it? He sent the Church to teach all things, yet you say that it is impossible to-day. Be sure that the Catholic Church has all necessary traditions embodied in her teachings. Within her fold each succeeding generation of Bishops have taught faithful men who have been fit to teach others also. But you refuse to be taught by that Church. You rely upon your own fallible judgment. And as long as you adopt that method you will never be sure, not only of the Christian traditions, but even of the true Christian doctrine to be derived from Scripture itself.

589. *You keep insisting, not only upon tradition, but also upon the teaching authority of your Church. Why follow her interpretations?*

Because we cannot safely follow the interpretation given by anybody else. All guides except the Catholic Church confess to being fallible. The Catholic Church alone claims infallibility, and proves her claim. I prefer to follow so sure a guide. Those who refuse to do so are at sixes and sevens as to the true meaning of Christianity.

590. *Have not laymen as much intelligence as Priests?*

Apart from the fact that Priests give, not their own human ideas, but the teachings of the Catholic Church, it is certain that the layman cannot know theological matters as do Priests, even as you are not as well acquainted with jurisprudence and urgery as lawyers and doctors. A specialist in a subject by years of study is bound to know more of that subject than the man in the street. If an average man is so liable to error in the interpretation of human law, how can he have the vanity to think himself expert in the interpretation of divine legislation?

591. *What special qualifications has the Catholic Church in the interpretation of Scripture?*

Very many.

1. The New Testament was written by members of the Catholic Church. She existed before a line of the New Testament was written. Protestantism came on the scene centuries afterwards. The Gospels are really the family papers of the Catholic Church, and she alone, possessing the family traditions, can interpret what those family papers really mean.

2. The Catholic Church carefully and jealously preserved the Bible through the ages, so that Protestants would have no Gospel were it not for her.

3. She has been much more faithful to Scripture than any of the Protestant Churches. Whilst many Protestant leaders are prepared to sacrifice the Bible in order to appear scientific and modern, the Catholic Church consistently demands that every jot and tittle of God's Word must be accepted in the original sense intended by God.

4. The Protestant Churches owe their separate existences to the fact that each denies that the others really know what Scripture means.

5. The Catholic Church was established by Christ as the rule of faith, and He declared that a man is to be regarded as a heathen if he will not hear the Church. The Catholic Church is the only qualified interpreter of Scripture.

592. *The Bible tells us to prove all things. I. Thess. V., 21. The Catholic Church demands that her adherents prove nothing, accepting all on her authority, and without question.*

Have you proved all things? Your own fantastic interpretations show that you have not. The text you quote has a meaning very different from that you attribute to it. It refers to conduct. The full text is, "Prove all things; hold fast that which is good. From all appearance of evil refrain yourselves." In other words, "Reflect, test, examine your conscience before you act, and do the right thing." In the same way, St. Paul said that one who desires to receive the Holy Eucharist must "prove himself, and so let him eat, for he that eateth and drinketh unworthily, eateth and drinketh judgment to himself." I. Cor. XI., 28. Your interpretation of Catholic requirements is just as fantastic. The Catholic Church does not demand that her adherents prove nothing. She wants them to examine the reasons for their Catholic faith, and prove the claims of their Church. We prove that she is the only possible Church historically, Scripturally, and logically, and that she must be infallible. Then when she speaks in the Name of Christ we reasonably accept her teachings. If I consult a doctor whom I know to be competent, I accept his decisions. I do not fight every inch of the way, disputing, arguing, and challenging his statements. So, once I know that the Catholic Church is divinely qualified to speak the truth in religious matters, I accept her decisions and definitions. Nothing could be more wise than that. In fact, it would be sheer folly to do otherwise.

CHAPTER TEN

THE CHURCH AND HER DOGMAS

593. *Being tied to dogmas, are you not the least fitted of all men to speak about religion?*

No. Other men give their own personal opinions, which are not necessarily any better than the opinions of their fellow men. I am able to give the exact doctrine of Christ, and Christ said, "My doctrine is not mine, but His that sent me." The Catholic Church also says, "My doctrine is not mine, but that of the Christ who sent me." One who has the infallible Catholic Church as guide to save him from mistakes is the best fitted of all men to speak about religion.

594. *Do you honestly give your own opinion, or the opinion of your Church?*

In matters of history, I state historical facts, and since they are facts they are my own belief. On questions of faith and morals, if the Church has given any definite teaching I give that teaching, and since it is true, it is of course my own conviction. Where the Church has given no definite teaching but leaves it a free matter, I give what I consider the most probable explanation.

595. *Why not preach charity, instead of speaking always with self-satisfaction of your "only right dogmas"?*

With so many conflicting Churches in existence, it is a vital matter to find the truth. If the Catholic Church were self-satisfied, she would be content to have the truth herself and not bother about those without it. As for charity, it is better to exercise charity than talk about it, and there can be no greater charity than to point out the right road to those who have missed the track.

596. *What is truth?*

Truth is an exact knowledge of things just as they are.

597. *Authority bears no relation to truth.*

It bears a tremendous relation to truth. The whole system of educating to truth supposes authority in a body of teachers. God is truth itself and the source of all truth. When God speaks, what He says has authority, and the authority of His words is an absolute guarantee of the truth of what He says.

598. *Truth is too big a thing for one religion to corner?*

Reason should tell you that the God who made both the universe and man must know the truth about both. It should tell you that if God definitely tells man anything, the information must be sound. It would justify the fact that God has spoken, if you would but examine the credentials of the Catholic Church. And finally, it would show you that the Catholic Church is big enough to contain all the truth revealed by God on the subject of religion.

599. *Dogma will not save a single soul.*

Alone it will not. But since the Catholic Church is the true Church which Christ commands us to hear, the conscious and deliberate rejection of her dogmas can forfeit salvation.

600. A man could be orthodox on every question, yet be lost.

That is true, for St. James tells us clearly that faith without works is dead. But that does not give any man permission to be unorthodox.

601. People will never know the dogmas of the Church to be true unless she changes them.

If people do not know the dogmas of the Church to be true, it is not because of any fault in the dogmas, but because of a fault in themselves. They are either inadequately informed, or wrongly informed. Certainly they would never know the dogmas of the Church to be true if she did alter them. Any alteration of them would be at the expense of truth. There is some hope for people as long as the Church keeps her dogmas intact—as she will do, of course.

602. Your unchanging dogmas are an insult to man's evolving intelligence!

Rather do you insult reason when you suggest that their truth must change before intelligent men can accept them. If what was true in religion two thousand years ago is not true to-day, it never was true. If I can disbelieve it now, it should have been disbelieved then. Christ taught absolute truth, and His doctrine will remain itself for all eternity. If the dogmas of Christianity changed, every intelligent man should abandon Christianity. Intelligent men are rapidly abandoning Protestantism with its constantly shifting positions. The Catholic Church refuses to change her dogmatic teaching, and she is daily receiving intelligent men into her fold.

603. By what process of reasoning do you hope to win men of clean lives and unshackled intelligence to your dogmas?

The process is this. Catholic dogmas, being the truth, set the mind of man free from human errors on the subject of religion. And I argue that most normally intelligent men wish to be free from error. Again I reason that men of clean lives are well fitted to appreciate the lofty moral standards of Catholicism. The only type of which I despair is the man whose intelligence is shackled by prejudice, or by inability to rise above the crude notions usually taught in the name of a so-called rationalism.

604. Do you think that your old-fashioned dogmas have any appeal?

The dogmas of the Catholic Church clearly express the exact teaching of Jesus Christ, the Son of God. If they seem old-fashioned to some men, these men have simply out-grown the truth to their own detriment.

605. Cannot men persuade themselves to accept any so-called truth in matters of religion?

They can, and they do. This accounts for the rationalistic position, with its refusal to believe in any save irreligious notions. But Catholics do not persuade themselves to think their own religious doctrines. They accept them from the Church established and guaranteed by Christ—a matter of hard historical fact.

606. Your dogmas are a crime of hostility to freedom of thought and expression.

Hostility towards freedom to do wrong, or express false blasphemies and irreligious doctrines is not a crime. It would be a crime to be indifferent to these things. True religion gives freedom from error, and freedom to love and serve God.

607. So Catholics must strangle their reason and swallow anything the Church teaches, however unlikely?

The strangling of reason is left to people who are ready to believe anything they hear about the Catholic Church. But the Church herself asks no man to strangle his reason, and says that it is a heresy to say that it ought to be strangled. Nor must Catholics accept anything, however unlikely. If a thing seems unlikely, they should suspend their judgment until they secure evidence of its truth or falsity, and then decide accordingly.

608. But by the mere fact of accepting the teachings of the Church, Catholics are accepting other men's reasonings.

They are not. Where other men's reasonings are concerned, Catholics should test them for themselves, and if they prove faulty, should reject them. But the Catholic Church says that when God has revealed a truth it is no longer a question of men's reasonings, and that we are not morally free to assert the opposite. We are obliged to accept doctrines revealed by God, because we know that God cannot be mistaken. But of course we make sure that God did say the things we accept on His authority.

609. Did not Tertullian say, "I believe because it is impossible"?

Yes. But the context shows that he used those words in the sense in which St. Paul spoke of Christ crucified as being unto the Gentiles foolishness. I. Cor. I., 23. He did not mean that he was prepared to believe things repugnant to principles of right reason. There are mysteries in the natural order, and still more there are and must be mysteries in the supernatural order. If God could do only those things which are possible to men, He would be no God at all. But things which are above reason are not necessarily against reason.

610. Will you receive understanding from any source other than your Church?

Yes. For knowledge of science, I go to scientists; of history, to historians; of law, to lawyers; of medicine, to doctors; of other religions, to textbooks of other religions; for knowledge of the religion revealed by Christ, to the Catholic Church.

611. At least concerning Christian doctrine, you believe what the Church teaches, and consider further investigation sinful.

I certainly believe implicitly the official and defined teachings of the Catholic Church since Christ said, "If a man will not hear the Church, let him be as the heathen." But I may investigate as much as I wish. The more I find out about the truth taught by the Catholic Church the better the Church is pleased. It is one thing to deny a doctrine; quite another to investigate its full significance. But not all the investigation in the world will ever prove a single dogma of the Catholic Church untrue.

612. Yet has not the Church changed quite a lot of her dogmatic teaching in deference to modern thought?

She has never changed a dogma, nor has she changed in any essential Christian truth. She does change in many secondary ways according to the needs of the time, but this occurs chiefly in matters of discipline. She has never modified her methods and teachings in deference to modern thought, very little of which really exists in average society to-day concerning religion—certainly not as much as in the middle ages.

613. *Has not the Catholic Church added dogma after dogma, of which the early Christians knew nothing?*

The Church has never added a single teaching of dogmatic value which was not contained in the original teachings of the Apostles. Where doubts have arisen, she has officially defined the right doctrine, not giving a new doctrine, but clearly expressing the exact significance of the old doctrine. And that is exactly what a teaching Church is for. Meantime the early Christians, by believing in the doctrines of Christ, believed these truths also at least implicitly, though they could quite well have been ignorant of the later terms used to describe them.

614. *Did not Christianity borrow many doctrines from Greek, Egyptian, Persian, and other mythologies? Cardinal Newman at least admits that Catholicism is a mixture of paganism and Christianity.*

To this I reply firstly that there are naturally certain similarities between religions from the mere fact that they are religions. Religion is natural to man, and naturally issues in expressions suitable to man. But similarities do not of themselves argue to derivation. Secondly, Cardinal Newman remarks that in some things Christianity could certainly make use of good elements in paganism. Even paganism has some elements of truth mixed up with its errors. Christianity, in its development, could select those elements of natural truth, remove all pagan and erroneous associations so that they cease to be pagan, and make use of the purified truth to better express Christian notions. Always, however, the motives why these things are observed among Christians are absolutely new and distinct, and cannot be found in pagan rites.

615. *If there is anything more polytheistic than Christianity in Greek or any other mythology, where is it?*

In Greek or any other mythology.

616. *You have God the Father, God the Son, God the Holy Ghost, Mary the Mother of God, Satan the God of Evil, invisible Angels and Saints, etc.*

Polytheism teaches several gods. Christianity teaches but one God. The three Divine Persons share the one Divine Nature, and are but one God. The other beings you cite are declared by the Church to be creatures, and cannot be used as an argument for the plurality of gods. If we taught that they are gods, you could rightly accuse us. But if we solidly maintain that they are not gods, it is irrational even for a rationalist to accuse us of ranking them as gods.

617. *Will priestly sophistry deceive all the people all the time, with the spread of science?*

No sophistry is likely to deceive all the people all the time. But Catholic Priests do not rely upon sophistry, and your supposition that they are opponents of true science is absurd in view of the fact that they have done as much, if not more than any other body of men in the world to spread science and genuine education. If the Priests are deceiving the people, who are deceiving the thousands of Priests themselves? Or are the Priests not deceived, but an entirely dishonest body of men?

618. *Why did scientific study advance so rapidly after the Reformation? Was it not because the Catholic Church forbade it?*

No. Never was scientific study neglected by Catholics before the Reformation. In physical science the invention of instruments—and very many of them by Catholics—has given us much more data than men possessed prior to the Reformation, but this progress would have come in any case, whether the Reformation had occurred or not. It is due to the ordinary development of human thought. The Reformation had no more to do with it than the signing of Magna Charta had to do with the discovery of America. America was discovered after the signing of Magna Charta, not because of it. The invention of a printing press by a Catholic contributed to the more rapid diffusion of other men's findings and promoted study and progress. But even then, a Catholic invented the printing press, not because he was a Catholic, but because he thought of it. Religion is not a factor in such matters. If a Christian became a pagan, and after that invented an excellent remedy for indigestion, you could hardly trace a connection between that and his paganism.

619. Why are scientists of standing so opposed to the Catholic Church?

If some happen to be, it is not because they are scientists of high standing. Hosts of scientists of high standing have been excellent Catholics. Ampere, Fallopio, Galvani, Laennec, Laplace, Magellan, Marconi, Mendel, Pasteur, Lapparent, Volta, and hundreds of others were convinced Catholics.

620. Is it not because non-Catholic scientists have superior intellects and better data?

No. It is because, being perhaps experts in their own line, they consider themselves expert in every line, and condemn the Church on insufficient data. Other scientists, equally expert in their scientific lines, realize that they are not therefore qualified in matters of religion any more than they would be fitted by a knowledge of medicine to speak on economics as an expert. These sensible scientists have studied at least the foundations of their religion, proved its reasonableness, and have never dreamt of abandoning their religion. There is no conflict between science rightly understood and Catholic dogmas rightly understood. Any apparent conflict is due to a misunderstanding either of science or of Catholic dogma.

621. Statements of dogma cannot be an exact science!

What is science? It is knowledge proved by strictly logical demonstration from facts or from evident principles. In religion we start from the historical fact of revelation, and from principles guaranteed by God. By strictly logical demonstration we prove exactly what must be believed and what must be done if we desire to fulfill the Will of God. Believe me, there is a most exact science of religion to be found in the Catholic Church.

622. Your dogmas must cramp the free play of a man's intelligence.

They no more cramp a man's intelligence than an excellent telescope diminishes his power of sight. They give additional light upon the most important matters. For example, the dogma that there is a hell saves me from the mistake of thinking that there is no hell—surely a vital matter. And the more a man uses his intelligence in the right studies, the more he will find that the credentials of the Catholic Church are quite in order, and that her dogmas contain nothing against reason.

623. Should not a man be ruled by his own opinions?

Not where it is a question of the religion revealed by God. To decide what one will believe or not believe for oneself is faith in one's own ability, but not faith in Christ. Christian faith believes what Christ taught and because Christ taught it, without reference to one's own likes or dislikes.

624. I use my reason to think for myself in these matters.

You will not get very far that way. Christ never said, "Blessed is the man who thinks for himself, for of such is the kingdom of Heaven." If Christ has done the thinking for you on a given subject, all you have to do is to accept His teaching. How will you find it? He has left an authorized Church. Use your reason in order to discern this Church, and then reasonably be taught by it.

625. Is it consciousness of weakness that makes the Catholic Church dread free inquiry?

She does not dread free inquiry into her truth and authority. At the same time, she knows the great capacity of the human mind for going astray. She dreads, therefore, prejudice, ignorance, and the fantastic conclusions of the illogical and half-educated.

626. If it be a sin to doubt Catholic dogma, how can you weigh evidence for and against? St. Paul tells us to prove all things.

To admit that Christ is God, and then to doubt an exact statement of His teaching is certainly a sin, for that implies a denial either of His knowledge or of His veracity. But we do not need to doubt a thing before we can begin to study it. I do not doubt the fact that the earth moves round the sun, yet I am perfectly free to weigh all the evidence for or against that proposition. St. Paul believed in the dogma of the Trinity, yet he could not prove that dogma save by proving that God had revealed it and that it must be accepted on God's authority.

627. If a man changes from Protestantism to Catholicism, does he not do so by his own judgment?

Of course he must judge that Protestantism is false, and Catholicism true. But that judgment is preliminary to faith. Having made that judgment and acted upon it, he becomes a Catholic. From that moment he is guided in what he believes, not by his own human judgment or opinion, but by what Christ has actually revealed as taught to him by the Catholic Church.

628. What is your opinion of rationalism?

It is the name of a system accepted by illogical people who wish to imply by the self-chosen title that they are really guided by reason.

629. Has not rationalism made havoc of Christianity, reducing the Bible to a myth, and quenching the fires of hell by humanitarian principles?

It has not made havoc of Christianity. It is making havoc of Protestantism. But Protestantism is not really Christianity. The Catholic Church alone is the true representative of Christianity, and she is not affected by rationalism. The Bible is as authentic as ever, and humanitarianism has not affected the fires of hell, even as it had nothing to do with their creation. As has been well said, the only way to abolish hell is to abolish one's own by leading a good life, and serving God.

630. Is not rationalism on the increase, people becoming indifferent to your Christianity?

Outside the Catholic Church, yes. The Protestant principle, "Do not be told by the Catholic Church what to think on religion, but be free to think for yourself," is proving fatal to Protestantism. Men have simply asserted their freedom to think Protestantism itself, and indeed all religion, useless. Catholics, who do not accept the principles of freethought are not affected to any great extent.

631. If you do not fear rationalism, why do you forbid Catholics to read rationalistic writings?

We do not fear rationalism. We do fear lest some individual Catholics be taken in by its sophistries, thinking that, because they themselves do not see the solution of difficulties proposed, there is no solution. Rationalistic writings constitute a danger for shallow and untrained minds, and rather a waste of time for educated men.

632. We rationalists can never become Catholics.

But rational men can do so. If you are not a Catholic, it is not sound reasoning that keeps you outside the Church. Defective information, mere want of thought, prejudice, moral cowardice, heredity, environment, and a hundred other factors may conspire to keep men outside the Catholic Church. But sound reason never does. Sound reason is the greatest ally of the Catholic Church in the natural order.

633. Why could not the Catholic Church keep a man like Joseph McCabe?

Because he was a man like Joseph McCabe. The Catholic Church keeps no man against his will. McCabe lost the faith as any man can do, and departed from the Church just as the Jews from Christ, saying, "This is a hard saying: who can hear it!" Intellectual pride blended with obstinacy of will could take any man out of the Church.

634. Would you question his honesty of purpose?

Yes. McCabe has sought to make money and court popularity by reviling the Church he quitted. He claims to know history, yet quotes as facts things he must know to be untrue—calumnies which Ernest Renan, as good a rationalist as McCabe, had refuted twenty years before McCabe rehashed them. Though he claims to be an unbeliever in Christianity, regarding that religion as a complete fraud, the whole of his distorted book, "Twelve Years in a Monastery" panders to Protestant sentiment!

635. It is strange that two highly intellectual men should be affected so differently, you being attracted to join the Catholic Church, McCabe impelled to leave it.

It is not strange. Intellectual attainments have really little to do with it, in the ultimate analysis. Brains alone cannot bring a man to Christian truth, and brains alone will not keep him in it. Christ did not say, "Come to Me, all ye intellectual people, and I will refresh you." If knowledge of religious truth and faith in it depended upon brains, heaven would be filled with the intellectual, and hell with the dull-witted. Goodness and brains do not always go together. You can have intellectual and cultured scoundrels. Christ appealed to men of good will. He demanded humility of all the human children who wished to be children of God. "God resists the proud and gives His grace to the humble." Where is human wisdom before God's infinite knowledge? Where is old age before His eternity? Or human strength before His omnipotence? God rightly demands that we acknowledge our true position. McCabe forgot it. He forfeited God's grace, left the Church, and in doing so left the Christ who established it. Meantime, McCabe left the Church after twelve years in a monastery; I joined the Church, and have been twenty years in a monastery. I became a Catholic with nothing to gain from this world's point of view, entered Religious Life, and took the same three vows which McCabe renounced. The odds are against insincerity when a step is costly to human nature. But not when a man leaves the Church for an obviously lower standard of living.

636. But when two intellectual men disagree, how can the ordinary man hope to decide?

The fact that McCabe and myself disagree means simply that you must not reject the Catholic Church because McCabe rejects it, nor accept it because I accept it. McCabe's rejection of it does not make it false; my acceptance of it does not make it true. It is either false or true independently of McCabe and myself. A man with ordinary elementary education can arrive at as sound a judgment as any other, provided he has a sincere desire to know the truth, to love and serve God, and prays earnestly for God's guidance. Any ordinary man can easily ask a Priest to explain Catholic doctrine to him. If he be sincere in his inquiry, he will notice how it rings true of its very nature. God's grace will enlighten him, and he will experience a distinct interior sense of obligation to accept the doctrine of Christ as taught by the Catholic Church. In other words, God will offer him the gift of faith—to be accepted or rejected. If he accepts, he becomes a Catholic, and all later reading of history, philosophy, and Scripture will but confirm the choice he made under the influence of God's grace. A Cardinal Newman and a bricklayer can equally become Catholic—a Joseph McCabe and a chimney-sweep can equally lose the gift of faith. Thus the Catholic Church, in her various phases, can appeal equally to the highest intelligence and to the simplest of men—which is as it should be with a Church established by Christ for the salvation of all men. And all men remain free to accept or reject the Church even as they were free to accept or reject Christ in the days of His life upon earth. Each man has the responsibility of saving his own soul.

637. But there are many individual dogmas of the Church which my reason could never accept. Take, for example, your dogma of God.

Catholic dogma concerning the existence and nature of God is in perfect harmony with the conclusions of sane philosophy, which have already been discussed.

638. I am referring to the doctrine of the Trinity. You have no sufficient reason for believing in that contradictory doctrine.

No contradiction is involved in the doctrine of the Trinity. The reason why we believe it is because God says that it is true, using terms which express it as nearly as possible in human language. As God ought to know His own intimate nature, His describing it is the best of possible reasons for believing in it.

639. Has not the Christian doctrine of the Trinity a mythological origin?

No. Christ taught us this doctrine both implicitly and explicitly in giving us His revelation. And He definitely ordered His Apostles to baptize in the one Name of the Father, and of the Son, and of the Holy Ghost.

640. But Indian philosophy taught this Trinitarian doctrine long before Christianity.

It did not. In the Vedic philosophy there are traces of *a* trinity, but not of *the* Trinity. The idea of Father, Son, and Holy Ghost is not to be found in it. That philosophy taught a pantheistic notion, all things being a kind of emanation from God to be reabsorbed into Him. It has no distinction such as ours between the Creator and the creature, and Brahma, Vishnu, and Siva bear no real resemblance whatever to the Christian doctrine of three divine and equal personalities sharing the one divine nature. The Indian notion no more resembles the Christian doctrine than does the hegelian Thesis, Antithesis, and Synthesis. You might just as well try to account for the notion of the Trinity from any notion of triplicity wherever it occurs.

641. The idea of the Trinity was derived from ancient Egyptian mythology. The Oracle of Serapis used to reply, "First God, then the Word, and with them the Holy Spirit. All these are of the same nature and make but one whole, of which the power is eternal."

Your only reason for attempting to derive the doctrine from Egyptian mythology is that you do not wish to admit that it is from God. The Egyptians derived their religious notions from their own every-day life. They had a multiplicity of gods, a god for every locality, each associated with some animal as a symbol. Later the idea grew that the gods resided in statues combining human figures with animal heads. Legend made the gods marry, sometimes two goddesses to one male god, thus forming a triad. Or again, the number three was derived from the family unit of father, mother, and child. The mother was the counterpart of the father, and that father lived again in his child. Religious idealization attributed these notions to a supreme god, and the Egyptians spoke of Osiris, Isis, and Horus, father, mother and child. But Isis and Horus were both inferior to Osiris, and all three mere myths. Nor does even the mythical notion imply a tri-unity or trinity in anything like the Christian sense of the word, nor any true divinity of infinite perfection.

The Oracle of Serapis certainly never used the words you quote. The books of Trismegistus Hermes, or the Hermetic Books, which are the great source of Egyptian mythology are full of Neo-Platonic and post-Christian interpolations and additions, and are unreliable. The attributing of the expressions "Father, Son, and Holy Spirit" to the Oracle of Serapis is but a subterfuge of enemies of Christianity who wish to suggest that the doctrine was never revealed by God. Anyone can attribute anything to anybody. It is a different matter if you ask for proof of authenticity. Men who will not believe in the doctrines of Christianity with evidence, will swallow oceans of oracles without evidence. Their eagerness not to be credulous when the historical Christ speaks is absurd in the light of their immense credulity when anybody merely mentions the magic words Oracle of Serapis. Their dislike of Christianity at once makes possible any anti-Christian assertion. But this is not rational.

642. Explain fully to us the Trinity, in the Christian sense of the word.

No man on earth can explain fully the Trinity. The finite mind cannot fully comprehend an infinite being. Even did God condescend to explain the doctrine fully to you, you would lack the capacity necessary in order to comprehend it. It is a revealed mystery to be accepted as true merely because God teaches it. However, we can explain the doctrine which Christians must believe. There are three divine Personalities in one divine Nature—the Father, the Son, and the Holy Ghost. These three Persons are equal in all things; equally God, equally eternal, powerful, etc. God is an infinitely perfect and purely spiritual Being, active in His knowledge and love. The knowledge God has of Himself is a living Personality called the Son. The idea of intellectual generation is not foreign to us, for we ourselves speak of our own thoughts as concepts and as the offspring of our intelligence. The mutual and reciprocal love between Father and Son is also a living personality—the Holy Spirit. There is no contradiction in this doctrine. We do not speak of one divine nature, yet three divine natures; nor of three divine persons, yet one divine person. We speak of one Divine Nature, yet of three Divine Persons, nature, and personality being quite different aspects of our consideration. It is as if, when dealing with the Persons, we viewed numerical distinction, as in the addition of $1+1+1$ into 3, yet when dealing with the Nature in which all three Persons share, that fusion which results in unity by multiplication of the same three figures—$1 \times 1 \times 1$ equals 1. Yet whilst the absence of contradiction is clear, the full significance of the tri-une nature of God is beyond the limited capacity of the human mind. We know the fact by revelation, and believe it implicitly because God has revealed it.

643. *If Christ be the Son of God, there must have been a time when He did not exist, for no son can be as old as his father.*

Christ is the name given to the Second Person of the Holy Trinity in His assumed human nature. As the Christ, therefore, He was not eternal, but began in time. But before the Second Person appeared on earth in this human form, he existed as the Eternal Son of God, equal with the Father in all things. But in His divine nature, if He be a son, how can He be as old as His Father? I'm afraid it is impossible to express an eternal fact in terms of time. Time is successive duration. We speak of growing old as time goes by. But in eternity there is no succession of time, and there can be no such thing as age when we speak of God. Father, Son, and Holy Ghost always exist, not existed; and they exist not for a long time, but without time. What we call now is only the indivisible instant which is the last moment of the past and the first moment of the future simultaneously. Our time is based upon the coming and going of movement. But there is no such thing in God. Yet the Second Person of the Holy Trinity is truly a son. A son is a being or person who derives from his father the same human nature possessed by the father. In the one God, the Second Person shares through the First Person exactly the same Divine Nature. And from that point of view He is the Son. But He differs from earthly sons in that He does not receive a numerically distinct nature, nor does He exist subsequently to the Father. He eternally participates in the Divine Nature through the Father. The word son in human language is the nearest inadequate approximation we can find to express the truth by analogy. To say that it completely expressed the reality would be to fall into that anthropomorphism which you would be the first to ridicule. You cannot object to the treating of God as if He were merely a kind of glorified created human being, and then refuse to believe on the score that Catholic theology does not explain Him in terms which would reduce Him to the same level as ourselves.

644. *What does the term Holy Ghost mean?*

It means Holy Spirit. "Ghost" is Anglo-Saxon for spirit, "spiritus" in Latin meaning a breath. Thus the word spirit is associated with human breathing as a kind of intangible impulse. Christ used the term to bring home to us that the Third Person of the Holy Trinity is the impulse of love invisible and intangible between Father and Son. Since love tends to union, and union with and in God is holiness, the Third Person is termed the Holy Spirit.

645. *You teach that the Holy Ghost proceeds from the Son, yet is responsible for the birth of that Son!*

The eternal Son of God, in becoming man, took a human nature from the Virgin Mary. Thus was born a being who was both God and man. As God, this Second Person of the Holy Trinity always existed, and from Him in eternity the Holy Ghost always proceeds, as from the Father also. In this sense the Holy Ghost does not give being to the Son. But the human nature, which began in time, was due to the operation of the Holy Ghost, and was assumed by the Son. There is no inconsistency in this doctrine.

646. *Let us leave these mysterious inner activities of God, and turn to external creatures. How do you view the theories of creation and evolution?*

Creation is not a theory. It is a fact revealed by God. Evolution is a fact within certain restricted spheres, but a mere theory when made of universal application. We have to admit evolution in knowledge, or in growth from babyhood to manhood. As a universal theory, however, evolution from nothing is absurd. Yet granted that God created something, it is quite possible that God endowed His original creation with power to evolve. Did he create vegetables, and animals separately, or did He create a vast rotating nebula and give it the power to evolve into various forms of being and life? The latter idea has never been proved. It is a matter of speculation, with no certainty attached to it, save that science quite discredits spontaneous generation of life. Did man himself evolve from lower living beings? It is absolutely certain that his soul did not. The soul is an intelligent spirit, and an intelligent spirit cannot evolve from matter. Moreover, God has revealed that the soul is created immediately by Himself. Did man's body evolve from lower animals, God creating the rational soul when some lower animal had sufficiently evolved towards manhood? Despite conjectures in favor of this notion, the evidence is against it. The missing link is still missing, and reason discounts the probability that a purely animal soul could develop an animal body beyond its own powers, lifting it to the higher stage needed for a rational soul.

647. Your creation supposes that God made all things out of nothing?

Yes, according to the right interpretation of that expression. God says that that is how things began, and He must know. Thus we read, "My son, look upon heaven and earth, and all that is in them, and consider that God made them out of nothing, and mankind also." II. Mach. VII., 28.

648. Does not the axiom hold, "Out of nothing, nothing can come"?

Yes. Granted absolutely nothing, nothing could ever be at all. Nothing could never become something. Nothing has nothing to work upon, and no faculties with which to operate. We are therefore forced to admit an eternal God.

649. Do you mean that God made beings out of nothing?

That phrase must be correctly interpreted. God did not make the universe out of nothing as carpenters make tables out of wood. He did not make nothing into a universe. The sense is this: God made the universe, but did not make it out of any pre-existing thing. Apart from God, before creation, there was nothing. God willed, and there was something. Thus created beings began. God does not need any previous being to work upon. He simply wills a thing to be, and it is.

650. All things are created out of spirit, i.e., out of God.

That would not be creation, but mutation of existent being. But God could not become what He was not before. Finite being cannot be made out of infinite being any more than infinite being can be made out of finite being.

651. Does not Scripture say, "Of Him, and through Him, and in Him are all things"?

Yes. But that does not mean that things are made out of God. It means that all things derive their beings from God's activity, are preserved by His continued providence, and exist always in His immense omnipresence.

652. Science says that the process of creation took millions of years; Genesis says that it occurred in six days. Why cling to a story which reason discredits?

Reason in no way discredits the account in Genesis. I am speaking of genuine and enlightened reason, not of the notions of people who think their own opinions always reasonable, whether they are so or not. It is possible to interpret the Hebrew word for day as meaning a period of indefinite length. But there is no need to adopt this interpretation, and we can admit that Moses had in mind days as we know them, of twenty-four hours each. Did God, then, create and establish all things as they are within a period of six ordinary days? No. To arrest the attention and assist the memories of those for whom he wrote, Moses used the analogy of days, with mornings and evenings, as the people living at the time he wrote knew them. He used these days to typify the objective reality of God's creative work during long periods of time. This is a purely literary device quite compatible with inspiration, and above all, when we remember that the main purpose of the author was to show that God is the Author and Lord of all things. In its religious significance, the account makes use of the seven ordinary sections of the week, bidding men worship God and rest upon the seventh. Scientifically, each day applies to a long correlative objective period, required for the slow astronomical and geological formation. In other words, Moses dedicated seven consecutive days in honor of God's work, considered as having occurred in seven consecutive periods. And as, after the sixth day, God is described as having abstained from further labor, so after six days of labor man was to abstain on the seventh. Thus Moses impressed upon the people that the week must end in a day devoted to religious duties.

653. But apart from the time required, science contradicts the very sequence of events as given by Moses.

Moses had no intention of giving the exact order in which things were produced. It is obvious that he intended to re-arrange the order to suit himself. His order is logical, not chronological. He describes eight divine operations in general, confining them descriptively to six days, allotting two operations to the third day, and two to the sixth day. It is clearly an intentionally artificial arrangement. When a book has no intention of giving a scientific account, nor of recording the chronological order of events, it is absurd to quarrel with it because it does not. I could write the life of a man according to the chronological sequence of years, or with an arbitrary arrangement of time, dealing with him, say, as lawyer, writer, philanthropist, politician, etc.—the sections chronologically overlapping, or being subject to inversion. That would not interfere with the historical value of my work. Science has nothing to say about an arrangement of matter which abstracts from science, and follows the legitimate canons of literary structure.

654. You believe that you can accept science without sacrificing the Mosaic account of creation?

It will take science all its time to clarify its own conclusions. But apart from that, no proven scientific conclusion will ever necessitate the rejection of a single jot or tittle of Scripture. Truth can never contradict truth, and the Biblical account is absolutely true in its own order. It does not profess to give a technically scientific account, but it does give the truth in a popular style adapted to the Hebrew mentality of the times when it was written.

655. Is it not a concession to rationalism to say of every unpalatable Biblical story, "I have not got to believe it absolutely"?

I have never made that concession. We have to believe the Bible absolutely, but according to the exact sense intended by the Bible. If you think that we do not believe it absolutely because we do not subscribe to what you think ought to be the sense, that is no fault of ours. Nor is such an attitude of mind rational.

656. Is it true, as Genesis says, that the earth is 5000 years old?

Genesis does not say that. It is impossible to calculate the age of the earth from the Book of Genesis. It could be millions of years old, without the Mosaic account being affected.

657. *Did Moses know the age of the earth?*

There is no evidence as to whether he knew or not. If he did know, he said nothing about it in his writings. Not intending to write a scientific text-book, he did not think fit to touch upon the subject.

658. *How old would you declare this earth to be?*

I could not possibly tell you. God has not told us, and He alone was there when creation began. The earth probably existed some millions of years before it became habitable by man. It is possible that the first man appeared ten, twenty or a hundred thousand years ago. In this matter we have nothing very reliable. We have but the ever-changing opinions or conjectures of scientists to go upon.

659. *Isn't it new to hear a Catholic admit that the earth could be millions of years old?*

It is probably as new as the evidence the sciences of astronomy and geology have been able to provide. Before the evidence of geological stratification was available men could but conjecture. Some were erroneously of the opinion that they could calculate the age of creation from the Bible, but the Church has never embodied anything dogmatic in her teaching on that question. It is a purely scientific question, not one of faith or morals.

660. *This limitation of the teaching authority of the Church to questions of faith and morals is very convenient.*

It is not a matter of convenience. It is a question of the will of Christ, who gave as much jurisdiction as He thought fit.

661. *Do you not teach that God's creative activities extended also to the production of angelic beings?*

Yes. Scripture often speaks of the angels. Christ Himself taught their existence. Human experience of their influence leaves no doubt on the subject. And it is reasonable that God should have completed the heirarchy of created beings by producing purely spiritual creatures in addition to merely material and semi-material beings. Not all evidence depends upon sense-experience. I have never seen an angel. I am not now in a normal condition to see one, and do not expect to do so until I reach heaven. I still belong to the material world. But I believe the word of God, who should know whether or not angels exist.

662. *I do not believe that any being without body, form, or shape can exist.*

In that case, of course, you are purely a materialist. Nor only that. You are an atheist, for such an assertion denies the very existence of God. God is a pure spirit, and can certainly create beings of a purely spiritual nature.

663. *Our Protestant clergyman admits that angels are not personal beings, but says that they are impersonal messages or good influences from God.*

That is but a concession to an unbelieving rationalism. And it is quite against the Word of God. Scripture insists that they are personal beings. Christ said, "Their angels always see the face of my Father, who is in heaven." Matt. XVIII., 10. Messages and influences are not permanent, and don't see. St. Peter says, "God spared not the angels who sinned." II. Pet. II., 4. Impersonal influences do not sin.

664. *What form have these angels?*

We cannot speak of the form or shape of purely spiritual beings. God has no form or shape. Shape supposes dimensional arrangement, and dimensions suppose quantity of matter. Angels can exert spiritual force, and even will the action of natural physical forces with God's permission. If at times they have appeared to men in bodily forms, they have but assumed appearances not proper to them, and most probably formed from the material atmospheric elements in order to manifest their presence in a way in keeping with man's lower level.

665. Then they are nothing like your winged statues?

No. God told the Jews to carve angels, with wings spread, to represent to men those swift spiritual beings to whom distance is as nothing. Exod. XXV., 18. But God did not say that they were exact representations of angels.

666. Will you explain a little more clearly what angels are?

Angels are purely spiritual beings. A brick is a purely material being. Man, with body and soul, is partly material and partly spiritual. God has no material body, and is purely spiritual. To complete the external manifestations of His perfections, He created beings of a purely spiritual nature—angels. The angels, then, are definite beings which have the qualities belonging to our souls, but not those of our bodies. Now our souls have two chief faculties—intelligence and will, and these are possessed by angels. But since they are purely spiritual they cannot be seen by our eyes any more than can God Himself.

667. Has every one a good angel to defend and protect him?

Yes. Christ took an ordinary little child and said, "Despise not one of these little ones: for I say to you that their angels in heaven always see the face of my Father." Matt. XVIII., 10. There is no reason why one child should have an angel appointed to guard it rather than any other, and no reason why an angel, once appointed, should desert its charge during life. In fact, the farther a child wanders from God as it grows up, the more the need of a guardian angel's care and protection.

668. Do not the lessons of earthquakes and similar disasters prove such belief in guardian angels to be humbug?

No. Angels are not supposed to stop earthquakes. They co-operate in the work of our salvation, inspiring good thoughts, and making us uneasy when temptations suggest themselves. I do not disbelieve in angels because they do not do what they are not supposed to do. A guardian angel could, were it God's will, prevent temporal calamities, but that is not ordinary, and is not ordinarily to be expected. Temporal and natural events depend upon temporal and natural causes. Nor do temporal calamities really matter. It is the supernatural life of the soul that really counts. It is enough to remark that God has appointed certain supernatural means for our supernatural safety, and amongst those means are guardian angels.

669. The Catholic burial service asks God to bless the grave and send His angel to keep it. If there is an angel by every Catholic grave, what does he do there?

All who are Christians have to admit that God has done much for men by the ministry of angels. The body of a Christian is holy. It has been consecrated by Baptism, and will one day rise again glorious and immortal. The Church speaks in a human way, and confides the body which the relatives cannot keep to the custody of God's angels. It is a very beautiful thought. But when you speak of an angel by every grave you evolve a difficulty from your imagination. An angel is not a creature subject to the laws of space. If you picture some diminutive winged animal sitting perpetually upon a tombstone, you are entertaining a ludicrous thought. But such a picture in no way corresponds with reality, and there is not a Christian who would not laugh at your simplicity. An angel is a spirit whose being is not commensurate with space, and whose powers are of the intellectual and volitional orders.

An angel could operate in London and New York at one and the same time, yet ever remaining in heaven. And when the Church commits a grave to the care of an angel she asks that that angel may intercede for the soul which inhabited the body we bury with so much sorrow, and commits the body to its care also since it will co-operate in the resurrection of that body as God's ministering spirit in due time.

670. Is the devil a supernatural being?

No. He is a natural angelic being, in a state deprived of supernatural grace.

671. Satan is a mythical being.

He is quite content to seem a mythical being. He has no desire to be detected in his operations, and is not likely to inform you that evil suggestions are from him.

672. Who is Satan?

The word Satan in Hebrew means one who is adverse, and it can refer to any adversary. In that sense Christ said on one occasion to Peter, "Go behind me, Satan, thou art a scandal unto me." Matt. XVI., 23. Satan therefore does not always refer to the devil. But since the devil, once Lucifer or the angel of light, is the greatest of all enemies to God and mankind, the word Satan has been applied in a special way to him. Of all adversaries, he is *the* adversary.

673. Do you make him also a person rather than an influence?

God endowed him with an imperishable personality. He is a person who influences. A person is an intellectual being who is master of his own freely chosen activities. It does not matter whether he be of a spiritual nature, as God or the angels, or of a semi-spiritual nature, as man. The devil has intelligence and freewill. He can exert a spiritual influence suggestive of evil. Many people say that they do not believe in the devil. That is quite in keeping with his wishes. But Christ definitely warns us against the evil influence of Satan.

674. Our minister told us that evil spirits are not persons, but evil thoughts, and that when Christ spoke of Satan falling like lightning from heaven (Lk. X., 18) He really saw a falling star, but lacked our present knowledge of astronomy.

Christ, being God, knew all things. Your minister lacked either knowledge of Scripture, or any real belief in the divinity of Christ.

675. Is the devil responsible for all sin?

Indirectly, yes, for he caused the fall of our first parents. Directly, no. Scripture tells us that the three great enemies of man's soul are the world, the flesh, and the devil. Men sin for mere worldly prosperity, or induced by sensual passion. At times, however, Satan directly tempts them. But Satan can do no more than suggest evil to our will; he cannot compel our assent. Man can always refuse consent to evil by the help of God's grace. "God is faithful, who will not suffer you to be tempted above that which you are able." I. Cor. X., 13.

676. Can you imagine a good God creating a devil?

I certainly cannot. But then, God did not create the devil. Let me explain. God did not create the devil as a devil. In other words, God did not create any evil spiritual being as evil. The angels, as created by God, were good beings of a spiritual nature, endowed with intelligence and freewill. Goodness alone is the terminus of God's creative action. But some angels misused their freedom of will and rendered themselves evil by their opposition to the God who is goodness itself.

677. Are there many devils?

Yes. St. John tells us that Satan was cast out of heaven, and that his angels were thrown down with him. Rev. XII., 9. The devils besought Christ, "If thou cast us out," Matt. VIII., 31, and said that they were legion. Mk. V., 9.

678. Of more interest to me are the dogmas concerning the formation of man. Why not admit that man has evolved out of the past?

Out of the past what? Man has evolved in many things. God meant him to do so. But he did not evolve out of nothing. Evolution supposes something evolving. We are forced to admit a Creator. If you will not admit that, you will have nothing turning its non-existent self into something.

679. May not Catholics believe in creative evolution, or emergent evolution?

Creative evolution is a contradiction in terms. Evolution supposes an existent something progressively improving itself. Creation supposes the production of being where previously there was no being. No Catholic, therefore, can believe in *creative* evolution as if there were no need of a Creator. Many Catholics believe in a *created* evolution as a possible hypothesis in a limited degree.

680. Too many have accepted the evolutionary theory in part or entirely for the Church to condemn it.

That so many have accepted the evolutionary theory does not make it true. If it were against God's revelation the Catholic Church would condemn it no matter how many held it. The number who hold an error could never influence the Catholic Church; nor does she mind whether her decision be popular or not. She is concerned with what God teaches, not with what men think. However, one can hold the evolutionary theory to a certain extent. Nobody holds it in full, for all evolutionists are very hazy about origins.

681. Restricting the question to man, what does Catholic dogma say concerning his evolution?

It says that his soul is certainly not the result of evolution, but that it is immediately created by God. There is no dogma concerning the precise mode of formation in regard to his body. But the Church stands to the ordinary teaching that his body has not evolved from lower beings, but that it also was produced by the special intervention of God. The idea that the body of man has evolved from lower animals is scientifically and philosophically highly improbable, and it cannot be held with either safety or prudence. Science has proved nothing concerning the origin of man's body, and is merely in the conjectural stage. And in view of the mind of the Church, no Catholic would be justified in denying the literal Biblical account. If he may not deny it, must he therefore believe it? He must accept it as more probable than the evolutionary hypothesis. Presumption stands for the literal sense until the contrary has been demonstrated.

682. Aquinas compares Adam's wisdom with that of Solomon, whilst anthropology shows that the first type of man was demi-witted and of small brain development.

Anthropology does not show that. That is part of the evolutionary guess. There is no scientific evidence whatever as to what degree of culture the first man possessed. Meantime it is certain that Adam had all the knowledge necessary and fitting for his circumstances. Genesis shows us that he knew the nature and diversity of animals, whilst Ecclesiasticus XVII., 5-6, tells us that God filled him with knowledge and understanding, and created in our first parents science and wisdom. The fact of their knowledge must be admitted. Its degree is open to speculation, but in no way can we admit that our first parents were demi-witted, nor can science possibly demonstrate such a deficiency.

683. Did God really take a rib from Adam and make a woman therefrom?

We are bound to believe that Eve was formed from Adam. It is revealed doctrine that "God hath made of one all mankind." Acts XVII., 26. "For the man is not of the woman, but the woman of the man." I. Cor. XI., 8. Nor has reason anything to say to the contrary. It is as easy for God to make a woman that way as to make Adam from the earth or the earth from nothing.

684. Besides Adam and Eve we read only of Cain and Abel. Whom did Cain marry?

Your knowledge is inadequate. Had you read on, you would have seen in the fifth chapter of Genesis that Adam begot Seth, and after that lived on for some 800 years, begetting sons and daughters. Cain very probably married a sister. He could even have married a niece! But that would involve the marriage of a brother and sister at some stage, or indeed of several brothers and sisters. With the cessation of necessity, such close inter-relationship was forbidden. But special conditions naturally prevailed in such special circumstances as the starting of the human race. God exercised a special providence to safeguard the earliest human beings from the evils usually associated with close inter-marriage. And after all, a sister would not be so closely related to Cain as Eve was to Adam. Cain's wife was not made out of his own rib! Whom Cain married precisely is not mentioned, as not being very important. One book cannot give all the names that have occurred in history, and the Bible gives but a summary outline of chief events.

685. Do you believe with science that man has been on earth tens of thousands of years, or do you believe the Bible story?

Science has nothing very definite to say on the subject, and in any case, the age of the human race cannot be calculated from the Bible. I certainly believe the Bible account in its own proper sense. As far as that account is concerned, man could have been on the earth a hundred thousand years. No one can say with certainty exactly how long.

686. You have distinguished between the body and the soul of man, the soul being a spirit. Yet how can a man belong to the material and the spiritual worlds at once? They exclude each other.

A material world cannot be a spiritual world, nor can a spiritual world be a material world. But the two can exist simultaneously, even as in one man's head we have material brains and spiritual thoughts. We cannot say that a man's material brains so fill a man's head that they leave no room for thought. Even in purely physical things you can have material copper and electric force occupying the same wire. They are in different orders of being.

687. Is it revealed doctrine that the soul of man is immortal?

Yes. Revelation confirms the conclusions of reason which I have explained already. The account in Genesis of man's formation proves it. God is immortal, and cannot die. He made man in His own image and likeness. But our bodies are nothing like God in appearance, and are mortal. Therefore the real image of God is in our soul, and it resembles God by immortality. Both Old and New Testaments insist upon the immortality of the soul.

688. *Man has not got a soul—he is a soul. Genesis II., 7, says that man became a living soul.*

That does not deny the distinction between body and soul in man. If God breathed a living soul into man's body, then man's body is a distinct thing, and man is rightly said to possess both a body and a soul. To say that a man is a living soul is but to use a figure of speech, alluding to the complete thing by the name of its principal part. A man's saying that he intends to take sail for Europe does not prove that the boat is a sail and that it has not got a sail. The immortality of the soul and its distinction from the body are obvious in Scripture. Thus we read, "The souls of the just are in the hand of God. The torment of death shall not touch them. In the sight of the unwise they seemed to die." Wisd. III., 1-2. Christ said, "Fear not them that kill the body but are not able to kill the soul." Matt., X., 28. If body and soul were not separate things one could not be killed without the other. St. Paul remarks, "While we are in the body we are absent from the Lord." II. Cor. V., 6. When he was out of the body he expected to be present to the Lord. But if the soul is dead it is present to no one. Again, he desired that the union of body and soul should be dissolved in order that he might be with Christ—a thing he declared to be far better. Philip. I., 23. Or again, in Heb. IX., 27, "It is appointed unto man once to die, and after this the judgment." Judgment follows death, and the dead body not being able to give an account of itself then, it is the living soul which experiences judgment.

689. *Immortality was unknown to the Jews, and was rejected by the Sadducees because it was not in the Pentateuch.*

The immortality of the soul was well known to the Jews. The Sadducees were a small minority who were remarkable among the Jews precisely because they denied it. The majority of the Jews, therefore, held it. They were well aware of the apparition of the soul of Samuel to Saul in I. Sam. (Kgs.), XXVIII., 15. Our Lord quoted the Pentateuch against the Sadducees, proving immortality from Exod. III., 6. "I am the God of Abraham, and the God of Isaac, and the God of Jacob." And He said, "He is not the God of the dead, but of the living." In other words, He is, not was, their God.

690. *David asks, "What man shall deliver his soul from the grave?" Ps. 89, 48.*

The verse means that no man can avoid death and free his soul from the necessity of being separated from the body.

691. *Does he not say, "He returneth to earth, and in that day all his thoughts perish"? Ps. 146, 4.*

When man's soul departs from his body, that body returns to dust, and all his thoughts and schemes for this earthly life are over.

692. *Ecclesiastes III., 19, tells us that the death of man and beasts is equal, and that man hath no pre-eminence over the beast.*

Human experience does show us that man can no more escape death than the beasts. But man's condition is not the same, for his soul lives on, still capable of knowledge and love, happiness or misery. Thus the same Book, in XII., 7, tells us that "the dust shall return to the earth as it was, and the spirit shall return unto God who gave it." The fate of the soul differs from that of the body.

693. But in IX., 5, we read, "The dead know not anything, neither have they any more a reward, for the memory of them is forgotten."

Those last words obviously show that it is useless to depend upon a reward as far as recognition by fellow men is concerned. The writer is speaking from the point of view of people still living in this world. To all practical purposes as far as this world is concerned the dead are removed from this world and know not anything as far as the evidence of our own senses goes. But that the soul has passed beyond the conditions of life as we know them does not prove that the souls of the departed are not quite conscious in other conditions. In I. Pet. III., 19, we are told that Christ preached to the souls of the departed. Such a proceeding implies that they were conscious of His doctrine.

694. Ezechiel XVIII., 4, says, "The soul that sinneth, it shall die."

The word soul here does not refer exclusively to the immortal part of man's nature. Ezechiel is pointing out that not only the sins of our parents, but also each man's own personal and individual sins deserve punishment. In verse 24 he says that, if the just man turn from his righteousness and do evil, he shall die, and all his righteousness shall not be remembered. But his prevarications will be remembered, a thing which will matter nothing to a soul if it merely ceases to exist, but very much indeed if it be still living.

695. You quoted the text, "Fear not them that are not able to kill the soul." But Christ went on to say, "Fear him who can destroy both body and soul."

Christ meant that we should fear God rather than men. Men have no influence in one's final judgment, whatever they may do to the body. But God cannot only destroy the body; He can condemn the soul to an eternal existence which is destruction indeed—the wreckage of all one's hopes and desires. It is simply a living death forever.

696. St. Paul says, "The cross to them indeed that perish is foolishness; but to them that are saved the power of God." I. Cor. I., 18.

All, whether good or bad, perish as far as this earthly life is concerned, by natural death. But the cross is folly to those who are spiritually dead in sin. When a man commits serious sin he drives God's grace out of his soul. His soul is then dead to a spiritual and supernatural life until he recovers God's grace by repentance.

697. But St. Paul tells us that Jesus alone hath immortality. I. Tim. VI., 16.

He means that through Christ alone can man attain to everlasting happiness. That he intends, not immortality as such, but a happy immortality is clear from his immediate addition of the words, "dwelling in the light," as opposed to the unending darkness of eternal misery.

698. The doctrine of the resurrection of the dead denies that the soul is still living.

It does not. It refers to the resurrection of the body. If the individual soul ceases to exist, there could be no resurrection of the same personality. The material body could be recalled, but another soul would have to be created. This would mean two successive personalities, of which the second would not be the first. Deny the immortality of the soul, and you deny any possibility that you yourself will rise again.

699. *It is more comforting to think that those who persisted in sin are not conscious.*

It would be still more comforting to think that they did not persist in sin. However comfort or discomfort has little to do with it. There are a thousand things we would like to be true, but that does not make them true.

700. *This sin business worries me. Is it possible that mortal man can sin against Almighty God? I can see that he can sin against his fellow mortal men.*

It is possible precisely because we are mortal men and He is Almighty God. What is sin? Sin is a crime, and crime is a breaking of the law. Now God created us, and He certainly has the right to lay down laws according to which we must conduct ourselves. If men will not obey those laws they sin against God just as those who refuse to obey the state are criminals in the eyes of state law. As a matter of fact, it would be impossible to sin against one's fellow men if one could not sin against God. Every sin supposes the violation of the rights of another. Rights and duties go together. If I have a duty it is because another has a right. But whence come the rights of my fellow men? What is their foundation? Since man did not make himself, he certainly did not make that which is less than himself, his rights. The very foundation of these rights is God the Creator, the Author of all morality. And every sin against your fellow man is a sin against the Author of the law—Almighty God. Without God you have rights with no assignable title and no real sanction.

701. *Was the sin of our first parents the eating of an apple, or the committing of adultery?*

It was not a sin of adultery. Disorder in their passions was subsequent to their first sin. Their higher faculties had perfect control over their lower faculties until they had rebelled against God. Only after that did things lower than themselves, even their own passions, rebel against them. There is far less reason why lesser things should obey man than for man to obey God. Nor were they expelled for eating an apple. Nowhere is an apple mentioned. They disobediently partook of the tree of knowledge of good and evil. The fruit of that tree could not communicate knowledge to them, but where before they had not known the evil of sin, they now had the sad knowledge of what it meant to be at variance with God. Their violation of God's prohibition was an implicit blasphemy, and a denial in practice of God's right to dictate their conduct.

702. *How can God blame anyone for doing what he must do?*

He cannot and does not. But for every free choice in the direction of evil man will have to render an account. Man is free, and no man must do moral evil.

703. *Why did not God make their will power strong enough to resist the temptation?*

He did. They need not have consented to it. God had to choose between giving man freedom of will or not. If man were not free, he would necessarily love and serve God. Man would have to love God. But God did not want a forced love from intelligent creatures. He wished to be freely chosen for His own sake. So He left man free. Yet if man is free, he is free not only to love God, but also to reject God. But God thought so much of man's freely-given love that He preferred to risk not being chosen.

704. At least God could have given men a stronger will.

What do you mean by stronger will? Do you mean a will with a stronger propensity towards the good? But freedom means freedom from inclinations imposed by any outside agency. It means indifference and personal decision. Any intrinsic strengthening of man's will in one direction means diminishing his freedom in the opposite direction. God gave man the truth; He gave him grace; but always man remained his own master physically, although morally of course he was bound to obey God.

705. God knows all. He knew the pair must fall when He made them.

God does know all. He therefore knew that they would be free, and that there was no *must* fall about it. There was no necessity to fall, and they could have resisted the temptation. You may say, "But they did fall, and God must have known that they would fall." That is correct. But the fact that God knew this did not make them fall, nor place the responsibility upon God. If I find out by some means that you are going to sail for Europe next week, when you have sailed I do not tell everyone that I made you go. Knowledge as such does not cause events. Events are responsible for the knowledge one has of them.

706. Anyway God need not have made a serpent or devil to tempt them.

God did not make any devils. He made angels in quite a sinless condition, but also free, even as man. By misuse of their freedom of choice, some angels turned themselves into evil spirits. In his evil will Satan then tempted man. God permitted this, for man had to prove the reality of his devotedness to God. Anybody can serve God if he is never tempted. Man's real glory is to be tempted to abandon God, yet not to consent.

707. You say that man fell. Evolution says that man did not fall, but that he has experienced a steady rise from brutality.

History denies this steady rise. It is full of falls, and is, in fact, but a catalogue of ups and downs. Nations rise to a high state of civilization and decay. If evolution wants to maintain a steady uplift, history itself proves it wrong.

708. What do you mean by original sin?

Actual sin is a deliberate personal transgression of God's law. But original sin, which is inherited, does not mean that I have personally and maliciously transgressed. We must notice the difference between nature and grace. Nature is our being and all that our condition demands as rational animals. Grace means a gift or quality over and above all that our nature legitimately demands. Now nature is fitted to know God only by deduction from created things. Yet over and above this God's sheer goodness chose to give us what is in no way due to us, the supernatural destiny to see Him face to face in heaven, and the grace to attain this Vision. He promised this to Adam and, provided Adam were faithful, to all his children. And in this supernatural matter He regarded Adam as father of the human family. Adam failed. He and his children were deprived of this supernatural destiny and of the gift of sanctifying grace. This deprivation of grace is called original sin. It is called sin in so far as we lack that quality which renders us pleasing in God's sight as heirs to the Vision of Himself in heaven.

709. Does God create every soul now in a state of sin?

No. God's creative activity terminates in good only. But the soul cannot normally be infused into a child of Adam without its contracting the privation of the original gratuitous gifts it was destined to receive had Adam not fallen. I say normally because God did anticipate the merits of Christ in one case, preventing the soul of the Virgin Mary from contracting original sin. Do not imagine, however, that God creates a separated soul and then infuses it. By simultaneous action the soul is created and blended with the body, thus completing a nature in a state of sin. The stain of original sin, also, differs from the stain of personal sin, which is *committed*, not *contracted*. Original sin supposes a lack of grace which would have been present, but it does not suppose a personal and malicious disposition.

710. What proof have you that original sin is inherited?

The very best—the word of the God who created us. In Ps. L., 7, we read David's testimony, "In sins did my mother conceive me." The original Hebrew has "in sin," not "in sins." He is speaking, not of his own personal sins, nor of any actual sin of his father or mother. He is speaking of original sin derived from Adam and the first fall, tracing back to the very first beginning of human life a sin handed on with human nature from parent to child. In Jn. III., 6, Christ demands that a man be born again of water and the Holy Ghost in Baptism. A birth means a life. Re-birth means the acquiring of some new principle of life not secured by our natural birth. And Baptism gives the principle of supernatural life without which we were born into this world, and the lack of which constitutes the very essence of original sin. St. Paul tells us clearly, "By one man sin entered into this world . . . in whom all have sinned." Rom. V., 12. Experience confirms this revealed doctrine. Our very proneness to evil argues to a privation of original rectitude. As Chesterton has well remarked, men may deny original sin, but almost the only thing they know about original innocence is that they haven't got it.

711. To brand me with sin is as unjust as hanging me for a murder I did not commit.

Original sin does not brand you with the positive guilt of actual and personal malice. It is a privation of a grace and of a destiny to which no human being has a natural right. God offered that destiny to Adam and to all his children, regarding Adam as head of the human family. Were you a married man with a family, I could certainly agree to grant to you and to each of your children a substantial recompense, provided you fulfilled certain conditions specified by me. If you failed to comply with my conditions, I could certainly cancel that recompense. Nor could your children justly complain later that I had robbed them of anything due to them. Original sin is the deprivation of a right to a happiness which was never due to us. The privation of grace is essentially the privation of something gratuitous.

712. I can understand inheriting the effects of the first sin, but why the sin itself? If my father is a thief, I share in his disgrace, but my soul is not stained by his sins.

Your father was not constituted the head of the whole human race, and is but the intermediate transmitter of an individual human nature. If we inherited original sin as something of positive personal malice, it would be unjust. But we do not. Death in a state of positive and serious personal malice merits hell. But if a child dies with no personal sin, but only original sin, whilst it can never attain to the very Vision of God, and thus suffers the privation of a gratuitous destiny, it will never endure the positive suffering of the lost in hell. It will be rendered happy according to its natural capacity.

713. Why inherit the first sin of Adam, and not his subsequent sins?

Only in the matter with which the first sin was connected was Adam constituted the supernatural head of the race. After his sin as head of supernaturally elevated human nature, he sinned as a private individual and independently of God's universal decree for the human race as such.

714. Why was I born without my consent, when I have to inherit original sin?

Before you existed your consent could hardly be requested. Also I would not need to be asked if someone offered to invest a few thousand dollars for me before I was able to be consulted. Yet the gift of life with a prospect of eternal happiness is more valuable than any earthly fortune. After all, if God permitted original sin, it was only because He knew that a greater good would eventuate in the Incarnation of His Son for us men and for our salvation. Christ has restored to every man the possibility of attaining the original supernatural destiny first offered us through Adam.

715. You suppose, of course, the validity of your dogmas concerning the person and work of Christ.

Those dogmas are valid. I do not suppose their validity.

716. Who was Christ?

Christ was the Second Person of the Holy Trinity, existing in the human nature which was born of the Virgin Mary, yet retaining ever His Divine Nature. He is, therefore, God and man at one and the same time. As man He could die for His fellow human beings; as God He was able to expiate the insult offered to the Divine Majesty, and thus restore to men the possibility of eternal happiness.

717. Is not there an important error concerning the date of Christ's birth?

It is true that there has been a miscalculation in our calendar. Christ was born probably some six or seven years before the traditional date. But this error is not of great importance. At most it shows that those who compiled our calendar were mistaken in their estimate. The important thing is that He should have been born, and should have paid the price of our redemption.

718. How did the idea that Christ was the Messiah get abroad? Who first knew it and taught it?

God first knew it, and from all eternity. He promulgated the doctrine from the very beginning of the human race, and continuously by the prophets of the Old Testament; Christ taught it clearly as the Gospels prove, and confirmed His claim by miracles; the Apostles and the Catholic Church have promulgated the doctrine throughout the world.

719. The evangelists never made reference to the miraculous birth of Christ.

They certainly did. The angel reassured Joseph in his bewilderment, "Fear not to take Mary . . . for that which is conceived in her is of the Holy Ghost." Matt. I., 20. To Mary herself God had revealed, "The Holy Ghost shall come upon thee, and the power of the most High shall overshadow thee. And therefore also the Holy which shall be born of thee shall be called the Son of God." Lk. I., 35.

720. Were not Mary, the brethren of Jesus, and the Jews completely surprised when Jesus came forward as the Messiah?

After the events at Christ's birth, and her receiving a special message from the angel that her child would be the Son of God, it is absurd to say that Mary was taken by surprise. As for the brethren of Jesus, He had no brethren in the first degree. Any relatives, even in the third or fourth degree, or even in the same tribe, were entitled brethren by the Jews. And of course some of these were surprised, unless we are to suppose that God made a special revelation to each one of them concerning

Christ. The Jews generally were surprised because they had built up in themselves despite the prophecies so very different a concept of the coming of the Messiah.

721. Have not older religions spoken of gods with sons on earth?

Some of them have made uncertain and vague claims, but none has made any precise claim in the full sense in which Christianity declares Christ to have been the Son of God. Nor is there a shred of evidence to show the reality of their claims, vague as they are.

722. I have discovered 27 virgin-born saviors in my studies of mythology.

You would find it very difficult to name them. However, granting that you have read of some such claims, a little further study would show you that a critical and comparative examination such as Christian doctrine has had to undergo leaves these mythological claims devoid of reality, whilst the Christian fact emerges unscathed.

723. You will not admit that Christians thought it fashionable to have a virgin-born Savior, so invented or borrowed one in desperation?

Such an admission would do violence to both reason and history. The invention theory supposes that the writers of the Gospel were liars, a theory abandoned by all the critics of Christianity worth while. The borrowing theory involves the old post hoc ergo propter hoc fallacy. That one thing is prior to another does not prove that it is the cause of that other. And nowhere in heathenism can you find any real parallel with the Christian doctrine. Pagan mythologies are characterized chiefly by the complete absence of an historial element. The great German critic Harnack pointed out that the one thing fatal to all mythological references or theories is the intense repugnance felt by the early Christians for everything connected with heathen idolatry. A profound critic, he writes, "Early Christians strictly refrained from everything polytheistic and heathen, and the unreasonable method of collecting from mythologies of all peoples parallels for orginal Christian traditions is valueless."

724. Whence came the ancient ideas of mothers and savior-sons reconciling us with God?

A belief in a God, a sense of sin, and imagination building upon ordinary human ideas would be enough to give rise to a mythology on the subject. Yet we can even admit lingering vestiges of the knowledge of our creation by God, and of God's primitive promise to put enmities between the woman and Satan. But no mythology has produced anything like the Christian doctrine, and it is certain that adversaries have dishonestly accredited virgin-births to ancient mythologies in their efforts to discredit Christianity.

725. Was not the Babylonian Astarte selected as the goddess prototype of Mary?

No. Astarte was a mythical non-historical person; Mary was historical. The legends concerning Astarte make her a goddess associated with all that is licentious and immoral. The historical Mary has never been regarded as a goddess, and was the purest woman who ever set foot on this earth.

726. I believe that the early Christians imported their notions of Mary and her miraculous son Jesus from the Egyptian Isis, virgin-mother of Horus.

Even according to the primitive Egyptian legends Isis was not a virgin-mother in any sense of the word. Your theory has been exploded by scholar after scholar. As a parallel it is altogether deficient, and your theory of connection is pure guess work, against all the facts. You might just as well point to the story of any woman who ever had a child in the whole of ancient literature and cry in triumph that the

Christian doctrine must have been drawn from that source. Many people are prepared to put implicit faith in any guesses which militate against Christianity, yet they ignore the most obvious facts in its favor. They keep demanding evidence, yet do not really want it, and will not accept it when it is offered to them.

727. Are there not great similarities between the life of Buddha and the story of Christ?

No. Buddhism knows nothing of God in the Christian sense of the word. It is definitely pantheistic. It knows nothing of the Holy Spirit. The very story of Buddha is not the story of a birth from a virgin. And in any case, it is certain that Buddhism was not known by the early Christians, and the Gospel writers never heard of its traditions. Nor, had they heard of them, could we conceive of their appropriating or using them.

728. Is there any fundamental difference between Jesus and Socrates, Plato, Aristotle, and other great thinkers?

There are many and vast differences. Socrates and others taught the uncertain philosophical conclusions of their own limited and finite minds; Jesus taught infallible and divine truth. The fruit of the teaching of the philosophers is a merely temporal proficiency in an imperfect human knowledge and conjecture; the fruit of the doctrines of Christ is eternal happiness. In themselves the philosophers were men; but Jesus was God.

729. What proof is there that Christ was God?

His perfect fulfillment of the Messianic prophecies of the Old Testament; His personal character; His teaching; His miracles, and chiefly His resurrection; His work in establishing a Church which has outlived empires and human institutions against tremendous opposition; the perpetual vitality of His sway over human hearts.

730. Did Christ ever say that He was God?

Yes. He declared His divinity when He said, "I and the Father are one." Jn. X., 30. The Jews knew it, and said, "For a good work we stone thee not, but for blasphemy; and because that thou, being a man, makest thyself God." Again, Christ accepted the supreme homage implied by the words of Thomas, "My Lord and my God." Jn. XX., 28. He could not have let such an expression go without correction, had He not been God. We know that, if any ordinary man claimed to be God, he would either be insane or untruthful. But Christ was not insane. He was ever a model of self-control, and the wisest teacher and legislator the world has seen. Nor was He a liar. His moral character forbids the possibility of a lie in so grave a matter. Christ really lived. He was not insane. He was not a liar. He claimed to be God. He accepted the adoration due to God. He is God.

731. Christ claimed, not to be God, but to be the Son of God.

In the case of Christ the one does not exclude the other. St. John admits personal distinction when he says, "The Word was with God," yet asserts identity in the divine nature when he adds, "And the Word was God." Jn. I., 1. Christ showed the co-equality of the three Divine Persons in the one single Divine Nature when He ordered the Apostles to baptize in the one name of the Father, Son, and Holy Ghost. Matt. XXVIII., 19. And He proclaimed His own identity in the Divine Nature with the Father by His words to Philip, who had requested, "Lord, show us the Father." "Philip," replied Christ, "have you not known Me? He that seeth Me seeth the Father also."

732. *Might not Christ have been mistaken?*

No sane man could so delude himself. Such an hallucination, being not temporary but permanent, would suppose in him a pathological state of insane enthusiasm. But Christ's wisdom and balance of mind absolutely excludes this. His wisdom at the age of twelve astonished the doctors of the Law. The people were lost in admiration of His doctrine, saying, "Never did man speak as this man speaks." His replies to His enemies showed the utmost prudence and genius. His tranquility under provocation and suffering does not argue to madness. Add to all this the authority of the life He lived. Very few philosophers fulfill all their own advice as did Christ. No, there is no possibility that Christ was deluded.

733. *Could we not say that Christ was a sincere humanitarian?*

He was sincere. He was not a mere humanitarian. The humanitarian is merely kind to his fellow men from motives of human and natural sympathy, not from motives of religion. St. Paul tells us the uselessness of humanitarianism from the religious point of view when he writes, "If I should distribute all my goods to feed the poor, and have not charity, it profiteth me nothing." 1. Cor. XIII., 3. Christ was essentially religious, not a mere humanitarian. He demanded that the love of God should be the motive of all our good works, not the love of our fellow men for their own sakes, God being simply ignored.

734. *If Christ were aware of His Divinity, why did He begin His ministry with doubt and temptation?*

The temptation of Christ does not suggest that He doubted His Divinity. His clear calm replies show anything but doubt. At perfect peace interiorly, He allowed an external temptation in order to teach us how to behave on similar occasions.

735. *You cannot deny His words, "The Father is greater than I."*

I do not wish to do so. Christ was at once God and man. In His created human nature He had deliberately subjected Himself to God's will. But, since in Him there was but the one personality, He had to use the personal pronoun "I," whether referring to His divinity or to His humanity. If He referred to His divinity He was equal to the Father. As regards His humanity, He was less than the Father. All such difficulties are solved by a correct notion of Christ as God made man, yet made man in such a way that He never ceased to be God. Had He ceased to be God, all the real value of His life and death for us would have been lost.

736. *Would God be born as an infant?*

Our speculations as to what would or would not be avail nothing against the fact that He was born into this world as an infant. He could have become man in some other way. But, granted that He wished to be born of the human nature which was to be redeemed, He needed to be born of a human mother. And this necessitated His being born as an infant. Redemption was thus manifested in both sexes, even as both sexes co-operated in our fall, Mary replacing Eve and Christ replacing Adam. By this means, also, the Son of God was enabled to exemplify the virtues of every stage of human life from infancy to manhood.

737. *Where is the Divine Wisdom in decreeing that Christ should be descended from three women of ill-fame, Rahab, Thamar, and Bathsheba?*

Firstly, there is no more difficulty why Christ should be descended from these more proximate sinners than that He should be descended from a sinful first parent. Secondly, the immediate source of Christ's human nature was purified from all inherited sin, Christ receiving a true human nature from Mary without the co-operation of a human father. Thirdly, the women you mention were not lawful wives, and there is a deep significance in the coming of redemption by them. The Jews regarded themselves as the lawful children of God, and thought that redemption was to be confined to them. They thought that they could not lose their inheritance, behave as they might. Yet Christ, the actual Redeemer, rejected the apparently lawful nation, and established a Church for all nations. The Jews do not recognize the Christian Church as the lawful spouse of the Messiah. Yet, as the Redeemer came by ancestry from unexpected women, so redemption has been given to men by an unexpected Church, illegitimate in Jewish eyes.

738. *If a man really did the good works you ascribe to Christ he would be popular. Yet the Jews crucified him.*

Christ was not unpopular with all. Many believed in Him and followed Him. But no man would be popular even to-day with all if, after such evidence of power, he turned round and lashed the vices of men, divorce, birth-control, impurity, drunkenness, dishonesty, irreligion, and blasphemy. Men will take all the benefits they can get, and the one who will offer benefits only will be popular. But if the same man starts to probe the conscience of the moderns, and to interfere with their private vices and self-indulgences, his popularity will soon go. Christ not only conferred physical benefits; He demanded morality and self-denial. Egotism rebelled and crucified Him at the instigation of the Jewish leaders.

739. *Did Christ make a mistake when He said that "this generation" shall not pass till the end of the world come? Matt. XXIV., 34.*

No. In that chapter of St. Matthew He blends prophecies concerning both the destruction of Jerusalem and the end of the world. Many who were then living witnessed the destruction of Jerusalem. And even as regards the end of the world, the Christian generation will not pass away until it comes. Many superficial readers confuse the two prophecies, forgetting that Christ had no intention of giving exact information concerning the final end of all things. "Of that day and hour no one knoweth, no not the angels of heaven, but the Father alone." Matt. XXIV., 36. In reference to this matter, there are three great generations to be considered; that of the unwritten law from Adam to Moses; that of the written law and the prophets, from Moses to Christ; and that of the Christian dispensation. God is not going to give any further revelation to man. All previous prophecies have been fulfilled in Christ, and Christ has declared that His revelation shall last till the end of time. This Christian generation shall not pass away till Christ comes, and when He does come it will be the end of the Christian era. We cannot complain that a thing has not happened before the time for it to happen has arrived.

740. *If Christ were God, He could not be guilty of an unjust action. Yet when casting devils out of a possessed man, He accepted their suggestion that they should destroy swine which were the property of an innocent man.*

The ordinary laws of justice which prevail between men cannot be applied to Christ in this matter. It would perhaps be unjust for an ordinary man to do such a thing, granting that he were capable of such power. But God alone is capable of such things, and the very divinity of the power Christ exercised on that occasion is proof enough that He had the right to do whatever He did. God has dominative rights over all that He has created, not only over vegetables and animals, but over men also. No man has rights against God, for all rights are granted by God. Now Christ was God. And there is no more difficulty in this case than in any of the temporal afflictions God permits in life. He has the supreme right to dispose of His own creation as He pleases. If He permits a drought that ruins thousands of farmers,

He is within His rights, for He has no obligation to send rain, or to establish laws which will infallibly bring rain when wanted. All this is viewing the question absolutely. But in this particular case you select, the temporal loss of those pigs was deserved, because the Mosaic law forbade the keeping of those—to the Jews—unclean animals. There is nothing unjust in this episode.

741. Where was Christ's knowledge of future glory when He prayed to be freed from the necessity of dying.

You must remember that there were in Christ two natures, one human, the other divine. Christ suffered in His human nature, and experienced a natural human shrinking from all that awaited Him. To that natural apprehension He gave expression conditionally, saying, "If it be possible, let this chalice pass from me." But with His divine knowledge He knew God's absolute will of both His passion and subsequent glorification, for He added, not conditionally but absolutely, "Not my (human) will, but Thy will be done." Long before this He had predicted that He would be put to death and that He would rise again from the dead. But despite His knowledge of the glorious sequel, His present sufferings were sufferings all the same. Knowledge of subsequent relief does not necessarily destroy the dread of a painful operation.

742. Christ found out His mistake on the cross, and knew that it was all in vain when He cried, "My God, why hast Thou forsaken Me."

Christ knew that His death was not all in vain. He died to give those who want it the means to save their souls. As those who want to save their souls have the means provided by the merit of Christ's death, His sacrifice was a perfect success, accomplishing all that it was intended to accomplish. It was certainly never meant to save men even against their wills. The cry of Christ on the cross, therefore, in no way expressed a conviction that all was in vain, but indicated a desolation of soul and a mental suffering in the passion which no other external expression could manifest more suitably. The words were uttered for our sake, and bespoke a suffering which was part of the price demanded of one enduring the penalty due to our sins.

743. Then Christ's sacrifice fails because He cannot create in men the will to be saved!

Christ can be said to have failed only if He did not succeed in accomplishing His purpose. But His purpose was to give men the means of salvation, should they will to make use of such means. All who sincerely wish to be saved can be saved. Meantime, even God cannot endow a man with freewill who has to do the right thing in spite of himself. That would be the end of freedom, of morality, and of merit. Salvation would be a physical necessity of nature, on a par with blood circulation, and man would no longer conform to the very definition of man. He would be another type of creature altogether.

744. The idea of atonement by human sacrifice fills me with horror, and must be abhorrent to a good and merciful God.

You would not abhor the death of Christ for mankind did you understand the full significance of the action. Far from being opposed to the goodness and mercy of God, it is the supreme manifestation of that goodness, God so loving the world as to give His only begotten Son.

745. But why should the innocent be condemned to death for the guilty?

It was not so much the condemnation of the innocent as the free offering of the Son of God in His human nature for the salvation of His sinful yet brother human beings. Man, bought by so great a price, is taught his true dignity in the eyes of God, learns how evil sin really is, and is moved to love One who has proved His love in so convincing a way.

746. Would Christianity be anything shorn of the crucifixion?

Absolutely speaking there could have been a Christianity without a crucifixion. God could have condoned the sin of mankind, and, without demanding just expiation, He could have sent His Son in human form to teach another type of Christian doctrine. But that is all in the realm of possibilities. We are concerned with facts, and as facts stand, Christianity could not be shorn of the crucifixion. Nor could the Jewish religion. All sacrifices from Adam to Christ were figures of the crucifixion. Abraham's willingness to offer Isaac predicted God's willingness to offer His Son, even as the Paschal Lamb foreshadowed Christ as the true Lamb of God who would die on the cross. Any value in the Old Testament sacrifices was derived by anticipation from the cross. God willed that the scales of justice should be balanced, and for that a man had to die for the sin of man. Yet since the infinite majesty of God had been offended, the human being chosen to expiate this infinite offense must be of infinite dignity. God the Son, therefore, became man, remaining true God, and in His human form was offered on Calvary.

747. What justification has vicarious punishment?

None, unless the one in whose debt we are chooses to accept it.

748. It would be condemned by civilized humanity.

It would not, unless it were the penalizing of one man against his will for another's crime. But who would condemn me if I chose to pay the fine of some poor man who had offended against the laws of the state?

749. Why is it praiseworthy if practiced by God?

It is praiseworthy to safeguard justice, and yet at the same time to exhibit untold love and mercy. Christ is God. Mercifully He took a human nature, and in that human nature expiated the sins of all those who wish to avail themselves of His generosity by fulfilling the conditions He appointed.

750. You have said that the greatest of Christ's miracles was the resurrection, yet Loisy, a progressive Catholic theologian, says that it was not an historical fact, but a spiritual fact only.

Loisy was a Catholic, but is so no longer, having been excommunicated from the Church for heresy. His assertion is worth only the evidence he can give, and he can give absolutely no genuine evidence for his conjecture. If the resurrection is not an historical fact, there is no such thing as an historical fact in existence.

751. But no one has ever returned from the dead!

That is a complete denial of the historical value of the Gospels. You have no proof whatever that no one has ever risen from the dead. You may not have personally witnessed such an event, but not all beyond your personal experience is necessarily false or non-existent.

752. Are the accounts of the resurrection as given by the Synoptics identical in every particular?

They are identical as regards substance and fact. They record different but not mutually exclusive particulars. Each gives its own independent summary, not pretending to give all and only that which occurred.

753. *A lawyer, versed in criticism, said that the accounts lack corroboration.*

Your lawyer friend gave only his fallible human opinion. Equally qualified jurists have come to the opposite conclusion, and the arguments of your jurist can all be refuted.

754. *The evidence of St. Paul is merely hearsay.*

Even had not St. Paul seen the risen Christ personally, his evidence would not be unreliable. If we demanded that no historian should set down anything except that which he had actually witnessed for himself very little history would be written. So long as the historian knows that the source of his information is reliable he is free to record his information. St. Paul did have the testimony of many and independent eye-witnesses, and would quickly have detected conflict in their accounts. But in addition to the evidence of other eye-witnesses, St. Paul personally saw the risen Christ. In Acts IX., he is converted by Christ in person. In I. Cor. XV., 8, he writes, "And last of all He was seen also by me." In I. Cor. IX., 1, "Have not I seen Christ Jesus Our Lord?" Again in I. Cor. XI., 23, "For I have received of the Lord that which also I delivered unto you." St. Paul could hope to gain nothing in this world or the next by lying. His doctrine led to his martyrdom in this life, and as for the next, he himself taught that God hates liars.

755. *St. Matthew speaks of the dead appearing to many at the death of Christ, but fails to give the name of even one of them, or of those who received such visitations.*

St. Matthew wrote a summary of events concerned with a principal character. If he had to describe in detail all connected with accessory incidents he would never be don... The proof that the Gospels as a whole are reliable history covers all these minor incidents. If a reliable historian relates that a man was killed during a street accident he is describing, and with the death of whom he is chiefly concerned, no one reasonably says, "I shall believe that man to have been killed only when you give me the names and addresses of every person in the street at the time." The absence of the names makes no difference to the fact that many came forth from their tombs as St. Matthew records.

756. *Why were not such marvelous events as Christ's death amidst preter-natural darkness and earthquakes, and His resurrection recorded by the Roman historians of the day?*

Christ lived and died in a remote corner of the Roman world, and had caused no political disturbance. Again, the Romans had supreme contempt for the Jews, and reports connected with Jewish religious happenings held very little interest for them. Suetonius mentions Christ briefly in his biography of Claudius; Tacitus speaks of His execution under Pontius Pilate; Phlegon, the freedman of Hadrian, records the eclipse of the sun at the death of Jesus; Celsus, the pagan philosopher, boasted of much knowledge concerning the life of Christ; Pliny the Younger mentions the Christians quite clearly together with their doctrines, but again is interested only in the manner in which their existence affected Rome and Roman dominion. Josephus, the Jewish historian who was born at Jerusalem about 37 A.D. records Christ's death on the cross under Pontius Pilate, and His appearance on the third day after His death to His disciples.

757. *Christ was buried on Friday and rose on Sunday. Where are the three days and three nights?*

We must take into account the Jewish methods of calculation prevalent at the time. The Jews used the expression three days and three nights for three periods of daylight and darkness as opposed to three periods of daylight only. Friday, Saturday, and Sunday were three periods of daylight to be taken as including periods of darkness. Whether the periods of darkness were complete or not, the Jews would speak of the whole section of time as three days and three nights. Thus in the Book of Esther V., 1, the Jews were told to fast for three days and three nights. Yet after two nights according to our way of calculating, but in the third period of daylight, the fast ended.

758. Christ rose with a material body and ascended into Heaven. What happens to His body in Heaven?

Christ rose with a material body, but not in a material body limited by all the conditions of matter as we know them. He rose with the same, yet with a changed body, the change in no way altering its identity. St. Paul predicts a somewhat similar and mysterious change in our own bodies after our own resurrection. "So also in the resurrection. It is sown in corruption, it shall rise in incorruption . . . It is sown a natural body, it shall rise a spiritual body." I. Cor. XV., 42-44. The body therefore shall rise with powers of which we have no experience yet, and strangely participating in the qualities proper to spiritual beings. It is a mystery, for our present ideas are drawn from our present conditions, and we should not be surprised that we lack the capacity to understand the conditions of a state of which we have as yet had no experience at all.

759. Let us turn from your dogma of Christ to those dogmas concerning your goddess Mary.

It would be mortal sin for any Catholic to regard Mary as a goddess. If a Catholic expressed such a belief to a Priest in confession he would be refused absolution unless he promised to renounce such an absurd idea. If you wish to attack Catholic doctrine, at least find out what Catholics do believe before you begin.

760. If you call her Queen of Heaven do you not do her an injustice in refusing to her the title of goddess?

It would be the greatest possible injustice to regard her as a goddess. It is just to honor her even as God has honored her, which we Catholics do. Jesus is King of kings and Lord of lords, and His mother certainly possesses queenly dignity, holding the highest place in Heaven next to her Divine Son. But that does not, and cannot change her finite and created human nature. To regard her as a goddess would be absurd.

761. Yet you insist that she is the Mother of God!

Jesus Christ is true God and true man, and as He was born of Mary she is truly the Mother of God. The Second Person of the Blessed Trinity was born of her according to the humanity He derived from her. She is not a goddess, for God did not take His Divine Being from her. But she is the Mother of God since the Second Person of the Blessed Trinity was truly born of her in His human nature.

762. How could Mary be the mother of the One who created her?

Mary owed her being, of course, to God, but this under the aspect of His eternal Nature. Subsequent to her creation that human nature was born of her which the Son of God had assumed to Himself. She was, therefore, the mother of Christ. But Christ was one Divine Person existing in two natures, one eternal and divine; the other temporal and human. Mary necessarily gave birth to a being with one Personality and that Divine, and she is rightly called the Mother of God.

763. Does not the Catholic Church insist also upon the biologically impossible dogma of the Immaculate Conception of Mary herself?

The dogma of the Immaculate Conception of Mary has nothing to do with biology. It does not mean that she was conceived miraculously in the physical sense. She was normally conceived and born of her parents, Joachim and Ann. But in her very conception her soul was preserved immaculate in the sense that she inherited no stain of original sin, derived from our first parents.

764. According to Catholic doctrine the Sacrament of Baptism destroys original sin. Would you say that Mary did not need Baptism?

Mary did not need Baptism in so far as that Sacrament was instituted for the destruction of original sin. She received that Sacrament in order to participate in its other effects, and chiefly in order to receive the Christian character which that Sacrament impresses upon the soul.

765. If Mary was sinless, she could not have needed redemption! Yet is not Christ the Redeemer of every child of Adam?

In so far as the sin of Adam involved the whole human race in condemnation Mary needed redeeming. But there are two ways of redeeming. God could allow one to be born in sin and then purify the soul by subsequent application of the merits of Christ, or He could, by an anticipation of the merits of Christ, exempt a soul from any actual contraction of original sin. Thus He exempted Mary from any actual inheritance of the sin, and she owes her exemption to the anticipated merits of Christ. In other words, she was redeemed by Christ by prevention rather than by subsequent purification.

766. Is there any evidence in Scripture that Mary was indeed never actually subject to original sin?

Yes. In Gen. III., 15, God said to Satan, "I will put enmities between thee and the woman . . . thou shalt lie in wait for her heel." The radical enmity between Satan and that second Eve, the Mother of Christ, forbids her having been under the dominion of Satan, as she would have been had she ever contracted original sin in actual fact. In Lk. I., 28, we read how the Angel was sent by God to salute Mary with the words, "Hail, full of grace." Grace excludes sin, and had there been any sin at all in Mary she could not have been declared to be filled with grace. The Protestant version translates the phrase as "thou that hast been highly favored." But the Greek certainly implies "completely filled with holiness." However, complaints that our doctrine exempts Mary from the contracting of original sin are becoming more and more rare in a world which is tending to deny original sin altogether, and which wishes to exempt everybody from it.

767. St. Paul says that One died for all, and therefore all were dead. II. Cor. V., 14.

Such texts must be interpreted in the light of other passages where God reveals that Mary was never under the dominion of Satan. Mary is included in these words of St. Paul juridically in so far as she was born of Adam, but she was not allowed to be born in sin to be afterwards redeemed. She was redeemed by prevention.

768. St. John knew the Mother of Christ better than the others, yet he does not mention her Immaculate Conception!

In Rev. XII. he shows clearly his knowledge of the deadly opposition between Mary and Satan. His Gospel he wrote to supplement the Synoptic accounts, and sufficient details had been given concerning Mary herself by St. Luke. Omission to mention a fact in a given book is not proof that the writer did not know of it, and above all if it does not fall within the scope of his work.

769. Did the early Church know anything of this doctrine?

St. Augustine, in the 4th century, wrote, "When it is a matter of sin we must except the holy Virgin Mary, concerning whom I will have no question raised, owing to the honor due to Our Lord." St. Ephrem, also in the 4th century, taught very clearly the Immaculate Conception of Mary, likening her to Eve before the fall. The Oriental churches celebrated the feast of the Immaculate Conception as early as the 7th century. When Pope Pius IX. defined the Catholic doctrine in 1854 he gave, not a new truth to be added to Christian teaching, but merely defined that this doctrine was part of Christian teaching from the very beginning, and that it is to be believed by all as part of Christian revelation.

770. Your infallible Church allowed St. Bernard to remain in ignorance of this doctrine.

Since the Church had not then given any infallible definition on the subject St. Bernard naturally could not be guided by it. St. Bernard believed that Mary was born free from sin, but he was puzzled as to the moment of her sanctification. He thought the probable explanation to be that she was conceived in sin, but purified as was St. John the Baptist prior to her actual birth. But he did not regard this opinion as part of his Faith. Meantime his error was immaterial prior to the final authentic decision of the infallible Church. St. Bernard believed all that God had taught and all that the Catholic Church had clearly set forth in her definitions prior to his time.

771. Did not St. Thomas Aquinas deny the doctrine of the Immaculate Conception?

His opinion was probably much the same as that of St. Bernard. Before the definite decision of the Church was given theologians were free to discuss the matter. But the Church has since defined that the soul of Mary was never subject for a single moment to the stain of original sin. Both St. Bernard and St. Thomas would have been very glad to have had the assistance of such a definition.

772. Why did the Church withhold that honor from Mary for so long a time?

Since Mary always possessed that honor the Church did not withhold it from her. The definition that Mary did possess such an honor was given by the Church when necessity demanded it. There was no real dispute about this matter in the early Church. In the middle ages theologians attempted a deeper analysis of the privileges of Mary and, with no infallible decision of the Church to help them, some theologians arrived at defective conclusions chiefly because of the defective psychology of the times. Some theologians held that Mary was preserved from original sin from the very moment of her conception; others said from the moment of her animation; yet others that she was purified at a moment subsequent both to her conception and to her animation. All admitted that she was sanctified prior to her actual birth. Now that the Church has spoken there is no doubt on the subject.

773. Did not Franciscans and Dominicans attack each other bitterly over the Immaculate Conception?

They indulged in much controversy, but it was a free matter for discussion until the Church had given her definite ruling. The Catholic Church demands unity in doctrines which have been definitely decided, liberty in matters still undecided, and charity always. I admit that her ideals of charity have not always been maintained by her wayward children in theological controversies, but that is no fault of the Church.

774. Did not Philip III. and Philip IV. ask the Popes Paul V., Gregory V., and Alexander VII. to define the Immaculate Conception in order to stop the wrangling, the Popes replying that the doctrine was not definable as not being in Scripture?

The Popes have never given such a decision. Paul V. in 1617 forbade anyone to teach publicly that Mary was not immaculate. Gregory V. in 1622 ordered the discussion to stop until the Church should have given an official decision. Alexander VII. said that the Immaculate Conception of Mary was the common doctrine of the Church and that no one must deny it. None of these Popes gave a dogmatic definition, but rather a disciplinary ruling. Pope Pius IX. defined the doctrine finally in 1854.

775. Why call Mary a virgin, seeing that she was a mother. The linking of the two terms is an insult to reason.

The assertion that an omnipotent God is limited by the natural laws, which He Himself established, is an insult to reason. Jesus, the child of Mary, was conceived miraculously without the intervention of any human father, and was born miraculously, Mary's virginity being preserved throughout. I do not claim that any natural laws were responsible for this event. I claim that God was responsible, and the only way you can show that the doctrine is not reasonable is by proving that there is no God, or that He could not do what Catholic doctrine asserts.

776. Where does it say in Scripture that Mary was ever a virgin?

Isaiah the prophet (VII., 14) certainly predicted a supernatural and extraordinary birth of the Messiah when he wrote, "The Lord Himself shall give you a sign. Behold a virgin shall conceive and bear a son; and his name shall be called Emmanuel." St. Luke says, "The angel Gabriel was sent from God . . . to a virgin . . . and the virgin's name was Mary." When Mary was offered the dignity of becoming the mother of the Messiah, a privilege to which any Jewish maiden would ordinarily look forward with eager desire, she urged against the prospect the fact that she had no intention of motherhood. "How shall this be done, because I know not man." She does not refer to the past, but by using the present tense indicates her present and persevering intention. The angel assured her that her child would be due to the miraculous operation of the Holy Spirit, and that she would not be asked to forfeit the virginity she prized so highly, and then only did she consent. Luke I., 26-38. When Jesus was born Mary had none of the suffering usually associated with childbirth. The child was born miraculously, Mary herself in no way incapacitated. She herself attended to her own needs and those of the child. "She brought forth her first-born son, and wrapped him up in swaddling clothes, and laid him in a manger." Lk. II., 7.

777. Did not Mary, to cloak her own sin, persuade St. Joseph that her child was of the Holy Ghost?

No. That is absolutely false. Mary, saluted by an angel as full of grace, was the purest and holiest woman who ever lived on this earth. And, as a matter of fact, with sublime confidence in God, Mary refrained from explaining the event to St. Joseph, leaving all to God. As St. Matthew tells us, "Behold the angel of the Lord appeared to him in his sleep, saying, 'Joseph, son of David, fear not to take unto thee Mary thy wife, for that which is conceived in her is of the Holy Ghost.'" I., 20. What you suggest has been said by certain people merely because the Catholic Church honors Mary. Their hatred of the Catholic Church is so great that they dislike all she loves, and are willing to overlook any injury to Christ in fostering their hatred.

Yet how can they hope to please Christ by dishonoring His mother? Every true child bitterly resents disrespect to his mother, and Christ was the best son who ever lived. The more we honor Mary the more we honor Christ, for the honor we show her is because of Christ. If He were not the central figure, Mary would have been forgotten long ago.

778. If Jesus was born of a virgin why does He say nothing about it?

We do not know that He said nothing about it. The evangelists do not record any special utterances of Christ on this subject, but they do not pretend to record all that He ever said. St. Luke tells us that when He met the two disciples on the way to Emmaus, "beginning at Moses and all the prophets, he expounded to them in all the Scriptures, the things that were concerning him." XXIV., 27. There is every probability that He explained His advent into this world according to the prophecy of Isaiah. Meantime the Gospels do record the fact that Mary was a virgin, and their words are as reliable in this as when they record the utterances of Christ.

779. To prove Davidic descent both Matthew and Luke give the genealogy of Joseph, useless were not Joseph the father of Christ.

The genealogy of Joseph was that of Mary also. They were kinspeople of the same Davidic stock. The Jews as a rule counted their generations only in the male line, and such a generation alone would appeal to the Jews for whom Matthew above all wrote. The same St. Matthew records that the angel told Joseph that the child was conceived miraculously by the Holy Ghost and not through the intervention of man. St. Luke in turn left no doubt as to his mind on the subject when he carefully wrote that "Jesus himself was beginning about the age of thirty years; being (as it was supposed) the son of Joseph." III., 23.

780. St. Matthew says that Joseph knew her not till she brought forth her first-born son. I., 25.

Nor did he. And the expression "till" in Hebrew usage has no necessary reference to the future. Thus in Gen. VIII., 7, we read that "the dove went forth from the ark and did not return till the waters dried up." That expression does not suggest that it returned then. It did not return at all, having found resting places. Nor does the expression first-born child imply that there were other children afterwards. Thus Exodus says, "Every first-born shall be sanctified unto God." Parents had not to wait to see if other children were born before they could call the first their first-born!

781. Matt. XIII., 55-56, says, "His brethren James and Joseph, and Simon and Jude: and His sisters, are they not all with us?"

The Jewish expression "brothers and sisters of the Lord" in Scripture merely refers to relationship in the same tribe or stock. Cousins often came under that title. In all nations the word brother has a wide significance, as when one Mason will call another a brother-mason without suggesting that he was born of the same mother. The same St. Matthew speaks explicitly of "Mary, the mother of James and Joseph" in XXVII., 56, obviously alluding to a Mary who was not the mother of Jesus but who was married to Cleophas, the brother of Joseph.

782. There would not be two girls in the one family called Mary.

There certainly could be. And St. John, XIX., 25, writes that there stood by the cross of Jesus "His mother, and his mother's sister, Mary of Cleophas." But even here, Mary of Cleophas need not have been a sister in the first degree of blood-relationship, but rather of the same lineage in more remote degrees of either consanguinity or affinity.

783. Why are Protestants, who believe in Scripture, so convinced that Mary had other children?

They are not inspired by love for Christ, or for the mother of Christ, or for Scripture in their doctrine. Their main desire is to maintain a doctrine differing from that of the Catholic Church. But it is a position which is rapidly going out of fashion. Learned Protestant scholars to-day deny as emphatically as any Catholic that Mary had other children. When Our Lord, dying on the cross, commended His mother to the care of St. John, He did so precisely because He was her only child, and He knew that Mary had no other children to care for her. The idea that Mary had other children is disrespectful to the Holy Spirit who claimed and sanctified her as His sanctuary. It insults Christ, who was the only-begotten of His mother even as He was the only-begotten of His Heavenly Father. It insults Mary, who would have been guilty of great ingratitude to God, if she threw away the gift of virginity which God had so carefully preserved for her in the conception of Christ. It insults St. Joseph. God had told him by an angel to take Mary to wife, and that the child to be born of her had no earthly father but was the very Son of God. God merely gave St. Joseph the privilege of protecting her good name amongst the undiscerning Jews, and He chose a God-fearing man who would respect her. Knowing that her child was God Himself in human form, Joseph would at once regard her as on a plane far superior to that of any ordinary human being, and to him, as to us, the mere thought of her becoming a mother to merely earthly children would have seemed a sacrilege.

784. You urge these privileges granted to Mary as the foundation of your devotion to her, yet Christ said, "Rather blessed are they who hear the word of God and keep it."

Would you presume to say that Mary, whom the angel addressed as full of grace, did not hear the Word of God and keep it? You have missed the sense of the passage to which you allude. In Luke XI., 27, a woman praised the one who had the honor to be the mother of Christ. Christ did not for a moment deny it, as you would like to believe. The sense of His words is simply, "Yes, she is blessed. But better to hear God's word and keep it, and thus attain holiness, than to be My mother. You cannot all imitate Mary by being My mother; but you can do so by hearing God's word and keeping it." The thought that those who hear God's word and keep it are rather blessed than Mary because she did not is simply absurd. "Henceforth," declared Mary prophetically, "all generations shall call me blessed." Lk. I., 48. And Elizabeth saluted her with the words, "Blessed art thou among women." Lk. I, 42.

785. How do you prove Mary's bodily assumption into Heaven?

No Christian could dispute the fact that Mary's soul is in Heaven. Christ certainly did not suffer the soul of His own mother to be lost. The doctrine of her bodily assumption after her death is not contained in Scripture, but is guaranteed by tradition and by the teaching of the Catholic Church. That Scripture omits to record the fact is no argument against it. Omission is not denial. Meantime early traditions positively record the fact, and negatively we note that, whilst the mortal remains of a St. Peter and of a St. Paul are jealously possessed and honored in Rome, no city or Christian centre has ever claimed to possess the mortal remains of Our Lady. Certainly relics of Our Lady would be regarded as having greater value than those of any Saint or Apostle, so nearly was she related to Christ. And it was most fitting that the body of Mary, who had been preserved even from the taint of original sin, should not have been allowed to corrupt. After all, it was just as easy for God to take her glorified body to Heaven at once as it will be to take the glorified bodies of all the saved at the last day. However the definite sanction of this doctrine by the Catholic Church is sufficient assurance of the fact.

786. Christ is said to have saved us. What does being saved mean?

A man is saved who is free forever from the prospect of going to the eternal misery of hell. The soul that is saved has necessarily been separated from this earthly life of probation, and has gone either to purgatory for a time, or immediately to the eternal happiness of heaven.

787. Do you deny that we Protestants are assured of salvation by our belief on Christ?

No one can be sure of salvation until he is safely dead, finishing this life in a state of grace. During this life a man, no matter how just he may be, is able to forsake the path of justice and lose all the merit of previous goodness. You may think this hard, but a murder on Tuesday could not be excused on the score of almsgiving to a beggar on the previous day. Previous good actions do not justify subsequent bad ones. Thus God says, "If the just man turn away from his justice and do iniquity .... all his justices that he hath done shall not be remembered." Ezech. XVIII., 24.

788. Faith in Christ is the only thing that will save sinners.

All the faith in the world could not save a sinner who intends to go on sinning. A man must repent of his sins, and try to live a good life.

789. "He that believeth in Me hath everlasting life." Jn. VI., 47.

Faith in Christ is one condition of eternal life. If a man·sees the facts and will not believe, he cannot be saved. If he does believe he can be saved, but it does not follow that he must be saved. By mere belief in Christ no man has certainty of salvation. St. Paul believed in Christ yet had to write, "I chastise my body and bring it into subjection: lest perhaps, when I have preached to others, I myself should become a castaway." I. Cor. IX., 27. In the following chapter, verse 12, he warns all of us, "He that thinketh himself to stand, let him take heed lest he fall."

790. Christ said that he who believes "cometh not into judgment, but is passed from death to life." Jn. V., 24.

This does not suppose an exemption from judgment. "We must all be manifested before the judgment seat of Christ." 2 Cor. V., 10. Your text means, "If you have faith and all other necessary conditions, you will not meet with the judgment of condemnation; and even now, if you be in God's grace, you have a title to this merciful judgment since you have passed from the death of sin to that life of grace which is intended to yield only to eternal happiness." Thus Christ says, "He who perseveres to the end, he shall be saved." Matt. XXIV., 13. Those who do not persevere in God's grace will not be saved. St. Paul says, "With fear and trembling work out your salvation." Philip. II., 12. Why, if they were already saved and had nothing to fear? Again he speaks of those who were once illuminated and who were already then fallen away. Heb. VI., 4-6. You claim to be assured of salvation and that you cannot fall away, whilst Scripture tells us of some who were as believing as you are, yet who did fall away!

791. We owe the great principle of justification by faith alone to the early reformers.

All decent Protestants are getting rid of that principle as rapidly as possible. Faith alone without a good moral life is not enough. Everyone is disgusted with the man who professes a Christian life yet who lives an evil life, and no one really believes that to be the road to salvation. St. James tells us that "Faith without works is dead in itself." II., 17. Martin Luther knew that this text was the end of his doctrine, so he rejected the Epistle of James, calling it an epistle of straw. But Protestants have had to accept that epistle. Far from owing gratitude to Luther for his principle of justification by faith only, most Protestants are heartily ashamed of it.

792. A man cannot save himself by his own good works.

Good works prompted by purely natural motives cannot save a man. Thus St. Paul says, "If I should give all my goods to feed the poor, and have not charity, it profiteth me nothing." 1 Cor. XIII., 3. Yet good works inspired by faith in Christ and love for Christ are necessary. "By works a man is justified, and not by faith only." James II., 24. Indeed the "Son of man will come in the glory of His Father . . . and then will He render to every man according to his works." Matt. XVI., 27.

793. What does the Catholic Church teach concerning the guidance given to individual Christians by the Holy Spirit in the work of their salvation?

The Holy Spirit dwells not only in the Church, preserving her from error, but also in the soul of every Christian who is in the grace of Christ. In the individual soul the Holy Spirit inspires love for God and the desire of Christian virtue, and in that sense He is called the Sanctifier of the soul. But since God cannot contradict Himself, the Holy Spirit never inspires any individual in a way at variance with the teaching and discipline of the Church established and guaranteed by Christ. And since man can easily deceive himself or still more easily be deceived by Satan who can pretend to be an angel of light, the Church applies certain tests to see whether a given influence be really of the Holy Spirit. Thus St. John warns us, "Believe not every spirit, but try the spirits if they be of God." 1 Jn., IV., 1. What are the tests? Firstly, negative. Is the notion I think inspired in any way at variance with the doctrine of the Catholic Church? Since it is already certain that the Holy Spirit guides the Church and that He cannot contradict Himself, it is certain that any ideas conflicting with Catholic teaching and discipline cannot be attributed to the Holy Spirit. Secondly, and granted this negative test, there is a positive test. Does the supposed inspiration incline the recipient to sane conduct rather than to some form of religious mania? Does it tend to foster humility rather than pride; obedience rather than self-will; purity, charity, and holiness? No impulse can be accepted as being of the Holy Spirit unless it can pass all these tests.

794. How does Catholicism differ from Calvinism as regards predestination?

Calvinism taught that some men were predestined to heaven no matter what they might do; others were predestined to hell no matter how they might try to serve God. But the Catholic Church teaches that God sincerely wills all men to be saved and that none should be lost. Anyone who does his best with all goodwill and dies sincerely repentant of his sins can certainly attain salvation through the merits of Christ. Every such man will have the necessary grace offered to him.

795. Does not the Catholic Church teach that grace is usually given through the Sacraments?

Grace is given directly in answer to prayer, but many very necessary graces are normally to be obtained only through the Sacraments instituted by Christ.

796. What is a Sacrament?

A visible rite or ceremony which signifies and confers grace. Thus Baptism is a visible rite. The pouring of the water on the forehead signifies the cleansing of the soul by the grace which the action bestows.

797. I trust in Christ and have no need of sacramental rites.

It is presumption to trust in Christ, yet to despise means established by Him and declared by Him to be necessary. The Christ in whom you trust certainly believed in such ceremonies. He anointed the blind man's eyes with saliva and earth, and He instituted the various Sacraments of the Church. If you study Scripture closely you will notice that the visible is again and again employed in the work of invisible sanctification. Your denial of sacramental and visible rites is opposed to the whole tenor of Scripture almost from beginning to end.

798. Who made the Sacraments?

Since there is no proportion between the visible action and the giving of interior grace of a supernatural character, it is evident that God alone could institute a Sacrament. It calls for His infinite power. Jesus Christ, therefore, at once God and man, instituted the Sacraments.

799. Why have you seven Sacraments, since Christ did not institute seven?

There are seven Sacraments precisely because Christ did institute seven. Had He not done so, there would not be seven. The Catholic Church emphatically denies that she has the power to institute a Sacrament. Far from instituting Sacraments, she has never even claimed the power to do so. From the very beginning Christians have always had seven, receiving them from the Apostles, who received them from Christ. Protestants were deprived of several of these Sacraments at the time of the Reformation. In the Church of England, however, many are returning to the doctrine of seven Sacraments as instituted by Christ, though of course their return to the doctrine cannot make all the Sacraments valid for them.

800. You connect Baptism with original sin?

Yes. Baptism was instituted by Christ for the destruction of original sin, and to restore that grace forfeited by our first parents which is absolutely necessary for the attaining of our eternal destiny. Christ Himself insisted that one must be born again of water and the Holy Ghost.

801. How can a man be born again?

Just as the soul is the life of the body, so grace is the life of the soul in the supernatural order. Now life is attained by birth. We are born into this earthly existence from our earthly parents. But we are born without the principle of God's grace which carries with it a right to a life of eternal happiness with God. Thus a man must be born into the life of grace by water and the Holy Spirit, if he wishes to possess the birth-right to eternal supernatural happiness.

802. Do you insist that Baptism is necessary to salvation?

Yes. Christ came to save men, and He has the right to dictate the conditions of salvation. If you offered me a fortune provided I would go to London via Suez, particularly insisting that I should go via Suez, it would be little use my saying, "Oh, I'll go via Panama—it's a much more sensible route." You would reply, "But I want you to go via Suez, or there will be no fortune." Now Christ distinctly commanded Baptism as a condition of salvation, and no arguments of men, who cannot save us, are of any avail against the authority of Christ. It is necessary to be baptized, or we shall never see God and rejoice in the happiness of Heaven.

803. *Then are all the unbaptized lost, whether it be their own fault or not?*

No one will ever be lost save through his own fault. Christ is God, and, as God, can work with secondary causes or without them. The ordinary means of salvation is by Baptism, and one who is convinced of the necessity of Baptism yet deliberately refuses to receive it cannot be saved. But God can supply the grace usually given by Baptism, and does so without the actual sacramental rite in two cases. If an unbaptized person dies a martyr for Christ he is credited with Baptism of blood. Baptism of desire counts for the man who repents of his sins and dies with the sincere will to do God's will, yet who, through no fault of his own, does not realize the necessity of actual Baptism by water, or is unable to receive it.

804. *Would you explain more fully this Baptism of desire?*

Every human being has a conscience which dictates a natural law of moral obligation at least when he comes to the age of reason. If a pagan knows nothing of Christianity, and is ignorant of it through no fault of his own, he can at least repent of his personal sins against his conscience, and desire to do the right thing. God gives every man the grace to do this much. Now we know that a man should receive Baptism. If the pagan knew this he would receive Baptism. This sincere desire to do all that God would require implicitly includes the desire of Baptism, and God takes the will for the deed, granting sanctifying grace. Thus such a pagan would be saved. As is clear, anyone who has attained to the use of reason would be capable of this Baptism of desire.

805. *Then an unbaptized infant cannot attain Heaven?*

An unbaptized infant cannot attain Heaven. Christ has said very definitely, "Unless one be born again . . . he cannot enter the Kingdom of God." Jn. III., 3. I am not more severe than Christ in my denial. He declares that the ordinary principle of life received by human generation is insufficient. We must receive an additional life of grace by baptismal rebirth. An unbaptized infant has received natural life only and had one birth only. If it dies without Baptism it has no claim to the supernatural happiness of Heaven.

806. *Is it not unjust that such a child should be lost through no fault of its own?*

Injustice is not involved in this question. When treating of original sin I explained how such a child lacks that supernatural grace which is not due to human nature, and without which no one can enter Heaven. Christ offers that supernatural grace to such of Adam's children as receive Baptism. It is His sheer goodness that He does so, and those who have been baptized have but to congratulate themselves. Unbaptized infants, who have never committed any personal sins, will never endure any actual and positive suffering. But they will be content with natural happiness only, and will not be able to complain that they do not possess the supernatural happiness of seeing God face to face, and being happy with His own supreme happiness. If I bestow a gift upon a beggar in the presence of another, that other cannot tell me that I am obliged in justice to give him a gift also. Since the fall of the human race, we are all beggars before God as regards supernatural happiness. I admit that it would be unjust if a child innocent of any personal sin had to suffer the miseries of Hell. But such is not Catholic doctrine, as I have explained.

807. *Do you suggest a special state for unbaptized infants?*

Yes. We call it the Limbo of unbaptized children. The word Limbo is derived from the Latin word *Limbus*, which means a bordering place. Limbo is an intermediate state of purely natural happiness. In that state unbaptized children will receive all the happiness proportionate to their natural capacity.

808. Why does not the Catholic Church baptize by immersion?

Such a method of Baptism, though valid, is not necessary. From the very beginning Baptism was administered both by immersion and by infusion or pouring water upon the forehead.

809. By relinquishing immersion you lose the significance of the original rite.

Immersion was never thought necessary in the Christian Church. After St. Peter's first sermon three thousand people were baptized, and it is most unlikely that it could have been by immersion, above all in the light of recent research into the water supply available in Jerusalem itself at that time. The Didache, or Teaching of the Twelve, written about the year 90, says, "Thus baptize . . . If you have not fresh water, baptize in other water. If you cannot do it in cold, use warm. If you have neither, pour out on the head water three times in the name of the Father and of the Son and of the Holy Spirit." Either form then is valid. If immersion were necessary, what would you do with bed-ridden invalids and the dying? Nor is the significance lost by pouring. The true significance is that grace washes the soul as water washes the body. The true sign of washing is retained by any true ablutions. Washing does not always imply the taking of a plunge-bath. Burial with Christ is signified by washing away the death of sin and the resurrection to the new life of grace. In any case Christ left the practical application of such matters to His Church, saying, "Whatsoever you shall bind upon earth shall be bound also in Heaven." Matt. XVIII., 18. And He promised to be with His Church, preserving her from any misuse of this power.

810. The Didache proves nothing.

It is evidence of the instructions circulated amongst Christians whilst St. John the Apostle was still living.

811. Scripture nowhere says that infants were baptized.

It nowhere says that they were not, and implicitly demands that they should be.

812. Do we not read only of adult baptisms in the New Testament?

No. We read of some adult baptisms, but they were not administered precisely because the subjects were adults, but because they happened to be converted as adults. Acts XV. commemorates the reception of two complete households into the Church by St. Paul, and we are not told that the adults only in those households were received. Christ told the Apostles to teach and baptize all nations, and the term all nations certainly includes men, women, and children. Again St. Paul tells us that Baptism is the Circumcision of Christians, and we know that Circumcision was administered to children. Col. 2, II. Or is the New Law to be less perfect than the Old, containing no purifying rite for infants? Your ideas are opposed to the whole tenor of Christianity. Christ is the second Adam. If the children of Adam are born subject to original sin and its penalties, so they can be born again of Christ into the life of grace. Or is Adam to be able to ruin all, yet Christ be unable to save any except adults? "What is of the flesh is flesh; what is of the spirit is spirit." Children by virtue of their natural birth are of the flesh, and Our Lord insists that unless one be born again he cannot enter the Kingdom of God. Do not be misled by the English translation, "Unless a man be born again." The original Greek does not use the word man in this text. It says, "Unless anyone be born again," and a child is someone.

813. *Christ Himself was not baptized in His infancy, but as an adult.*

Christ was baptized as an adult because only then did He institute this essential rite of the New Law. You could not expect Him to receive it before instituting it. Yet remember that He had received the rite of Circumcision which is figurative of the Baptism to be received by Christian children, and that rite He received in infancy.

814. *John told his converts to repent and be baptized.*

He was speaking to adults, and undoubtedly adults must repent of their personal sins before they can come to God. Yet children who are incapable of personal sin and repentance are born in original sin, to destroy which is the primary purpose of Baptism.

815. *The Bible says, "Believe and be baptized." How can children make an act of faith?*

The command to believe and be baptized was addressed to adult listeners only who, without faith, would not even see the necessity of Baptism. But children belong to their parents, and the parents may certainly give their children to God, professing faith on their behalf and promising to bring them up as Christians.

816. *Christ said, "Suffer little children to come to Me . . . for of such is the Kingdom of Heaven." He does not mention that they should be baptized.*

That text has no reference to Baptism. Christ's purpose there was to insist upon humility. He impressed the moral lesson that only such as cultivate the dispositions of a child before God will enter Heaven. But he never said that all children, even the unbaptized, will necessarily go to Heaven. He would contradict His own doctrine if He said that. And if the text had any reference to the Baptism of children at all, it would tell against your position. You have no right and no warrant to refuse baptismal regeneration to children who have had their natural birth, but not their supernatural rebirth.

817. *I was baptized in the Church of England. What is the religion of my Baptism?*

The Catholic religion. Baptism, if valid, makes a Christian. Now Catholicity is the only true form of Christianity. Therefore everyone validly baptized is radically a Catholic, even though he be unaware of it.

818. *Do you deny that Baptism can belong to the Anglican Church?*

Yes. All the Sacraments were instituted by Christ, and belong to Christ. Now Christ founded the Catholic Church and committed His religion to her keeping only. Therefore the Sacraments, without exception, belong to her. Not a valid Sacrament is proper to the Church of England or to any other Protestant Church. There is but one Lord, one Faith, one Baptism. If Baptism administered by an Anglican be valid, the subject is baptized *in* the Church of England but not *into* the Church of England. Christ instituted Baptism into the Catholic Church, not Baptism into the Church of England.

819. *If that be so Anglicans are Catholics after all, a thing which I have heard you repeatedly deny.*

In virtue of their valid Baptism they are radically Catholics. But despite affiliation with the Catholic Church by valid Baptism, one can exclude himself from the true and visible Church by conscious heresy or schism. If a child is baptized validly in the Church of England, that child is a Catholic and remains a Catholic until it comes to the age of reason and adopts heretical and schismatical Anglicanism for itself. For example, if I receive an adult Anglican together with his infant son into the Catholic Church, and it is certain that both have been baptized validly, I have to ask the father to abjure heresy and to profess formally his submission to the Catholic Church. But nothing is done as regards the infant son. It is simply taught Catholic doctrine and brought up as a Catholic. Its Baptism, although performed in the Anglican Church, made it a member of the Catholic Church. In that sense every valid Sacrament, even marriage, belongs to the Catholic Church. Usually, however, converts to the Catholic Church are baptized again conditionally, lest there should be any radical defect in their first submission to that rite.

820. What is Confirmation?

Confirmation is a Sacrament instituted by Jesus Christ as a complement to Baptism. As there is a sacrament of spiritual birth, so there is a sacrament of spiritual virility, conferring the grace required for growth in good will, fidelity, and Christian courage.

821. Does the New Testament say that Christ instituted this Sacrament?

Not explicitly. But we know that the Apostles conferred the gift of the Holy Spirit by the laying on of hands in a sacramental rite distinct from Baptism. Acts VIII., 14-17. They would not have confirmed the faithful by this distinct right unless they had been commissioned to do so by Christ. Christian tradition and the authoritative teaching of the Catholic Church are absolute guarantees that Confirmation is a genuine Christian Sacrament.

822. Is Confirmation absolutely necessary for salvation?

No. But it would be wrong and sinful to neglect it through indifference. Christ certainly did not institute this Sacrament needlessly. It confers graces of the utmost use in the spiritual life, rendering us stronger in the struggle for virtue, and therefore rendering our salvation the more assured.

823. What is Confession?

Confession is a Sacrament instituted by Jesus Christ by which those who fall into sin after Baptism may be restored to God's grace. Confession is called the Sacrament of Penance because it supposes that the recipient is truly repentant of his sins. It involves the admission of one's sins made to a duly approved Priest in order to obtain absolution.

824. All men are equal. How can a Priest set himself above others and presume to be their judge?

All men equally share a common humanity, but not all are equal in office and responsibility. Also no man could have the right to set himself above others in this matter. If Christ had not endowed His Priests with power to forgive sin they could not possess it. But He endowed them with this power, and they forgive sin not in their own name but in the name of Christ. A criminal has to answer to the state for his crimes against civil law. How then can a fellow citizen act as judge and pass sentence upon him? In his official capacity he is delegated by the state and acts in the name of the state. Now Christ died to pay the price of our sins and He surely has the right to say how forgiveness shall be applied. We cannot deny the right of Christ to administer forgiveness through agents of His own choosing, nor can we insist that He must forgive us on our conditions whilst we ignore His conditions.

825. We Protestants believe that God alone can forgive sin.

And that is the Catholic teaching also. But the question concerns the way in which God has chosen to administer that forgiveness. We Catholics add that God can delegate His power if He wishes, just as the supreme authority in the state can delegate a judge to administer justice. Would you deny to God that power?

326. But can you prove that God did delegate that power to men?

Yes. Christ was God, and in St. Jn. XX., 21-23 we read these remarkable words, "As the Father hath sent Me I also send you. When He said this He breathed on them; and He said to them: Receive ye the Holy Ghost. Whose sins you shall forgive, they are forgiven them; and whose sins you shall retain, they are retained." Now Christ's mission was to destroy sin, and He gave that same mission to His Apostles. Knowing that their merely human power as men was quite insufficient, He gave them a special communication of the Holy Spirit for this special work. To say that Christ did not confer a true power to forgive sin is to rob the whole ceremony and the words of Christ of any real meaning. And it was obviously a power to be exercised, Christians applying to the Apostles for forgiveness.

327. Give me one instance where any Apostle ever forgave sin.

St. Paul certainly exercised the power of binding and loosing from sin and the effects of sin in the case of the incestuous Corinthian. In 1 Cor. V., 3, we find him saying, "I have already judged him that hath done so"; and in 2 Cor. II., 10, he justifies his forgiveness of the repentant man by saying, "If I have pardoned anything, I have done it in the person of Christ."

328. I believe that the Apostles received the power, but it was for them only and has not been handed on in the Church.

Christ commissioned His Church to teach all nations till the end of the world. The Apostles had to hand on all essential powers to their successors. And the conditions of salvation must be the same for us as for the first Christians. If those subject to the Apostles had to obtain forgiveness from their fellow men, there is no reason why we should be exempt. We share the same privileges as the early Christians and must have the same obligations. Till the Reformation all Christians went to confession. In the 4th century we find St. Ambrose defending Confession by saying that if a man can forgive sin by baptizing, he claims nothing greater when he claims the power to forgive sin through the Sacrament of Penance. That Priests possessed such power was Christian doctrine in his time and is still the doctrine of the Catholic Church. The Greek Church, which broke away from the Catholic Church in the ninth century, has retained this Apostolic practice. Protestantism gave up the practice in the 16th century because it was uncomfortable and mortifying. But once admit such a principle, and one could abolish every uncomfortable commandment of God.

329. Forgiveness through the mediation of a Priest is opposed to the doctrine that Christ is the only Mediator.

One Mediator redeemed us. The Priest does not redeem us; he is but an accredited agent of the one Mediator. Confession is but one way of applying the mediation of Christ to men even as Baptism is another. And if Baptism is a Sacrament for the destruction of sin which we ourselves did not commit but which we inherit from Adam, another Sacrament is most fitting for the destruction of sins which we do personally commit after our Baptism. Christ certainly thought so, and instituted the Sacrament of Confession. If you believe in one Mediator, so do we; but we listen to that one Mediator and do as He has commanded us.

330. What is wrong with confessing our sins directly to God in prayer?

Since it is God who has been offended, God has the right to lay down the conditions of forgiveness. You cannot insist that God must forgive you on your own conditions. And Christ certainly did not give His Priests power to forgive sin knowing that no one would have to seek forgiveness from Priests at all.

831. Is it possible to secure forgiveness without confessing to a Priest?

Catholics who are unable to find a Priest are forgiven if they make an act of perfect contrition or sorrow, but such an act supposes at least the intention of going to Confession when the opportunity presents itself. For perfect sorrow supposes the will to do God's will. Protestants and other non-Catholics can also secure forgiveness by perfect sorrow, if they are not responsible for their ignorance of the law of Christ. For lack of knowledge would be a condition of true sorrow in those who do not comply with the actual law. Such people would go to Confession if they realized the obligation. But who can know that he has such perfect contrition? Perfect contrition implies a hatred of the sin to be forgiven, not from any motive, but because it has offended God. It implies intense sorrow for having committed it; the will to make full reparation of the harm done; and the firm purpose to avoid committing it again. What certainty has one that he possesses such dispositions? Is his sorrow supernatural? Is his conviction of forgiveness merely self-persuasion; a case of the wish being father to the thought? He has no definite and personal revelation that he is forgiven. Catholics who receive sacramental absolution are at least not left in such doubts and anxieties, for even though their sorrow be not as perfect as it should be, the Sacrament itself will supply for certain defects.

832. But people can simulate sorrow, or deceive the Priest by telling him only so much as they wish.

Catholics know that they cannot deceive God. God uses the Priest as His agent or instrument. Even though the penitent have not supreme sorrow, yet he must be genuinely sorry and is obliged to confess all grave sins. If he deceives the Priest then, although the Priest utters the words of absolution in good faith, God does not apply the effects of those words to the soul. A Catholic goes to Confession when he wants his sins forgiven. He knows that if he merely pretends sorrow or deceives the Priest in serious matters, not only are none of his sins forgiven, but he goes away with an additional mortal sin of sacrilege. He does not go to Confession for the sheer joy of adding to his sins. If he is not sorry and does not intend to make a genuine Confession, he just stays away and goes on with his sins. Only when sincerely desirous of recovering God's grace does he present himself in the confessional. He is not so foolish as to go through the farce you suggest.

833. Then a Priest can absolve only on certain conditions?

Yes. The penitent must tell fully and sincerely all his serious sins; he must be truly sorry for having committed them; determine to try to avoid them for the future; and promise to make good any injury to others whether by defamation of character or by theft of money or goods.

834. Do not Catholics sin because they know they can get absolution in Confession?

Does a man break his leg because he knows that a doctor can set it? Catholics regard sin as a very great evil and no Catholic thinks that he is morally free to commit any sin, with or without Confession. If he does commit sin he knows that he can get it forgiven provided he repents and determines to try to serve God for the future. Above all he knows that Confession gives him no permission at all to commit the same sins again, and if he has the intention of doing so he knows that the absolution is null and void. Might I ask whether Protestants can sin because they know that they can get forgiveness without Confession? Or is there no forgiveness for Protestants?

835. *Confession is like washing a child and letting it play in the mud again.*

It is not. The Church washes the child and forbids it to play in the mud again. But if it does play in the mud again in spite of the prohibition, of course she is prepared to wash it again if it be truly sorry—as any true mother would do. If readiness to forgive is to be the cause of further sins, what will you say to God who declares that if a man's sins be as scarlet they shall be as white as snow provided he repents?

836. *Even though the Church forbids it, I know a Catholic who does confess and sin again.*

He does not sin again because of his Confession; nor does his fall say that he was not truly repentant when he confessed. Christ said something about forgiving seventy times seven. How often would you forgive? And isn't it better to try, fail through weakness, and repent, than to abandon all efforts to return to God's grace?

837. *But if Confession does not stop sin what is the good of it?*

Confession is an immense help in the prevention of further sin. Remember that Christ did not institute this Sacrament precisely to prevent further sin, but to forgive sin once it has been unhappily committed. To prevent sin there are other Sacraments, and other means such as good example, religious instruction, prayer, and the grace of God. But if, in spite of these helps, a man falls through strong temptation, as anyone is likely to do, it is a very great good that his sin can be forgiven.

838. *It is easy to confess to a fellow man and get forgiveness. But it is not so convenient to remain in humble doubt.*

The humiliation of Confession is an inconvenience not found in Protestantism, and from that point of view Protestantism is easier. On the other hand Christ was too merciful to leave us without some definite assurance of forgiveness, and He gave us a very definite Sacrament to alleviate our anxiety.

839. *Did not Priests invent Confession in order to obtain the money required for absolution?*

No money is ever paid for absolution. If absolution cannot be given, $10,000 would not obtain it. If it can be given, it cannot be refused, and it would be mortal sin on the part of any Priest to suggest payment for it. Moreover, if any man came to me and offered to purchase forgiveness from me I would tell him that he was suggesting a mortally sinful procedure, and send him away with his money and without absolution unless he retracted his ideas and repented of his sin. In that case I would absolve him, without of course touching a penny of his money. Meantime no Priest would be so foolish as to invent Confession. Priests would gladly be free from the burdensome duty of sitting for hours in the confessional. Had Christ not imposed it, and Priests could prove Confession unnecessary, they would be the first to demand its abolition.

840. *Do not Priests use the confessional to obtain all domestic and state secrets?*

No. Catholics tell their own sins only. The Priest finds it hard enough to listen patiently to that much, without wishing to hear all household secrets, nor will he allow penitents to speak of other people's misdeeds. In any case no Priest can make use of knowledge acquired whilst hearing Confessions. One of the strictest laws of the Church obliges him never to betray what he hears in the confessional.

841. *Did not the Lateran Council in 1215 first oblige auricular Confession?*

No. It decreed that Catholics must go to Confession at least once a year, merely specifying how often one must go. If the idea of auricular Confession were then introduced for the first time, and Christians were not used to it, there would have been an uproar of protest throughout the whole Church. But all Christians were perfectly familiar with auricular Confession, and no protest arose.

842. Do Priests themselves go to Confession?

Of course. The obligation falls upon them as upon the laity. Nor can any Priest give himself absolution. He must kneel at the feet of some other Priest in order to secure forgiveness.

843. Who hears the Confession of the Pope?

Any Priest to whom the Pope chooses to confess.

844. Did not St. Augustine warn Priests that the hearing of Confessions is dangerous to virtue?

The only reference that remark of danger has to the Sacrament of Confession is to prove that St. Augustine knew quite well of its existence. All he desired to do was to insist upon the virtue required in the Priest who undertakes the duty. Even so, a warning against a possible danger does not suggest that Priests yield to that danger. One could give a lecture upon the danger of drink without suggesting that the listeners were subject to its influence.

845. Is it not demoralizing for young girls to be asked by the Priest whether they have been guilty of improper behavior?

Priests have no obligation to examine the conscience of the penitent. The penitent must do that. If a young girl, or anybody for that matter, has been guilty of improper conduct, then such conduct is demoralizing. But the confession of that sin, sorrow for it, and the resolution not to commit it again, is not demoralizing.

846. When will Catholics realize that Priests are sinful beings like themselves?

All Catholics know that Priests are human beings who need Baptism and redemption by Christ just as everyone else. But they also know that they are not acting in their ordinary capacity as human beings, and that the value of absolution does not depend upon the personal worthiness of the Priest. Meantime God alone knows whether men, including Priests, are actually and personally in a state of sin.

847. When will they see the folly of confessing to such men?

Only when they completely forget their Christian faith, for Christ Himself appointed this means of forgiveness.

848. We Protestants regard Confession as an intolerable burden.

Why should you worry about a thing which does not affect you? Let Catholics, who do go to Confession, do the worrying. They find it full of compensating consolations. Your only worry should be your ignoring of the words of Christ as recorded in St. John XX., 21-23.

849. The shame of having to tell their sins keeps Catholics away from their Church and from Christ.

How do you know? Catholics know that God commanded Confession as a means of recovering His friendship and that for this the price is negligible. They know that shame did not keep them from committing the sin as it should have done, and they will not let false shame keep them from confessing it. They know that they fully deserve the humiliation involved; but it is better to manifest it to one man who is strictly obliged to forgive it and forget it, than to have it manifested on the Last Day, when every man's unforgiven crimes will be made manifest to the bitter humiliation of those who died with unrepented grave sins. They know that if they feel too ashamed to tell it, they have but to ask the Priest to help them, and that he will do so in such a way that they can acknowledge what is required without any offense against delicacy. Their sins have offended God, not the Priest, and no Priest has any reason to feel hurt personally or to exhibit anger. Also, far from despising a penitent, a Priest rather admires the humility and sincerity of those who confess their sins with deep sorrow. The difficulties of Confession are imagined by those who have never been to Confession.

850. Can a Priest forgive blasphemy against the Holy Spirit, which Christ says shall not be forgiven in this world or the next?

There is no sin too great to be forgiven provided one sincerely repents of it. Christ really referred to evil dispositions of soul which are so hardened that one will lack the will to repent. Blasphemy against the Holy Spirit is not blasphemy as commonly understood, but a determined resistance to the very grace of the Holy Spirit which is meant to save us. Thus the Pharisees who saw the miracles of Christ could not deny them to be miracles; yet rather than yield to the grace being offered them, they said that Christ wrought them with the help of the devil, and not by God. A man who rejects the very means God adopts to convert him is little likely to make good use of other graces offered by God, and Our Lord warns us very strongly to beware of sinning against the light, since it seldom ends in repentance. Yet even such a man with the help of special grace could repent of his bad dispositions and thus be converted and forgiven. Any unforgivableness, therefore, is on account of a man's bad dispositions, not on account of the nature of the sin. There is no absolutely unforgivable sin such as cannot be forgiven even though a man repents.

851. Will a Catholic who is convicted of murder go to Heaven if he confesses his sin to a Priest?

If he has confessed his sin sincerely and with genuine sorrow, his sin will be forgiven and his soul saved.

852. What of the thief who is not discovered by the police?

The Priest orders him to make restitution, giving back to the owner the money or goods stolen. Only when he promises to do so will he receive absolution for his sin before God. But the penitent is not obliged to give himself up to the police. It is their business to prove the crime and arrest him.

853. Will the Priest tell the police or is it a sacred secret?

The Priest will certainly not tell the police. He can never act upon information submitted to him for the purpose of absolution before God.

854. Is not such a Priest an enemy to the state?

No. State laws control men in their capacity as citizens of the state. But a Priest does not hear confessions in his capacity as a citizen of the state. He is acting, not as a human being, but as an agent of God. You might as well oblige God, since He knows all things, to reveal all crimes to the police. The Priest would never have known had he not been doing a duty in the name of God. In any case, he is obliged by both the natural and positive laws of morality in this matter to die rather than reveal such things.

855. What is the Holy Eucharist?

It is a Sacrament instituted by Christ, in which Christ Himself is truly, really, and substantially present that He may be offered in the Holy Mass as the Sacrifice of the New Law, and also that He may be received by us in Holy Communion for the spiritual refreshment of our souls.

856. Are there any signs in the Host proving that He is bodily present?

No. It is a mystery of faith. All external appearances remain as before consecration, but the substance of bread and the substance of wine are changed into the substance of Our Lord's body and blood. The reason why we believe is not in the Host as such, but in God. He has revealed this truth, and we believe because He must know and could not tell an untruth.

857. Did not the Jews think that they were asked to eat the very body of Christ? Yet He refuted them by saying that His body would ascend to Heaven and that the flesh profits nothing. Jn. VI., 63-64.

When Christ promised that He would give His very flesh to eat, the Jews protested because they imagined a natural and cannibalistic eating of Christ's body. Christ refuted this notion of the manner in which His flesh was to be received by saying that He would ascend into Heaven, not leaving His body in its human form upon earth. But He did not say that they were not to eat His actual body. He would thus contradict Himself, for a little earlier He had said, "My flesh is meat indeed and My blood is drink indeed." VI., 56. He meant, therefore, "You will not be asked to eat My flesh in the horrible and natural way you think, for My body as you see it with your eyes will be gone from this earth. Yet I shall leave My flesh and blood in another and supernatural way which your natural and carnal minds cannot understand. The carnal or fleshly judgment profits nothing. I ask you therefore to have faith in Me and to trust Me. It is the spirit of faith which will enable you to believe, not your natural judgment." Then the Gospel goes on to say that many would not believe, and walked no more with Him; just as many to-day will not believe, and walk no more with the Catholic Church. According to the doctrine of the Catholic Church Christ's body is ascended into Heaven. But by its substance, independently of all the laws of space which affect substance through accidental qualities, this body is present in every consecrated Host.

858. We Protestants believe that Christ's body is really present in the Eucharist, but not by transubstantiation.

The majority of Protestants believe that His body is really absent. Those who do say that they believe in His real Presence yet deny transubstantiation illogically admit an effect yet deny the only process by which it can truly occur. If there be no transubstantiation or conversion of the substance of bread into the substance of Christ's body, then the substance of bread remains after consecration, and it is bread and not the body of Christ. People make a kind of bogey of transubstantiation as foolishly as a man would do somewhat similarly if he admitted a railway from New York to San Francisco, yet refused to admit that it could be called the transcontinental railway.

859. The Apostles' Creed, the Athanasian, and the Nicene do not mention transubstantiation. There is no record of such a doctrine until 1564 when Pius IV. put it into his creed. Are we to believe the early Christians, or the doctrine of a thousand years later?

The doctrine is not in the three Creeds you mention. But they do not contain the whole of Christian doctrine. They are partial statements insisting upon certain doctrines against special errors of those times. It is true that Pius IV. included the doctrine in his profession of faith, but you are wrong when you say that there was no mention of the doctrine till then. In 1551, 13 years earlier, the Council of Trent taught the doctrine explicitly. In 1274, 290 years earlier, the 2nd Council of Lyons insisted upon the admission of transubstantiation by the Greeks as a condition of return to the Catholic Church. In 1215, 349 years earlier, the 4th Lateran Council consecrated the word transubstantiation as expressing correctly the Christian doctrine of Christ's real presence by conversion of the substance of bread into the substance of His body. In 1079, 500 years earlier, Berengarius declared in his retraction, "I acknowledge that the bread is substantially changed into the substance of Christ's body." Everybody who possessed the true Christian faith, until this year, 1079, believed in the substantial change, and there was no need to insist upon the word, since no one denied the nature of the change. In the 4th century all the great Fathers and writers admitted that by consecration bread was changed into Our Lord's very body. Ignatius, Bishop of Antioch, who died about 107 A.D., wrote, "Heretics abstain from the Eucharist because they do not confess the Eucharist to be that very flesh of Jesus Christ which suffered for us." And that doctrine is all that is expressed by transubstantiation. At the Last Supper Christ said, "This is my body which is given for you." Lk. XXII., 19. Now He either gave them His body or He did not. But He gave them His Body, for we dare not say, "Lord although you say, 'This is my body,' it is certainly not your body." However it was not His body according to appearances and visible qualities, and it could have been His body only according to substance. Therefore Our Lord first taught this doctrine of substantial change at least implicitly.

860. *The elements do not change, for there is no chemical difference after consecration.*

Which elements do not change? In every material thing there are two sets of elements quite distinct—substance and qualities. And no man has ever seen substance; he has seen qualities only. Thus I see the squareness of a block of iron, but it can become round, still remaining iron. I can feel its hardness, though it can become soft in the furnace, the substance being unchanged. If it be black, it can become red; if it be cold, it can become hot; if it be heavy, by great heat I can render it a vapor. The qualities, then, differ from the substance, or we could not change one without changing the other. And if we can change qualities without changing substance, God can certainly change substance without changing qualities. Any chemical differences are dependent upon qualities. Granted the permanence of the same accidental qualities the same chemical reactions will be apparent. Father Faber, whilst yet an Anglican, well said, "I am worried about the Roman doctrine because, whatever may be said of the proofs for it, I do not see how any man can disprove it. If they say that the substance changes, but that all appearances remain the same, then they say that something changes of which no man has any experience and yet which reason must postulate as the reality underlying all appearances and separate from them." When you say that the elements do not change their chemical properties, I simply reply that the elements of external qualities do not change their chemical properties, and that no Catholic has ever imagined that they do. But the substance underlying those external appearances certainly does change. The fact that qualities remain unaltered is a fact of experience; the fact that the substance changes is revealed by God, and cannot be known in any other way. Yet is it not more than sufficiently guaranteed when God says so?

861. *We have only the word of the Priest for the fact.*

No Catholic Priest would himself believe it were it not the doctrine of Christ. It would be the height of folly to believe it without solid evidence that Christ had taught it. God created substance and qualities, and we cannot deny to Him perfect control over them and ability to change them at His pleasure. And when Christ says, "This is My body," we have to accuse Him of falsehood or else admit that it is His body not according to the senses, but according to the underlying substance which is imperceptible to the senses.

862. Is Christ's body anatomically and physiologically present?

Christ's real body is present. Anatomical structure and physiological modifications belong to qualities possessed by substance. After the consecration we have the substance of Christ's body present without any external manifestation of His anatomical or physiological appearances, and the qualities of bread remaining as the object of sense perception without any substance of bread. That substance of bread has been converted into the substance of Christ's body. And as substance is the basic reality, we rightly say that the Blessed Sacrament is the very body of Christ.

863. Is Christ's body subject to processes of digestion?

The substance of Christ's body is not subject to processes of digestion or to any chemical reactions. The qualities of bread of course behave in their normal way, undergoing a change as they are affected by digestion. Our Lord's substantial presence ceases as these qualities cease to retain those characteristics proper to bread.

864. If poison were present before consecration would it be safe to consume the Eucharist?

No. People would be poisoned. The Church has never taught that poison could be converted into Christ's body, and in any case you are dealing with chemical activities proper to qualities, and not proper to substance as such. All such objections are based upon notions excluded by Catholic teaching. And it is of little use to refute what the Catholic Church does not teach.

865. Christ is in Heaven. How can you put Him in the tabernacle?

No Catholic denies that Christ is continually present in Heaven. He is not so present in the Eucharist that He ceases to be present in Heaven. He is in Heaven according to His natural though glorified form. The same Christ is in the Eucharist substantially, but not in the same way as He is present in Heaven. Substance as such abstracts from limitations of place and space. Locality directly belongs to the qualities of bread which remain after consecration, and indirectly only to the substantial presence of Christ's body underlying those apparent qualities.

866. Is not the Priest who can accomplish this thing akin to the miracle man of primitive religions?

No. The miracle-man claimed to perform his wonders by his own marvelous powers. The Priest says that the power of Christ effects the change in the Eucharist, and that he himself is but an instrument employed by Christ, and taking a very secondary place. The miracle-man depended upon the superstition and credulity of the bystanders. The Priest forbids superstition and credulity, and insists upon faith in God, a supernatural faith based upon rational foundations. The miracle-man attributed preternatural effects to natural causes, whether spiritual or material. The Catholic Church attributes supernatural effects (a vast difference!) to a supernatural cause. The miracle-man could never prove any direct commission from God. The Catholic Church can prove her direct commission from Him to the satisfaction of every intelligent man willing to inquire into her credentials with sincerity. The miracle-man tried to perform things wholly unbecoming to God, by means which have no resemblance to those relied upon by the Catholic Church, and for a purpose and end totally different.

867. *I heard you say that Christ is offered in the Eucharist as the Sacrifice of the New Law.*

That is true. That offering of Christ in the Eucharist is known as the Mass, and the Mass is the Sacrifice of the New Law.

868. *There is only one sacrifice for Christians—that of Calvary.*

The Sacrifice of Calvary was a Sacrifice not only for Christians but for the whole human race from the moment of the first sin. But whilst the death of Christ upon the Cross was the one great absolute Sacrifice, the Mass is a true and relative Sacrifice applying to the souls of men the fruits of Calvary. Anyway the doctrine which denies that the Mass is the true Sacrifice in the Christian dispensation is simply anti-scriptural.

869. *How do you prove that the Sacrifice of the Mass is Scriptural?*

By religion we honor God, and the chief and highest form of worship has ever been by the offering of sacrifice. Now God demanded continual sacrifices of various kinds from the very beginning of the human race until the coming of Christ, and it is not likely that the Christian and more perfect religion would lack a continual and regular offering of the highest act of religion. All the various sacrifices of the Jewish dispensation represented and prefigured the Sacrifice of Christ on Calvary, and derived all their value by anticipation from His death upon the Cross. And if the Jews had to honor God by regular sacrifices, so too must Christians in the higher and more perfect New Law. But there is this difference. Whilst the Jewish sacrifices were anticipations of the Sacrifice of Christ on Calvary, the Mass is a recollection and constant application of that one great Sacrifice to the souls of men.

870. *It is little use your telling us what ought to be, unless you can prove it as a fact from Scripture.*

I can do so. The Old Testament predicts that Christ will offer a true sacrifice to God in bread and wine—that He will use those elements. And this prediction is every bit as clear as the prediction that He will also offer Himself upon the Cross. Thus Gen. XIV., 18, tells us that Melchisedech, King of Salem, was a Priest, and that he offered sacrifice under the form of bread and wine. Now Ps. 109 predicts most clearly that Christ will be a Priest according to the order of Melchisedech, *i. e.,* offering a sacrifice under the forms of bread and wine. We must, then, look for some form of sacrifice differing from that of Calvary, for the Crucifixion was not a Sacrifice under the forms of bread and wine. You may say that Christ fulfilled the prediction at the Last Supper, but that the rite was not to be continued. However, that admits that the rite was truly sacrificial—and the fact is that it has been continued in exactly the same sense. It was predicted that it would continue. After foretelling the rejection of the Jewish priesthood, the Prophet Malachy predicts a new sacrifice to be offered in every place. "From the rising of the sun even to the going down my name is great among the Gentiles: and in every place there is sacrifice and there is offered to my name a clean oblation." Mal. I., 10-11. The Sacrifice of Calvary took place in one place only. We must look for a sacrifice apart from Calvary, one offered in every place under the forms of bread and wine. The Mass is that Sacrifice.

871. *Were all the conditions of a sacrifice verified in the Last Supper? And are they still verified in the Mass?*

Yes, to both questions. For a true sacrifice we need a Priest, an altar, a victim, and a covenant with God. Christ was truly the great High Priest, and He gave the power of Priests to His Apostles, commissioning them to do repeatedly as He Himself had done in their presence. "Do this," He said, "in commemoration of me." The power was to persevere in the Church, even as Malachy had predicted. As victim, Christ offered Himself at the Last Supper. Taking bread and wine He said, "This is My body . . . This is My blood . . . *As often* as you shall eat this bread and drink this chalice, you shall show the death of the Lord until He come." 1 Cor. XI., 24-26. The separate forms of consecration represented the separation of His body and blood when He ratified the Sacrifice by His death on the Cross next day. The victim, then, is Christ under the appearances of bread and wine representatively separated. This does not interfere with the value of Calvary, for Christ's real death occurred there, and without it this representative function would be useless. Continuously through the ages the Sacrifice of the Mass has been offered daily in the Catholic Church, and is to-day offered in every place from the rising of the sun even to its going down, as Malachy predicted.

As for the altar, years after the death of Christ St. Paul said, "We have an altar whereof they have no power to eat who serve the tabernacle." Heb. XIII., 10. Finally, there is the covenant with God. "This chalice is the new testament in my blood," said Christ. 1 Cor. XI., 25. It had legal documentary value in the sight of God. The Catholic Church alone fulfills Scripture in the Sacrifice of the Mass.

872. Christ's blood is not shed in the Mass, and without shedding of blood there is no remission.

Christ offered Himself with the shedding of blood on Calvary. Without that shedding of blood there would be no remission of sin. Yet since the Mass is but an application of Calvary with its shedding of blood there is no real difficulty. There is a difficulty for one who denies the Sacrifice of the Mass, for without that there is no fulfillment of Malachy's prophecy that there will be offered in every place a clean oblation, without shedding of blood, from the rising to the setting of the sun.

873. Did not Pope Innocent III. in 1208 first teach the dogma that the Mass is a sacrifice?

No. He merely insisted upon the doctrine which had always been held by Christians that the Mass is a sacrifice in the true sense of the Gospel teachings. If the idea was not Catholic doctrine until 1208, why did St. Irenaeus in the year 180, over 1000 years earlier, write that Christ commanded His disciples to offer sacrifice to God, not because God needed it but that they might become more pleasing to God? And he goes on to show that the continued offering of the Eucharistic Sacrifice is the fulfillment of the prophecy of Malachy which manifestly predicted that the Jewish people would cease to offer to God, and that a new and pure sacrifice would be offered to Him in every place by the Gentiles. Adv. Haer. IV., 17, 5. If Irenaeus, Bishop of Lyons, could write that in the 2nd century, it is of little use to assert that Catholics did not believe the Mass to be a true sacrifice until the year 1208.

874. Catholics speak of the Mass as if it meant the real death of Christ, and calculate its mathematical value!

No Catholic has ever believed that Christ is really slain in the Mass. They have never gone beyond the words of Scripture, "As often as you do this you shall show the death of the Lord until He come." Nor did any theologians attempt a mathematical calculation as to the efficacy of the Mass. They knew that mathematics could never express it. The theological value of the Mass is a perfectly legitimate question for any man to ask who seeks deeper knowledge of Christian doctrine.

875. According to Cardinal Vaughan, Catholics think the Mass better than Calvary!

That sweeping statement is not justified by Cardinal Vaughan's qualified doctrine. "So far as the practical effects upon the soul are concerned," he writes, "the Holy

Mass has in some senses the advantage over Calvary." And he was quite right. No Catholics think that the Mass in itself is better than Calvary, for it is Calvary re-applied, depending upon and deriving all its value from Calvary. "As often as you do this," said Christ, "you shall show the death of the Lord until He come." And that death took place upon the Cross. Yet the Mass has this advantage that whilst the death of Christ upon the Cross occurred in one place only and before a few people, Calvary re-applied in the Mass can occur in many places and before multi-tudes.

876. Christ offered the Last Supper in the evening. Why do you not have Mass in the evening instead of the morning?

It is not essential that Mass should be offered in the evening, but simply that the Mass should be offered. Mass in the evening of course would be quite valid. But the Church, making use of her God-given power to regulate all that pertains to disciplinary matters, has decreed that it should be celebrated in the morning. This law is in honor of the fact that Christ rose from the dead in the early morning, thus completing His work of redemption.

877. Why does the Catholic Church give Communion under one kind only?

For many grave reasons. This custom inculcates in a practical way that Christ is completely present under either kind. It excludes the heretical doctrine that it is absolutely necessary for Communion to partake of the chalice. It removes the danger of irreverence to the Precious Blood by upsetting or spilling it. It spares the recipients the danger of infection by their drinking from the same chalice. It enables a Priest to celebrate Mass and distribute Communion without keeping the congregation an undue length of time, a reason which has particular force in the Catholic Church where hundreds go to Communion at early Masses. It secures uniformity of practice throughout the Church, for whilst flour is easily obtained for the purposes of bread, and easily kept, wine cannot be secured in sufficient quantity in many countries, above all in foreign missions.

878. Jesus gave Himself under the forms of bread and wine. You are not justified in withholding the cup from the laity.

The fact that the Catholic Church does so is sufficient proof that she is justified in doing so. However, let us view the theology of the matter. Jesus gave Himself under both kinds, yet He was completely present in either kind. He who receives either kind receives the whole Christ. In any case, Christ being risen dies no more. It is not possible now to separate Christ's body and blood in actual fact. Wherever Christ is, there He is whole and entire. He is wholly under the appearances of bread and wholly under the appearances of wine. In receiving the Blessed Sacrament under the form of bread the communicant receives the Blood of Christ also. In receiving under the form of wine alone he would receive the Body also. There is no possibility of receiving the Body of Christ without the Blood of Christ.

879. Whatever the theory may be, I object to the anti-Christian practice.

The practice is not anti-Christian. Reception under one kind only is quite suf-ficient for Holy Communion. Our Lord said simply, "If any man eat of this bread he shall live forever, for the bread that I will give is My flesh for the life of the world." Jn. VI., 52. In the early Church Communion was at times given to little children by giving them a few drops of the consecrated wine only. The martyrs would often take into the arena with them the Blessed Sacrament under the form of bread only, wrapped in linen, to give themselves Communion before death. The practice is quite in accordance with the doctrine of St. Paul, "Whosoever shall eat *or* drink unworthily shall be guilty of the body *and* of the blood of the Lord." 1 Cor. XI., 27.

880. *"Eat OR drink" is not in my Protestant Bible.*

It is not in the Authorized Version, but you will find it in the Revised Version. Protestant scholars admit that the substitution of *and* for *or* in the Authorized Version was an inexcusable mistranslation of the Greek for polemical purposes.

881. *So the Priest always has the wine, but does not give it to the laity!*

The Priest does not always receive under both kinds. If for some reason he cannot celebrate Mass, yet desires to receive Holy Communion, he receives under the form of bread only, just as any other communicant. If he celebrates Mass, he must consecrate both kinds for the sake of the Sacrifice, the separate consecrations being necessary for the representation of Christ's death by the shedding of His blood on the Cross. Having consecrated under both kinds the Priest must consume both kinds. But even in doing so, he receives no more than the laity, for both Priest and lay communicant receive the complete Christ, and more than the complete Christ cannot be received. But your objection proceeds from a complete misunderstanding of the nature of the Eucharist. The idea of the officiating Priest having a "drink of wine" which is denied to the laity does great injury to the reverence due to the Presence of Christ, and is utterly absurd. About an egg-cup full of wine is used in the celebration of Mass, and in any case if a Priest did merely want a drink of wine there is no need for him to vest himself elaborately and spend half an hour saying Mass in order to have it.

882. *Could a Priest be in mortal sin yet give the true body of Christ?*

A Priest commits a grave sin of sacrilege if he celebrates Mass whilst he himself is in a state of mortal sin. But that would not render the consecration invalid. The words of consecration have their effect quite apart from the state of the celebrant's soul. He consecrates in virtue of his priesthood, not in virtue of his being in a state of grace or of sin. It is his loss if he be not in God's grace, but the communicant suffers no loss in receiving Communion from his hands. It is the priesthood of Christ in him that consecrates, and that is not less efficacious because a Priest sins personally.

883. *At what age can children receive Holy Communion?*

Any baptized child could receive Holy Communion with profit. The early Christians frequently gave Communion even to infants. However, the Church for wise reasons requires in her present discipline that children should have attained sufficient reason to be able, after due instruction, to know that the Blessed Sacrament differs from ordinary food, and that by receiving it they are receiving Christ.

884. *Has a child of seven sufficient reason?*

As a rule, yes. The law of the Church to receive Holy Communion once a year obliges all Catholics who have come to the use of reason, and this law begins to oblige from about the age of seven. The average child of seven certainly has enough sense to realize that the reception of the Holy Eucharist is a religious act. It can know who Our Lord is, and the fact that He is present in the Blessed Sacrament. Such a child is quite capable of approaching with sincere faith and devotion.

885. *You have spoken often of Priests. Do you regard their ordination as a Sacrament?*

Among the seven Sacraments is that of Holy Orders. Its institution by Christ, its visible rite, and the fact that it gives grace are all clearly shown in Scripture. Thus St. Paul says that Christ "gave Apostles, Evangelists, Pastors, etc., for the work of the ministry." Eph. IV., 12. Ordaining by the imposition of hands is often mentioned, and Timothy was told not to neglect the grace of God "which is in thee by the imposition of hands." I. Tim. IV., 14. Rightly ordained Priests alone have the right to teach the Gospel authoritatively and carry on its sacred ministry.

886. *Does not St. Peter say that all Christians are a holy priesthood?*

Yes, and in a certain sense it is true. Baptism implies a certain consecration to God, and the obligation to offer the sacrifice of praise by a sincere life of prayer and of good works. He points out that, as the Jews were a chosen race, so the baptized are the chosen race to-day. But the Jews had in addition specially chosen men consecrated as Priests among themselves. Thus, whilst Christians are a chosen race now, offering the sacrifice of praise and of a pure life to God, certain men must be chosen from among them to offer the special Sacrifice of Christ's Body and Blood, and to forgive sins. In this sense not all Christians are Priests.

887. *You include marriage among the Sacraments?*

Yes. Every valid marriage between baptized Christians constitutes the Sacrament of Matrimony.

888. *Christ did not institute marriage. It existed long before His advent to this world.*

Prior to Christ it existed as a matrimonial contract, but Christ elevated it to the dignity of a Sacrament of the New Law. Christ therefore instituted matrimony as a Sacrament. He blessed marriage by His presence at Cana, and declared its indissolubility when He said, "What God has joined, let not man put asunder." Henceforth, what was formerly a union by human contract was to be regarded by Christians as sealed by God in a new and special way.

889. *How can marriage be a Sacrament?*

A Sacrament is a visible rite instituted by Christ for the signifying and giving of grace. Marriage is a visible rite, witnessed by men. It has been elevated by Christ to sacramental dignity. It signifies something very sacred, the union of Christ with His Church, as St. Paul tells us. Eph. V., 22-33. There is but one Christ and one true Church. So there must be but one husband and one wife in each case. As there is no divorce between Christ and His Church, so there can be no divorce between husband and wife. And as the union between Christ and the Church results in the production of grace, so this sacred union in marriage conveys grace to the contracting parties that they may rightly fulfill their duties to each other, and to their children, for the love of God.

890. *Marriage is a legal status not subject to any law spiritual.*

If no law spiritual governs marriage, why did Christ say, "But I say unto you that whosoever shall put away his wife and marry another committeth adultery"? Christ was not the civil ruler, and He had said explicitly, "Render to Caesar the things that are Caesar's." If marriage belongs solely to civil authority, Christ would have left it to civil authority. And why did St. Paul say, "Marriage is a great Sacrament, but I speak in Christ and in the Church"? He did not say, "But I speak from the viewpoint of civil authority." Again, elsewhere he writes, "Let her marry to whom she will, only let it be in the Lord." I. Cor. VI., 39.

891. *According to your doctrine polygamy would be wrong. But the Bible permitted it.*

Christ clearly tells us that, whatever concessions were made in the Old Law, it was God's intention from the very beginning that a man should cleave to his wife, not to his wives, and that they should be two in one flesh. God had made concessions because of the hardness of men's hearts in the less perfect Law, but those concessions were withdrawn in the more perfect Law. Christ restored the primitive law, and said, "Henceforth what God hath joined together, let not man put asunder." Mk. X., 2-9.

892. *Christ allowed divorce for one reason. He said, "Whosoever shall put away his wife, except for fornication, maketh her to commit adultery." Matt. V., 32.*

Christ allowed permanent separation if adultery be committed, but He does not allow divorce and re-marriage in the sense you intend. When He said, "Whosoever shall put away his wife, except for the cause of fornication, maketh her to commit adultery, etc.," the sense He intended was this, "Whosoever shall put away his wife (I am not speaking of mere separation without re-marriage, for that is lawful in the case of fornication), but whosoever shall put away his wife . . . he that marries her commits adultery." This is the only possible interpretation in the light of parallel passages. Thus St. Mark records Christ's words absolutely, "Whosoever shall put away his wife and marry another, committeth adultery against her." X., II. In St. Luke, also, we have the words without any parenthesis: "Every one that putteth away his wife, and marrieth another, committeth adultery, and he that marrieth her that is put away from her husband, committeth adultery." XVI., 18. St. Paul tells us clearly, "A woman is bound by the law as long as her husband *liveth;* but if her husband die, she is at liberty." I. Cor. VII., 39. For a Christian, then, there is no such thing as divorce and re-marriage whilst the first partner is still living. Attempted re-marriage results in a sinful union only. You can have divorce and give up Christianity, or you can have Christianity and give up divorce You cannot have both.

893. *The civil law admits divorce and re-marriage.*

Civil law and divine law are not always in harmony. Politicians at times exceed their powers and make laws which are contrary to those of God. Thus they have legislated concerning matrimony with no reference to the will of Christ who raised the marriage contract to the dignity of a Sacrament.

894. *Your law imposes a great hardship upon the innocent party.*

It is the law of Christ, not a law made by the Catholic Church. And it is at times hard upon the innocent party. But since when were we dispensed from the observance of God's laws on the score that obedience to them is inconvenient?

895. *What can one do if the husband is absolutely impossible to live with, or is guilty of adultery?*

Brutal cruelty and ill-treatment afford lawful grounds for separation, as also does adultery if it has not been condoned. But this separation does not break the bond of marriage. Death alone can do that, and neither is free to marry again whilst the other is still living. For grave reasons a Catholic can obtain ecclesiastical permission to have the separation rendered legal by a civil decree of divorce in order to avoid legal difficulties, but this must be on the understanding that such a decree leaves neither party free to contract another marriage whilst the other party is still living.

896. *Are there not many cases in history where the Pope has granted a divorce and permission to re-marry for various reasons?*

You would find it very difficult to prove one such case. Many decrees of nullity have been issued, but they are not divorces. Yet even supposing that you could prove that some individual Pope had granted such a divorce, that would be no argument against the doctrine of the Catholic Church. It would but prove that such an individual Pope acted against his conscience and against the teaching of the Church. An appeal to the lapse on the part of an individual Pope proves nothing against the Church. You cannot disprove a law by pointing to a criminal who has broken it. The Catholic Church has always taught that divorce of a true marriage with the right to re-marry is not allowed.

897. Did not the Pope grant divorces to Louis XII. and Henry IV. of France, and very nearly to Henry VIII. of England, being prevented in this case by fear of Charles V.?

The two prior marriages you mention were declared to have been null and void from the beginning. Therefore no true marriage had ever existed. Louis XII. proved conclusively that he had not been a free agent, having been compelled by his father, Louis XI., to submit to the ceremony. So too, the first marriage of Henry IV. was declared null and void because Marguerite de Valois had been forced into the marriage by her mother, Queen Catherine, for political purposes. The free consent of both parties is necessary for a true and binding marriage contract. In the case of Henry VIII., the power of Charles V. was a motive why his marriage with Catherine of Aragon should not be declared null without rigid proof of its invalidity. At the same time, the enmity of Henry was to be avoided if at all possible, and theologians did all they could to see whether the first marriage were really null and void. But it was impossible, and at the risk of losing England to the Holy See a negative decision had to be given. Henry promptly declared himself head of the Church in England, and took the divorce Rome refused to grant.

898. Did not the Pope give Napoleon a divorce?

No. Napoleon married Josephine in 1796, a marriage validated by a dispensation from the Pope. From that marriage Napoleon never secured any divorce by lawful ecclesiastical authority. He forced a declaration of nullity from some unauthorized clerics, and they put him through a second marriage ceremony in 1810, but this attempted re-marriage was a mockery. The whole thing was a violation of the laws of the Church, and the Church has never acknowledged the second marriage as valid at all.

899. Marconi secured a divorce and was re-married in the Catholic Church.

Marconi secured a decree of civil divorce from the state, but from the Catholic Church he secured a decree of nullity. The civil divorce broke no real bond of marriage, but merely released the parties from any further civil obligations. The Church declared that the form of marriage Marconi went through with Miss Beatrice O'Brien on March 16, 1905, was null and void, and that both were really single people mistakenly believing themselves to be married. Nullity was proved by sworn evidence given by Marconi, Beatrice O'Brien, a Protestant, and many witnesses. The defect in the first marriage was not that it took place in the Anglican Church but that neither party consented to a marriage until death in the Christian sense of the word. They attempted to contract marriage until they should grow tired of each other, both lacking the knowledge that such a temporary contract is not a valid Christian marriage.

900. Were they living in adultery, and were their children illegitimate?

Even though objectively their marriage was invalid, they were both in good faith believing their state to be lawful, and therefore they were not guilty of a sin of adultery. Nor would any children have been illegitimate, for children of a putative marriage are entitled to legitimacy.

901. *After being refused a divorce by the civil courts did not the Duke of Marlborough secure one from the Pope?*

No. A civil divorce was granted in 1920, and both parties had married again before the case was put to Rome in 1926.

902. *The Duke became a Catholic and promptly secured an annulment.*

The Duke was a Protestant when the decision was given. Nor was it promptly given. The application was made to the Southwark diocesan court in 1925. This court, after scrutinizing all the evidence, gave judgment in February, 1926, that the first marriage was invalid from the beginning. Rome, not opposing the decision, but lest it might have been given too easily, called the case to the Holy See. The whole matter was reviewed, sworn testimony being obtained in America and England. The Holy See arrived at the same decision as Southwark and decreed nullity accordingly, six months later. You can hardly call that promptly.

903. *Why was the Duke's first marriage invalid?*

On November 6th, 1895, the Duke of Marlborough went through a marriage ceremony with an American girl, Consuelo Vanderbilt. Both were Protestants, and normally such a marriage would have been valid. However, Miss Vanderbilt had secretly promised to marry another man of her own choice, but the mother forced the girl to marry the Duke. The marriage was not a success, and they separated in 1905, by mutual consent. In 1920 they secured a civil divorce, and both married again. In 1925 the decision of the Catholic Church was sought as to whether the first marriage had ever been valid according to Christian principles. Rome sought all the evidence possible. Miss Vanderbilt's mother deposed on oath, "I forced my daughter to marry the Duke, thinking her objections merely those of an inexperienced girl." Her aunt deposed on oath, "This marriage was forced on the girl, who desired to marry someone else altogether." Another friend of the mother deposed that "it was no question of persuasion, but of absolute constraint." Rome could not but decide that, abstracting altogether from the civil decree of divorce, the parties had never really been married at all.

904. *It looks as if money had weight with Rome.*

Not at all. Not all the money in the Bank of England would be of any avail to secure an annulment from the Church if the first marriage had ever been valid. Meantime the trial at Southwark, with three judges and two other officials, lasting three months, cost $40 in expenses. The retrial in Rome lasted six months. There was much more expense in securing sworn testimonies from America and England, and in the number of legal men employed. This trial cost $200 in expenses; not a very great burden to the parties concerned. Moreover, the law of the Church is that litigants bear expenses only if they are able to afford them. In the ten years between 1920 and 1930 some 120 matrimonial cases were tried in Rome. In 69 cases the litigants paid expenses. In nine cases a nominal fee only was paid. In 39 cases the expenses were totally remitted. Nor did the offerings make any difference in the decisions given. Sixty-six per cent. of those who paid, and 89 per cent. of those who could not pay, obtained favorable decisions.

905. *It comes to the same thing. We Protestants get a divorce from the state whilst Catholics get an annulment from their Church.*

There is all the difference in the world between the two positions. A civil divorce claims to break the bonds of a valid marriage, bonds which the Catholic Church rigidly declares to be unbreakable. A decree of nullity does not break the bonds of a valid marriage at all. It declares that the marriage was never a true marriage and that there is no bond to break. It declares that the reputed marriage was null and void as a contract from the beginning. Had it been valid, the bond could not be broken save by the death of one of the parties.

906. What is the Sacrament of Extreme Unction?

It is a Sacrament instituted by Christ in which a Priest anoints with blessed oil those who are sick and in grave danger of death. This Sacrament gives grace which is of great spiritual assistance to the dying, and even at times affords relief from the physical illness.

907. When did Christ institute such a Sacrament?

That is not known. But the fact that He did so is evident from the words of St. James. "Is any man sick among you? Let him bring in the priests of the Church, and let them pray over him, anointing him with oil in the name of the Lord. And the prayer of faith shall save the sick man: and the Lord shall raise him up: and if he be in sins, they shall be forgiven him." James V., 14-15. When St. James says that he must be anointed in the name of the Lord, that he shall be saved, and that the Lord will raise him up, he shows most clearly that Christ Himself was the author of the commission to administer this sacramental rite.

908. My spirit is quite out of sympathy with that kind of thing.

I do not think so. Extreme Unction is the same *kind* of thing as Baptism. If you agree that grace can be given by the application of water in Baptism, as you do, you should find no difficulty in admitting that grace could be given by the application of oil, should the same Christ decide to institute such a Sacrament.

909. My future depends upon Christ, not upon being anointed with oil.

If it depends upon Christ, it depends upon the means appointed by Christ for the communication of His grace. He at least says that He wants to save you by Baptism. "He who believes and is baptized shall be saved." That is one condition. The inspired word of God also tells us that if anyone be sick, he should call in the priests of the Church and be anointed with oil in the name of the Lord. If your spirit is out of sympathy with that kind of thing, then it is out of sympathy with the Christian religion. And it is a fact that the more a man's spirit is out of sympathy with the Catholic Church and her rites, the more it is out of sympathy with Christianity itself.

910. I do not expect to win a race when it is over.

Nor do I. But the race is not over until the soul has definitely left the body, and no one knows with absolute certainty just when it does leave the body. If the soul has gone when the Sacrament of Extreme Unction is administered, the Sacrament cannot avail. But if the soul still be there, it certainly can avail unto salvation.

911. You anoint even the unconscious, yet a medical friend tells me that, in his opinion, death takes place with final unconsciousness and before the heart stops beating.

That may be the opinion of your friend. But it is no more than his opinion. The Catholic Church says that a man may be anointed within from half an hour to two hours of apparent death, according to the type of death. Not that a man is certainly still living but that there is a probability that the soul has not yet departed from the body, and the benefit of the doubt must be given to the unconscious man. Your medical friend has no certainty. The only certainty that a man is really dead, on the admission of the highest medical authorities, is cadaveric rigidity and initial decomposition. All other signs of death have probability only, unless of course a man has been smashed to pieces in a violent accident. This probability is shown by the fact that expert doctors, after the most diligent examination, have pronounced people dead who have later regained consciousness. I am very glad the law prevents doctors from giving certificates of death as soon as "final unconsciousness" appears, and before the heart stops beating. Until the heart does stop, one could not know whether a particular lapse into unconsciousness is to be final or not. And even when the heart has stopped, there is no absolute certainty that the soul has actually departed in that moment. There is but a solid probability which does not exclude all doubt. And the Church rightly gives the benefit of the doubt to the subject.

912. *These seven Sacraments of the Catholic Church are to assist us in the sanctification of our souls, and to prepare us for a happy eternity. But will you maintain that your Catholic dogmas concerning the future state in no way violate reason?*

I am quite prepared to maintain that.

913. *No one on earth knows anything about the life beyond.*

You are very dogmatic. However, I prefer to accept the authority of the God who made me and who must certainly know what is awaiting me. It is your word against the Word of God. I prefer the latter.

914. *Will the future differ from this life?*

Yes. This life is adapted more to our material nature, the soul conforming its activities to the body it animates. In the next life the body will be adapted rather to our spiritual nature, the soul dominating. Whether the new conditions will be pleasant or unpleasant depends upon our conduct here on earth.

915. *Your pleasant or unpleasant conditions suppose the dogmas of heaven and hell, dogmas which reason cannot accept.*

The dogmas of heaven and hell guarantee the conditions. Nor is there anything in those dogmas which conflicts with sane reason.

916. *Is a man definitely judged at death?*

Yes. "It is appointed unto men once to die, and after this the judgment." Heb. IX., 27. Retribution follows immediately after death. Souls are judged individually at once, so that probation comes to an end with this life.

917. *I believe that all men will get a second chance. Christ said, "Thy kingdom come. Thy will be done on earth as it is in heaven." At some future time on earth there will be a kingdom in which God's will must prevail.*

The kingdom of Christ is already in this world, though not of it. That kingdom is two-fold, perfect in heaven, imperfect on earth. We pray that God's kingdom of grace may be extended in the souls of men, and that they may so fulfill the will of God that they may attain that final happiness of the kingdom of heaven. But the words you quote in no way refer to another temporary state, or to any second chance.

918. *When Christ comes again, will He not teach and rule us?*

When Christ comes again it will be to judge mankind, not to teach and rule us in this world. He has put His Church on earth to do the teaching, and if men will not listen it is their own fault. Now is the time of our probation and we must make good use of the present life instead of relying upon future opportunities for preparation.

919. *Did not Christ promise that we should reign on earth with Him for a thousand years, and that during this Millenium Satan would be bound?*

That has no reference to a further probation on this earth. The thousand years are to be interpreted in the Hebrew sense of a long and indefinite period of time. Even to-day we say, "I could listen to such music for a week," without intending precisely seven days. The thousand years refer to the long period between the advent of Christ and the end of the world. The supply of grace is more plentiful and God's mercy more copious, so that Satan's power is truly diminished. And those who, for the love of Christ, have learned to rise above things of earth and live for God truly reign with Christ.

920. *St. John tells us, "Blessed is he that hath part in the first resurrection. In these the second death hath no power." Rev. XX., 6.*

The first resurrection is the mystical resurrection from the death of sin. We rise with Christ in Baptism, and those who die still retaining the grace of their baptismal rebirth possess a permanent title to the glorious second and actual resurrection of the body at the last day. On such as these the second death will have no effect. The first death is the dissolution of soul and body. The second death is the eternal living death of hell.

921. *What do you mean by hell?*

Hell is the eternal lot of misery awaiting those who die in a state of grave sin and at enmity with God. Before the general resurrection, the soul alone experiences this misery; after the resurrection, the body will be re-united with that soul and will share in the misery, being tormented by created elements even as the person forsook God during life for the enjoyment of created things. The chief misery will be the sense of having lost the happiness of the Vision of God; the other will be the torment of fire.

922. *What evidence have you that such a hell exists?*

The very best. The God who made us tells us that He also has made a hell. There is a hell in which both the bodies and the souls of the lost will be afflicted. Thus the gentle Christ Himself warns us, "It is expedient for thee that one of thy members should perish rather than that thy whole body go into hell." Mk. IX., 29. Remember that all shall rise some day, the good and bad alike, the body sharing in the fate of the soul. "All that are in the graves shall hear the voice of the Son of God. And they that have done good things shall come forth unto the resurrection of life; but they that have done evil unto the resurrection of judgment." Jn. V., 28. Those who are lost will go to everlasting fire. Christ calls it "unquenchable fire." Mk. IX., 44. He tells us of the grim sentence, "Depart from me you cursed into everlasting fire which was prepared for the devil and his angels." Matt. XXV., 41. Such a solemn utterance of the judicial sentence demands the literal sense. Judges do not speak in metaphors at such moments, "Let him be hanged—but of course only metaphorically!" And it will be conscious suffering. Our Lord says, "Their worm dieth not, and the fire is not extinguished." Mk. IX., 43. And again, "There shall be weeping and gnashing of teeth." Matt. XIII., 49. Continued conscious suffering is the fate of the lost. And reason demands such a fate. When a man sins gravely, he chooses between God and a thing forbidden by God. He cannot have both, and he prefers to renounce God rather than the created good. If he dies without repentance his will is still alienated from God. He would do the same thing again if he got the chance. And as long as these dispositions last, he must do without God, and happiness. These dispositions lasting forever once this probationary life is over, so will the penalty.

923. Do you maintain that there is a real fire in hell?

Yes. The fire of hell is a real and created fire which will affect even the bodies of men who die at enmity with God. I grant that it will differ in various characteristics from natural fire as we know it. Christ chose the word fire as being that element best known to us which produces results most similar to the effects of the fire of hell. Yet fire as we know it depends upon combustion. The fire of hell will not depend upon being constantly fed with fuel, but upon God's will, the principle of all existing things. If God can will that fire should exist with the aid of fuel to which He gave its properties, He certainly can produce and conserve fire by simply willing it, and without the aid of created fuel. Thus He manifested to Moses a bush in flames yet unconsumed.

924. How can fire affect a spiritual being such as the devil?

By the restriction of its activities according to the limitations of the created agent of torture, and by the intellectual apprehension of the suffering fire normally causes. But difficulties concerning its method of action make no difference to the fact that it exists.

925. Heb. II., 14, tells us that the devil is to be destroyed. Who then will keep the fire of hell going?

The text means that Christ will destroy the power of the devil over the souls of the redeemed. Satan will never be personally destroyed. And in any case he does not keep the fire of hell going. If Satan had anything to do with it that fire would have been destroyed long ago. He has never enjoyed it. However, the torments of hell are dependent upon the will of God.

926. Why does the Church offer us hell when we have hell in this life?

The Church offers hell to no one. She does all she can to prevent people from going there. Meantime hell is not in this life. Those in hell are irrevocably lost, and no one is irrevocably lost while still in this life. Until his very last breath every man has the opportunity offered him to save his soul. Nor are the ills and sufferings of this life hell. They are often a very good medicine curing us of over-attachment to this earthly life. Again, Christ Our Lord endured more bitter sufferings during life than others are called upon to endure, and in no way could He be regarded as experiencing contact with hell.

927. Where is hell?

It is a place of suffering awaiting men after death, if they fail to depart this life in the grace and friendship of God. Information concerning its locality has not been revealed in terms of longitude and latitude, even could such terms avail. God has revealed that there is a hell, but not where it is. And the latter information is immaterial; nor can any argument be based upon its absence. If the cables reported an earthquake at Potosi, your ignorance of the locality of Potosi would not disprove the earthquake. Our not knowing where hell is makes no difference whatever to hell. God has told us that it is a reality and that a man is a fool who does not fulfill the conditions necessary to avoid it.

928. Your Church will have increasing difficulty in getting intelligent men to believe in hell.

The stream of converts from the ranks of intelligent men is sufficient answer to that suggestion.

929. *Such a doctrine is against the weight of enlightened reason.*

It is not. It is reason enlightened by God that accepts the doctrine. If you are speaking of natural enlightenment, then the first thing that such enlightenment admits is its own deficiency and limitation; the historical value of the Gospels, and the fact that those Gospels teach eternal punishment. It is the very unenlightened man who will admit eternal happiness because he likes it, and deny eternal punishment because he doesn't. The forces producing both are obviously in this world—good and evil. Meantime the Catholic Church has plenty of evidence that there is a hell. Opponents have not a scrap of evidence that there is not. And no man can explain the terrible sufferings of Christ, granted His knowledge that there was no hell to save us from, and that we would all get to heaven in the end, whether He suffered or not. He did not go through His crucifixion for nothing.

930. *Modern progressive scientific theology has no time for hell.*

The idea that there is no hell is neither progressive nor scientific. It is not progressive, for it is not progress to leave people ignorant of a chasm yawning beneath their feet. If to take the truth from people and leave them in error be progress, then only could you call this progress. Nor is it scientific. There is not a jot of evidence that there is no eternal hell, whilst God says that there is one. The men who deny hell go by their feelings, shutting their eyes to facts. No scientist does that. I feel that there ought not to be cancer. But there is cancer.

931. *I cannot see how any clear-minded person can believe in hell.*

That does not alter the fact that many clear-minded people do believe in its existence.

932. *Many pretend to believe and are hypocrites.*

Very few would pretend to believe in hell. An immense number pretend to themselves that they do not believe, and they do so in order to carry on as tranquilly as possible in evil conduct. Those who want to suppress hell are not characterized by a real desire to defend the honor of God, to be more scrupulous in the observance of His laws, and to be more faithful in the fulfillment of their duties.

933. *Believers' lives must be overshadowed by stupendous horror!*

There is no reason why that should be at all. They have only to repent of their sins sincerely and resolve to avoid grave violations of conscience, which alone can lead to hell. It is the man who does those things which God strictly forbids who has reason to be overshadowed, and even then by the horror of his conduct chiefly, and secondarily by the prospect of the fate such conduct deserves.

934. *Where this terrible dogma does not embitter happiness, it destroys character.*

That is a gratuitous assertion. I believe in hell. Since it exists I would much rather know than not know. And the knowledge does not embitter my happiness. As for my corrupt character, you at least have not sufficient evidence to judge me on that point.

935. *If I could rob people of their faith in hell I should not feel any regret.*

That is because you do not understand the Christian religion, nor the nature of the eternal moral law. Hell exists, and since it does exist, it is treason to the God of truth and treachery to man to try to blind men to the fact.

936. *Treachery to man! Are you pleased to know that there is a hell?*

Since there is one, I am glad to know it. I do not want to think that there is not a hell if there is one. And I am glad that there is a hell. I am glad that the state has penalties attached to the breaking of its laws. If there were no such penalties, its laws would fail to preserve the peace and well-being of the community as they should. In the same way I am glad that God has a deterring penalty attached to the violation of His commandments.

937. *Is your desire of hell for your fellow men due to your humanitarian sentiment or to the effete doctrine of your infallible Church?*

I do not desire hell for my fellow men. I desire to save them from it. A truly humanitarian sentiment makes me glad that evil conduct is not a matter of indifference. It would be a dreadful thing if all men thought that they could sin with impunity. Your talk of an effete doctrine of an infallible Church is absurd.

938. *I am human, and I can't believe in a burning hell, above all for souls Christ came to redeem.*

I cannot believe that Christ came to redeem people if there be no hell from which to save them! But beware of your imagination. If you imagine a hell which is in any way opposed to the justice and love of God, that is not the hell you are asked to believe in at all. God is just, merciful, and truthful. He says that there is a hell, and you are asked to believe in the hell which He knows to exist, not in any vague speculation of your own as to its nature. Hell is as much a mystery of faith as is grace, and you are asked to believe in the fact of hell because God knows the truth and could not tell an untruth. You are not asked to comprehend fully its nature, and your inability to believe in the hell you imagine does not mean that you are unable to believe in the hell which God created "for the devil and his angels."

939. *How could a mother be happy in heaven with her child in hell?*

She could not, were her view of things limited by her present inadequate ideas. But with an unclouded view of what really constitutes goodness, and of what really constitutes evil, she will have very different estimates in heaven which will render happiness not only possible but a fact. Let us try to grasp it. Hell being a fact, our lack of understanding makes no difference. And in any case, Christ loved the child more than did the mother herself, yet He is happy in heaven. So there must be some way out. You see, we cannot interpret heaven in terms of this life. Here we are natural beings, our natural love directly awakened by our fellow beings. But in heaven God Himself will be the direct object of our love. We shall love God, what God loves, and as God loves. All other beings will be loved in God. Thus Christ said concerning the difference of human love in heaven that marriage shall not exist, but that men will be "as the angels of God in heaven." Matt. XXII., 30. Merely natural love will change to supernatural love in and through God, and people will be lovable in so far as they resemble God. If a son dies unrepentant, having identified himself with wickedness, then he will be the opposite of God. The mother will experience an absolute necessity to love God, who is pure, just, holy, and truth itself. And she will find complete happiness in doing so. Her natural love for her son gives way to a supernatural love for him if he is pure, just, holy, and truthful. But it gives way to her love for God if her child is impure, unjust, wicked, and essentially a liar, as is the father of lies himself. Her transfer to heaven has changed her reasons for loving her son, and if he dies in such evil dispositions she has no supernatural reason to love him. All her happiness is in God, and that happiness cannot be disturbed. This may sound difficult. It must. For we are trying to explain conditions of heaven by ideas drawn from our earthly experience, ideas which do not go far enough. The explanation gives a solution as far as the limited mind of man can go. And if it astonishes human reason, we should be more astonished still if our limited powers could fully grasp the matter.

940. *Is any person so bad as to deserve eternal punishment?*

Yes. The man who deliberately and finally despises and rejects the Infinite Love of God deserves to be deprived of it forever.

941. *Surely he did some virtuous actions. Are they to be of no avail?*

They would have counted for very much, had the man wished. But if he subsequently commits mortal sin and dies without repenting of it he forfeits any benefits of previous virtue. Refraining from adultery on Friday is no excuse for the commission of murder on Saturday.

942. *You damn people whose wills are so weak that they cannot avoid sin!*

None but deliberately willed and unrepented mortal sin meets with eternal punishment. If inherent weakness is so great as to destroy real responsibility, God would not accuse the man of mortal sin. But such is not the case with the normal man. The normal man is able to refuse consent of the will to evil inclinations and suggestions. Some people are only too ready to call their own cowardice inherent weakness. They could have refused to sin, but chose to sin, and afterwards fell back on the lame excuse of "weak moments."

943. *However bad people may be, I think it is against right ideas of God to speak of His punishing anyone forever.*

Then what are you going to do with Satan? He is a creature of God even as we. Is he going to reform? Will he ever come out of the eternal fire prepared for the devil and his angels? No. And granting the fact that God is punishing one of his creatures like that, responsible human souls can certainly meet with the same fate. I do not like the thought of anyone suffering in hell any more than you do. But that will not make me deny the existence of hell. Hundreds of things we do not like are facts.

944. *How can you reconcile hell with God's love, justice, and mercy?*

If I could not, that would but prove something wrong with my own ideas on the subject. For it is certain that God is loving, just, and merciful; and He has revealed that there is a hell. So the ideas cannot be repugnant. However God's love, justice, and mercy demand that there be a hell. His love demands a hell, for the more He loves goodness, the more He must hate sin. To the man who says that God loves too much to send a man to hell, I simply reply that He sends no man there; men go there. And God has loved too much not to let them go there if they scorn, reject, and throw God's love back in His face. Again, His justice demands that if a man dies rejecting an infinite goodness he should endure a penalty of a never-ending nature. If there were no eternal punishment, a man could cry to God, "You say 'Thou shalt not.' I say 'I shall.' Do your worst. You cannot punish me forever. What care I for your commandments or for yourself! You must either make me happy in the end, or annihilate me, when I shall have escaped your power." It is impossible for the drama of iniquity to end like that. That would not be justice. And as for God's mercy, already it is a mercy that man has the thought of hell as an emergency brake to stop his headlong rush into vice. The truth that there is a hell has mercifully saved many a soul from a life of blasphemy and sin, and still more often from death in a state of sin. And remember that God's mercy is offered to every man over and over again during life. Mercy is asked for, not forced upon people. Some men who are loudest in their protests against God's injustice would be the first to complain if God forced anything upon them, even His mercy. But men cannot have God's mercy and reject it at one and the same time.

945. But Christ who came as the revelation of God, was so kind and gentle!

That intensifies the force of the arguments for hell. Only a grim reality could have forced Him to speak as He did. He taught heaven and hell equally. You cannot have heaven because you like it and reject a hell taught with the same authority because you do not like it. Think of His passion and death. If there were no hell to save us from; if we all had to go to heaven whether He were crucified or not; then His sufferings and death were foolish. Men wish to abolish hell. There is but one way to do so. Let each man abolish his own hell by repenting of his sins and endeavoring to serve God.

946. You make Christ cruel.

I do not. Due punishment for not doing as Christ commands is justice, not cruelty. Parents know that it is not cruelty to inflict reasonable and deserved punishment upon children who are rebellious. And God has more right to your obedience than any parents to the obedience of their children. It is a blameworthy weakness in parents if they allow their children to do just as they please with no fear of the consequences. And God is not so foolish as to give serious laws to His rational creatures on the understanding that nothing will happen if they break them. But there is no need to endure the extreme penalty. Keep the laws and you will be safe.

947. Your hell is full of non-Catholics, who commit grave sin and do not know how to make an act of perfect contrition.

We do not know how far they understand the gravity of sin. As for the act of contrition, you are leaving out the greatest factor of all—God's grace. In a flash God can enlighten the mind and move the will to a purely interior act of contrition of which the onlookers know nothing. And God alone knows how many are thus saved.

948. If you believe in Christianity you must believe that there are infinitely more people in hell than in heaven.

I have not to believe that, and I do not believe it. Yet I believe in Christianity. Why should you, a non-Christian, prescribe for me what I have to believe? You might at least leave that to Christians.

949. How many souls are lost according to the Catholic Church?

Various theologians have expressed various opinions. But these are merely private opinions. The Catholic Church has no official teaching on the subject, nor has any definite information been revealed to men by God. The one thing certain is that men can be saved and men can be lost, and that unrepented mortal sin is the deciding factor. That is enough for all practical purposes.

950. Are Judas and Adam in hell?

It has never been revealed that any particular soul is in hell. Christ said of Judas, "Better for him had he never been born." That does not look too hopeful in his case, for no matter what a man has to endure, if he attains eternal happiness in the end, much better to have been born. However, even of Judas, no man has absolute certainty. The question can be solved only by God. It is practically certain that Adam is in heaven, and not in hell. Thus Scripture says, "Wisdom preserved him that was first formed by God, the father of the world . . . and brought him out of his sin." Wisd. X., 2. Adam was the type of the second Adam, Christ, and it is to be expected that Christ, the second Adam, would see to it that the first Adam was fully liberated from Satan. The Greek Church, from very ancient times, has celebrated the feast of Adam and Eve.

951. *I am interested in your dogma concerning purgatory. Must I be a Catholic before I can understand that invention of your Church?*

No. You must be a non-Catholic to suspect that the Church did invent it. The idea that there is no purgatory is the invention of Protestants. The reformers corrupted the true doctrine, and many good Protestants, realizing this, are returning to the Catholic religion of their forefathers even as I myself have done. Meantime, if I could discover, or you could show me, when and where the Church invented this doctrine, I promise to spend the rest of my life exposing the Catholic Church as a merely human institution making outrageous claims upon men.

952. *Why make people afraid of such a horrible place as purgatory, when you know that it does not exist?*

I know that it does exist. And if you deny it because to you it seems a horrible place, you must deny hell also because it is far more horrible. And if you deny hell, you deny Christianity. And is it not a more horrible thought that there would be no purgatory? In that case you would have but heaven and hell. All not quite fit for heaven could not hope to escape hell. It is a much more pleasant thought that there are people not quite good enough for heaven, yet not bad enough for hell, and that these are sent to purgatory until they are purified sufficiently for heaven.

953. *What is the nature of your doctrine on purgatory?*

It can be summed up very briefly. At death the soul of man, if quite fit, goes at once to heaven; if not quite fit, to purgatory; if quite unfit, to hell. The soul which has repented of all its sins, and has fully expiated them in this life, is quite fit for heaven at once. The soul which departs this life in a state of unrepented mortal sin can never be fitted for heaven, and goes to hell. But a soul which has sincerely repented of its sins, yet has not fully expiated them, secures immunity from hell by repentance, and goes to purgatory until it has expiated all its deficiencies.

954. *Does God want to roast you merely because you have the misfortune to be alive? He knows that you had no say in the matter.*

God does not want to roast me. It is not a misfortune to be alive, though it is blameworthy to have misused one's existence. Nor did I want a say as to whether I should receive the gift of existence. People can leave me a fortune tomorrow without consulting me. But I did have a say in my infidelities to God's grace, and for that I am responsible and do not wish to excuse myself.

955. *Have you been so atrociously wicked as to deserve purgatory?*

There is no need to be atrociously wicked in order to need purification, any more than there is need to be on your death-bed before you need medicine. But there is need to attain to a high standard of purity and holiness before one could be fit to enter the glory of God's presence.

956. *Do the souls of Protestants go to purgatory?*

All souls, whether of Protestants or of Catholics, or of any other religion, will go to purgatory if they are not good enough for heaven at the moment of death, nor bad enough for hell. Non-Catholics may deny purgatory, but that makes no difference to purgatory.

957. Would God destine so good a man as General Booth for purgatory just because he was not a Catholic?

Purgatory is not a final destiny. Every soul that goes there is saved, and is ultimately admitted to the very Vision of God. Good Protestants as well as good Catholics will go there if they are not quite perfect at death. There is no dispensation. And where is the man who has not his imperfections?

958. A man has every chance to repent in this life.

He has. And if he does not, he will not even go to purgatory if his sins be grave. Purgatory is not a place for repentance, but for purification. If two men repent on their death-beds, one of whom broke one commandment and the other, all the commandments often, both are saved by their repentance. But they are not both equal before God. They will suffer relative purifications in purgatory.

959. This dogma of purgatory was invented by Pope Gregory in 600 A.D., and was made an article of faith by the Council of Florence in 1439.

If not invented until 600 A.D. why did St. Monica, in the 4th century, implore her son St. Augustine, as she lay on her dying bed, that he would pray for her soul whenever he went to the Altar to offer the Mass? And how would you account for the inscriptions in the Catacombs recording prayers for the dead offered by the Christians of the first centuries? Or, if you would go back earlier, what will you do with the teaching of Scripture itself? The Council of Florence merely recalled previous definitions.

960. What is your Romish reply to the challenge of Art. XXII. in the Book of Common Prayer?

That Article of the Church of England says that the Romish doctrine of purgatory is grounded upon no warranty of Scripture, but is rather repugnant to the Word of God. The reply is that the Article is quite erroneous, and that many Anglicans realize the fact. Thus an Anglican clergyman unsays that Article definitely in his book entitled, "The Catholic Religion—a Manual of instruction for members of the Church of England." He speaks of a place of mercy "provided in the intermediate state, in which evil will be completely purged. When this purification is accomplished, such souls enter into perfect peace," p. 193. On the following page he suggests that, at the Reformation, men were too eager and rejected much that was true—including the intermediate state. In no less than six different places he urges prayer for the dead just as Catholics pray for the dead, and, as he shows from Scripture, both the Jews and St. Paul prayed for the departed. On p. 379, he writes, "Still more desirable is the celebration of the Holy Eucharist for the repose of the soul of the departed." Thus this Anglican clergyman goes back to the Romish doctrine of purgatory. I am not quoting from a book unacceptable to the many. My copy is of the 19th edition, completing 207 thousand.

961. How can an Anglican clergyman, who has sworn to accept the Articles of religion, teach such doctrine?

I do not see how he can do so. Romish theologians are simple children compared with the capacity for mental gymnastics manifested by Rev. Vernon Staley, the author of the book, in his efforts to salve his conscience. He says in effect that the doctrine of purgatory is all right, but that Anglicans must not use the *word* purgatory. He admits the thing, but not its description. He calls it a place or process of cleansing, but he will not call it purgatory, which means the same thing. It is as if we Catholics had invented the word theatre. Then this exponent of Anglicanism would insist upon using the word play-house, and swear that he did not agree with the

Catholic Church concerning houses of entertainment. In substance he declares Article XXII. to be false and unscriptural.

962. *You speak of Scripture, but the Bible mentions only heaven and hell.*

It does not. It certainly mentions an intermediate state to which the soul of Christ went after His death on the cross. 1 Pet. III., 19. This state was neither heaven nor hell, but the Limbo of the Fathers of the Old Law. In addition to this, Scripture mentions the purgatorial state. In any case, it would not matter if the Bible did mention but two places. My mentioning only London and New York could not prove the non-existence of Paris. It would be a different matter if Christ had said, "There is no purgatory." But He did not.

963. *But the Bible does not mention purgatory.*

It does not mention the precise word purgatory. But the intermediate state of purification described by that word is there.

964. *How do you prove the existence of such a state?*

In Matt. V., 26, Christ, in condemning sin, speaks of liberation only after expiation. "Thou shalt not go out from thence till thou repay the last farthing." In Matt. XII., 32, He speaks of sin which "shall not be forgiven either in this world or in the world to come." Any remission of the effects of sin in the next world can refer only to purgatory. Above all St. Paul tells us that the day of judgment will try each man's work. That day is after death, when the soul goes to meet its God. What is the result of that judgment? If a man's work will not stand the test St. Paul says that "he shall suffer loss; but he himself shall be saved, yet so as by fire." 1 Cor. III., 15. This cannot refer to eternal loss in hell, for no one is saved there. Nor can it refer to heaven, for there is no suffering in heaven. Purgatory alone can explain this text. As a matter of fact, all Christians believed in purgatory until the Reformation, when the reformers began their rejection of Christian doctrines at will. Prayer for the dead was ever the prevailing custom, in accordance with the recommendation of the Bible itself. "It is a holy and wholesome thought to pray for the dead, that they may be loosed from their sins." 2 Mach. XII., 46. Prayer for the dead supposes a soul not in heaven where it does not need the help of prayer, nor in hell where prayer cannot assist it. Some intermediate state of purification and need, where prayer can help, is necessary. And the doctrine is most reasonable. "Nothing defiled shall enter heaven." Rev. XXI., 27. Yet not all defilement should cost man the loss of his soul. Even in this life human justice does not inflict capital punishment for every crime. Small offenses are punished by fines or by temporary imprisonment, after which the delinquent is liberated. Those who deny purgatory teach the harder and more unreasonable doctrine.

965. *God would not demand expiation after having forgiven the sin.*

What you think God would or would not do cannot avail against that which He does do. When David repented of his great sin God sent the prophet Nathan with the message to him, "The Lord hath taken away thy sin. Nevertheless, because thou hast given occasion to the enemies of the Lord to blaspheme, thy child shall surely die." 2 Sam. XII., 14. To forgive the guilt of sin, and purify the spiritual scar and stain, which that disease of the soul leaves, by expiatory suffering, is better than to leave the soul still unpurified and indebted to God's justice. I too could fully forgive a friend his offense should he have robbed me, yet still insist that he make good the damage he has wrought me.

966. *What is the punishment of purgatory?*

When the soul leaves the body, that which can think, remember, love, hate, be happy or miserable, has gone from that body. A corpse cannot do these things. And the soul, with these capabilities, goes into a new state of being as a separated spirit. And my true self, separated from the distractions of this world, will perceive clearly and fully its own unfitness for God's presence, a perception which will mean unspeakable suffering. The exact nature of this suffering we do not know, but it is compared in Scripture to the action of fire afflicting a sensitive body. Although it is not defined as a dogma that there is a real fire of purgatory, it is the general opinion of theologians that there is a real fire somewhat analogous to the fire of hell. However it be explained, the fact that purgatorial suffering awaits the imperfect has been revealed by God.

967. *When did God make purgatory?*

Heaven of course always existed. For where God is, there is heaven. Hell was made when the devil and his followers fell from grace. There was no purgatory for them. Purgatory, then, was made when men began to sin and die with sins repented of, but not fully expiated by the sufferings of this life. Men under the Old Law went to purgatory just as those do who live under the New Law.

968. *Where is purgatory?*

God has not deigned to satisfy our curiosity on that point, and the knowledge is not of practical importance to us. The fact that there is a purgatory has been revealed by God. And when He reveals a fact, we cannot say to Him, "Well, I for one refuse to believe it until You tell me more about it." God proves a thing by saying it, for He is truth itself. We have but to prove that He said it.

969. *How do you know that there are any souls in purgatory?*

I know that 100,000 people die daily. I refuse to believe that they all go to hell, and feel quite sure that they are not all fit for immediate entry into heaven. Moreover, you would find far more difficulty in endeavoring to show that there are no souls in purgatory.

970. *How do you know that you can help the souls in purgatory by your prayers?*

God would not have inspired the Jews to pray for the departed if such prayers were of no avail. Christians have always prayed for the dead, a practice fully warranted by the doctrine of the Communion of Saints. And if we can pray for our dear ones who are in trouble in this life, our prayers can certainly follow them in their future difficulties. All prayer is addressed to the same God who is as present to the souls of our dear departed as He is to us.

971. *Is your own personal conviction such that you will want others to pray for you?*

It is. All who have the Catholic faith believe in prayer for the dead. It is not a doctrine for the laity only. And I sincerely hope that friends will pray for me and have Masses offered on my behalf when God has taken me from this world. I shall need them. Nothing defiled will enter heaven, and if at death one's soul is not absolutely perfect in virtue proportionately to the grace it has received, it is defiled by imperfection of some sort. "If we say that we have no sin we deceive ourselves, and the truth is not in us." 1 Jn. I., 8. Masses and prayers offered for me after my death will help to expiate such imperfections as I unfortunately possess.

972. So you expect to get redemption on the nod! You are fortunate.

I am. And not a soul will be saved who does not owe it to the death of Christ on the cross, and who will not admit that this was a purely free and gratuitous gift wholly undeserved by men. Mass merely applies the satisfactory value of Christ's death to my soul. Meantime, those who deny purgatory and the necessity of expiation wish to obtain salvation much more "on the nod," as you call it, than Catholics.

973. Joseph McCabe says that purgatory is the most lucrative doctrine ever invented by Priests.

He is the last man from whom you should seek information about the Catholic Church. I am a Priest, and know as much about the Catholic Church as Joseph McCabe ever did. And my judgment is not warped by hatred. The doctrine of purgatory was revealed by God. It is not a lucrative doctrine invented for financial reasons. Popes, Bishops, and Priests all believe in it on exactly the same footing as the faithful, and it is my consolation that many Priests have already promised to offer Mass for me as soon as they hear of my death. And they will receive nothing for doing so.

974. Yet Priests accept offerings for Masses under false pretenses.

They do not. A Priest will accept an offering on the understanding that he will say a special Mass for the intentions of the person making the offering. In accepting an offering from one person he forfeits the support he would receive from another in exercising his ministry on that other's behalf.

975. It is a source of revenue which no Priest dare fail to utilize. The selling of Masses must be most profitable.

That remark shows that you do not understand the nature of Mass offerings at all. Priests do not sell Masses, and the people do not pay for Masses. The Mass cannot be bought or sold. Even were I to say that the Priest offers the Mass and is paid, not for the Mass, but for his time and services, any evil element such as you suggest would be excluded. It matters little whether a chaplain be given a salary for a year's service, or a special offering for a special service. However the explanation is deeper than that. In the Old Law the people brought tithes and percentages of their goods and dedicated them to God. The gift was directly made to God, and once given, ceased to belong to the giver and belonged entirely to God. Then God made use of these gifts for the support of His religious ministers, inviting them to be His guests. The same spirit characterizes Catholic practice. A Catholic wishes to offer the Sacrifice of the Mass to God. He is not compelled to do so. Now the Mass is a Sacrifice instituted by Christ, but it supposes the outward necessities, bread, wine, altar, vestments, and a living human being authorized by God to offer it in the name of Christ and of the Church. The Catholic offers to God all that is necessary, and indeed offers a personal sacrifice by contributing towards the upkeep of the altar and towards the very life of the Priest who is to stand at the altar on his behalf. Since he has made this offering to God, the Mass is applied according to his intention. Thus, when you attack the idea that the Priest sells the Mass to a Catholic, you are not attacking Catholic doctrine or practice at all.

976. Your harnessing purgatory to the idea of offering to God is most ingenious. So the Church is equal to God?

I do not harness purgatory to the idea of offerings to God. I give the simple Catholic explanation, according to the doctrine of Christ as recorded by St. Paul. "They that serve the altar partake with the altar. So also the Lord ordained that they who preach the gospel should live by the gospel." 1 Cor. IX., 13-14. And as a matter of fact purgatory does not necessarily come into it. It is a question of offering Mass for any intention whatever. Some Masses are offered for those we love and who have departed from this world. Nor is the Church made equal to God. She is but commissioned by God to attend to matters connected with His due worship. If I wished to give a friend a valuable plant, yet handed it to his gardener to be planted in his garden, I would not be elevating the gardener to the status of my friend.

977. How can you as an honest man support the extortion of hard-earned money from the poor?

I could not support extortion, but I can honestly say that only a person absolutely ignorant of things Catholic could imagine that money is extorted from the poor for Masses.

978. Don't Priests visit the bereaved and tell them that so many dollars are required per week for Masses?

No. Catholics are taught the truth from the pulpit in general. They are told that it is good to have Masses offered for the dead if possible; as indeed it is. Apart from that, the matter is left to the spontaneous desire of individuals. And they are never required to have such Masses offered.

979. If you do not extort, you press home the fact that, unless such Masses are said, the soul of the loved one will remain in purgatory.

That is not true. There are many ways in which we can help our deceased relatives and friends, apart from having Masses offered for them. We can offer our own assistance at Mass, and our Holy Communions; we can offer any prayers we wish, or our sufferings, and acts of Christian mortification. It is good to have Mass offered specially for them if possible. But that is not the only way in which we can help them. Nor has anyone ever maintained that a soul necessarily remains in purgatory until Masses shall have been offered.

980. Why don't Priests pray for the souls of the poor without payment of money which only the rich can afford?

Priests pray every day for the souls in purgatory without payment of money, and without any discrimination between the rich and the poor. When someone asks for a special intercessory Mass, offering the customary stipend, the Priest will comply with the request. But this is in addition to his personal prayers for the dead.

981. But would they say Masses for the poor?

Thousands of Masses are said every year for the poor by thousands of Priests, when no offering at all is made. As a matter of fact the law of the Church obliges a Parish Priest to offer Mass every Sunday and on every Holy Day of Obligation for his parishioners, excluding all private requests and offerings. And every Priest, in a spirit of charity, often offers Mass for the special intentions of poor people who cannot afford any offering.

982. The fact remains that the Catholic Church derives millions from Masses, as Joseph McCabe points out.

Naturally the offerings of millions of people would amount to millions. That is to be expected. A million people in Sydney contribute some millions yearly for various transport services; but the individual traveller is not unreasonably burdened, and the officials do not receive exorbitant remuneration. Your point proves nothing save the numerical strength of the Catholic Church, four hundred times as numerous throughout the world as the city of Sydney.

983. *So purgatory has been able to extort millions!*

It extorts nothing. The truth revealed by God inspires Catholics to have Masses offered for their departed friends and relatives. And those Catholics, who can afford to do so, desire by personal sacrifice to render the offering of the Sacrifice of the Mass their own special offering to God.

984. *From offerings for Masses in England about a quarter of a million is raked in yearly.*

Proportionately to their numbers that averages a penny per week from individual Catholics, and yields about sixty cents per week to the individual Priest.

985. *In the United States it means a sum of between one and two millions a year.*

The margin of difference is rather wide; however, taking the amount as two millions, on the Catholic population of the United States the average is again less than ten cents a year from the individual towards the support of Priests from this source. And at McCabe's maximum, the individual Priest would receive the average income of one dollar per week from such Mass-offerings.

986. *Setting out the millions at so much per head is unsound, if ingenious. Not every one pays, and those who do are made to feel it.*

My argument is not unsound. It is unsound to talk of millions without mentioning the distribution of the sources from which they come. Nor is any Catholic made to feel that he is paying. In fact, no Catholic is made to pay in any sense of the word, for there is no obligation to have Masses offered at all for one's personal intentions.

987. *Can any honest man be proud of all this?*

The New Testament says that he who serves the altar should live by the altar. And certainly the man who devotes the whole of his life to the welfare of his people can quite honestly accept a small percentage from the earnings of those to whose welfare he is devoted. The Priest has to live. He is more constantly at his work than the man who controls a transport system for the convenience of citizens and who derives his living from the small contributions of those who use those services. And the Priest's work is more important and more responsible. Moreover, the average Priest barely gets a living, and many have to be subsidized or they could scarcely live at all.

988. *At any rate, has not the soul of a rich man a better chance than the soul of a poor man?*

We cannot make such a comparison. The rich man who provides for the offering of Masses for the repose of his soul has a better chance of diminishing his purgatory than the rich man who makes no such provision.

989. *I want my question answered. A rich man leaves $1,000 for Masses for his soul. A poor man leaves but $1. Who has the better chance of entering heaven?*

If both died in a state of unrepented mortal sin, neither of them has any chance. If both died in a state of grace, both will certainly enter heaven. All souls which depart this life in a state of grace will eventually enter heaven. However some souls need more purification in purgatory than others. The question, then, is whether the wealthier man will secure the more rapid purification, and enter heaven more easily than the poor man. Not necessarily. The $1 may easily have been the greater generosity relatively than the $1,000. The dispositions of the poor man could easily have been more pleasing to God than those of the rich man. The very poverty and suffering of the poor man in this life was already expiation; so much so that Christ practically says that heaven belongs almost by special right to the poor, declaring that the rich with their life of comfort and self-indulgence will enter heaven with great difficulty. The poor man might scarcely need the few Masses he asks, whilst the rich man, with all his Masses, may have far more to expiate. Then, too, the departed can benefit by Masses and prayers within certain limits only. Anything over and above those limits would be applied to other souls. St. Augustine clearly taught in the 4th century, "There is no doubt that our prayers can benefit those who so lived as to deserve to be benefited by them." He recommends sacrifice on their behalf, whether of the altar, or of prayers, or of almsgiving, adding, "Although they do not benefit all for whom they are offered, but those only who deserved during life to benefit by them." But we can safely leave the adjusting of all these things to God.

990. How do Priests know when a soul escapes from purgatory?

Souls do not escape from purgatory as criminals from jail. When they are sufficiently purified for the Vision of God they are admitted to heaven. And no one knows when this occurs, unless God gives a special revelation, a favor we have no right to ask.

991. Then you might be praying for a soul not in purgatory at all!

That is quite possible. Granted that we believe in purgatory, that our prayers can help the dead, and that we do not know for certain whether our dear ones are emancipated from their purifications or not, we continue praying for them. We give them, rather than ourselves, the benefit of any doubt. We argue that our prayers may possibly benefit them, not that they may possibly be wasted. And we would certainly risk saying too many for them rather than allow them to run the risk of being deprived of help.

992. On that score, Catholics would go on praying and having Masses said as long as they live.

Quite so. Is it a fault to be generous as long as one lives? And are such earnest prayers harmful? I am a Priest. My own mother has gone to God. I shall certainly offer Masses for her as long as I am able to do so and am free from other obligations. If, long before my death, her purification is finished and she is enjoying the happiness of heaven, I know that not a single prayer or Mass will be wasted. There are other souls in purgatory, and no Catholic begrudges the application of his prayers and sacrifices to other souls should his own dear ones have no need of them.

993. I must confess that I find all this rather baffling.

You are outside Catholicity, and no more understand the spirit of the Catholic religion than a man standing outside a Cathedral can discern the wonderful beauty of the stained glass windows. But a reasonable man would say, "Well, I can hardly expect to perceive the real sense and design from here. But there must be something in it, and if I cannot enter the building I must be content to be without an understanding of that window's real beauty." But you stand outside the building of Catholic doctrine, stare at practices you cannot expect to understand from outside, and express astonishment that you see nothing in them.

994. I have heard Catholics speak of indulgences for the souls in purgatory? What are indulgences?

Do not mix up the ecclesiastical term indulgence with the modern idea of self-indulgence. An indulgence is not a permission to indulge in sin, but is a remission of punishment due to sin. Now in the early Christian Church certain sins were punished by long public penance, sometimes for days, at other times for years. But the Church was often indulgent, and loosed or freed Christians from all or part of their public penance, if they showed other good dispositions, or performed certain works of charity. The Church had that power in the name of God as surely as the state has the power in its own name to commute a sentence or even release a criminal altogether under certain circumstances. Christ said to the Church, "Whatsoever you shall loose upon earth shall be loosed also in heaven." Matt. XVIII., 18. That the merits of Christ and of the Martyrs and Saints of the ages are at the disposal of the Church is also a consequence of the doctrine of the Communion of the Saints. And that power of commuting or even of remitting penances and expiations exists in the Church to-day, being exercised by the granting of indulgences.

995. *What do you mean by an indulgence, say, of forty days?*

An indulgence of forty days means that the Church liberates us from that amount of expiation of our sins which would be equal to a forty days' public penance in the early Church. It does not mean forty days less purgatory. Such an indulgence is called a partial indulgence.

996. *What is a plenary indulgence?*

A plenary indulgence remits all the punishment due to our sins. If one gained a plenary indulgence perfectly at the hour of death, he would be exempt from any purification in purgatory. Such an indulgence would not increase one's merit, but would merely free from the penalties due to past sins. The conditions for the gaining of a plenary indulgence are as a rule earnest prayer for the Pope's intentions, and often, Confession and Communion. The Pope's intentions are for the peace of the world, the extension of the Kingdom of Christ, and the conversion of non-Catholics to the true faith.

997. *Can indulgences be applied to the souls in purgatory?*

Yes, but by God alone. We can but ask Him to accept indulgences on their behalf. But we can certainly offer them with a definite conviction of their normal acceptance by God for those we love, even as we can share our goods in this life with more needy friends. This too is implied by the doctrine of the Communion of Saints.

998. *If a plenary indulgence be applied to a certain soul in purgatory there would be no more need to pray for that soul.*

A plenary indulgence, of course, would be able to liberate a soul from purgatory. But we cannot know that we have satisfactorily fulfilled all the conditions necessary for the gaining of a plenary indulgence, and we cannot know for certain that God has actually accepted it, if gained, on behalf of the particular soul we have in mind. We know the general principle that indulgences are beneficial to the souls in purgatory, and we gain and offer them to God, leaving all questions as to their application to Him.

999. *Do you deny that indulgences were sold in the middle ages?*

They were never sold with the sanction of the theology of the Church. If unscrupulous individuals sold indulgences, such traffic in them would no more militate against the Church than would my own conduct did I myself adopt the practice privately.

1000. *Pope Leo X. sold indulgences in Germany to get money for St. Peter's. Do you think it right to sell pardons for sins?*

An indulgence is not a pardon for sin. It can be gained only by one who is not in a state of sin, and who has previously secured forgiveness of his sins by repentance and confession. Then, and then only, an indulgence is a remission of further penalties due to sin. It is absolutely wrong, of course, to sell indulgences. Pope Leo X. did not do so. There were abuses by some individuals in this matter, but they were never with the sanction of the Church. The Pope granted the favor of certain indulgences to those who would give alms towards the building of St. Peter's in Rome. But there is a difference between giving alms to a good work, and giving money to purchase something of equivalent value. Remember that Christ had a special blessing for the widow who gave her mite as an alms to the temple in Jerusalem. Would you accuse Him of selling that blessing for a mite?

1001. Are not Papal Bulls and indulgences still sold in Spain, and cannot any crime be committed and an indulgence obtained, if sufficient money be forthcoming?

A Papal Bull is simply a Papal document with a leaden seal or bulla attached to it. It need have nothing whatever to do with indulgences. Indulgences have never been for sale as far as the Catholic Church is concerned, and are not sold in Spain or anywhere else. If a man commits mortal sin, not all the indulgences in the world could forgive it. They are not for the forgiveness of sin, but can be gained only after such sins have been forgiven by other means. Since they can be gained only by people in a state of grace they are an inducement not to fall into sin. And they may be obtained, not by money, but by certain good works such as prayer, almsgiving to the poor, etc.

1002. After due purification in purgatory, you maintain that souls will be admitted to heaven. What is this heaven?

Heaven is the destiny in which a human soul will, if saved, be happy in the clear and immediate sight of God for all eternity. Before the resurrection of the body the soul alone enjoys this vision of God; after the resurrection, the body will be re-united with the soul and will share in its glory and joy.

1003. May not heaven and hell be our present thought-forms which will give way to other thought-forms when we leave the body and go to the unknown?

We do not go to the unknown, though we do go to the as yet unexperienced. Christ has revealed the essential elements of our future lot. Meantime heaven and hell are not our present thought-forms. Heaven is prepared independently of our thinking processes. Christ said definitely, "I go to prepare a place for you, that where I am you also may be." Thus our own thoughts do not make heaven. Also Christ said, "Depart from me you cursed into the everlasting fire which was prepared for the devil and his angels." Hell therefore is also independent of men's thoughts.

1004. How do you know that there is a heaven?

God has revealed the fact. "Be glad and rejoice," said Christ, "for your reward is very great in heaven." Matt. V., 12. That heaven is not in this life, nor is it to be on this earth. "I go to prepare a place for you. I will come again and will take you to myself, that where I am you also may be." Jn. XIV., 3. The conditions of heaven will differ from any we know in this life. "For when they shall rise from the dead they shall neither marry nor be married, but are as the angels in heaven." Mk. XII., 25. "They died . . . confessing that they are pilgrims and strangers on the earth. They that say such things do signify that they seek a country . . . they desire a better, that is to say, a heavenly country." Heb. XI., 13-16. And St. John tells us that, "God shall wipe away all tears from their eyes: and death shall be no more, nor mourning, nor crying, nor sorrow shall be any more, for the former things are passed away." Rev. XXI., 4.

1005. Where is heaven?

I cannot tell you in terms of longitude and latitude, as we mark out places on this earth. Such terms suggest a place in space, and space is measured by distance, and distance in turn is calculated from the material conditions of bodies which have nothing in common with spiritualized beings. It is quite useless, then, to ask for an explanation of heaven in terms of geography and geometry. Such a request would be like asking for the geographical location of God. Spirit beings have no "whereness" as we understand that notion. When Christ said, "I go to prepare a place for you, that where I am you also may be," He was speaking to human beings, and used a language they could understand, although it was necessarily an inadequate explanation. Heaven and our ideas in our present state have no really common ground to work upon.

1006. The fact remains that you do not know where heaven is.

If I did know, that would not make heaven any more real, and my not knowing does not make it less real. Heaven is no more destroyed by our ignorance of its "location" than New York would be because a school child could not say where it existed. Nor has the knowledge practical value for us. If a brick hurtles through the air and fractures your skull, killing you, it is immaterial to you whence it came. You are dead, and the brick was a fact. If a man dies in serious sin, he is in hell. It is immaterial where. His misery is a fact. If he dies in God's grace, he is in heaven. It is immaterial where. His happiness is a fact. God has told us enough for all practical purposes, and we must be content for the time being with as much as God has been pleased to tell us.

1007. Christ ascended to heaven beyond the clouds. To the moon? Or did He continue beyond the sun and the stars? Or is heaven everywhere?

The ascension of Christ until a cloud received Him out of the sight of the Apostles was a phenomenon sufficiently clear to impress upon them some higher state of being. As a matter of fact He ascended only relatively to those who were watching Him. Our notions of ascent and descent are regulated by direction from the center of the earth. To the man on the opposite side of the earth the direction taken by Christ would be in the direction of descent. However, relatively to those watching Him, Christ ascended, and after a few moments they found themselves looking at a cloud. How far did Christ go? He merely allowed His supernatural qualities to assert themselves, and His body took upon itself a nature independent of all earthly conditions and limitations. He simply passed into another state of being, even as the thoughts incorporated in these words on paper are passing into another state of being within your mind as you read. And His new state at once renders useless all calculations based upon visible qualities as we know them. You might just as well try to measure abstract beauty with a wooden ruler. Christ's glorified body is not subject to conditions of which we have experience.

1008. You teach that heaven will last forever, although Christ said that heaven and earth shall pass away.

Heaven there means the heavens. Our Lord couples the expression with the earth, and predicts that the visible universe will undergo a great change. The heavens, or the whole universe together with the earth, will some day cease to be as we see them at present. The visible order will change, but the teachings of Christ shall not change, nor shall His predictions lack fulfillment in due course.

1009. *I cannot conceive a future state altogether satisfying.*

There is a big difference between imagining a future life and conceiving it. I cannot imagine or picture the future life any more than you can. The only images we could form would be derived from this life, and they would fit this life, not the next. Not without reason does God say, "Eye hath not seen, nor ear heard, neither hath it entered into the heart of man, what things God hath prepared for them that love Him." 1 Cor. II., 9. Yet although we cannot imagine what the next life will be like, we can conceive the fact that it will be, and also the intelligible principles by which it will be governed.

1010. *Will not heaven be monotonous—always existing with no hope of change?*

In heaven we shall be with Christ and as Christ. This supposes conditions of which we have no experience on earth. It is little use guessing. We have but to accept the fact that there is a heaven, avoiding sin and serving God in order that we may attain to it. Speculate about heaven as we will, we must not miss our eternal happiness, for we cannot afford to be without it.

1011. *Would the soul of a mother be unhappy in heaven if she saw her child in suffering and sorrow upon earth?*

Let us take it for granted that she is aware of her child's sorrow. Could she be aware of it and perfectly happy at one and the same time? She could not, were she subject still to conditions of earthly life as we know them. But in heaven she is subject to entirely different conditions. Jesus Himself certainly knows of the child's sufferings, and He loves the child more than does the mother, yet is perfectly happy despite this knowledge and love. It must be possible, then, to be aware of a loved child's sorrow and yet to be quite happy in heaven. It may be explained as follows:—Even in this life we can love directly or indirectly. I may be very fond of a friend directly. By that very fact I am well-disposed towards anyone else who is dear to him, and if I meet such a one, say his mother, my love for my friend overflows to her. But it remains love of my friend directly. The mother participates in my love for him. Had I not that love for him, I would be indifferent to her. Now in heaven, the one absorbing love is love of God and that love renders one perfectly happy. All natural love is merged in that one great love as a drop of water in the ocean. A mother, then, is no more rendered unhappy by the knowledge of her child's suffering than God Himself could be rendered unhappy by it. Her outlook has changed. God's will makes her supremely happy. She realizes the spiritual and eternal good which God intends to draw from sufferings proper to our present state. And the conditions of her lot do not admit of sadness in any shape or form. We are dealing, of course, with a mystery, and cannot hope to comprehend it fully whilst still in this life.

1012. *You have spoken repeatedly of the day of resurrection and of judgment. Are all to rise from the dead, or only some?*

All are to rise from the dead. "The hour cometh wherein all that are in the graves shall hear the voice of the Son of God. And they that have done good things shall come forth unto the resurrection of life; but they that have done evil, unto the resurrection of judgment." Jn. V., 28-29. Thus, too, St. Paul tells us, "Behold I tell you a mystery. We shall all indeed rise again." 1 Cor. XV., 51.

1013. *What is the purpose of the resurrection?*

In order that complete man, body and soul, may attain an eternal destiny, and that the body which good people have mortified for the love of God, and which evil people have wickedly indulged for the love of self, may share the fate of the soul. Human beings in their complete nature will thus glorify God's mercy and justice.

1014. *What of souls already in hell, heaven, or purgatory?*

When their bodies rise from the grave, each soul will be re-united with its own proper body, the body sharing the fate merited for it by the soul. On that last day, of course, which will be the day of judgment for all mankind, purgatory will cease to exist. Our Lord tells us that there will be but two sentences. Matt. XXV., 34-41. The souls which have not finished their purification will be purified completely on the day itself, intensity supplying for any lack of duration. God will find no difficulty in arranging that.

1015. *What will the body be like?*

These self-same bodies will rise, but not entirely as they are at present because while the substance remains the same, the qualities of that substance will be changed. They can never completely change their nature so as to become purely spiritual beings, such as God Himself, or the angels. Thus St. Paul says, "The dead shall rise again incorruptible, and we shall be changed." 1 Cor. XV., 51-52. Our bodies, then, will not be purely spiritual, but rather spiritualized. They will share sufficiently in the spiritualizing influence of the soul to be rendered no longer subject to the possibility of death. Rightly, however, St. Paul says, "I tell you a mystery." For how all will eventuate, and exactly what will happen, is known to God alone. We know merely the fact that all human bodies will rise again at the last day.

1016. *Are you aware how many millions there will be? This makes me doubt even the existence of God!*

Now I must ask you to take this reasonably. That there will be millions of human beings proves the existence of God. How can their number disprove it? Each being is a reason for God's existence, and if anything, the multiplication of beings is the multiplication of reasons for His existence. Meantime I am not aware how many millions there will be on the day of judgment. I know merely that there will be many millions. But that affords no difficulty save for my imagination.

1017. *How could all be assembled at once on this small earth?*

With the data at present at my disposal I cannot say. But I can conceive of any possibility except that the general resurrection will not occur. Remember that we are warned that the heavens and the earth as we know them will be changed, a new order of things coming into existence. Remember, too, that we are dealing with an omnipotent God, who created the universe from nothing and who can certainly do with it what He wills. Were the earth not large enough to hold the millions of men, God could simply will its amplification until it could hold them, even as Christ amplified the substance of loaves and fishes. But whatever the explanation, doubts could occur only to the man who insists upon measuring the Creator by the creature and who believes that, because man could not do a thing, or could not imagine a thing, therefore God cannot do it. After all, I could not create a universe, nor could I imagine how it could have been created out of nothing. Yet I cannot deny that God did create it, for the whole universe cries out against such an absurd conclusion.

1018. *If we are judged individually at death, why are we all to be judged again at the last day? God must already know.*

God does not judge in order to discern guilt. At the particular judgment, which takes place as individuals die, God apportions to each soul relative remuneration or retribution. But at the end of the world, all souls will be re-united to their bodies. the souls of the just not losing their happiness, the souls of the lost not escaping their misery. The general judgment will then take place for the general manifestation of God's justice. All men will then acknowledge His attributes, even those who have denied them during this earthly life. But those who availed themselves of God's mercy will have nothing to fear on that day.

1019. When will the end of the world come?

No human being can say. Christ Himself refused to give any definite information on the subject. "Of that day or hour no man knoweth, neither the angels in heaven, nor the Son, but the Father." Mk. XIII., 32. The uncertainty is deliberate, so that men will be encouraged to live good lives in constant expectation of the possible end. So, too, the moment of our death is uncertain, and for all practical purposes death is the final coming of Christ for us. For the soul is at once judged and declared definitely to be a subject of heaven or of hell.

1020. Did not Christ Himself believe that the end of the world was at hand? I refer you to Lk. IX., 27.

In that text Christ says, "I tell you of a truth: There are some standing here that shall not taste death till they see the kingdom of God." But those words have no reference to the end of the world. Christ often called His Church His Kingdom. When He said to St. Peter, "I will build my Church . . . and give to thee the keys of the kingdom of heaven," He identified the two notions. Again, when He said that His kingdom was to be as a net holding good and bad fish He obviously referred to His Church in this world. And within thirty years of His death, that kingdom of Christ had spread throughout the known world, many, who had heard Christ, living to see its establishment. Meantime Christ's prediction that His Church would go to all nations, even to the uttermost parts of the earth, and His promise to be with it all days even to the end of the world, show that He did not expect the end of that world to be at hand. Also, He proved abundantly His divinity and knowledge of the future. It is absurd to say that He was not aware of the subsequent history of the world as it has actually unfolded itself.

1021. St. Paul thought the end was imminent, and told the Thessalonians that they would go to heaven with him.

St. Paul did not believe that the end was near. In 1 Thess. IV., 16, he says that the Lord will certainly come again, adding, "Then we who are alive, who are left, shall be taken up together with them in the clouds to meet Christ." But he does not say that he himself and his listeners would still be living when Christ comes. He could not intend such a thing, knowing that it is not given to any many to know the day or the hour of Christ's coming. He knew simply that there will still be some Christians living on earth in that day, and intended "such of us Christians as may still be living." When Christ comes, St. Paul's words will be fulfilled. Evidently some of the Thessalonians misunderstood his words, for in his second epistle to them he writes, "Be not easily moved . . . neither by spirit, nor by word, nor by epistle as sent from us, as if the day of the Lord were at hand." 2 Thess. II., 2.

1022. World events and the signs of the times prove that the end of the ages is at hand now in our own days.

I do not think there is a single age in the history of the Church when men have not said that. And history has proved them wrong. You may think present signs proof, but Christ said that it is not given to man to know. At best we can but conjecture, and your opinion is nothing more than a conjecture. Christ gave general signs, it is true, but He purposely left them obscure, telling us that the end would certainly come, but not telling us when.

1023. *Never in history were there such plagues and rumors of war as to-day.*

That is simply unhistorical. Hundreds of years ago the black death swept through Europe, and history is one long account of wars. I do not think that even the general signs given by Christ are approaching the completion of their fulfillment yet, and I do not think that the end is likely to occur in our own days. I do not claim to know, of course. You differ, thinking that the end is near at hand. But whether I am right or you are right, let us remember that as far as we are concerned individually, our own deaths will carry us to our personal judgments; and when our own deaths are to occur is God's secret. God can take me now as I am speaking to you, or you as you are listening to me. Let us both be ready to meet God with true sorrow for our sins and great love for Him when He does take us from this world.

CHAPTER ELEVEN

THE CHURCH IN HER MORAL TEACHINGS

1024. *Does not the Catholic Church permit the use of lies in the defence of her worn-out dogmas?*

Her dogmas are anything but worn-out. However to your main point I must reply by giving you the moral teaching of the Church concerning lies. The Church absolutely prohibits the use of any dishonest means, and declares that a deliberate lie is a sin under all circumstances. No good end in view can justify a lie.

1025. *May a Catholic make a false oath to non-Catholics on behalf of his religion?*

He may not make a false oath to anyone on behalf of anything. The mere fact of calling upon the God of truth to witness to a falsehood is a grave sin under any circumstances, and a sacrilege. Nor is this true only for a Catholic. It is true for any man at all. Every Catholic knows that it is never lawful to tell a deliberate lie, and that it is still more unlawful to confirm a lie by a false oath.

1026. *Your doctrines seem fair enough, but are they show-case doctrines for the public? In other words, does not your Church allow you to use mental restriction or reservation in your replies over the air?*

I have never used mental reservation in explaining any teachings of the Church. Nor would I be justified in doing so. Even though mental reservation can be lawful in certain circumstances, you must not think that the Church allows it as a regular thing. It can be lawful, for although no one is ever allowed to say what is not true, one is not always obliged to say what is true. In mental restriction no lie is told, but part of the truth is withheld. Thus, to save a small boy from a bully, another lad could say, "He ran down this street towards the station." But he does not add, "And he turned down the first street on the right." He reserves that information within his own mind, and the mental restriction is quite lawful in such a case. However, since it misleads, the Church says that mental restriction is lawful only when there are sufficiently grave reasons either of justice or of charity to justify it. It is not lawful whenever we please. But there is no sufficient reason for mental reservation when one is asked to explain the teachings of the Catholic Church, and in my replies I have never made use of it.

1027. *I object to the permission of mental restriction under any circumstances, since withholding part of the truth misleads the listener just as if the speaker had lied.*

If all that the speaker says is true, you cannot accuse him of lying. To be silent is not to lie. We may say that such a man is unjust, if he ought to speak yet refuses to do so. We may say that he is disobedient, if he is commanded by lawful authority to tell the rest, and will not. But he is not a liar, for he has not said what is untrue. Thus Christ said to the Apostles "Go up to the festival day, but I go not up to this festival day." Jn. VII., 8. Then, after they had gone without Him, "He Himself went, not openly, but in secret." The full truth was, "I go not in the ordinary way you would expect, and with you; but I intend to go another way known to Myself alone and of which I do not wish to inform you now." But Christ did not add the latter words, although He knew that the disciples would be misled. Yet we cannot accuse

Christ, who was truth itself, of telling a lie. As a matter of fact it is not only lawful not to say what is true, but at times there may be a grave obligation not to do so. However, in certain circumstances it would be quite wrong to make use of mental restriction. Its use supposes always a justifying reason, whether of justice or of charity.

1028. You speak of charity, yet are not Catholic children taught to hate Protestants?

No. They are forbidden to do so, and are taught to pray for them.

1029. Do Catholics take an oath never to buy from a Protestant what they can purchase from a fellow Catholic?

No. If a Catholic takes an oath injurious to an enemy because he is an enemy he commits a serious sin. Catholics are quite free to deal with whom they please in business. The ordinary Catechism puts the question, "Are we obliged to love our enemies?" and gives the reply, "We are obliged to love our enemies. Love your enemies; do good to them that hate you; bless them that curse you; and pray for them that persecute and calumniate you."

1030. How do you reconcile the conduct of bitter Catholics with the teachings of Christ?

It is impossible to do so. But if some individuals seem to lack charity you will find that such conduct is opposed to the teachings of their Church. Such bitterness is not justifiable, and arises from human weakness and lack of self-control. But bitterness is not common amongst Catholics, though they suffer much from anti-Catholic prejudice.

1031. Is a Catholic employer obliged to show special favor to Catholic employees?

No. He certainly may do so, provided his motive be positive charity towards them, and not in the least dictated by dislike of his non-Catholic employees; and also provided it involves no injustice towards those employees. Thus St. Paul says, "Let us work good to all men, but especially to those who are of the household of the faith." Gal. VI., 10.

1032. Would not such apparent preference of Catholic employees justify Protestants in boycotting Catholic labor?

No. No evil has been done. And even had it been done, you are not justified in rendering evil for evil.

1033. Is it a sin for a Catholic to employ a Mason?

No. The Freemason may have no personal antipathy towards Catholics at all, and even if he had, the law is, "Do good to those who hate you." If a competent Catholic applies for a position together with a Mason, a Catholic may employ his fellow Catholic by preference because he wants to do a good turn to a fellow Catholic from a motive of fraternal charity. But he must not consider as a reason for this the doing of a bad turn to the Mason. That would be quite un-Christian and un-Catholic.

1034. If a Catholic employs a Mason, what should other Catholics do?

They should behave just as they would otherwise. If a Catholic did do a bad thing by employing a Mason, who are his fellow Catholics to judge him and inflict a penalty? They must leave that to God. But, as I have said, a Catholic does not do any evil by employing a Mason. In purely business matters we Catholics object to being asked our religion, or to losing a position solely because we are Catholics.

And we must do to others as we would have them do to us, even if they themselves offend in this matter.

1035. Your charity does not make you bless the work of our good Protestant missionaries.

The Catholic Church cannot bless a false religion. We do admire the good dispositions and the zeal of those who do not realize that Protestantism is false. We have to love those who are mistaken, but not their mistakes. To ask the Catholic Church to bless the efforts of Protestant missionaries is just the same as asking her to bless Mahometan propaganda because there are some who sincerely believe in that form of religion.

1036. Scripture says, "Let brethren dwell together in unity."

As citizens we are brothers and should dwell together in civic unity. But those of our national brethren who have broken unity with the Catholic Church are not our brethren in religion. The Catholic Church did not break with them; they, or their ancestors, broke with the Catholic Church; and their duty is to return to Catholic unity. But meantime, let us maintain national fraternal unity as fellow citizens, and let not differences of religion affect our civic relations. By being a Protestant you do not offend me personally, and I have no reason to get upset about it. Likewise by being a Catholic I have not done you any injury, and you have no reason to feel personally offended.

1037. But your Church scatters curses, interdicts, and excommunications! Where is "Love your enemies" in this?

The Church condemns evil doctrine, and says that her condemnation falls upon such as knowingly and deliberately identify themselves with the condemned doctrine. The gentle Christ said, "If a man will not hear the Church, let him be as the heathen." St. Paul says, "If any man preach any other doctrine, let him be accursed." Gal. I., 8. St. Paul meant that in the Catholic sense I have explained. Love your enemies, by all means. But if you do, you will hate the evil which is to their harm. Hatred of that evil proves your love for them. If you did not love them, you would be utterly indifferent, and it would not matter to you what they believed or did. Or you might even rejoice to see them with the wrong doctrine, and deliberately refrain from uttering any warning. An interdict is but a suspension of public services in a given place when the people no longer deserve them, and then only in the hope that this grave penalty will bring them to a better frame of mind. Excommunication is but an official declaration that persons have behaved so badly that they have already cut themselves off from the grace of God, and therefore from the soul of the Church by their sin. And this official sentence, too, is but an effort to bring them to a better frame of mind. The intention is really to help such people in the end.

1038. Popes think it is right to excommunicate all who do not agree with them.

That is not true. Non-Catholics, who are unaware of their errors and who are not subjects of the Church, do not incur the penalty of excommunication. I wonder what you would say of St. Paul's words, "I have already judged ... with the power of Our Lord Jesus Christ ... to deliver him that hath so done ... to Satan." 1 Cor. V., 3-5. No Pope has ever spoken more severely than St. Paul in this passage.

1039. Can the Pope send people to hell by excommunication?

No. Excommunication cuts a man off from the visible Church on earth. But no man can be excommunicated save for mortally sinful conduct which supposes that he has already cut himself off from God's grace and from the soul of the Church. If he dies excommunicated and without repenting, his own unrepented sin takes him to hell, not the sentence of excommunication.

1040. But the moral theology of your Church is so dreadfully intolerant. If I follow apathetically the laws of that Church I might as well never have been endowed with freewill.

Catholics follow the laws of their Church not apathetically, but willingly. They know that her legislation rejoices in the authority of Christ. You might just as well say, "If I have to follow the ten commandments apathetically, I might as well have been born without freewill." You are mixing up physical freedom with moral freedom. Man is physically free to do good or evil, but he is not morally free to do evil. And as morally we are not free to disobey God's commandments, so we are not morally free to disobey the Church Christ commissioned to teach in His name.

1041. But Pope Pius IX. condemned liberty of conscience straight out.

He did not. He condemned the proposition that any man is free to embrace any religion he pleases. But this has nothing to do with liberty of conscience. It simply asserts the principle that, if God has given a definite revelation, it is man's duty to accept that revelation just as it is. Man cannot be morally free to reject a religion which he knows to have been revealed by God, and choose some other religion at his own pleasure. If a man does not know the true religion, and is erroneously convinced that it is right to be a Wesleyan or a member of any other non-Catholic Church, then Catholic moral theology so respects his conscience that it will not allow him to be received into the Church as long as he has this conviction.

1042. Protestantism is a great boon to Catholics in allowing you to broadcast your doctrines. Had the world remained Catholic you could not have done so, and Marconi would have been treated like other scientific men by your Catholic Church.

Protestantism is not a great boon to Catholics. Their greatest boon is their Catholic Faith which Protestantism would like to destroy. Wherever it could, Protestantism ever tended to persecution of Catholics. However, it was a boon in one way. If I had a malignant growth in my system the pain warning me of its presence would be a boon. At the time of the Reformation there were many evils, not in Catholic doctrine, but in the lives of many Catholic people. Protestantism gave warning of these evils, and the Catholic Church became keenly aware of the necessity of remedying these abuses. She did so, and thus indirectly Protestantism benefited the Church. And had the world remained Catholic I would certainly have been allowed to broadcast my doctrines, since they happen to be as Catholic as the Church herself. As for Marconi being treated like other scientific men by the Church, he would not suffer any harm by that. And he would not even meet with the reproof sometimes given to men of science, provided he kept within his proper realm of science and avoided dogmatizing erroneously in matters of religion. But Marconi has never done this.

1043. Had Christendom remained Catholic, could we have broadcasted Protestantism?

No. Why not? Because there is no reason why the broadcasting of truth should be prevented, but there is every reason why the broadcasting of error to people who already have the truth should be forbidden. Truth has a right to exist. Error of itself has no right to exist. He who would rid the world of all errors would do it a very great service.

1044. Would the Catholic Church abolish religious liberty in America if it had the power?

I am quite sure that we differ in our ideas of what religious liberty means. The Catholic Church would give everybody the liberty to be religious. But liberty to propagate any religion at all is another matter. The abuse and misuse of liberty and freedom are dangerous things. A man can be subject to erroneous religions and free from the true religion. Or he can be subject to the true religion and free from erroneous religions. However, you evidently mean freedom to maintain and propagate any religion or all religions. To that thought I would say this. If all in America were Catholics, the Church would rightly forbid the danger to their faith by the introduction of error. But if erroneous religions were already established and their adherents were in good faith, the Church would permit their continued existence and liberty. And such is the case at present. The non-Catholics in America have never been her subjects, and she is not called upon to adopt such general protective measures as would be the case in a completely Catholic nation.

1045. Do you approve the proclamation of religious liberty in Spain?

No. It was prompted by no desire for any purer religion, but by motives of hatred of all religion, or else simply by irreligion. It did not give the people liberty to be religious, for it restricted the liberty of good Catholics to practice their religion and educate their children according to the dictates of their conscience. Where is the religious liberty when the first move is to expel religious teachers and break up religious communities?

1046. Would a Catholic be justified in leaving the Catholic Church in order to join a Protestant form of religion?

No. No Catholic can ever have a just reason to leave the Catholic Church for any other form of religion. Nor could any man have a really sound reason for wanting to become a Protestant. In order to do so, one would have to ignore reason, if not violate it.

1047. What if he really believes Protestantism to be a more modern, helpful, and feeling religion?

He certainly might think it more modern, but that would not justify him in leaving the religion of Jesus Christ in the form prescribed by Christ for a more recent variation of human origin. He would not find it more helpful, for an erroneous religion, or form of religion, could not be so beneficial as the exact religion of Christ. And if he did find that it awakened more emotional feeling within him, that would not make it true. Religion is not primarily ordained for the providing of pleasurable experience to men, but in order to secure man's willed obedience to God.

1048. Could I give up Protestantism and become a Catholic in order to marry a Catholic?

If you are really convinced that the Catholic religion is false and your present religion true, you could not do so. You would be violating your conscience in a very grave matter. But you have probably taken your Protestant religion for granted, and have never gone deeply into the question. For the sake of the girl you can have the Catholic religion explained to you by a Priest. And if at the end of your instructions, you believe in it, you can become a Catholic for the love of God and for the religion's own sake. In this way you would not be becoming a Catholic for the sake of the girl, for you would become a Catholic in any case, even were you never to marry a Catholic. But if, at the end of your instructions, you still believed Catholicism false, you could not become a Catholic. That should be clear.

1049. *Did not the Pope forbid the liberty of the Press?*

He condemned the doctrine that the Press is quite free to propagate pernicious doctrine. Any sane man would admit that no one has liberty before God to propagate error and iniquity. There is no such thing as moral freedom to do what one likes whether God forbids it or not. And this the Pope clearly stated.

1050. *Why is there an index prohibiting books by the leading writers of the day?*

The Catholic Church exists to sanctify men. She must give them all that is necessary for their salvation, and safeguard them from all that could hinder it. Any Church which has no prohibition of dangerous books would not be doing its duty. Meantime if a leading writer publishes stuff which can lead souls to hell, then the Catholic Church forbids her children to be led by him. What sort of a Church would she be if she remained indifferent whilst the members she is supposed to be saving corrupt their minds and hearts?

1051. *Where is freedom in this?*

That should be obvious. Such prohibitions keep Catholics free from evil reading which could corrupt their faith or morals.

1052. *Is it mortal sin to read a book which one knows to be on the Index?*

Yes, unless he secures special permission for grave reasons to read it. The only books named in the Index are those which are sinful and immoral of their very nature, or which have been proved to give an entirely false and even blasphemous view of Christian doctrine.

1053. *Is the Bible on the Index?*

False translations of the Bible are on the Index. Catholics may read the safe translation provided for them, a translation which may be secured at any Catholic bookshop.

1054. *Does not the Church ban sex-books which can enlighten one as to the pitfalls of life?*

Some sex-books are banned, above all those which depend for their sale not upon their technical matter, but upon their lurid and suggestive style. Sex-books which are valuable to doctors and experts are allowed to them. As far as the ordinary non-professional human being is concerned, books treating of sex are not so valuable to the present-day generation as you think. Sex-knowledge is being spread by every possible means; but instead of people becoming enlightened to avoid the pitfalls of life, they are filling their minds with thoughts on a subject which is a pitfall in itself, and which would otherwise occupy far less of their attention. The criminal courts are certainly not one whit less busy because of the popular study of sex-questions.

1055. *Is not the Index an effort to suppress the truth?*

No. It is an effort to suppress error, which can poison the mind every bit as much as arsenic can poison the body.

1056. *It proves that your Church depends upon credulity rather than upon reason for its support.*

You miss the point. The Church is out for healthy reason, and forbids books which foster the credulity of her enemies. You might as well accuse a chemist of desiring the ill-health of his customers and not their health when he labels a bottle "Poison."

1057. Can books destroy peoples' faith if they are properly instructed?

What do you mean by properly instructed? If a Catholic has had long train-ing for years in logic, philosophy, history, Scripture, and theology, it is unlikely that reading would destroy his faith. But how many lay-people have had such training? Yet without it, few would be able to see through the fallacies latent in many books. So-called educated men who have had a good education in some mat-ters but not in others, have lost their faith through reading anti-Christian literature, not knowing sufficient in matters of religion to detect the errors of the books chosen.

1058. Will the Church be able to sustain this cunning censorship in per-petuity?

If parents prevent their children from reading harmful literature, would you call that cunning censorship, or wise parental control? The Catholic Church is the mother of all her spiritual children, and she exercises a wise parental control over their spiritual formation. Other churches have not the same interest in their mem-bers, and in any case no authority. The Catholic Church alone has a real sense of duty towards those whom she is commissioned to guide in the way of salvation.

1059. The real reason is because the Church is afraid that Catholics will find out the truth.

Let me give you a little parable. Almighty God established a paradise on earth, created Adam and Eve, and said, "Do anything you like, but do not eat of the tree which will give you acquaintance with evil. I forbid you to eat of that tree." But a certain wily serpent came along and said to Eve, "Why has God for-bidden you to eat of that tree?" And Eve replied, "God has commanded us not to touch it because He says that He knows that it is not good for us." The serpent replied, "The real reason is because God is afraid that your eyes will be opened, and that you will find out the truth and be equal to Himself." Adam and Eve ate of the tree and regretted it all their lives. Some Catholics have disobeyed the laws of the Church in this matter and have lost both their faith and their morals. But your explanation of the motives of the Catholic Church has a very familiar ring about it.

1060. You insist, then, that this prohibition of certain types of books is a reasonable measure?

I do. If it be in the interests of the public to have a "Pure Foods Act," is it not in the interests of Christians to have a "Pure Faith Act"?

1061. I suppose the inspectors under your "Pure Faith Act" would be Priests who would have to sin by reading the books first so as to be able to warn their flocks?

Priests have not always to be consulted. The moment a Catholic perceives a book to be dangerous to his faith or morals he knows from the doctrine concerning occasions of sin that he is obliged to cease reading it. Each is his own censor to a certain extent. In doubt, a book could be given to a Priest to read. The moment the Priest finds that the book is undoubtedly evil in itself, he closes it and forbids it. If it needs reading right through for purposes of refutation, he secures permis-sion from the Bishop and does it as a duty. Just as doctors have at times to attend to patients in a way which would be positively sinful for a non-professional man, so a Priest may have to study books to safeguard morals, books forbidden to those who have not the public duty. The Priest in this case would commit no sin, where others would do so.

1062. *Does the dictatorship of the Pope refer to spiritual things only?*

We cannot use the word dictatorship of the Pope in the ordinary sense of the word. The Pope has supreme authority according to the laws dictated by Christ in the constitution He gave to the Church. The authority of the Pope extends to both spiritual matters and to temporal matters in so far as they have connection with spiritual things. The Catholic Church is not a society of angelic beings, but of human beings who are composed of a spiritual soul and a material body. As a visible society of semi-spiritual beings it demands a spiritual religion expressed and regulated with the help of material means. This is in conformity with man's twofold nature. The Pope therefore has authority both in spiritual matters, and in temporal matters which are bound up with spiritual interests.

1063. *Is the temporal punishment of torture in accordance with the teachings of Christ?*

It is quite lawful to inflict pain as a punishment, or no school-master could punish a rebellious child. I am grateful now for many a punishment inflicted upon me by my parents in my childhood. In principle, the infliction of pain is lawful. The question rather concerns the degree of pain to be inflicted. Excessive pain is undoubtedly wrong, unjust, inhuman, and un-Christian.

1064. *But the history of your Church is one of excessive torture, unparalleled cruelty and injustice.*

You have read garbled accounts. No one denies the existence of cruelty and persecution in the history of the ages. But they have been exaggerated. Nor were they due to the Catholic point of view. They were in spite of the Catholic viewpoint, and due to the imperfect notions of the times, times in which Protestants were not less cruel than Catholics. My own course of reading as a Protestant bred in me the same repugnance for the Catholic Church as you now experience. I dreaded and hated the Church as a monstrous thing. Yet to-day I accept her as my mother, realizing that she has been caricatured by misunderstanding and misinformed writers. And over twenty years of association with the Catholic Church have only served to deepen my appreciation of her rational foundations, principles, and spirit.

1065. *Do you deny that your Church has been responsible for monstrous cruelties?*

I do. I say that such a doctrine is a monstrous fable. History shows that human beings, whether Catholics, Protestants, Mahometans or Pagans, have been guilty of great cruelties to one another. Even ecclesiastics, if you wish, through their own fault and not through any teaching of their Church, have been guilty of excessive cruelty. Such excesses cannot be justified, but it was their own personal conduct. It was not inspired by their Catholicity, but by their own mistaken, or even evil dispositions.

1066. *St. Thomas taught that heretics should be put to death.*

He had in mind such men as had been Catholics, and who labored to destroy the faith of other Catholics after their own lapse from the Church. And even then he puts the question speculatively. And he was quite logical. He argued that one who unjustly takes his neighbor's life by murder deserves death at the hands of the state. But he who destroys the faith of another robs him, not of his temporal life, but of his eternal life, which is far worse. The state, therefore, which is bound to safeguard the complete well-being of its citizens, would be justified in putting such a man to death, removing him permanently from among men to whom he can do so much damage. Speculatively, then, St. Thomas says that such a penalty would not be excessive. In practice he does not say that it should be done. **And** even if it were done, he writes that the Church whose mission is one of mercy must do all she can to win such a man from his sinful dispositions and destructive campaign, in order to save both his temporal and spiritual life if possible.

1067. Do you personally believe that all non-Catholics deserve burning at the stake?

No. Present-day Protestants are not ex-Catholics in bad faith, and even if they were I would not wish to burn them. Some of them might deserve it. Some Catholics certainly do deserve it, for if a traitor to his country deserves death, so too does a traitor to God who has a far greater claim to our loyalty than any country could possibly possess. However, thank God that neither non-Catholic people who might deserve it, nor bad Catholics who do deserve it, are likely to be burned to-day by their fellow men in this country. Your feelings are nearly as sensitive as my own on this point.

1068. What about the tortures of the Spanish Inquisition?

You have probably read many imaginary descriptions of that tribunal which pretend to be history. However let us be quiet about torture inflicted by Catholics four hundred years ago. Seventy years ago a young servant girl was transported for life to Tasmania for scorching linen whilst ironing, and that from England three centuries after the Reformation! We are rather in a glass house. In 1848 things occurred in Norfolk Island in the name of gentle English Protestant enlightenment which would make your hair stand on end. Here are the words of a document presented to Sir William Denison, of N.S.W.: "Floggings of the utmost brutality are incessant, as also the infliction of the 'Spread Eagle,' a species of racking and gagging with an instrument which cuts the tongue and mouth. Women are tortured by confinement in irons, iron collars around their necks, chained to the floor, and left on bread and water." And all this for the crime of stealing a tea-pot or a coat. These prisoners were our fellow Englishmen. Five are named from Middlesex; three from Surrey; others from Essex, Stafford, and Gloucester. Please don't ask me about the Inquisition. It makes me look up the records of what was done in the name of England after she had abandoned Catholic principles, and blush for our race.

1069. Llorente, secretary of the Inquisition in Madrid about 1790, says that during Torquemada's eighteen years some 8,800 persons in Spain alone were burned.

Llorente is discredited as an historian even by Protestant scholars. He was secretary to the Inquisition, some three hundred years after the death of Torquemada. But he was false to the Church and was expelled from Spain. After that he wrote his so-called and very biased history, pretending to make use of documents to which he said he had had access. When challenged even in his own day, he said that he had burned all the official papers upon which he had placed reliance. We cannot trust an historian who declares that he destroyed the original documents deliberately. Research has shown that about four thousand deaths occurred at the hands of the Spanish Inquisition during almost three centuries. But even did we accept 8,800 in a period of 18 years, that would work out at an average of some 500 a year. Sir James Stephens, in his History of English Criminal Law, shows that there were about 800 executions a year during the early post-Reformation period in England. Such severity was not due to Catholicism as such, but must be attributed to the general character of the times, which we are all glad have passed. If they have passed—the barbarity of the Great War leaves grave doubts!

1070. *Do you feel proud of yourself when you read of Torquemada?*

I do not feel very proud of myself. I am very proud of the Catholic Faith which, owing to God's sheer goodness, I now possess. But you have a wrong idea of Torquemada. He was head of the Inquisition in Spain, a great theologian and a good man. All the opprobrium associated with the Inquisition has been heaped upon his head, but unjustly. The cruelty and extravagance of other officials were despite him, and despite the protests and instructions of the Church. Popes Sixtus IV. and Innocent VIII. protested strongly against the excesses of disobedient officials, their protests proving that such excesses were not committed in the name of the Church. Yet even whilst we admit excesses, we must remember that they have been greatly exaggerated by partisan writers.

1071. *Why was the Inquisition established at all?*

On the same principle as that by which the U. S. Government passed the "Pure Foods Act" to prevent contamination of the foods we eat. The Inquisition was established and still exists in the Church to prevent the doctrine of Christ, which gives life to our souls, from being adulterated and contaminated. The Spanish Inquisition, of course, as a semi-political institution has lapsed.

1072. *You still justify an ecclesiastical Inquisition?*

Of course. It is as lawful and wise a tribunal as that for the censorship of films. And although the Holy See condemned brutal excesses, the Spanish Inquisition was as necessary for both Church and state in Spain as the Criminal Investigation Branch of the Police Department for the preservation of law and order in Chicago. There was no more need to suppress the Institution altogether because of abuses than there is to enforce prohibition because of individual abuses of drink, or to smash a pair of spectacles because dirt has spoiled their transparency.

1073. *How can you reconcile the Inquisition with the fact that God is love?*

The fact that God is love does not forbid the imprisonment of a criminal nor the hanging of a murderer. If love for the murderer does not prompt it, at least love for law and order, and love for other citizens suggests it. I am obliged to love my enemies, but not their crimes. Christ loved His enemies and prayed for them. Yet He told them that if they died in their sins they would be cast into hell for all eternity. Love does not forbid the punishment of crime. It insists that there should be some punishment so that men will not easily commit it.

1074. *But the Inquisition is not all! The Pope honored the Duke of Alva for the slaughter of 18,000 heretics.*

The Duke of Alva was a man of good and bad qualities. For his good qualities the Pope honored him by presenting him with a hat and sword. He did not honor him for the slaughter of 18,000 heretics, an event which happened afterwards. Alva was sent, not by the Pope, but by Philip II. of Spain to suppress a rebellion in Holland, then subject to Charles. In this expedition Alva showed himself to be a man of iron and blood, and Catholics condemn him for his conduct as much as any others could do. In reality he slaughtered about 6,000 heretics, not as heretics, but as rebels. In his vanity he himself multiplied the number three-fold, boasting that he had killed 18,000. However his disgraceful cruelty remains, but the Catholic Church was not to blame. If my parents teach me the right thing to do, and forbid me to do the wrong thing, you could not blame them were I to turn a criminal by my own choice. The same dear Alva took up arms against the Pope when it suited him later on! His spirit of obedience to the Church was not very remarkable.

1075. What about Cranmer, Ridley, and Latimer?

It is a grim fact that they were burned at the stake during the reign of Mary for high treason under laws framed by Cranmer himself during the reign of Edward VI. for the burning of both Protestants and Catholics who would not conform to the established Church of England!

1076. Did the Catholic Church protest against the massacre of Huguenots on St. Bartholomew's Day, Aug. 23, 1572?

Yes. That massacre had no connection whatever with the Catholic Church. The Church did not instigate the massacre, nor did the Pope have any knowledge of it beforehand. It was a purely political and deplorable murder engineered by Catherine de Medici, a woman almost completely irreligious. After its occurrence a lying report was sent to the Pope that it was a successful repression of a plot to murder the king. In thanksgiving for the king's safety, the Pope ordered a Te Deum to be sung in Rome. But when Gregory XIII. heard the real story he expressed his horror and condemnation, and refused to allow one of the leaders of the attack to be presented to him, saying, "I will not receive a murderer."

1077. Giordano Bruno was burned for saying that the earth moved round the sun. He died in 1600.

Bruno was not burned for that. His history would surprise, I think, even you. He apostatized from the Catholic Church and first joined the Calvinists. In 1580 he was excommunicated by them at Geneva. He went to England, but in 1584 had to leave because he proved to be a disturber of the peace, having among other things insulted the professors at Oxford by saying publicly that they knew more about beer than about Greek. He migrated to Germany, and was there excommunicated by the Lutherans in 1590. Returning to Rome he was excommunicated again by the Catholic Church, not for teaching the theory of Copernicus, but for blasphemy and heresy by denying the Divinity of Christ and asserting that He was but a magician. He was handed over to the secular authorities, and burned in the gentle style of those times as a traitor and as dangerous to the welfare of the state. Such, briefly, is the story of Giordano Bruno.

1078. Has not the Church always hindered the progress of science by her moral prohibitions?

No. The Catholic Church has ever conserved knowledge and encouraged true science. Her doctrine is that Catholic truth is of God, and that scientific truth is also of God. There cannot be a conflict therefore between Catholic truth rightly understood and demonstrated scientific truths. But the scientific truth must be demonstrated. A mere hypothesis may or may not be true, and as long as a doctrine is in the hypothetical stage the Church is prudent in her judgment. If the doctrine has no religious consequences, the Church is all encouragement in the pursuit of inquiry. If religious consequences are involved, she encourages inquiry, but forbids positive utterances until the hypothesis is proved definitely to be a fact. This has never hindered scientists, but has spurred them on to the securing, if possible, demonstrative proof of their theories.

1079. Why did the Church condemn Galileo? Were not the Cardinals wrong?

They were. But, as I have explained, the decision was not in any way connected with the infallibility of the Church. It was a reversible decision, and it was reversed in due time. The authorities at the time thought mistakenly that the theory of Galileo was opposed to Scripture, and also perceived as a fact that the propagation of the theory would tend to upset the faith of many of the simpler people. But this case does not justify the charge that the Church has consistently hindered scientific inquiry. As a matter of fact Galileo had not proved his case at all, and the Church encouraged men of science in every possible way to study the question and see whether his theory could possibly be demonstrated.

1080. Were not the Jesuits the very embodiment of the intolerant moral theology of the Catholic Church?

The Jesuits are members of a Religious Order whose members pledge themselves to love Jesus Christ as much as possible, to labor solely in His interests and in order to win as many souls as possible to His service.

1081. Did not Clement XIV. suppress the Jesuits because he was so shocked by their crimes, and die shortly afterwards from poison?

No. The Jesuits were very active in stemming the tide of the Reformation, and many of the Protestant princes and rulers were so persecuting the Church because of this that Clement XIV., in a moment of weakness and against his own convictions, suppressed the Order "for the peace of the Church." He did this under a great misapprehension, and under pressure. And the Order was rightly reinstated by another Pope. It is true that Clement XIV. died shortly after his action in suppressing the Jesuits, but to say that he was poisoned is sheer romance and without a trace of historical foundation. The anxiety of the whole case certainly undermined his health, and the medical certificate states that he died from a condition of scurvy and hemorrhoids, aggravated by worry. In other words, natural factors only accounted for his death.

1082. Pastor Chiniquy was a Priest who said that he left the Church because she was too intolerant.

He did not leave the Church voluntarily, but was expelled from it in 1851 by the Bishop of Montreal because the Church could not tolerate his immorality. He pretended repentance, promised to behave himself, and persuaded another Catholic Bishop to accept his services. But in 1856 he was again expelled for immorality. If Pastor Chiniquy is your only argument against the moral theology of the Catholic Church, there is nothing wrong with that theology. I think it was Dean Swift who gently remarked, "I wish when the Pope weeded his garden, he wouldn't throw the weeds over the fence into our grounds." But the Pope does not do this. Some foolish Protestants gather the weeds up carefully and cultivate them as precious plants.

1083. Does not the Bull Ad Extirpanda claim the right to force the Catholic Church upon unwilling men?

No. In that document the Pope commands Catholic princes to prevent the propaganda of those who would publicly labor to destroy the faith of those who already professed belief in Catholicism. The word exterminate does not mean in its Latin significance that such men should be killed, but that they should be banished or expelled from the country. Nicholas I., a Pope of the ninth century, had already said, "The Church has no sword but the spiritual. She is here, not to kill, but to give life." But she has to preserve the spiritual life of her subjects, and certainly has the right to appeal to the authorities in a Catholic state to protect their religious interests.

1084. Does not every Bishop swear to persecute and oppose all heretics, schismatics, and rebels against the Pope?

The Latin word persequor does not mean the same thing as the English word "persecute." It means that the Bishop must vigilantly watch against the inroads of heresy, and that he will enforce in his diocese and amongst his Catholic subjects the

laws preserving them from heresy, schism, or rebellion. Every Bishop swears that
he will maintain the discipline of the Church, in the interests of truth and morality.
Our own Archbishop took that oath. But if he were armed with a revolver and met
an unarmed Protestant in a secluded spot, he would not feel the least obligation in
virtue of his oath to put a bullet through the poor man.

**1085. The Church does not persecute because it cannot. Persecution in
the world to-day for religious opinions is impossible.**

Persecution in the world for religious opinions is not impossible to-day. It
occurs. In Russia and Mexico physical violence has been employed again and again.
In almost all Protestant countries Catholics are persecuted by moral antipathy. But
Protestants are not persecuted in Catholic countries. Persecution merely because of
religious opinions is against the very principles of the Catholic Church. You seem
to think that she would persecute if she could. The real truth is that she has no
desire to do so. In his Encyclical on Indifference in Religion, Pope Pius IX. set
out the Catholic attitude in the following words: "Catholics must in no way whatever
adopt the attitude of enemies towards those who are not united with us in the same
bonds of faith and charity. Rather they must strive to help them by all the duties of
Christian charity, assisting the poor, the sick, and those afflicted by any other calamities. Their first duty, of course, is to try to lead them out of the darkness of error,
in which unhappily they are, and to draw them to Catholic truth, and to that Catholic
Church which holds out her arms to them ever inviting them to her embrace, that
by faith, hope, and charity, and all other good works, they may attain eternal salvation." Such is the official doctrine of the Church.

1086. Why does the Pope object to the Christian religion in Italy?

He does not. The Catholic religion is completely Christian, and the Pope would
like to see Italy completely Catholic so that it would be completely Christian.

1087. Why does he object to the preaching of Protestantism in Italy?

He does not object to Protestants living in Italy, and worshipping God in their
own way according to their conscience whilst they are there. He does object to their
trying to destroy the faith of Catholics. He would have very little interest in his
people if he did not.

**1088. Then why, by broadcasting, try to destroy the faith of Protestants
here? Is it wrong for Protestants there, but right for Catholics here
where they are only a small percentage of the population?**

The fact that there is but a small percentage of Catholics here has nothing to do
with the question of right or wrong. If so, where Catholicism is the prevalent religion
you would have to admit its right to exclude Protestantism. Or again, you would
have to admit the truth of Mahometanism where that religion is in the ascendancy.
If Catholicism is true in Italy, it is true here; if false here, it is false there. Relative
numbers have nothing to do with it. Christianity was true when Christ and His
twelve Apostles were the only ones in the world who believed in it. Again, the broadcasting of Catholic doctrine will not destroy the faith of Protestants. If it affects
them at all, it is calculated to perfect their faith by leading them back to the full and
perfect religion of Christ in the Catholic Church. On the other hand, the propagation
of imperfect Protestant teaching tends to destroy the full faith of Catholics. Truth
carries its own right to exist. It is a good thing to spread knowledge of the truth.
But error has no right to exist. It is a good thing to destroy error. Now the Catholic
Church, having the truth, has a right to exist and teach everywhere. In fact, she has
to do so, for Christ commanded her to teach all nations. Protestantism has not the
same right. It retains some elements of Catholic truth, but many corruptions of

its own. However sincere Protestants may be, Protestantism is an erroneous form of religion, and it keeps people from the real truth. The Catholic Church therefore rightly objects to the propagation of error among those who have the truth, and rightly propagates the truth amongst those in error. It is a perfectly logical position. Of course you will say that this doctrine supposes the truth of the Catholic position. It does, and the truth of that position I have often shown.

1089. Is it a sin for a Catholic to attend weddings in Protestant churches?

The law of the Catholic Church forbids participation in a religious service that is not Catholic because it is an implied repudiation of the faith which a Catholic professes to be the only true faith. It is good for non-Catholics to realize this so that, knowing that Catholics must refuse, they will not ask them to assist at the religious ceremony itself and then be offended as if refusal were due to lack of friendship.

1090. May a Catholic act as best man or bridesmaid at a non-Catholic wedding?

A Catholic may not act as an official witness. A wedding in a church is not a merely social event; it is also a religious ceremony. Though non-Catholics may not see it, the Catholic position is alone logical. Protestants should choose witnesses of their own faith and spare Catholics the pain of having to refuse.

1091. Why is the Catholic Church so severe in her law in this matter?

For very good reasons. Firstly, loyalty to Christ forbids our sanctioning in any way a false form of religion, and Protestantism is a corruption of Christ's religion. If one may attend any religious services, irrespective of creed, then a Christian could assist at pagan rites. There must be a limit somewhere, and the Catholic Church says that those limits exclude any false form of religion, even though it be an adulterated form of Christianity. The presence of a Catholic at Protestant services is a silent approval of the error that one religion is as good as another. St. Paul says, "A man that is a heretic avoid." Tit. III., 10. St. John says, "If any man come to you and bring not this doctrine, receive him not into the house, nor say to him: 'God speed you.'" 2 Jn. V., 10. The law of the Church, too, protects the faith of Catholics. If they attend Protestant services, there is always a danger that they will participate actively in a shamefaced way, and also a danger of their drifting into indifferentism and weakening in their own faith. Their presence, also, can be a cause of scandal to other Catholics who may begin to think that it is right for them also to attend at non-Catholic Churches. Nor is such attendance a kindness to Protestants. The abstention of Catholics from their services is a lesson of the utmost importance to them. Our attendance would sanction to a certain extent their idea that their religion also is as good as our own. But our absence from their Churches gives them food for thought. An Anglican might say, "Well, I have seen Methodists, Presbyterians, Congregationalists, and people of many other religions at our services; but I have never yet seen a Catholic associated with us." And the fact that the vast Catholic Church denies their claims has led many a man from the chaos of the different Protestant Churches to the true religion.

1092. Catholics will be despised as narrow-minded Pharisees.

Would a Christian who refused to attend pagan rites be a Pharisee? And is it narrow-minded to limit one's conduct according to the dictates of conscience? If so, it is better not to be what you would term broad-minded. And it is rather absurd to suggest that you despise Catholics for being true to their convictions. You should rather despise them if they were not.

1093. *They will certainly lose their friends by such neglect of civil duties, and the causing of such discord.*

If any discord arise, it is unavoidable. It is good to have peace, but not peace at any price; above all when the price is the violation of conscience. If Protestants are angry because Catholics will not do what the Catholic conscience forbids, then it is not the fault of Catholics. In any case, are not religious obligations greater than civil obligations? And is not the loss of earthly friends better than the loss of the friendship of Christ—if the worst should happen?

1094. *But your attitude is an insult to Protestants. You even compare their religion with paganism.*

It is not an insult to Protestants that a Catholic cannot attend a Protestant service. Every man must be guided by his own conscience. How far would one have to give up having any convictions at all, lest he insult those with whom he has to disagree? Nor do I compare Protestantism with paganism. I compared the unlawfulness of a Protestant assisting at pagan rites with the unlawfulness of a Catholic assisting at Protestant rites. A Catholic would be as justified in acting according to Catholic principles as a Protestant would be justified in fidelity to his own. That was the whole of my comparison.

1095. *Are not Protestants good and sincere people?*

It is not a question of their goodness, but of the religious system they support. No Catholic may give the impression by his presence that Protestantism as a system is a lawful substitute for the true Church.

1096. *Protestants often attend Catholic services.*

You must not think that Catholics can do with their conscience what you can do with your conscience. A Protestant should say, "If Catholics really believe that their religion is the only form sanctioned by Christ, then I do not blame them for living up to their convictions. I would blame them did they seek to please men rather than God. And if I had their ideas I would do just as they do."

1097. *Do Protestants sin in attending Catholic services?*

That would depend upon their convictions. We do not judge Protestants on principles they do not hold. If they think one religion as good as any other, I suppose they could attend almost any religion with a good conscience. But if an Anglican, for example, thought his to be the only true Church, and that all others were wrong, he would sin by attending other forms of worship. Objectively, of course, a Protestant does not sin by attending Catholic services. One who has the wrong religion may attend services of the right religion. But he who has the right religion certainly cannot attend the services of a wrong religion. Catholics may not assist at any but Catholic services.

1098. *You must do to others as you would have them do to you.*

That cannot apply in matters of conscience. If so, I could say, "Well now, if I were a murderer I would like him to help me to strangle that man. And since he is a murderer, I must do to him as I would like him to do to me in similar circumstances, and help him to strangle his victim." That is absurd. In all matters where we can do it with a good conscience we must do to others as we would have them do to us. In any case, we Catholics do not wish any Protestant to violate his conscience and offend God in order to please us.

1099. *Let me give you a concrete case. You are a convert to the Catholic Church and a Priest. Now if your own mother died, would you attend her Protestant burial?*

Happily my own mother also became a Catholic. However, had she died as a Protestant, I would have attended her funeral, but would have taken part in none of the religious ceremonies associated with that funeral.

1100. *God says, "Honor thy father and thy mother."*

That commandment comes after the commandments dealing with God's personal rights, and it is to be observed for the love of God. It never demands that I dishonor God in order to honor my parents.

1101. *You would love your mother so little whilst pretending to love God!*

Love of my mother would take me to the funeral; love of God would prevent me from joining in the rites of a false religion.

1102. *There must be something radically wrong with your conscience!*

There would be, if I could take part in a religious service conducted in the name of a religion opposed to the Church established by Christ. It would be disloyalty to Christ, and I cannot sin even for the sake of my mother. She would not be my mother but for the love of God, and the more we appreciate God's gifts the less right we have to offend Him because of them.

1103. *Is it because she could not believe what you believe?*

As I remarked, she received the grace of the Catholic faith before she died. But had she not, it would rather have been because I could not believe what she believed, and could not honestly pretend to do so, that I would have refrained from any part in the rites of a non-Catholic religion. And my particular mother would have been the last in the world to expect me to do so.

1104. *Does not the Church absolutely forbid Catholics to become Freemasons?*

Yes.

1105. *You have never been a Mason. How can you know anything about it?*

I seem to know so much about Masonry that I have been challenged over and over again with the charge that I am an ex-Mason of the Royal Arch Degree. However I have never been a Mason. But just as I can speak about New York even though I have never visited that city, so I have authentic information about the origin and aims of Masonry.

1106. *Your Church takes the stand of an intolerant bully in this matter.*

She does not. If a man wishes to join a club and is presented with a book of rules, has he the right to say, "Here, you can't bully me like this. How dare you talk to me of obligations!" The officials would rightly reply, "Nonsense. You wish to be a member of this club, and these are our rules. We are not bullying you. You want to be a member of this club, and we cannot accept you unless you promise to conform to the regulations." So the Catholic Church has the right to legislate for those who choose to remain or to become Catholics. She simply says to Catholics, "If you join the Masons, you deprive yourself of the benefits of the Catholic faith." Where is the bullying in that? It is but an exercise of lawful authority. Christ said to His Church, "Whatever you bind on earth is bound also in heaven." St. Paul says "Obey your prelates and be subject to them, for they watch as having to render an account of your souls." Heb. XIII., 17. The Church has a grave responsibility, and men can disobey only by the renunciation of their Christian privileges.

1107. Why do you hate Masons?

I do not. The Masonic system and the Catholic system are not reconcilable, and no Catholic may join the Lodge without thereby renouncing his Church. But there is no reason why Catholics and Masons, making allowance for each other's persuasions, should not be personally friendly in this country, observing always true charity towards individuals.

1108. If you do not hate Masons, you at least hate Catholics who become Masons.

I have no hatred of Catholics who have become Masons. I am very sorry for the Catholic who does so, and would move heaven and earth to reach him before he died, were such a Catholic to send for me on his death-bed, as indeed has happened.

1109. When did the Church first forbid Catholics to be Masons?

Pope Clement XII issued the first formal prohibition in 1738. As modern Freemasonry began in 1717, this was just twenty-one years after its origin.

1110. In ancient times Priests used to be good Masons.

Masonry did not exist in ancient times. But if, since the decree of Pope Clement, a renegade Priest did join Masonry, he at once ceased to be a practical member of the Catholic Church by the mere fact of doing so.

1111. Was not Pope Pius IX. a Mason?

No. Those writers who have said that he was, have quoted only spurious documents, and have given such contradictory details that Pope Pius IX. must have been initiated on half a dozen different occasions and in as many places. Dudley Wright, in his book, "Roman Catholicism and Freemasonry," says that Pope Pius IX. was initiated as a Mason on August 15, 1839, at Palermo. Yet on the date given, Pius had been a Bishop for more than twelve years. The document upon which he relied has been proved a forgery over and over again.

1112. Why are Catholics forbidden to be Masons?

However tolerant individual Masons may be towards the Catholic Church, and with all due charity towards individual Masons, the Church forbids her own subjects to join the Masonic Lodge for many and good reasons. Masonry is a secret society of a character opposed to right moral principles; its oath is too sweeping and unjust; in the name of Masonic fraternity, much injustice has occurred in ordinary life, Masonry counting more than merit and capability; on the Continent of Europe Masonry aims at the destruction of the Catholic Church, and the Church could not but forbid Catholics to join her avowed enemy; nor could the Church distinguish between Masons of one country and of another—Masons claim worldwide solidarity, and all must fall under the ban; and, in any case, Masonry claims to be a religion derived from mythological sources, and as such is on a par with all other false religions as far as the Catholic Church is concerned.

1113. You say that Masonry is condemned as being a secret society.

Not merely as a secret society, but as one involving a particular kind of secrecy. A member takes a solemn oath to keep secret any matters heard within the Lodge with no previous idea of their nature and with no certainty of the extent to which he is committing himself. Many a man who has taken that oath has refused, because of it, to follow his conscience. Masonic friends of mine have admitted this to me. Secrecy is permissible only where legitimate business is concerned, and no man is morally free to bind himself blindly by an oath, when he is not even sure that injustice to others will not be involved. Albert Pike, an American Mason, tells us in his book, "The Inner Sanctuary," that it is the duty of a Royal Arch Mason to espouse the cause of a companion Royal Arch Mason, whether he be right or wrong. It is immoral to take any oath which is likely to involve such conduct.

1114. We Masons are bound to secrecy by our code just as you Priests by yours.

Our codes are totally different. I am bound only to safeguard the manifestations of conscience made to me by people in Confession, and to preserve such other natural and committed secrets as involve no injustice to others.

1115. Are Catholics forbidden to belong to all secret societies, or only to Masonry?

The Catholic Church does not condemn any society merely because it is secret in its own transactions of business. Every society may have its lawful secrets. A family is a society, and no family is obliged to call in strangers and exhibit all its affairs to the public gaze. But the Church does condemn those societies whose form of secrecy can be dangerous to religion, or to the state, or which can lead to the violation of conscience. Many Catholic societies which have their own legitimate secret business are permitted by the Church. But before giving her sanction, she makes sure that such secret business is limited to lawful matters, and that the constitutions of such societies are based upon Christian principles, containing nothing in any way opposed to the law of God.

1116. The Knights of Columbus form a secret society sanctioned by the Catholic Church. How do they differ from Masonry?

In all the points I have enumerated against Masonry. They do not constitute a secret society of the type condemned by the Church. They are prepared to submit all their affairs to ecclesiastical authority. Every member knows that he will never be asked to violate his conscience or injure other people's rights in virtue of his membership. Their society does not claim to be a new and universal religion, nor do any of its members profess their wish to destroy the Catholic Church.

1117. Masonry believes that one religion is as good as another. Is that detrimental to the Catholic Church?

Even did Masonry believe that, it would be detrimental to the Catholic Church. For if God reveals a definite religion, it is blasphemy to say that any other religion is as good as the one He has revealed.

1118. Do you think that Masons plot against the Catholic Church?

In some countries they do; in others they do not. However the spirit of Masonry the world over is anti-Christian and anti-Catholic, for it excludes all definite Christianity and yet claims to be a religion. "He that is not with me, is against me," said Christ.

1119. I deny that Masonry is opposed to the Catholic Church.

Senator Delpech, President of the Grand Orient in France, said on September 20th, 1902, "The triumph of the Galilean has lasted many centuries, but now He dies in His turn. He passes away to join the dust of the ages with the other divinities of India, Greece, and Rome, who saw so many deceived creatures prostrate before their altars. Brother Masons, we rejoice that we are not without our share in this overthrow of false prophets. The Romish Church began to decay from the day the Masonic association was established." The Swiss Lodge declared, "We have one irreconcilable enemy—the Pope and clericalism." Masonic documents seized by the Government of Italy declared that the ultimate idea of Masonry there was to destroy Catholicism and even the Christian idea altogether. Again in 1913 the Grand Orient of France said, "The aim of the Grand Orient is to crush Roman Catholicism in France first, and then elsewhere." Masonic journals in England replied to these quotations by saying that English Masonry did not sympathize with such extravagant utterances, and that it had no opinions, political or religious. But the American Pike replied, "It is idle to protest. We are Masons, and we recognize the French brotherhood as Freemasons in virtue of solidarity. Ours is a universal fraternity." The list of Grand Lodges published in 1907 shows that the United Grand Lodge of England recognizes practically all the Grand Lodges of the world. As the Ancient Scottish Rite for the installment of a Grand Master says, "There is a sacred bond uniting all the brethren of our Craft. However scattered over the earth, they all compose one body." Masonry as such is opposed to the Catholic Church. I know that there are many fine, broad, and tolerant men, who rather admire the Catholic Church, if anything. But the fact remains that no Catholic may become a Mason without renouncing his religion, and no Mason can become a Catholic without severing his connection with the Masonic Lodge.

1120. Masonry goes back to Solomon's temple, long before Catholicism began. How can you say that it began in 1717?

Masonry claims to go much farther back than Solomon's Temple. "The Freemason," an English Masonic periodical, August issue, 1926, says: "Freemasonry can stand and watch all religions as they pass in review." W. A. Waite, in his book, "Emblematic Masonry," 1925, p. 286, says: "Masons alone are truly ordained and have a succession more than Apostolic." A. Churchward, in the "Treasury of Masonic Thought," under the chapter on the Great Pyramid, says, "Masonry goes back 300,000 years before Christ to the Egyptian mysteries of Horus." There are many other such extravagant claims made by Masons. But whilst Masonry claims to be pagan in origin, and whilst it talks paganism, historically it is not so old. The best German Masonic historians, such as Begeman, laugh at the notion and admit that Masonry as it is to-day began with the Grand Lodge of England in 1717. Its organization was completed in 1722 with the new book of the constitutions and the three degrees of apprentice, fellow and master. The mentioning of Solomon's Temple in connection with Masonry is absurd. I might just as well found a society of Shintoists in 1933; include in my ritual the burning of a few joss-sticks; and then tell the world that really my society dated back to Confucius, adding as proof the allegation that he must have burned joss-sticks at any rate.

1121. Were there not mediaeval guilds or lodges of stone-masons before 1717?

There were older societies of stone-workers before that date, but having no connection with Masonry, and making no absurd pretentions to a fantastic heredity. The old guilds had ceased to exist, and the spirit of the new Masonry was a contradiction of that which prevailed in the earlier and non-connected Catholic guilds. Masonry was not even a revival of an older system. It was a completely new and quite independent organization.

1122. We Masons believe in God.

Not all do. I remember reading in a French Masonic Review these words, "Masonry teaches that there is only one religion—the worship of humanity. God is an erroneous concept of humanity." However, many Masons believe in a Supreme Architect, just as the pagan Aristotle did.

1123. *Our Great Architect is the same God as yours.*

God Himself would scarcely recognize the portrait as authentic. God is not merely the author of all things, He is the Father, Son, and Holy Ghost, in whose Name we have been baptized. The mere admission of a Great Architect suggests no intimate relations with Him, no knowledge of His intimate and personal life, no recognition of Jesus Christ His Son, no acceptance of God's revelation, and no obedience to His commands. I admit that some individual Masons subscribe to Christian teachings to some extent, but they do not do so as Masons.

1124. *We Masons meet in order to worship the true God.*

If so, how can you deny that Masonry is a non-Catholic form of religion? And even granting that your ritual is a worship of God, it is a worship opposed to the way in which He Himself wants you to worship Him. And what of the Masonic claim that the very rites are derived from ancient pagan mysteries?

1125. *That claim is not true. Every part of the Masonic ritual is based upon Biblical teaching.*

J. S. M. Ward, founder and secretary of the Masonic Study Society, writes in his book, "Freemasonry and the Ancient Gods," p. 330, that the Hindoo conception of the diety is the "same as that taught in our Lodges, with the same attributes, Brahma, Vishnu, and Shiva." Wilmshurst, Grand Registrar of West Yorkshire, wrote at the request of his fellow Masons a book called "The Masonic Initiation." On p. 105 he writes: "To the Jewish brother Masonry points to the Father of the faithful; to the Hindoo brother it points to Krishna; to the Moslem, it points to Mahomet." The Royal Arch Ritual gives the letters J.B.O. as denominating the Great Architect; the Hebrew Jehovah; the Syrian Baal; and the Egyptian Osiris.

1126. *I maintain that the Masonic Craft is Christian.*

It is not. Bro. T. J. Lawrence, in his book, "Freemasonry," 1925, p. 58, says: "Masonry does not even require a profession of Christianity. It freely admits Jews, Mohammedans, and others who reject Christian doctrine." Dr. Fort Newton, in "Brothers and Builders," says that, like everything else in Masonry, the Bible is a symbol of God's perpetual revelation, which God is still making through the Old Testament, the Koran, the Vedas, etc." That is the end of the Bible in the Christian sense. In the same book he writes that Masonry is not a religion, but the religion, and that Masons pursue the universal religion. That is the end of Christianity as the universal religion. It is because of its un-Christian character that the Free Presbyterian Church of Scotland, in 1927, made abstention from the Lodge a condition of its own membership. In the same year the Wesleyan Conference in England declared that the Christian message "is wholly incompatible with the claims of Freemasons." Even General Booth, shortly before he died, addressed a letter to every Officer of the Salvation Army saying: "No language of mine could be too strong in condemning any Officer's affiliation with any society which shuts Him outside its Temples; and which in its religious ceremonies gives neither Him nor His name any place. The place where Jesus Christ is not allowed is no place for any Salvation Army Officer."

1127. *But Masonry is not a religion.*

Mackey's Lexicon of Freemasonry will tell you that "all the ceremonies of our Order begin and terminate with prayer, for Masonry is a religious institution."

1128. *Masons have many charitable institutions.*

We do not condemn any good they are able to accomplish. Meantime the Catholic Church has charitable works on a much vaster scale. And she condemns the Masonic system, without casting reflection upon the sincerity of individual Masons or the good works of the Craft.

1129. I know of hundreds of Catholics who have joined the Masons, despite the prohibition of the Church.

You may know of many. Those who have done so have preferred the benefits of Masonry to the principles of their religion, selling their birthright, as did Esau, for a bowl of temporal porridge. They have cut themselves off from their Church, and deprived themselves of the right to the Sacraments. Law is law. If they want to be Catholics, they must submit to the laws of the Catholic Church. No one will compel them to do so, but if they will not, you cannot blame the Church for her refusal to regard them as practical members.

1130. Anyway they seem quite content to be Masons.

Who knows? Those who have completely lost their faith may be so. But there are many who have not lost the faith, and who but seem to be content. They are most miserable because they cannot practice their faith as long as they are Masons; and although they have not the courage of their convictions yet, they hope to renounce Masonry before they die, and to be reconciled with their Church. I, as a Catholic Priest, know this; for they have told me what they would not tell any fellow Mason on the subject—whilst they still intend to remain with the Lodge. A Catholic Mason is not a very happy man.

1131. Can a Mason become a Catholic?

Yes, provided he is sincerely convinced that the Catholic Church is the one true Church, and that he be prepared to sever his connection with the Lodge. He cannot become a Catholic whilst still remaining a member of any Masonic Lodge.

1132. Once a Mason, always a Mason!

That is merely a foolish superstition. If a man drops Masonry, altogether renounces it, and has nothing more to do with it, he ceases to be a Mason however much his fellow-Masons declare that he still belongs to them. Masonry does not grip a man body and soul for all eternity, with or without his will.

1133. May a Catholic join the Odd Fellows?

No, although that society does not fall under so strict a condemnation as Masonry. There are Catholic benefit societies which give all the temporal advantages to be secured in the Odd Fellows, or in other similar non-Catholic benefit societies. The Church naturally prefers her members to join Catholic societies. The majority of the Odd Fellows are non-Catholics, and no matter how good they may be, it is certain that their Lodge offers less suitable companionship for Catholics than a Catholic society. The Masonic Lodge is, therefore, absolutely forbidden; all other non-Catholic Friendly Societies are strongly discouraged.

1134. Why does the Catholic Church forbid cremation?

It was a pagan practice which Christians avoided from the very beginning. In the third century we find Christian writers, such as Minucius Felix, warning Christians against imitating the practice, and bidding them retain the custom of earth burial. In comparatively recent times Atheists and irreligious materialists have reintroduced it in order to destroy Christian belief and to impress in an imaginative way the doctrine that all is over at death. This, in itself, would be enough to justify the Church in her refusal to accept a practice credited with such closely associated ideas opposed to the doctrine of immortality. But there are many other reasons. It is opposed to human instinct and the better sentiments of the human heart. Filial piety protests against such treatment of, say, a deceased mother. Christian reverence for the dead also protests. The body that has been anointed in baptism and that has been the temple of the Holy Spirit during life, should not be treated as so much offal or refuse, but should be allowed to disintegrate according to the ordinary laws of nature in God's earth. Again, the whole liturgy of the Catholic Church for Christian burial, from time immemorial, is adapted to earth-burial, and she cannot be expected to change her sacred liturgy with fads of the times. If a Catholic is cremated, he forfeits the privileges of such Catholic burial, a liturgy of great benefit to the soul which inhabited that body. The man who does not bother about such things, and holds that once one is dead that is the end of it, and that nothing else matters, is saying just what the advocates of Cremation hoped that he would say. It is good to be buried in the Catholic way, in consecrated ground. That is the proper place for a Christian. We can add to these reasons the medico-legal aspect of the case. Cremation destroys all signs of violence or of poison, and thus prevents exhumation and medical examination for the detection of crime. Many murders have been discovered by such examination after burial, and if Cremation became a general practice, it would be an easy way out for the poisoner and murderer.

1135. *Is it a sin against the law of God to support Cremation?*

The natural law of morality does not forbid it, nor has God directly given a positive law in the matter. It is a disciplinary law of the Catholic Church, and a very grave one. The Church could suspend the law, and permit Cremation in certain circumstances, as in the case of an epidemic or in war time. But normally she insists upon retaining the law, and all Catholics are obliged to observe it. The Church speaks with the authority of God, and it is God who forbids Cremation through His Church. Any Catholic who would violate the will of the Church in this matter would, by the very fact, be violating the will of God.

1136. *Does not the Church oppose Cremation because she knows that it renders any idea of a resurrection impossible?*

No. Cremation does not affect the question of the resurrection. Cremation means but a more rapid separation of the elements of the body, and even if the ashes be scattered to the winds, God can quite easily reassemble those elements. What is impossible to us is not impossible to God. Remember that there is no such thing as the absolute destruction of matter. There can be merely a transformation of matter. However many changes matter may go through, it is always there, still in existence. And the God, who created matter, can easily transform it back again into the bodies which it formed previously. No matter how men treat human bodies, or where they put them, some day they will all rise again.

1137. *Why does not your Church condemn gambling and lotteries as sinful and immoral?*

Because they are not sinful and immoral in themselves. They can be made the occasion of sin, as when a passion for gambling leads a man to spend money which is not his own, or which is necessary for the upkeep of wife or children, or to pay his lawful debts. But if one can honestly afford it, he is free to invest in lotteries, or to indulge in the amusement of a wager, unless he is violating a law of the state.

1138. *Does not God forbid gambling of any kind?*

Nowhere does the law of God forbid gambling, provided no fraud, deceit, or injustice enters into it. If all is conducted fairly, and an investor keeps within his means, a man is free to purchase a proportionate chance of winning a bet or a lottery without offending God's laws in any way. But if a law of the state forbids gambling, such a law must be obeyed.

1139. *Christ drove the gamblers from the Temple.*

When Christ expelled the money-changers, and the buyers and sellers from the Temple, their crime was not gambling. Their crime was the conducting of secular business in such a place, and their own dishonesty in charging exorbitant prices for goods and exchange. But gambling as such was not involved in this matter.

1140. *It is dishonest to wish to get $5,000 for $1 in a lottery.*

If it be dishonest to invest $1 in order to secure a chance of winning $5,000, which may or may not be obtained, then it is equally dishonest to invest one's railway fare in order to secure a chance of discovering a possible nugget of gold, which may or may not exist, on some distant gold field. Every investment on the Stock Exchange, or for that matter every insurance policy, is an investment of money the return from which depends upon an element of chance.

1141. *Gambling and lotteries are the seeking of personal gain through another's loss, giving that other no adequate return, and adding nothing to the sum of the common wealth.*

There is nothing wrong with seeking personal gain. We are free to use our faculties and possessions in order to secure personal gain, unless justice or charity is violated. We are not free to do so by dishonest means; but gambling is not in itself dishonest. There is nothing wrong with gaining through another's loss when that other is quite willing to endure the loss and is in a position to meet the loss without violating his obligations to himself or others. Every gift you receive is a loss to the giver of the value spent on the gift. Meantime an adequate return is made to the investor in a gamble or a bet who happens to lose. The actual winner offered his partner or partners in the transaction an equal chance of gaining the contribution he himself invested. The losers had their proportionate opportunity, and were satisfied with the pleasurable risk afforded them. They were perfectly willing to take the risk, and nothing was taken from them against their reasonable will. That the transaction added nothing to the common wealth is not a factor affecting morality. Otherwise it would be immoral for you to give ten dollars to a beggar, for nothing would be added to the common wealth by that action.

1142. *"Thou shalt not steal" is at least as decisive against gambling as "Thou shalt not kill" against dueling.*

That is not true. No man has the right to alienate his life. Men have got the right to alienate their goods. And gambling is not stealing. If I take from Brown a dollar belonging to Brown against his will, I steal. But if we mutually agree to each putting a dollar in a hat and drawing lots as to which of us shall have the two dollars, we are not offending. We own our own money, and we can choose to renounce our possible possession of it in exchange for a lawful chance of winning the prize. I am willing that if he wins he shall have my dollar. He is willing that if I win I shall have his. There is no question of stealing from each other.

1143. *Can a man consent to be robbed?*

That is a contradiction in terms. If a man freely consents to my receiving his property, he is not being robbed. Imagine a man taking me to a law court on a charge of stealing his money, and there admitting that he freely consented to my having it!

1144. *I have seen young men get into serious trouble through gambling.*

You have seen young men ruined through their own lack of prudence and honesty. Excess and dishonesty are absolutely to be condemned. I speak as strongly as you against such things, and not for a moment does the Catholic Church sanction such sin. But if a man sinfully invests money in betting or in lotteries, money which he is obliged to use for the payment of just debts, or if he steals the money of others in order to so invest it, the fault lies in his personal dishonesty, not in any dishonesty of the lottery itself. The same type of man might also spend money on a motor car, neglecting to pay what he owes the butcher. You are allotting the dishonesty in the wrong place, transferring the innate dishonesty of an unjustified participant to the lottery itself.

1145. *"Thou shalt love thy neighbor as thyself."*

Good. And I would be as willing that the other should have my contribution should he win, as he would be willing that I should have his in the event of my winning. You overlook the element of free contract.

1146. *What does the Catholic Church do to wipe out the drink evil which causes so much misery in so many homes? We Protestants fight for prohibition.*

The Catholic Church drills into every one of her children that drunkenness is an unjustifiable sin. But we refuse to admit that prohibition should be enforced upon all. The particular abuses do not justify so sweeping a thing as abolition of drink altogether. You don't throttle a man because one tooth is aching. The Church does her duty in this matter in a sane way. Meantime, drunkenness is not the only evil. Drink itself is not forbidden by the law of God. Divorce and birth-control are forbidden. What is Protestantism doing to wipe out these evils? It scarcely alludes to them; or if it does, it does so in order to sanction them.

1147. *Why does your Church oppose prohibition?*

Nowhere does God forbid wine or alcoholic drink. And the Catholic Church insists upon justice. It is unjust to forbid all men to drink even in moderation because a few take it to excess. This is an unjust interference with individual liberty. And in any case you cannot force people to be virtuous. The failure of the American experiment has shown that. If a man cannot take drink moderately the Church advises him to take the pledge and practice total abstinence. But prohibition is like abolishing table knives because some men have used those implements for purposes of murder and suicide.

1148. *As there are no half-measures in this matter, your refusal of prohibition favors the continuance of a sin repugnant to Christ.*

What do you mean by no half-measures? For the man who cannot resist getting drunk, I admit that there are no half-measures. He must inflict rigorous prohibition on himself, and if necessary the law must forbid him to be served with drink. If you mean that prohibition must be inflicted on everybody, I deny your assertion. Such prohibition is as extravagant, and therefore as unreasonable, as the doctrine of a man who would insist that you must always employ a steam-roller to crack walnuts. Would you agree with his argument that because you are opposed to the use of a steam-roller to crack walnuts, you are opposed to the cracking of walnuts at all? We all agree about the sin of drunkenness. We disagree about the means to be employed in its prevention. Drunkenness is repugnant to Our Lord. But His first miracle was to change water into wine for the simple joys of a wedding-feast. He had no objection to the use of wine. He objects to the abuse of it. If some men abuse their liberty by thieving, we do not think to stop thieving by abolishing the use of liberty and locking everybody up in jail. And we are not the less Christian for sane conduct.

1149. *"Wine is a mocker; strong drink is raging; and whosoever is deceived thereby is not wise." Prov. XX., 1.*

The moral is that no man should be deceived into drinking to excess. Thus St. Paul wrote to the Ephesians, "Be not drunk with wine." Eph. V., 18. Yet in his first Epistle to Tim. V., 23, he writes, "Do not still drink water, but use a little wine for thy stomach's sake, and thy frequent infirmities." Our Lord Himself blamed the Pharisees that they accused John the Baptist of having a devil because he abstained from drink, but when they saw Christ Himself drinking wine in moderation, they said, "Behold a man that is a glutton and a wine-drinker, a friend of publicans and sinners." Matt. XI., 19. Let us have temperance by all means. But there is no warrant in Scripture or in reason for prohibition.

1150. *Does drink enter Catholic presbyteries?*

All of them have to keep special supplies of altar wine. Over and above this altar wine, reserved for sacramental use, drink enters some presbyteries, but not others. It depends upon the needs of the individual Priest. If a Priest took drink to excess, he would be guilty of sin, and a worse sin than a layman would commit, owing to the scandal given by violating the dignity and requirements of his sacred office. Otherwise there would be no harm whatever in a Priest taking drink in moderation.

1151. *Even Catholic Bishops drink!*

Some take it moderately; some do not take it at all. I have known one Bishop who would eat none but brown bread, and another who would never touch it as not agreeing with his health. The advice given by one Catholic Bishop to another I have recorded above in giving you St. Paul's words to Timothy.

1152. *Is there any virtue in taking strong drink?*

That all depends upon the intention with which one takes it. If taken in moderation for the sake of health so that one may the better fulfill his duties for the love of God, it is virtue to take it. If taken merely for the sake of taking it, such use of drink would not be virtuous.

1153. *The Catholic attitude to drink shakes my faith in Christianity.*

You have not understood the Catholic attitude. But, in any case, if you see a drunken man, it should affect your faith in that man, not your faith in Christianity. If the man professes to be a Christian, you must blame him for not living up to his belief. But Christianity is all right. If it told him to get drunk, it might be different. But it forbids him to do so. Don't lose your faith in Christianity, but persuade drunkards to live up to its obligations.

1154. *Does the Catholic Church make light of drunkenness. Isn't it sinful to cause blind misery and poverty in the home?*

The Catholic Church does not make light of so grave a sin. It is an evil which leaves every one of us very miserable indeed. Man has obligations to God, to himself, and to his neighbor. Such drunkenness violates all three obligations. Few things so destroy God's image and likeness in man as excessive drink. Other vices leave him with reason at least. But, as Father Burke so well said, "Reeling from the hotel, the drunkard has laid the image of God upon the altar of the meanest and most despicable of all devils—gluttony." As regards himself, the drunkard loses health, respect, friends, happiness, and much else. For if a man dies in almost any other crime, he has his wits about him and can call upon God for mercy and forgiveness. But if he dies in drunkenness, he is incapable even of an act of repentance. And as regards his neighbor, surely first and foremost come his wife, and his children, his parents and other members of his family not to speak of his duty to his employer and professional clients. Yet what greater misery can a man bring upon the woman who confided her youth and heart to him forever, than that which his drunkenness inflicts upon her? And his own children are filled with shame, disgust, and scandal. No prohibitionist can speak more strongly against drunkenness than the Catholic Church; for she has a heart full of compassion for the homes wrecked by this vice, and of indignation that God should be so offended.

1155. *How do Catholics observe the Lord's Day?*

They should sanctify Sunday by assisting at Mass, by prayer, and by abstaining from unnecessary servile works.

1156. *I think Catholic ideas most peculiar in this matter.*

That is merely because Catholic ideas do not happen to fit in with your own religious upbringing. Things we don't agree with usually seem peculiar to us. But the whole point is, are your ideas right, or are our ideas right? You have no proof whatever that your notions are right, or that Catholic ideas are wrong.

1157. *Did not God command us to observe Saturday, and not Sunday at all?*

No. The command as given by Moses in the Name of God to the Jews was that the Sabbath, and not Saturday, should be kept holy. The word Sabbath means rest. The law includes two elements; one essential, that one day in seven should be dedicated to God; the other ceremonial, that the particular day should be chosen. The Jews selected Saturday.

1158. *God is eternally the same. Having once demanded the seventh day of the week, even He could not change it to the first day of the week.*

On that argument He could not have changed from the Old Law to the New Law, nor from the Jews to the Christians. You should give up your Christian beliefs, and join the Jewish religion! Yet did not Christ say, "You have heard it said in the Law; but now I say unto you." And He deliberately abrogated certain Jewish legislation concerning marriage. He certainly admitted the possibility of some changes.

1159. *God's covenant with the Jews concerned one day in seven, and He said, "My covenant I will not break." Is God a liar, or is your Church wrong?*

God is not a liar, and the Catholic Church is not wrong. God Himself predicted in Isaiah II., 2-3, that He would establish a visible Church to which all nations would come, and that out of that Church the law would proceed to teach us His ways. In due time He sent His Son, who established the Catholic Church, and she tells us God's present law. God has not changed. If you decide to do different successive things, your decision does not change merely because the undertakings change successively. The Jews decided to observe Saturday, while Christians decided to observe Sunday. The seventh day as God's day was not changed. The Sabbath, God's rest day, was transferred from Saturday to Sunday.

1160. We Adventists observe Saturday as God commanded. Where are we wrong?

In believing the specified Jewish day to be still of obligation. You do not seem to understand that the Old Law was but figurative of the more perfect New Law, and that in the New Law Christ established the Catholic Church which clearly teaches the change of ceremonial day. If you want to keep the ceremonial day of the Jews, you may as well keep the lot, and abolish Baptism in favor of Circumcision.

1161. You Catholics got Sunday from Mithraism.

We did not. Sunday may have been the day celebrated in honor of Mithra. But this was not the reason for its selection by Christians. There is as much connection between the Christian choice of Sunday and Mithraism as there is between the fact that the Jews observed Saturday and the derivation of the word in English from Saturn. Had the Church chosen Wednesday for some reason of her own, you would alter your charge and cry in triumph, "Ah! The day sacred to Wodin."

1162. What are the reasons for the selection of Sunday rather than Saturday?

After Christ's resurrection and the establishment of the Church of the New Law, Christians kept the substance of the Old Law in this matter by still retaining one day out of seven. But the Apostles, as I have said, changed the specification of the day to Sunday. This they did for several reasons. Firstly, in order to honor the resurrection of Christ from the dead on Sunday morning. St. Paul shows that this is the bed-rock foundation of our faith when he says, "If Christ be not risen, then is our faith in vain." Secondly, the advent of the Holy Ghost gave life to the Church on Pentecost Sunday. Thirdly, the change was calculated to impress upon our minds the transition from the Old Law to the New Law. Finally, Saturday had special significance as being dedicated to the completion of God's creative work. But God's redemptive work is greater than His creative work, and as a mark of honor the first day of the week was dedicated to the superior redemptive work of God.

1163. Does Scripture in any way justify such a change as a fact?

Yes. Christ, of course, accepting the Old Law prior to fulfilling and perfecting it by His new revelation, observed Saturday. But He Himself prepared the way for the change of day. He defended His disciples when the Jews accused them of not observing the Sabbath strictly in the traditional sense. Matt. XII., 1-8. He rebukes a too severe an interpretation of the Sabbath law. Lk. XIII., 10-16; XIV., 1-5; Jn. V., 9-18; VII., 22. He shows His authority to do as He may please with the Sabbath. Mk. II., 27-28. Nowhere does He re-assert the obligation of observing the Jewish Sabbath. Never does He quote this Jewish Law. In marked contrast, the New Testament pays special honor to Sunday. Christ rose on Sunday, and appeared to His Apostles on Sunday. He chose the following Sunday to appear to them when St. Thomas was present. Fifty days later He chose Sunday for the bestowal of the Holy Spirit upon His Church. The first Christians themselves observed Sunday from the very beginning. "On the first day of the week, when we were assembled to break bread." Acts XX., 7. St. Paul rebuked the Galatians because of their tendency to revert to Jewish customs, and above all in their observance of Jewish days as if they were still binding. Gal. IV., 9-10. To the Corinthians he wrote, "As I have given order to the churches of Galatia, so do ye also. On the first day of the week let every one of you put apart . . . what it shall well please him" towards the collection on behalf of the Church. 1 Cor., XVI., 1-2. In Rev. I., 10, St. John tells us that he was in the spirit "on the Lord's day," i.e., on the day on which Christ rose from the dead, and which was already dedicated to Him as sacred in a special way.

1164. Geiermann, a Catholic writer, says that the Church changed the day in the 4th century at the Council of Laodicea.

You have misunderstood him. The Church then merely gave a special precept ordering the faithful to keep to the Apostolic practice of observing Sunday. But the change was not made in the 4th century for the first time. Thus St. Augustine wrote in the 4th century, "The Apostles and their contemporaries sanctioned the dedication of Sunday to the worship of God." Two centuries before Augustine, Tertullian had written, "We, as tradition has taught us, observe the day of the Lord's resurrection." St. Justin Martyr, who died in 167 A.D., wrote, "On Sunday we meet to celebrate the Lord's Supper and read the Gospels and Sacred Scripture, the first day on which God changed darkness, and made the world, and on which Christ rose from the dead." Earlier still, St. Ignatius, who died in 107 A.D., says, "If we still live according to the Jewish observances, we confess that we do not accept the grace of Christ. Those who once lived according to the Old Law have come to a new hope, no longer observing the Jewish Sabbath, but the Lord's day on which our Life rose from the dead." Thus tradition goes back to the indications given in Scripture and recorded above. Yet it is right to say that the Catholic Church changed the day in so far as the Apostles were representatives of that Church; for they, with the authority of Christ, sanctioned the change.

1165. This changing of the law proves that the Catholic Church is founded and governed by Satan.

The foundation of the Catholic Church is a matter of history, and history shows that Christ Himself founded her. You would find it quite impossible to say when, where, and how Satan founded the Catholic Church. As for Satan governing the Catholic Church, do you think Satan would be so insistent on the preservation of the doctrine of Christ? The Catholic Church says that anything impure, filthy, or wicked, is absolutely forbidden. Is that Satanic? She warns against all sin, and urges her children to be holy. It does not sound very devilish. You neither understand Scripture nor the Catholic Church to which you are so opposed.

1166. Could not a person keep Sunday holy without going to Mass?

A Catholic could not, when there is nothing to prevent his attendance at Mass. It is a mortal sin to miss Mass, and if he put himself into a state of mortal sin he vitiates all else he might attempt to do. That is, of course, unless he makes an act of perfect contrition, after which he could do some good actions; but he would not have fulfilled God's essential law.

1167. Could he not pray and read his Bible all day?

I doubt it. But if a Catholic did do that, he would be doing what God does not command, and neglecting the thing God does command.

1168. Why is it mortal sin to miss Mass on Sundays?

Christ said, "If thou wilt enter into life, keep the commandments." Now one of these commandments is, "Remember that thou keep holy the sabbath day." Thus God demands the sanctification of one day in seven in a special way. His very use of the word "Remember" implies a grave obligation not to forget or omit this duty. It is a mortal sin to disobey God in this matter. But how are we Christians to observe this commandment? Who is to tell us? Our Lord says, "If a man will not hear the Church, let him be as the heathen." Matt. XVIII., 17. We must, then, hear the Church. Now the Catholic Church tells us that the central factor in the religion of Christ is the Mass, and that the chief thing in the sanctification of Sunday is to be present at the offering of that Sacrifice to God. This obliges under pain of mortal sin, unless sickness or other grave difficulties prevent such assistance at Mass. Remember that men are not only individual beings. They are also social units in a collective nation. And as they are obliged to worship God in their individual capacity, so too collectively. God has always demanded public worship, and from the earliest Apostolic times Christians met regularly for religious exercises in common.

1169. Why should Catholics be thus burdened?

Religion is a debt to God. We Catholics pay this debt regardless of our own comfort and pleasure. We do not pay earthly debts when it gives us pleasure, and refuse to pay them when it displeases us. It is a matter of honesty and justice.

1170. Why are not Catholics taught good living, instead of going to Mass and giving money?

You wrongly suppose that the Church insists upon attendance at Mass and money-giving, and that she is indifferent to truth and good living. You should ask Catholics who do attend Mass what they are taught, instead of making prejudiced guesses.

1171. Many go to Mass and are as bad as non-church-goers.

Would you have them continue in their sins and discontinue going to Mass? That is what the average non-church-goer does. It would not be so bad if he did so and kept silent about others. But it is intolerable that he should rail at those who do attempt to offer some worship to God.

1172. All the same the one who goes to Mass is no better in God's sight than the one who does not.

He may not be in other things, though even that is unlikely. But he is certainly better in God's sight in so far as he attends Mass. If the church-goer has faults, I do not justify them; but those faults will be less grave than the sin of the man who neglects the greatest of his debts—that to Almighty God.

1173. Catholics go to Mass and then are free to do what they like on Sunday.

By going to Mass Catholics have remembered to keep holy the sabbath day, which is required. For the rest, Catholics are not allowed to do as they please afterwards. They are forbidden all unnecessary servile works, and are of course forbidden, as always, any sinful conduct. But they are not forbidden lawful relaxation from ordinary pursuits.

1174. To keep a day holy means to keep it pious, godly, and sacred.

Catholics do keep the day holy. The day is consecrated to God by definite duties of religion. Innocent recreation does not desecrate it. Eating one's meals on Sunday is not in itself a pious act, yet it does not desecrate the day. To keep a day pious does not mean that every single act must be one of piety. Any act which is not sinful can be offered to God's greater honor and glory, even as David offered his dancing before the Ark of the Covenant. When the Pharisees complained to Christ that the disciples were doing what their traditions held to be unlawful, Christ replied that the Sabbath was made for man, not man for the Sabbath.

1175. Is playing tennis keeping a day holy and as a day of rest?

Playing tennis is not sinful. It is neither holy nor wicked of itself. It is mental and bodily refreshment of one's forces. But how far will you go? If I may not play tennis, may I exercise my limbs by walking? If I may not use my legs, may I use my eyes in reading? If not that, may I use my lungs by breathing? Where are you going to stop in the use of one's faculties? Religion was not meant by God to be a strait-jacket of gloom.

1176. Our Protestant ministers forbid sport on Sunday.

If so, they do so on their own authority, not on the authority of the Scripture.

1177. Anyway, those who take up games and sport on Sunday drop their Church after a time.

That may be true of many Protestants who know that their ministers forbid such things unreasonably, and therefore give up going to church at all. It does not affect Catholics. We have easily the largest number of church-going people, even though we refuse to adopt the man-made prescriptions of Protestant ministers.

1178. After Mass, Priests even organize picnics and outings.

The Catholic Church is the only Church which can oblige her people to worship God definitely on Sunday, and many of her churches are filled three or four times on that day. There is nothing wrong with innocent recreation provided it does not interfere with one's duties to God and attendance at religious worship. Sunday is a day on which we must avoid hard bodily labor, worship God, and take lawful rest. But God never intended us to sit glum and gloomy from Saturday until Monday, as if that could offer Him the greatest possible honor and glory. Of course the Catholic Church may be guilty according to the standards of many Protestants, but she has never admitted those standards. The Catholic goes to an early Mass, slips home, has his breakfast, and then enjoys God's sunshine in innocent recreation. His greatest critic is the man who breakfasts in bed, and reads the Sunday papers until 11 a.m., religiously refusing to play the piano. If he feels like it, such a man goes along to some service at a popular church or chapel in the evening, believing himself to be one of the chosen few who have gone to church that day, forgetting the legions of Catholics who have done so whilst he was still in bed.

1179. I want you to reconcile such conduct with Christ's commands.

Innocent recreation on Sunday is not opposed to Christ's commands. You decide upon your own notion of what Christianity means, and calmly demand that I reconcile Catholic practice with your notions, as if your ideas were infallibly correct. That is the way with Protestantism. Protestants won't accept the authority of the Pope, believing his claims arrogant. Then each proceeds to set himself up as his own Pope. Why should I accept your tests of what Christianity should be as possessing any value? Another Protestant, with different ideas, will want me to reconcile Catholic practices with his notions. If Catholic teaching could square with every peculiar idea of each Protestant inquirer, it would have to be as changeable as the chameleon.

1180. If sport on Sunday were no harm, Christ would have said so.

Let us put it the other way round. If it were sinful, it is possible that Christ would have said so. We certainly cannot expect Him to describe all that is not sinful. Sleeping is not sinful, yet nowhere does Christ solemnly assure us that it is no sin to go to sleep. Christ omitted any explicit reference to sport on Sunday just as he omitted to refer to the wearing of shoes, sleeping at night, or the breathing of the air God gives us.

1181. *What do you mean by servile work?*

Work which in olden times used to be given to servants and slaves, and which is chiefly performed by bodily labor and for bodily needs. Liberal and more intellectual works are not forbidden.

1182. *Would work for an hour be servile, but not for ten minutes?*

The term servile refers, not to the time spent in the work, but to the nature of the work. If the work is of a servile nature in itself, it cannot be done even for ten minutes without genuine necessity. If not servile of its very nature, it would not become servile if done for ten hours.

1183. *God says, "Thou shalt do no manner of work," yet you permit housework on Sundays.*

God forbade the ordinary work of the Jews by which they earned their living, and the work they allotted to their slaves and servants. Christ Himself rebuked the Pharisees for their letter-of-the-law interpretation of this commandment. God's chief purpose was that all might be free for religious duties. We have to note what God intended, and fulfill the intentions of the legislator, in addition to making allowances for the vast difference between the spirit of the Old Law and that of the New. The Catholic Church forbids all unnecessary servile work on Sundays. If such work can be done during the week, it is not necessary on Sundays. Our Lord Himself said that one would be justified in laboring to release an ox from a pit on the Sabbath. A man cannot find time always on week days for all things necessary to be done, and certainly some housework is reasonably necessary on Sundays.

1184. *You claim to legislate in purely spiritual things, yet order fast and abstinence on certain days. There is nothing spiritual in forbidding people to eat meat.*

I have never said that the Church legislates only in spiritual matters. Men are not purely spiritual beings, and in our composite nature, spiritual legislation must in some way affect our material being. The laws of the Church cover material things in so far as they affect our spiritual welfare. There is nothing spiritual about meat in itself. But spiritual virtue is exercised when we abstain from meat from a motive of self-denial, gratitude, and obedience to God.

1185. *Is there any Scripture warrant for fasting?*

Yes. When the Pharisees complained to Christ that His disciples did not fast, He replied that they did not whilst He was with them, but that they would when He had gone from them. Mk. II., 18. Now the Catholic Church, ordered by Christ to teach all nations whatsoever Christ had said to her, tells us that at certain times we must fast in expiation of our sins. St. Paul wrote to the Corinthians, "Let us exhibit ourselves as servants of God, in patience, in fastings." A Christian spirit of reparation says, "I indulged my senses at the expense of God's law; I will therefore now mortify them at the expense of my own comfort." However it is part of Christian law, and those who say that the Catholic Church obliges fasting whilst other Churches do not, complain as usual that the Catholic Church is fulfilling the Christian law whilst others are not. And the Catholic Church appoints special days, for if it were left to individuals they would fast very irregularly, or not at all. It is much better to make it definite.

1186. Why forbid meat on Fridays? Christ said that nothing from without defiles a man, but that it is disposition of soul that counts. Mk. VII., 15.

It follows that meat is not evil in itself, and that the Church does not forbid meat on Fridays because she thinks that meat will defile men. That should be evident from the fact that the Church permits meat on other days, as she could not do if she believed meat to be evil. Therefore it must be a question of the day, and not of the meat. Why then does the Church forbid meat on Fridays? Because on that day Christ gave His life for us in misery and suffering. If a Catholic eats meat on that day, the meat does not defile him, but his interior disposition of ingratitude and disobedience certainly does. If a man is not prepared to give up a little meat on the day Christ gave up His life, he is not worthy to be ranked as a Christian. The Friday abstinence has kept Our Lord's sacrifice and death before the minds of millions of Catholics for centuries. To the vast majority of the Protestant Churches which abolished this beautiful practice merely because the Catholic Church had the grace to fulfill it, Friday is just like Tuesday, or Wednesday, or Thursday, and their members do not think week by week of the greatest event that ever occurred in history for love of us. I have never yet received a convert into the Church who has not seen the beauty of this devotedness to Christ, and of the loyalty with which the Church recalls Friday as the day of the greatest event in our redemption. That non-Catholics should be silent about this Catholic custom I could understand. But that they should still profess to be Christians and then blame the Catholic Church for such a generous and loving act in honor of Christ merely because they do not do it themselves is astonishing.

1187. The Bible says that Anti-Christ will bid men abstain from meats. 1 Tim. IV., 3.

The reference is to men who teach that meat is evil in itself and who declare that it is wicked to eat it under any circumstances. But Catholics do not believe or teach this. Almost any butcher will tell you that he supplies many Catholic customers regularly with meat.

1188. When did the practice of Friday abstinence from meat begin?

In the very earliest ages of the Church. The practice is mentioned in the Didache or Doctrine of the Twelve Apostles, a booklet written by one of the immediate followers of the Apostles in the year 90.

1189. Who said that every man will go to hell if he eats meat on Friday?

No one. The Catholic Church says that it is a mortal sin for a *Catholic* to eat meat on Friday knowingly and wilfully, without a sufficiently grave and excusing reason. Then that Church says that if a man dies in unrepented mortal sin, he will go to hell.

1190. I don't blame Catholics for voluntarily abstaining from meat on Fridays, but to do so because ordered to do so is making a virtue of necessity.

That is not true. No Catholic is physically compelled to abstain from meat on Fridays. It is a moral obligation, adding the virtue of obedience to that of Christian mortification. On your method of reasoning you should say that a man should voluntarily abstain from stealing, and that it is wrong to do so because God has said, "Thou shalt not steal." And do the laws of the land destroy the virtue of citizens because there is a moral obligation to observe them?

1191. Ought not Catholics to abstain from intoxicating drink on Fridays?

There is no law obliging them to do so. Of course there is always the law of conscience forbidding drinking to excess on any day. Yet, although there is no law forbidding drink in moderation on Fridays, it would be a very good and meritorious action if a man did abstain voluntarily from alcoholic drink on that day in a spirit of mortification and self-denial. But that would not dispense him from the obligation to abstain from meat. Let a man fulfill the law, and then do more if he wishes. Obedience is better than sacrifices prompted by one's own opinions.

1192. Would it not be better for the Church to forbid intoxicants rather than harmless meat?

It would not. The Church wishes to forbid a thing which most of her people will miss. Practically all eat meat; not all by any means drink intoxicants. All are united in a common act of mortification. There is a tendency in men to think that all laws should conform to their own pet ideas. A man likes his meat and dislikes drink. So he suggests that the Church should rather forbid drink than meat. But drink does not affect all men; meat affects practically all.

1193. Who made the law of celibacy?

The Catholic Church, with God's approval and authority, following the example of Christ and the Apostles.

1194. Did not Pope Gregory VII. originate it in the 11th century?

No. He merely enforced the already existing law more rigidly in his efforts to correct abuses. Over 300 years before Gregory VII. was Pope, the Greeks met the Latin Bishops at the Council of Trullo, and admitted, "We know that the law of the Roman Church is to demand that married men, from the moment of their ordination, must separate from their wives forever." St. Jerome, over 300 years before that, wrote, "The Apostolic See accepts married men to be Priests provided they live no longer as husbands to their wives." Marriage was never allowed after ordination. If a single man were ordained, he had to practice celibacy. If an aspirant were already married, he had to practice celibacy from the day he became a Priest. Pope Siricius, in 385 A.D., said, "All we Priests are obliged by an inviolable law dating from our ordination to be continent and chaste, and thus offer the sacrifice of our bodies to God." This same Pope wrote also, "I have heard that a Priest of Christ has married, defending his action by saying that the Priests of the Old Law married. But the Church, the Spouse of Christ, has always loved chastity. Wherefore any Priest who claims a privilege from the Old Law which is unlawful in the New must know that he is deprived by the authority of the Apostolic See of the ecclesiastical honor he has so misused, nor can he celebrate the divine mysteries." Pope Siricius was not beginning a new law in the Church, but blaming an individual for not observing a law that had long been in existence. In 314 the Council of Neo-Caesaria had also said, "If a Priest marries, let him be degraded." The Apostolic Constitutions gave the law, in the 2nd century, "If a Priest or Deacon is not already married, he can never contract marriage." Thus right back to the 2nd century you have explicit testimony that in the Catholic Church once a man became a Priest he had to renounce marriage, and practice celibacy.

1195. Are there not Oriental Churches united to the Catholic Church, yet without the law of celibacy?

Yes. They have been exempted from the law obliging all Priests of the Latin Rite. The Church has tolerated the ancient custom of marriage in those Eastern Churches which have sought re-union with her, allowing married men to be ordained amongst them, though marriage subsequent to ordination is forbidden. But in the Western Latin Church the full law must be observed.

1196. God commanded all men to marry when He said "Increase and multiply."

That is a general precept for the whole human race, and a general blessing upon marriage. But it does not bind each and every individual. If it did, every single marriageable man in the world is breaking God's commandment and is in a state of sin. Or when would a man begin to sin by not being married? At 18? 19? 20? Or only when he could afford to support a wife? And would you accuse Christ of violating God's will? Or if you exempt Him because of His divinity, would you blame the Apostles? Was St. John the Baptist so very evil? Or St. Paul, who wrote, "I would that all were as myself . . . unmarried"? 1 Cor. VII., 7. You quote the Bible, and then give a teaching radically opposed to the doctrine of that Bible.

1197. The Bible says that a man must leave father and mother and take a wife. Matt. XIX., 5.

The sense is simply that one who does take a wife has a duty to her and to his children which is so binding that he must leave even his parents in order to fulfill it in his newly adopted state. But Christ gave a special blessing to those who would renounce father and mother, and the prospects of a wife and children also, for His sake. Matt. XIX., 29 says, "And everyone that hath left house, or brethren, or sisters, or father, or mother, or wife, or children, or lands for my name's sake, shall receive an hundredfold, and shall possess life everlasting."

1198. St. Paul says that a Bishop must be the husband of one wife. 1 Tim. III., 2.

St. Paul does not say that a Bishop must be the husband of a wife, but insists upon the expression "one wife." Had he meant that it was necessary to have a wife, he would have been violating the law himself. In the early Church, owing to the scarcity of single men eligible for the Priesthood, married men who wished to be ordained could be accepted provided they had not been married twice. Those presenting themselves must have been the husband of but one wife. That is all that the text means. Catholic Bishops and Priests do not violate that law. A law forbidding a man to have had more than one wife does not order him to have one; nor is it violated by a man who has never had a wife at all. However, as Christianity grew and vocations became more plentiful, single men only were accepted, and had to remain celibates, according to the advice of St. Paul which I have quoted.

1199. St. Paul says that if a man cannot rule his own house, how shall he take care of the church. 1 Tim. III., 4.

That does not suggest that a Bishop must be married, but belongs to the same context as that which you have just quoted. If a man who has been married, but not to more than one wife, be chosen, he must be one who has been faithful and who has ruled well his own house. That discipline was most wise at a time when such a man could be chosen. But such discipline no longer holds.

1200. "Forbidding to marry," is given as one of the signs of false Churches.

The Catholic Church does not forbid people to marry. The vast majority of Catholics marry with the blessing of the Church. The text refers to people who declare all marriage evil, as did many early heretics. Marriage is not evil, nor is any Catholic forbidden to marry, as you would suggest. It is true that Priests may not marry. But no one can be obliged to become a Priest; in fact every one who is a Priest could have married instead of devoting his life to an ecclesiastical vocation, had he wished.

1201. Priests are only natural human beings. Why are they forbidden to marry?

Because they do not wish to be only natural. They wish to be supernatural. St. Paul was human, but he did not marry. And like St. Paul, Catholic Priests wish to centre their interests in Christ and share their hearts with no one else. Meantime, they are not forbidden to marry *as human beings*. They are forbidden *as Priests*. Prior to their choice of the Priesthood, every Priest could have chosen marriage instead had he wished.

1202. Are Priests different from other men?

As human beings—no; as called, not to the state of marriage, but to the Priesthood—yes. For this reason, whilst like all others who for one reason or another do not marry, they are obliged to avoid all sins against chastity; they also take upon themselves an additional obligation to do so under pain of sacrilege by vows of chastity offered to God.

1203. It is against nature to suggest that Priests are exempt from ordinary temptations.

No one suggests that they are exempt from ordinary temptations. But it is not against nature to rise above these temptations. It is one thing to be tempted; quite another to yield to the temptation. Anybody could avoid sin if never tempted. But the merit and glory of a Christian is to be tempted yet not to give way to the temptation. Priests undertake to resist such temptations with the help of God's grace.

1204. Protestants do not believe in your oath of celibacy. They know that Priests do not live up to it.

Upon what do you base that outrageous assertion?

1205. They are ordinary men, and as such cannot resist their natural inclinations.

Do you mean that no one with human nature can be pure and chaste? That every young couple entering matrimony can be quite sure that the other has led an evil immoral life up to that moment? If you do not mean that, do you mean that a young man in the world can lead a good life, but suddenly becomes corrupt when he gives himself to a life of closer union with God? Do you think that the devoting of oneself to a life of prayer and to spiritual things makes it much harder to live a good life than it was before? If a man wanted an immoral life he need not become a Priest in order to attain his desire; nor would he dream of taking a solemn vow of chastity for the sheer joy of making himself doubly guilty in breaking it. And do you, a Protestant, include in your indictment all unmarried Protestant ministers and celibate clergymen?

1206. Priests violate a fundamental law of nature ordering production of the race.

It is a fundamental law of nature that those who do exercise the functions of marriage should do so for the propagation of the race, and no Church fights against the contraceptionist as does the Catholic Church. But it is not a fundamental law of nature that every individual must marry. Many single people never get the chance. St. Paul also says that a single life for the love of God is the better thing, and the Catholic Church asks the better thing of her Priests so that they can be more free to devote themselves to the cares of all, that they may set a lofty example of self-restraint, and that they may more closely imitate Christ.

1207. *You would be much happier if you were married.*

If that were so, will you blame me for denying myself what you admit to be a happiness? However supernatural happiness more than compensates me for the loss of that natural happiness. No word of mine could make you think that I am gloomy or miserable. And I am sure that your estimate of me will make you admit that there is at least some girl in the world the happier for not having had me inflicted upon her as a husband.

1208. *Why inflict such a burden upon human nature?*

If anyone is to complain, let the Priests do the complaining, who have to endure the burden. And believe me, if Priests were left free to marry, very very few would ruin their work and influence by taking upon themselves the duties of married life with its necessary division of their interest from their ecclesiastical vocation. Priests do not want to be free to marry.

1209. *Our Protestant ministers do not pretend to be better than other men—they marry. Is not this more honest?*

Few Protestant ministers would thank you for that remark. There is, however, no need to pretend to be better. There is need to be better. Christ said to His Apostles, "You are the salt of the earth, but if the salt lose its savor! . . . You are the light of the world. So let your light shine before men that they may see your good works, etc." Your ministers may marry—but the Apostles did not, even as their Master did not. Of course it is more honest to marry than to live a life of unchastity in an unmarried state. But provided one lives a clean and chaste life in in the single state, thus imitating Christ, it is not more honest to marry.

1210. *Do you condemn Protestant ministers for marrying?*

Not for a moment. They break no commandment of their Church. It is true that God commands His Priests to remain single through the legislation of the Catholic Church. But her legislation in this matter has nothing to do with Protestant clergymen.

1211. *If it is right for one set of ministers to be celibate, it must be wrong for others not to be celibate.*

You might just as well say that, if it is right for me to obey one set of laws in America, it is wrong for another man to follow a totally different custom in China! And the Catholic Church differs much more from other religions than America differs from China.

1212. *Priests ought to marry to set a higher example.*

No one could give a higher moral example than Christ, and a Priest sets a higher moral example by not marrying. When he encourages young people to live pure and chaste lives in a single state he is not telling them to do what he is not obliged to do himself. He is unhampered by domestic cares so that he can go to the poorest mission for the love of God, and can attend those dying of contagious diseases without thought of carrying infection to wife and children. And it is certain that our people have more confidence in their Priests precisely because they are single men, above all in the Confessional. Even in the Greek Orthodox Church, it is a known fact that the people go to confession by preference to single Priests rather than to married Priests.

1213. *Why more confidence in a single man as a Confessor than in a married man?*

Because single men can give undivided attention to their duties, and have more time to study and know the law of God upon which they must base their advice. Then, too, people feel that one who has renounced earthly affections for the love of God has more opportunities of living a disinterested spiritual life, and that his words will be correspondingly more helpful. And last, but not least, a single man is not so likely to share his thoughts and worries with a better-half, or betray a confidence through indiscretion or inadvertence.

1214. *How can Priests advise as to the duties of the married state when they have no practical experience of it?*

"The lips of the Priest shall keep knowledge, and they shall seek the law at his mouth." Mal. II., 7. The married state is not exempt from God's laws, and the Priests must know those laws. Every Priest studies all the possible duties of marriage from a moral point of view during a long course of theology before he enters a Confessional at all. If you say that a Priest cannot explain those laws to people because he himself is not married, will you say that a trained lawyer has no right to explain the law of the land to a plumber concerning that individual's trade because he himself has never so much as soldered a jam-tin?

1215. *Priests condemn prevention of life by birth-control yet prevent life by their celibacy!*

Those who undertake the duties of married life are forbidden deliberate and artificial birth-prevention. Priests called, not to married life, but to a different state altogether, have neither the rights nor duties of the married state. There is a vast difference between preventing children by setting God's natural laws in operation yet frustrating their effects, and simply omitting to have children. No one is obliged to set the natural productive laws in operation. So, too, the obligation to pay bills is not violated by the man who has no bills. I may omit having creditors, but if I have them, I must not prevent them from receiving what is due to them. That should make it clear. Human beings may omit those actions which God intends to result in life, but if they exercise them and then prevent human life, they violate God's law.

1216. *Where is there a warrant for the convent system outside your Catholic traditions?*

There is more than sufficient warrant for convent life in Sacred Scripture. But even were the only warrant to be found in Catholic traditions, that surely would be quite a natural place to seek a warrant for a Catholic custom. Where else would you want me to find a warrant for it? In Totemism?

1217. *Perhaps I should call them Nunneries rather than Convents.*

If the word Nunnery sounds more suspicious and suggestive of evil to you than Convent, then I think you should. Otherwise you would not be speaking with all the bigotry and uncharitableness you might.

1218. *Is not the convent system borrowed from the pagan Vestal Virgin system?*

No. The convent system occurs in history after the Vestal Virgin system, but not because of it. Chronological succession does not always imply derivation. It is true that the Vestal Virgins were women, and unmarried, claiming a religious significance. But there the likeness ends. Christianity is the negation of paganism, and the Christian motive is quite the opposite of the idolatrous motives of paganism.

1219. Where did Christ tell us to shut ourselves away in monasteries or convents?

Nowhere. But He invited some people to renounce all things and to follow Him by close imitation. "If you wish to be really perfect, sell all you have, give to the poor, and come, follow Me." If a man marries he cannot do that. He has a duty to his wife and children, and cannot sell the house and furniture over their heads, leaving them stranded. From the very beginning many Christian young men and women renounced the prospects of marriage and property for the love of Christ. The Church arranged community houses wherein the members were to own nothing, merely receiving shelter from the weather and necessary food and clothing. For the rest they were to give themselves to prayer and to works of piety and charity, instructing children, preaching the Gospel, nursing the sick, or feeding the hungry and destitute. Later these houses were called monasteries, after the Greek word Monos, meaning alone or single. The fact that those who have renounced all in accordance with the invitation of Christ live in monasteries or convents makes no more difference than if they lived in tents.

1220. Monks and nuns run away from temptation for selfish moral reasons, trying to be good in an easier life.

I am grateful for that admission that they try to be good. Meantime, if to take definite means to live a better life is to be guilty of a selfish moral end, then I wish that more men would labor for that selfish moral end. Those who enter monasteries or convents may escape certain classes of temptations, but they always have self with them, and at times the temptation to go back to the easier life they left. Nor must you think that monastic or convent life is one of idleness. Every monastery and convent is a hive of industry, each member being engaged at set hours in very definite and continuous duties of various kinds.

1221. By locking up Nuns you stand for a system that makes prisoners of our womanhood.

I do not. I believe that female criminals should be made prisoners, but convents are not prisons. They are private residences. Many people are under a delusion concerning convents. They speak of locking people up, and always with the idea of a prison in their minds. Now in prisons we lock people in to keep them in, and away from the outside world which does not want them. And they are kept in against their will. But in convents the doors shut the outside world out in order to keep it out, and away from the individuals who do not want it. And the Nuns stay there because they desire to do so. Throw open the doors of a prison. The inmates will thank you, and joyfully depart. Throw open the doors of a convent, of the strictest convent you can imagine. The good Sisters will close the door again from the inside and continue the life they prefer. If you call that a prison, then your definition of a prison sadly needs revising.

1222. Your Church is pretty clever, making thousands of weak women virtual slaves.

The thousands of Nuns are not weak, but women of very strong character as a rule. If a girl of weak character enters a religious Order, she soon leaves and resumes an easier life in the world. I admit that, if the Catholic Church were merely human, she would be pretty clever. But she would be too clever. She could not possibly induce so many to devote themselves to such a life unless God Himself inspired them to do so.

1223. Why are Nuns never allowed out of their convents?

Surely you have seen them at times travelling by train, or tram; or in the public streets for purposes of shopping or other business.

1224. Why can't they travel without a companion, even when visiting their own homes?

It is the rule of convents that members do not travel alone. The presence of a companion is a protection, and at the same time preserves the good Sisters from the scandal evil-minded people would be so ready to propagate if they were seen travelling and entering houses alone. I wonder whether you would always have the charity to believe that it was the home of her relatives, should you see a young Nun entering or emerging from a house by herself?

1225. It is a sad fact that Enclosed Orders never let the Nuns out, or allow them to have contact with the outside world.

It is not a sad fact. It is a fact that those who enter Enclosed Orders will not go again beyond their convent walls. In what are called the Active Orders not all contact with the outside world is renounced. Where the work of the Nuns involves such contact, it is permitted. But apart from that, the Nuns gladly return to their quiet and spiritual detachment. However, there are some Nuns who have chosen to enter convents where the rule permits them to avoid all further contact with the world. Feeling called by God to such a life, they enter an Enclosed Order. But remember that there are no Nuns who cannot leave their convent whenever they definitely will to return to that life in the world which they voluntarily abandoned.

1226. You say that any Nun could give up the life?

Yes. There is not a single Nun who cannot leave any convent, if she insists that she wants to go. No one will detain her by force and against her will. She can secure a dispensation from her vows on making due application through her superiors or directly to the Bishop.

1227. Do you know of any Nun who has left after final vows, going back to the world and to sanity?

I know of many Nuns who have left, even at times with a dispensation from final vows. Some were sane before they left, and remained sane after they left. Some were not quite well-balanced before they entered, were discovered not to be eminently sane, and were sent away without being allowed to take their final vows, or, if they had taken them, were advised to apply for a dispensation. For religious life demands the utmost sanity in aspirants.

1228. Why oblige young immature women to take vows at all?

No Nun is ever obliged to take vows as a young immature woman, or at any other stage of life. If you can find one Nun who was compelled in any way at all to take her vows, then the Catholic Church says that her vows are quite invalid and not binding. If a Nun freely takes her vows for life, of course she understands that it is as permanent a contract for her as for the woman who freely vows fidelity for life to a husband.

1229. Nuns are martyrs to a cruel system.

They are less martyrs than a girl who ties herself to a husband for the rest of her life, in very many cases at least.

1230. *Do they stay because they love the life, or because they fear the anathemas of the Church?*

Because they love their self-chosen life. Not one of the Nuns would have entered unless she had chosen to do so. Nor is any Nun allowed to take her final vows until after at least four years of experience of the life to see whether she is satisfied even after entering. You might as well suggest that no married woman remains faithful to her self-chosen state because she loves and is happy, but that she does so only through terror.

1231. *Anyway you allow misguided women to live unnatural lives away from the sunshine, and from good men who would bestow upon them their love.*

Most things that Christ taught and recommended seem to be misguided to those who are completely irreligious. No one claims that Christian and materialistic principles are in harmony. However, the good Sisters have private grounds for recreation in the sunshine, contrary to the creation of your melodramatic imagination. As for their being away from men who would love them, they do not wish for such love, and what kind of a man would force his attentions upon an unwilling lady?

1232. *The dreadful vows have warped their minds and made them love darkness rather than light.*

Who told you that the vows were dreadful? Have you tried them? I have taken exactly the same vows of poverty, chastity, and obedience as the Nuns, and they are no more difficult for a Nun to keep than for myself. I do not find them dreadful. And the evidence of one who has experienced a thing is worth the assertions of ten millions who have never tried it. As for the minds of the Nuns being warped, kindly consult the thousands of parents, Catholic and non-Catholic alike, who confide their children to Nuns for their intellectual and moral formation. Finally, if the Nuns have learned to love their life, of what do you complain? If you say that they only think themselves to be happy, well, they are quite satisfied, and you have no cause to be unhappy about them. Let them do the worrying.

1233. *Christ did not die that Nuns should live such a strange and hard life in these civilized times.*

He did not die that the unmitigated sensuality of these civilized times might continue. St. Paul chastised his body and brought it into subjection, and said that those that are Christ's have crucified their flesh with its concupiscences. Do people crucify the flesh with cocktails and comic operas, soft linen and other luxuries, with a Rolls-Royce or two thrown in? If Christ were to condemn anything in these days of civilization, it would not be the humble, pure, and mortified Nun. If the Nun's life seems strange to you, remember that the life of Christ seemed strange to the worldlings of His day, who said that He had a devil. But at least, since you regard the life of a Nun as being hard and mortified, you will never pretend that a convent is a house of unbridled luxury and sensual indulgence.

1234. *What does the silver ring worn by Nuns mean?*

That they prefer to give their hearts entirely to Christ rather than to any earthly lover. As the ordinary wedding ring signifies that a woman has vowed absolute and permanent fidelity to her husband, so the ring worn by a Nun signifies that she has vowed fidelity to her vocation of poverty, chastity and obedience.

1235. Why do they lose their hair and wear such ugly dress?

They sacrifice their tresses as a sign that they renounce worldly vanity. Their habit is designed according to the rules of complete Christian modesty, and is most successful in warding off evil attention. Half-dress in a loose immodest fashion, and see the attention, and the kind of attention, that a girl will draw upon herself. If she wants to avoid such attention she could not do better than to dress as a Nun. No one would look at her twice.

1236. Are not superiors very hard on young Nuns?

No, not in general. An individual superior might be exacting; but remember that superiors are not allowed to exact more than the rules of the Order demand, and every Nun has had those rules carefully explained to her before she has made her profession. If she makes her profession, she does so because she wishes to live a life of obedience under such discipline.

1237. It is cruel that young Nuns should teach tiresome children all day and then return to live with elderly and cranky Nuns.

I am glad you admit that the Nuns have taken up a tiresome duty for the love of God, expecting no other reward save His approval. You must admire the way in which they voluntarily consecrate their lives to God, and to the training of little ones to fit them for the service of God in their earthly lives. However, they have not always to return to the company of elderly Nuns. There are many communities of quite young members of their Order. Also, even elderly Nuns are not cranky because elderly. Age most often tends in religious life to sweeten character. If some are cranky, would you turn them out after their years of service and devotedness in their young days, and allow only young Nuns to remain? Have you any elderly relatives? Are they cranky because elderly? Do you regard them as a burden and threaten to turn them out into the street? Are young people never to live with elderly people, and is it always a misery to do so? The bright young Nuns would be the last in the world to take your advice, even if you offered it to them.

1238. If Nuns are so happy, why have they such sombre and gloomy faces?

Nuns have not gloomy faces. You mistake gravity for gloom. Nuns are serious women, if you like, but their hearts are as light as feathers. Half the put-on excitement of modern butterflies in these days of jazz and cosmetics is to deaden the conscience, and conceal even from themselves if possible the jaded heart of lead so many worldly women carry always with them.

1239. To my mind Nuns are the most unhappy beings in the world.

To your mind. But things are not always what they seem. You measure Nuns by your idea of happiness. The man who said, "Eat, drink, and be merry," was branded as a fool by Christ. If you ever fall ill, go to a Catholic hospital and let the gloomy Nuns nurse you back to health. It will be an eye-opener to you.

1240. I have never seen a Nun smile or look pleasant.

You know Nuns only from a distance, if you know them at all. Nuns do not mistake excitement for happiness, but there are plenty of smiles in their own convent environment. In the streets you may not have seen a Nun laugh. But the sight of poor humanity in the streets, rushing and struggling, and worried even in the midst of its giggling, is not calculated to make a thoughtful person laugh. Yet as for looking pleasant, I'll guarantee that the tranquil face of a Nun is a much more pleasant thing than the face of the average woman of the world.

1241. *They will never again look upon their loved ones, but die and be buried!*

We all have to die some day and be buried. As for never again seeing loved ones, even if that were true in the case of a Nun, a girl who voluntarily leaves America for China can quite easily die and be buried in China without seeing her loved ones again in this life. And if she goes, knowing the conditions, she does not burden everybody with constant complaints about it.

1242. *There is a Carmelite Convent in my suburb known as the Death Order.*

You must have been reading Stevenson's Suicide Club, and then eaten cucumbers and gone to bed with the fond hope that you would not have a nightmare after all! There is a Carmelite Convent in your suburb at Dulwich Hill, but it is not a Death Order. It is an Order devoted wholly to the life which alone really counts—that of God's grace. The Nuns are well cared for bodily, even though simply; and they attain to an age beyond that attained by the average person in the world.

1243. *It costs a girl $7,500 to enter this Order!*

Do you think anyone is likely to pay $7,500 to enter a Death Order when one can so easily commit suicide for nothing? People do not save up cash for the joy of committing luxurious suicide! But let me explain the real facts. The Carmelite Nuns have to live. But according to their rule their life is devoted chiefly to the salvation by prayer of people who have not got the sense to pray for themselves. Consequently they do not teach in schools, and have no regular means of income. If a girl wishes to enter the Carmelite Convent, she must be able to provide a small dowry to be invested, so that the interest will provide her with the bare necessities of life. And nothing like $7,500 is demanded.

1244. *People may not enter until they are twenty-one.*

That rather spoils your case. You ought to say that they are rushed in before they know their own minds whether they like it or not, manacled hand and foot, and left to the final fate of all who enter this Death Order for the destruction of unwanted females.

1245. *The Nuns are kept behind menacing iron grilles even when talking to visitors.*

You have got things wrongly again. The grille is not to keep the Nuns in, but to keep people out.

1246. *There are high walls round this Convent inside which the Nuns are imprisoned.*

Those walls, too, are not to keep the Sisters in, but to keep curiosity-mongers out, and to give the Sisters undisturbed tranquility in their attention to God and to their spiritual lives.

1247. *They never come out.*

That sounds dreadful, doesn't it? But when one undertakes to enter upon a permanent state in life, it is intended to be permanent. I have become a Priest, and dreadful to relate, I can never cease to be a Priest. A girl marries a man, and dreadful to relate, she remains married to him. Yet you are wrong. A good many girls do come out of that Convent. Those who enter undergo a long probation before they are finally accepted, and many leave during this period of probation. It is far easier for a girl to come out from the Carmelite Order than it is for one to get into it. Believe me, the doors are opened more easily from the inside than from the outside.

1248. Did not Henry VIII. suppress monasteries and convents because they were immoral?

If you knew anything of Henry VIII. you would never suspect him of being shocked by immorality. He was quite immoral himself, and did not regard immorality as being a reason for the suppression of anything except his own conscience and his marriage with Catherine of Aragon. However he did suppress monasteries and convents. It was not because they were immoral, but rather because they stood for strict morality, and were a rebuke to his own low standards. But chiefly he wanted to confiscate their property which they used for the relief of the poor, but which he wished to use for the relief of Henry. The career of Henry was one of lust and of murder, things not usually associated with zeal for religion.

1249. Are not Nuns married to Priests?

No. Who in this world could persuade thousands of good women to forego theatres, dances, and worldly amusements, and to take a strict vow of perfect chastity in the sight of God, merely that they might be at the service of Priests who offer them no remuneration, and who strangely enough bind themselves by similarly strict vows under pain of sacrilege? Have some sense.

1250. I am a broad-minded Anglican Protestant, yet I cannot but suspect convents.

Is one broad-minded whose mind suspects evil and unspeakable proceedings in every building to which she does not happen to have access? And what of your own Anglican Sisterhoods? They model themselves on the lives of our Catholic Nuns. Those modest ladies, living prayerful and retired lives, do not throw their private rooms open to the public. Are you going to besmirch their characters also? If so, you will have the strange spectacle of a Catholic Priest defending Anglican Nuns against the attacks of an Anglican woman who rightly calls herself a Protestant, but wrongly calls herself broad-minded.

1251. Convents should be open to public inspection.

Inspection of what? Even if admission were free to the public, the public would not wish to inspect convents. It is rather dreary work to walk through empty corridors, inspect ordinary kitchen tables, wooden chairs, and bedrooms which differ little from the common boarding-house variety. In fact it would be a pity to destroy your ideals. All your delight in the idea of inspecting convents is based upon what you imagine you would find and which in reality does not exist. Where ignorance is bliss, it is folly to be wise. An actual visit of inspection would only mean the destruction of your castles in the air. Surely you would prefer not to be disillusioned by the finding of nothing blameworthy in convents.

1252. Until such inspection is granted I cannot consider convent life above board.

Is the Wesleyan religion not above board because the minister's Manse is not open to public inspection? If women wish to live bad lives, could they not obtain such lives without bothering to enter convents, renouncing money and all worldly pleasures? The last thing an immorally inclined woman would think of would be to enter a convent as a Nun.

1253. *But if everything is clean and upright, why not throw them open to the public?*

If everything is clean and upright in your own home, why do you not throw it open to public inspection, instead of regarding it as private premises? Why not ask all passers-by, complete strangers, to walk in and inspect your private rooms? If I came to your house and told you that I suspected you of leading an evil life, and that I insisted upon inspecting every room in order to try to prove my suspicions, what would you say? Think it out, and you will have your answer.

1254. *Our Protestant Churches are open to the public.*

Catholic Churches are still more open, and for longer hours. But convents are not churches, nor are they public institutions. They are the private homes of ladies who wish to live together in the service of God.

1255. *Would you personally vote for the systematic inspection of convents by the police?*

No. Nor would any reasonable man. Why should the private dwellings of any citizens who transgress none of the laws of the land be subjected to such an indignity? But submit your reasons for the inspection of convents to the Chief of Police. He will soon put you right. The police do not even want to inspect convents. Should any violation of the law occur within a convent there would be no difficulty whatever as regards police inspection, just as in the case of any other private dwelling.

1256. *How can we know of convent scandals when they are closed to public inspection? We must believe the accounts given by Maria Monk and others until we see otherwise.*

You cannot know of convent scandals, not because convents are closed to public inspection, but because the scandals don't happen. That you must believe in such scandals until you see otherwise looks fairly hopeless, since you intend to keep your eyes tightly shut against any good in the Catholic Church at all.

1257. *Convents have laundries and schools. Surely these are public institutions.*

If the Sisters conduct an institution, that institution is distinct and separate from the convent proper, and may be inspected at any time by any authorized person. But the right to inspect a public institution does not give the right to inspect the manager's private home. Would you insist that he must show you the kitchen, dining-room, bath-room, in his personal quarters, and let you see for yourself that there were no dead bodies under the linoleum?

1258. *Public inspection would be the end of the system.*

It would not. The only fear of a novice when she enters is that she will be found unsuitable and not be accepted. Open the doors, and the Nuns will close them again, as they did in the first place, imploring the Church to let them do so with her blessing. They are happy in their self-chosen state. If you threw open the doors of married life and released married women from all further obligations far more would depart from their husbands than Nuns from their convents. Your ideas on this subject are not prompted by philanthropic interests in the good Sisters, but by your blind hatred of the Catholic Church.

1259. Martin Luther, the good man who started Protestantism, left the abominations of the monastery. He was an ex-Monk.

He was. But if he was so good a man, and the monastery so evil, he was a mighty long time living an iniquitous life before he got his conscientious scruples. Yet hear a few facts. After Martin had left the Catholic Church, he gave permission to Philip of Hesse to commit bigamy and have two wives. Does that sound good and Christian? And to Philip he said, "Provided you keep it quiet." Does that sound straight? He called his enemies "Coarse donkeys, cursed sows, epicurean swine, putrid puddles, and the cursed broth of hell." It does not sound much like Christian charity. To his friend Weller he wrote, "Why do I drink too much, talk too much, and like good meals too much? It is when the devil prepares to torment me and mock me." Preaching against his fellow-Protestants, the Anabaptists, he says, "The Anabaptists say that reason is a torch. Does reason shed light? Yes, like dung would shed if set in a lantern. Reason is a prostitute. Throw dung in her face to make her hideous. Reason ought to be drowned." But I spare you. Phrases such as these are legion in the writings of Luther, and the greatest tribute to the Catholic Church is that a man like Martin Luther felt impelled to leave her.

1260. What about Maria Monk?

Maria Monk was a woman of no religion, who was arrested for vagrancy and sent to jail in Montreal in November, 1834, by Mr. Justice Robertson. The following year she entered a Magdalen Asylum for fallen women managed by Catholic Nuns. She was not a Nun, but an inmate. After a short stay there, she left and began to pose as an escaped Nun, relating horrible charges against the Sisters. She said that she had been a novice there for four years. Judge Robertson exposed her, saying that she had been in jail at the very time she was pretending to have been in the convent. However, she wrote a book called, "The Awful Disclosures of Maria Monk," and lectured on the Protestant platform, going from town to town as fast as the refutation followed her. Discredited entirely in the end, she fell back upon the streets. In 1849 she was arrested for stealing from a man who was consorting with her, and died in prison whilst undergoing her sentence.

1261. You must convince me that she gave false evidence in her book.

On October 24th, 1835, her own mother swore that she had never been a Nun. Dr. Robertson condemned her as a fraud. The Protestant Press in Montreal denounced her book as a tissue of lies. Before Benjamin Holmes, J.P., on November 14th, 1835, different people swore to all the places in which she had been engaged in domestic service during the very period in which she said she had been in the convent as a Nun. The President of the Bank of Montreal and a group of Protestant gentlemen visited the convent she had attacked, and found that the rooms and corridors in no way fitted her descriptions. Dolman's Magazine, October 9th, 1849, says: "The notorious and unfortunate Maria Monk was sent to jail for stealing from a consort in the streets, and died last Friday in prison." Chamber's Encyclopaedia says: "Her lying story deceived many credulous people." If this does not convince you, I challenge any one on earth to convince you of anything you do not wish to believe. I only wish you were as exacting in demanding proof of evil in the Catholic Church as you are in demanding its refutation.

1262. Montreal is a Catholic city; we can understand the verdict on Maria Monk.

Dr. Robertson, J.P., was a Protestant. Maria's mother was a Protestant. The gentlemen who inspected the convent were Protestants. All the Protestant papers in Montreal denounced Maria Monk.

1263. *Why is her book allowed to be published, if not true?*

As long as there is a credulous public, or section of the public, wanting such books and prepared to pay for them, publishers will be found to seek the profit from them. In many countries, as a matter of fact, her book is forbidden as indecent literature.

1264. *What about the revelations of Mrs. Shepherd?*

She is not a reliable witness. Her whole record is criminal. She died in 1903, but not before becoming a celebrity on the Protestant platform. Under the name of Miss Douglas she was arrested for forgery, and served sentences on other counts under the aliases of Parkyn, Edgerton, and Margaret Shepherd in Bodmin, Cornwall, and London jails. The Salvation Army tried to reform her, but she betrayed them, and Miss Florence Booth said, "The woman is undoubtedly a fraud." She deceived even W. T. Stead, who wrote later to a friend, "The less you have to do with the lady in question, the better for your peace of mind and for your pockets." Margaret Shepherd never was a Nun. She came into contact with Nuns only through being sent to the institution for fallen women at Arno's Vale, Bristol, England. She took to writing obscene books, and exploited the credulity of unthinking Protestants. Even Protestant clergymen wrote to the papers warning the public of her true character. That you should have to fall back upon such witnesses is a tribute to the Catholic Church you so dislike.

1265. *If Nuns can leave convents so easily, why all the fuss when Sr. Ligouri ran away from the convent at Wagga, N.S.W.?*

Any fuss was caused by bigoted Protestants who hoped to work up a scandal against the Catholic Church, and who persuaded the Sister to sue the Bishop for $25,000 for wrongful arrest and detention in the Reception House for deranged people. The verdict was given for the Bishop. In his summing up, after all the evidence of that famous case of 1921 had been taken, Judge Ferguson said that she herself had refuted any idea of any unkindness shown her whilst a member of the community. He remarked that the conducting of the case for the plaintiff was marked by sectarian feeling, adding that "questions were asked designed to show that people of her faith could not be believed on oath," and that other questions "were intended to bring into question the propriety of the convent system." No breath of scandal, however, resulted. The Judge also pointed out that Sr. Ligouri had no difficulty whatever in leaving the convent, but that, instead of leaving in daylight, fully dressed, she departed at midnight, half-dressed, and without shoes, leaving no word whatever as to her intended destination. She had no relatives in Australia, and the convent authorities had every reason to suspect mental derangement. They sent to find her having a duty to provide for her. The Judge said, "I am amazed that the convent authorities are called upon to excuse themselves for having sent to search for her. What would have been thought of them if they had not done so?" In her disturbed state of mind she sought refuge with complete strangers who happened to be Protestants, and the Orange Lodge took up her case to the bitter disappointment of its hopes. Sr. Ligouri left the convent in circumstances which would lead anyone to conclude that in her own interests she should not be let loose upon the world in such a deficient mental state. She would not have been retained in the community, and would certainly have been given a dispensation from her vows. But out of charity the Nuns insisted upon making provision for her until they could give her into the keeping of her own relatives. The "Ligouri Case" was a complete fiasco as an argument against convent life.

1266. *I am interested in your moral theology concerning those who contract marriage. Why does the Catholic Church forbid mixed marriages?*

For many reasons. Marriage is a Sacrament, and those who desire to receive that Sacrament should be duly and validly baptized Christians. The Church, however, has no certainty that any non-Catholic has ever been validly baptized at all. Again, it is a sacrilege to receive a Sacrament whilst one is in a state of grave sin. The Catholic party prepares by a good confession, whilst the non-Catholic more often than not gives no thought whatever to the matter. Then, too, any children of the marriage have the bad example of one of the parents who never fulfills Catholic duties, even if the poor children be brought up as Catholics at all. The Catholic party is constantly subject to discouragement in the practice of his or her religion, and is even exposed to the danger of a complete loss of faith and of salvation in the end. Nor are mixed marriages, as a rule, in the interests of the parties themselves from the point of view of mutual happiness. Marriage is difficult enough in any case when the first glow of love begins to settle down to the realities of life. It is vastly more difficult when the Protestant does not understand Catholic ways, has no sympathy at all with the Catholic party on the most vital of all matters—religion, and even resents the claims of the Catholic Church. Mutual misunderstandings result, and the Protestant, not making the Catholic as happy as he expected, does not make himself as happy as he dreamed.

1267. *I have heard that the Church openly forbids mixed marriages, but secretly fosters them to secure the control of the children.*

That is not true. The Catholic Church has never fostered mixed marriages, and barely tolerates them when she can do nothing else.

1268. *Why should religion come before marriage?*

Because marriage is not the most important thing in life, whereas religion is.

1269. *Where does the Bible forbid mixed marriages?*

It would not matter if the Bible did not forbid them. Not every detail of Christian practice is there. Christ gave the Church the power to make such legislation as she might think necessary at various times. However that God does not approve mixed marriages between people with the true religion and people without it is clear from Scripture. In the Old Testament He strictly forbade the Jews to marry outside the true religion. "If you embrace the errors of these nations that dwell among you, and make marriages with them, and join friendships . . . they shall be a pit and a snare in your way, and a stumbling block in your side . . . till He take you and destroy you from this land which He hath given you." Joshua XXIII., 13-14. St. Paul, writing to Christians, says that a widow is free to marry, "but," he adds, "let her marry in the Lord." 1 Cor. VII., 39. In dealing with marriage in general, he writes to the Ephesians, "But I speak in Christ and in the Church." Eph. V., 32. He gives the solemn warning as regards marriage with unbelievers, "How knowest thou, O wife, whether thou shalt save thy husband? Or how knowest thou, O man, whether thou shalt save thy wife?" 1 Cor. VII., 16.

1270. *Catholic men know that Protestant wives are best. Why prevent them from having the best wives?*

Good Catholic men who desire to marry Protestant women never think of them as Protestants except to wish that they had been Catholics. They do all in their power to persuade them to become Catholics. They love them at times for their character, or because they have happened to meet them at the psychological moment when they were romantically inclined. Or even at times they only think they love. There are many explanations, but never yet has a Catholic man loved and wanted a girl precisely because she is a Protestant. He may love her. He has never loved her Protestantism.

1271. *Why do Catholic women make such bad wives for Protestant husbands? They seem so proud and selfish.*

Good Catholic women often make bad wives for Protestant husbands. But it is not because they are proud and selfish. Their religion teaches them humility and self-denial. But the same religion teaches that a Catholic may not give way one jot or tittle in matters of Catholic obligations. The deepest thing in man is his religious conviction. If two people marry and have no religious sympathy, are alien to each other on that point, then each will say and do a dozen things daily that will disgust and further alienate the other. The Protestant party has not the same principles nor the same rigid conviction as the Catholic. He makes concessions and expects the Catholic to do the same. Very often the Catholic cannot and is accused of pride and selfishness. Peace goes and the Protestant is sorry he ever married a Catholic. It all comes from the difference in religion. I would advise every Protestant man who is determined never to become a Catholic to choose a wife from among his fellow Protestants. A Catholic wife is suitable for a Catholic but often makes a bad wife for a Protestant.

1272. *If a Protestant marries a Catholic will the Catholic Church recognize that marriage at all?*

Yes, provided it takes place according to Catholic rites.

1273. *Marriage is a contract between the parties themselves. Why should they have to be married in the Catholic Church?*

Marriage is a public as well as a private contract, and society rightly insists upon public conditions for validity. And since marriage is also a Christian Sacrament committed to the care of the Church, the Church reasonably and properly lays down the conditions for the lawful and valid reception of that Sacrament.

1274. *Catholics cannot attend a Protestant Church. How can the Protestant marry in the Catholic Church?*

To be married by a Priest is not against the principles of a Protestant who says that one religion is as good as another; but it is against the principles of a Catholic to be married by a Protestant minister. If it were against the principles of some given Protestant, he should stick to his principles and refuse to be married in a Catholic Church. But in this case both parties would refuse, and the marriage would be cancelled.

1275. *What would the Catholic Church do to a Catholic who marries in the Protestant Church?*

The Catholic Church regards her as a lapsed Catholic. Whilst still obliged to attend Mass, she is not allowed to receive the Sacraments. Individual Catholics would be obliged to treat her kindly and with charity. She would not therefore be treated badly personally or insulted. It is a matter for her own soul. She cuts herself off from the grace of God, and forfeits her right to the spiritual privileges of her religion.

1276. *I have known Priests to worry Catholics who have married outside the Catholic Church.*

A Priest has the obligation to try to save souls, and he has to inspire Catholics to observe the laws of their Church. If a Catholic is living as the Catholic conscience forbids, a Priest would be little like Christ if he simply left that soul to perish. And after all, the Priest would find it much more pleasant to sit at home enjoying a quiet book and allowing his flock to go its own way. But what sort of a shepherd would he be? You should admire the Priest who is a man of duty.

1277. Would the Catholic Church recognize a marriage between a Catholic and a Protestant in a Registry Office?

From the aspect of civil law the parties would contract certain civil obligations. But before God and in conscience the marriage would not be valid, and the Catholic party would be living in a sinful alliance, violating her conscience. She would be deprived of the Sacraments of the Church until she repented and had her marriage rectified according to the laws of the Church.

1278. You dare to say that no marriage outside the Church is a true marriage, that the Catholic party is living in sin, and that the children are not acceptable in decent society?

You make one mistake. The Catholic Church does not say that the children are not acceptable in decent society. Civil society is regulated by civil law, and a marriage legal in civil law obtains legal effects. Children of such a marriage are legitimate and acceptable in civil society. But whilst the marriage is regarded as legal by society, it is not valid in conscience for a Catholic, and such a person lives in sin. A marriage which civil law regards as valid need not necessarily be valid in God's sight. No state on earth could force me to say that a definite civil law is infallibly the law of God, and no state could possibly prove such a claim to infallibility.

1279. By a recent law, made by men in 1908, your Church makes it a sin for a Catholic to marry in a Protestant Church.

It has always been a sin for a Catholic to marry in a Protestant Church. But in Australia, prior to April 19th, 1908, such marriages, though sinful, were regarded as valid by the Catholic Church. Since 1908 such marriages are invalid. If a Catholic wishes to contract a valid marriage now, he must do so in the Catholic Church. This law is not a new law. Wherever the Church was solidly established, the Church applied this law. And the law was applied to Australia on April 19th, 1908, by what is known as the Ne Temere Decree. As for its being a man-made law, you forget that Christ commissioned His Church to legislate for the well-being of the Sacraments, and of those who would receive them. If the state can say, "Unless you come before my Registrar, your marriage will be regarded as null and void," so the Catholic Church can say, "Unless your marriage comes before my official minister, as far as I am concerned, I shall consider it no marriage." And God sanctions the view of the Church in this matter rather than any legislation of the state. Christ elevated the natural contract of matrimony to the dignity of a Sacrament, and it is as much a Sacrament as Baptism, Confirmation, Ordination, or any other. And as such it belongs to the Church.

1280. Why come between two lovers? God says love one another as I have loved you.

That we must love as God has loved us shows at once that not any kind of love is lawfully indulged. Christ never loved us so as to break God's laws because of us. Such love would be unlawful. God and conscience come first always. No human love can come before one's love for God, and he who loves God observes the laws of His religion.

1281. *Civil law says that the marriage of a Catholic and a Protestant in a Protestant Church is valid. Why don't you acknowledge the law of the land?*

The state holds the marriage to be valid in state law. And all Catholics hold the marriage to be civilly legal. But the state says nothing whatever about God's view of the matter, and the Catholic Church declares the marriage null and void before God, and therefore in conscience. Even after that declaration, if the parties do not get a civil divorce, they cannot marry other people without bigamy in civil law. So you see that civil law is not affected as such.

1282. *I mean, why don't you acknowledge civil law as binding before God and in conscience.*

We acknowledge that in the case of each and every law which does not conflict with the law of Christ. In the matter of marriage there are laws which conflict with the law of Christ, and these state laws are not valid before God. As I have said, if every state law is necessarily the law of God, then you claim infallibility for the state, an infallibility you deny to the Catholic Church with scorn on the principle that there is no infallible body of men on earth.

1283. *Render to Caesar the things that are Caesar's!*

A state law opposed to the law of God is not rightly the thing of Caesar, and in so far as it is thus opposed to the law of God, it is to be ignored. Obedience must be rendered to God rather than to the State.

1284. *How can the Catholic Church hope to win the confidence and respect of non-Catholics?*

She does not hope to do so if it means watering down Christian obligations. Christ could have kept many of His Jewish followers by saying that He did not mean His words, "The bread which I shall give is My flesh." The Jews said, "This is a hard saying. Who can accept it?" But Christ let them go rather than keep them by mitigating His doctrine. The Catholic Church does likewise. If men say, "This is a hard saying," the Church will never mitigate Christian obligations in order to win them. She is here to accommodate men to Christian teaching, not to accommodate Christian ideals to the moods of men.

1285. *If two married Protestants both become Catholics, have they to be married again in the Catholic Church?*

No. They were both Protestants at the time of their marriage, and the Catholic Church declares such marriages to be binding before God. The law of the Church in this matter extends to marriages in which at least one of the parties is a Catholic.

1286. *If two Protestants, married in a Protestant Church, get a divorce, could one of the parties marry a Catholic in the Catholic Church provided he or she becomes a Catholic?*

No. The marriage of two Protestants in a Protestant Church is valid before God, and nothing can dissolve that marriage except the death of one of the parties. Divorce does not give even such Protestants the right to marry again whilst both parties are still living. And becoming a Catholic has no effect upon the validity of such a marriage.

1287. *If a Catholic did marry outside the Catholic Church, would Christ cast a stain upon little children held up by Him to be the essence of goodness and innocence?*

Christ would cast no stain upon them. Nor does the Catholic Church. Their goodness and innocence are not affected. But note this. The state says, "Unless you observe my laws your marriage will not be lawful wedlock, and your children will be illegitimate." On your principle, the state has no right to cast such a slur on innocent little children, and has no right to lay down any conditions of marriage, but must sanction promiscuous cohabitation as being quite all right.

1288. *Tell me plainly. Are the children of a mixed marriage outside the Catholic Church illegitimate?*

This means that, whilst the civil legitimacy of such children remains unaffected, the refusal of the Catholic party to comply with the marriage laws of the Catholic Church deprives the children of religious recognition and privileges. Such recognition and privileges are reserved by Canon Law for those children only who are born of the marriages of Catholics celebrated according to Catholic requirements. No one can reasonably object to that.

1289. *Can the child of a mixed marriage outside the Church go to heaven?*

If the child is brought up as a Protestant it has the same chance as any Protestant in similar circumstances from other points of view. If brought up as a Catholic, it has the additional helps of the Catholic religion just as any other Catholic child, except that it has the bad example of a non-Catholic parent ignoring obligations which the child is taught to be essential, and the weak faith in many cases of a Catholic who thinks so little of her religion as to marry outside the Church.

1290. *Why sanction a mixed marriage at all in the Catholic Church? Is the Church afraid of losing the Catholic? Or the money?*

It is not a question of the money. If the conditions demanded by the Church are not fulfilled, $100,000 would not secure the marriage according to Catholic rites. Nor is the Church afraid of losing one of her members. She is afraid that one of her members will lose the advantages of the Catholic faith and perhaps her soul. The loss of one person out of 400 millions does not affect the Church very much from the point of view of numbers. But the loss to such a soul will not bear description. The Church sanctions such a marriage when there are reasons grave enough to warrant risking the dangers attached to mixed marriages. But she takes every precaution by exacting promises that the Catholic will be free to practice her religion, that all children will be Catholics, and that the Catholic party will set a good example and do her best to convert the non-Catholic party.

1291. *Could the Pope, besides giving a dispensation for a mixed marriage, dispense from the obligation of bringing up the children as Catholics?*

No. It is divine law that no Catholic may hand over any child to what he or she knows to be a false religion.

1292. *Why must the Protestant promise that all children will be Catholics?*

You must try to see this through Catholic eyes. A non-Catholic does not, as a rule, believe that his is the only true religion, and on the principle that one religion is as good as another, his conscience does not forbid that his children should be brought up in the Catholic religion. But a Catholic is in a very different position.

He believes that his is the only true religion, and does not believe that one religion is as good as another. Now how can a Catholic in conscience hand over his children to what he knows to be a wrong religion? How say, "I shall have all the benefits of the true religion, but my children won't!" Or, "God will be worshipped by me in the way He commands, but not by my children!" Even God could not authorize a Catholic to cling to the true faith himself, yet deny that faith to his children. Without securing the promises no Catholic could conscientiously enter upon such a marriage.

1293. Should not the children be of the mother's faith?

No. The children must be brought up in the Catholic faith, whether it be the faith of the husband or of the wife. A religion is not true because it is the religion of the wife. If so, then when the wife is Anglican, Anglicanism would be true; when a Christian Scientist, Christian Science would be true; when Catholic, Catholicism would be true! Again, if a man married a Catholic and had three children of the marriage, they would have to be Catholics, and would have the true religion because their mother was a Catholic. If she died, and the man married a Seventh Day Adventist, further children would have to be Seventh Day Adventists, and would have the true religion because their mother was an Adventist. So three children would call the Pope the Vicar of Christ, and the others would call him the Beast and Anti-Christ, and all would be right!

1294. That all must be Catholics is very one-sided in favor of the Catholic Church!

It must seem like that to you, but in reality it is not. Parents co-operate with God in giving existence to children. But why is any man at all created? That he may save his soul and attain heaven. Marriage therefore has as its chief purpose the creating and training of children for their eternal destiny. And religion is therefore all important. Now the Catholic believes that there is but one true religion. It does not matter whether others agree or not. And he believes that all other religions are wrong. Again it does not matter whether others agree or not. That is the Catholic conscience. It follows that no Catholic can in conscience consent to hand over his children to what he believes to be a false religion. Nor can a Catholic say, "Give me the girls and you take the boys." The soul of a boy is just as dear to God as the soul of a girl. There can be no compromise. As for the one-sidedness, look at things this way. The Protestant who believes that one religion is as good as another need not mind if the children are brought up as Catholics. He does not violate his conscience and does not ask the Catholic to violate hers. They are square. The fact that the Catholic Church feels bound in conscience to demand all the children shows that she is conscious of having the truth and being the true Church. The fact that Protestants do not demand the children shows that they are not really conscious of possessing the truth.

1295. If a Catholic cannot sign away the children, how can a Protestant do so?

If a Protestant wants to marry a Catholic, and his conscience does not protest against it, he may sign the promise in regard to the children. But if the Protestant really believed the Catholic faith to be evil, and that his personal religion was the only true religion, then he has no right to promise that any of his children will be Catholics. He should abandon the marriage rather than thus violate his conscience. He should demand that the children be brought up in his faith. But then of course a dead-lock would result. He would have to refuse compromise, and as the Catholic is also obliged to refuse marriage unless the written promise is given, the marriage would be cancelled. It is better to part with a human being than to part with loyalty to conscience in so grave a matter.

1296. Why must the promise be made in writing? Surely you can take a man's word for it!

In many cases, yes. But sad experience has shown that some were not in good faith, and even granting good faith at the time there is no guarantee that such dispositions will persevere. Human nature is mutable. Why does the law of the land demand both signatures for the marriage itself in writing? Surely at the moment of marriage both are in good faith? The promise concerning the children is just as important as the marriage itself. On that promise the eternal welfare of the children may depend, surely a great responsibility. All serious contracts demand permanent signed records, and as no one resents them in other matters, so no one should resent them in this. Death could carry off the Catholic partner, and it may be very necessary to have written records of the promise. And if a man really intends to grant such a condition he should not mind putting his signature to it.

1297. Why are not mixed marriages celebrated before the Altar?

Marriage is a Sacrament and a very holy rite. The normal subject is a Catholic only. When non-Catholics present themselves as partners in the marriage ceremony, the Church does not grant the full privileges which are the right of Catholics only. The marriage is valid, of course, even though celebrated elsewhere than before the altar.

1298. If this restriction were abolished there would be fewer marriages outside the Church.

The number of marriages outside the Church might be diminished, but the number of mixed marriages might greatly increase. By this law the mind of the Church is kept constantly before Catholics, and they do not think lightly of entering upon such alliances. If a Catholic would marry outside the Church because of such a law, she has little love for her religion, and would not be much of a Catholic whatever concessions were made in her favor.

1299. The law will not prevent mixed marriages. They will always be.

That may be so. But the law diminishes their number. The Church cannot accept mixed marriages as the normal thing, and she would not be wise to treat them as normal.

1300. Is it fair to mar the happiness of a young couple?

Is it fair to ask the Church to admit to her Sacraments those of any religion or of no religion? People who are complete strangers to her cannot expect her to make as much of them as of those who are her own children. The parties do not resent their exclusion from the Altar nearly so much as the Church resents mixed marriages.

1301. Why such lack of respect for the non-Catholic and the guests?

The law is not prompted by lack of respect for the non-Catholic party or for the guests. It is prompted by respect for religious rites and for the worship of God. The non-Catholic has no more right to intimate Catholic religious practices than an unnaturalized citizen to all the civic rights of true subjects. The non-Catholic party may be as good as gold. But that is not the point. The point is that she is not a Catholic, and the Church is quite within her rights in saying how far she will admit non-Catholics to a participation in her privileges, even as a club is within its rights in saying how far non-members may participate in its privileges. But such restrictions as regards non-members cannot be construed as an insult. The

Catholic Church is not bound to manifest equal approval of Catholic marriages and of mixed marriages alike.

1302. *Would Christ be so intolerant?*

He would sanction all prudent measures for the good of souls. In the Old Law God gave drastic laws and penalties affecting those of the true religion who tried to contract mixed marriages, and the Catholic Church is but similarly zealous for the true religion of Christ.

1303. *Why is the Catholic Church opposed to birth-control?*

She is not opposed to the controlling of the number of children by lawful means, such as by self-control and by mutual consent to abstain from the use of marital privileges. But she is opposed to birth-control as commonly understood to mean the prevention of conception, after indulgence in actions calculated to result in the generation of children. The use of such privileges and the deliberate frustration of their normal effects is a very grave sin against the law of God. And for this reason the Catholic Church cannot but forbid it.

1304. *Why is birth-control wrong?*

It is opposed to the natural dictates of morality. It is obvious, for example, that the accompanying pleasure in eating and drinking is secondary and in view of the primary end, that the individual life may be preserved by due nourishment. We have supreme contempt for the glutton who does not eat to live, but rather lives to eat. No decent man eats merely for the sake of eating, even prepared to vomit in order to be able to eat again! And as appetite for food is an instinct ordained to the preservation of the individual life, so sex appetite is ordained to the preservation of the life of the race. The pleasure attached to the indulgence of sensual passion is but secondary, and in view of the primary purpose, the production of children. The birth controller satisfies passion for the sake of passion, and violates the moral order established by God. The use of marital privileges together with the deliberate frustration of the justifying purpose is but reciprocal vice. It leads, too, to many sins of injustice, being often practiced without the consent of one party. It is destructive of marriage, for it often leads to the divorce court when those who have based their marriage on sensuality have tired of each other. And violated nature exacts a penalty sooner or later. When birth-control is practiced in early married life, it leads to sterility and the impossibility of having children when they are wanted later on. The health of women is often gravely affected, neurosis, fibroid tumors, and other evils resulting. The health of women is undoubtedly better where there is a higher birth rate than where there is an artificaly low one. Finally it logically leads to the destruction of the human race by implying that one may indulge in the act of procreation for pleasure and yet frustrate the purpose of God in permitting that act.

1305. *Is it not only recently that the Catholic Church forbade it?*

No. But the recent publicity and advocacy given to this wretched vice have led to new statements of the permanent Catholic doctrine. This vice ruined pagan Rome, and Origen wrote against the pagan Celsus in the third century, "At least the more our people obey Christian doctrine, the more they love purity, abstaining from even lawful sex-pleasure that they may the more purely worship God. Christians marry as do others, and they have children; but they do not stifle their offspring. They are in bodies of flesh, but they do not live according to the flesh." In the fourth century St. Augustine wrote, "Relations with one's wife when conception is deliberately prevented are as unlawful and impure as the conduct of Onan who was slain." St. Thomas Aquinas, in the thirteenth century, taught clearly the constant doctrine of the Christian religion that birth-control is a grave sin. He writes, "Next to murder, by which an actually existent human being is destroyed, we rank this sin by which the generation of a human being is prevented." Contra Gent., Bk. III., c. 122. It is not a new law by any means.

1306. Where does God forbid it?

God is the author of the natural moral law, and I have already shown that birth-control is opposed to that law. However, in Gen. XXXVIII., 10, we read that Onan was slain by God for this sin. "And therefore the Lord slew him, because he did a detestable thing." The gravity of the punishment shows the gravity of the crime, and Cornelius a Lapide remarks, "If God so punished Onan, what must He think of Christians?" In the Book of Tobias we find the Angel Raphael instructing the youthful Tobias. "Hear me, and I will show thee who they are over whom the devil can prevail. For they who in such manner receive matrimony as to shut God out from themselves, and from their mind, and to give themselves to their lust as the horse and mule which have not understanding, over them the devil hath power." VI., 16-17. And the prayer of Tobias is full of significance, "O Lord, Thou knowest that not for fleshly lust do I take Sara to wife, but only for the love of posterity in which Thy name may be blest." VIII., 9. In the New Testament St. Paul repeatedly says that the lustful and sensuous will not inherit the kingdom of heaven and that even marital relations must be honorable. Such relations are justified only provided the conception of children be not deliberately and artifically prevented. The honorable nature of marriage is destroyed if it be turned into a merely sensual satisfaction. Christian marriage is a great symbol of the union between Christ and His Church. Can you imagine the Church deliberately preventing the spiritual life of grace in the souls of those whom her union with Christ should bring to God? Not only the natural law, but the positive revelation of God excludes birth-control.

1307. God dispensed from other laws given to the Jews.

He has never dispensed from such laws as involve the principles of natural morality. The violation of some laws is wrong because God has forbidden a thing, or commanded some disciplinary measures. But contraception is not wrong because God forbids it. Rather God has forbidden it because it is wrong in itself; and God could not dispense from it, even as He could never sanction an essentially wrong thing.

1308. Does contraception prevent souls from existing which God intended to be born?

People who practice contraception certainly prevent souls from coming into existence. Did God ordain them to be born? Certainly not by His absolute will, or He would not permit people to succeed in their crime. But He does ordain them to be born conditionally, that is, provided the parents do the right thing He intended them to do. If they fulfill the conditions required for the generation of children, He intends children to result. At the same time, whilst commanding parents to observe the law of nature, He leaves them physically free to serve Him or to rebel, as in the case of any other commandments. Those who practice contraception violate God's law, and deprive Christ of children to redeem. And if they die in such sin they will most certainly be lost. If they say that conscience does not reproach them, then they have warped their conscience, and will have to answer for it.

1309. Do you deny that one can follow his conscience?

One should follow a right conscience. But conscience can be warped just as any other judgment. Therefore a man needs some test by which he can know his conscience is true. What is that test? He must see whether his conscience squares with the known law of God. The Church tells us clearly that law in this matter, and once we know the law from the mouth of the Church, conscience bids us follow it.

1310. Celibacy denies life to millions. Is not that birth-control?

Not in the sense in which birth-control is forbidden. Birth-control affects those who enter married life, or those who live as married people without warrant. If people use privileges proper to the married state, they sin if they deliberately frustrate children. But there is no obligation to enter the married state.

1311. Your arrogance in interfering with the domestic relations of man and wife is astounding!

It would be arrogance did I pretend to be the legislator. But it is not when I simply declare what God demands. He, as Creator, has full rights over His creatures, and the right to make conditions upon which they may use the faculties He gave them, forbidding their use in a way which offends and insults Him.

1312. Your teachings on birth-control come with no weight from bachelor Priests.

You seem to think that it is a law made by unmarried men. Get that idea out of your head. God made the law. The celibacy of Priests has nothing to do with the question. God's law has the same force whether a bachelor Priest declares the law, or a married layman. Would you say that the teachings of Christ are to be accepted in every case except when He refers to marriage, your exception being based on the fact that He was never married?

1313. Who is likely to be right, the unmarried man who views things through the distorting spectacles of his Church, or the reasonable man who loves truth for its own sake?

The man who knows what God says about the matter is likely to be right rather than the one who knows little or nothing of God's law. Meantime the birth controller does not love truth for its own sake. Rather he loves sensuality for its own sake. Violation of Catholic teaching in this matter is also a violation of reason, and those who violate Catholic ideals have to warp their reason to do so, or just ignore it.

1314. Will the Church ever change her teaching on this point?

No. This is not an ecclesiastical law, but a divine law. No one on earth can ever dispense man from it. The Catholic Church is not here to allow God's laws to be broken, but to see that they are kept, so far as possible. Of course she cannot force all her subjects to observe the law, even as God does not force all people to keep other commandments of moral obligation.

1315. Many Catholics practice birth-control, as is evident from their small families.

That is not evidence. Only on a man's own admission could we know that he is not limiting his children by practicing continence, he and his wife agreeing to abstain from marriage rights by mutual consent. But even if it be true that many Catholics sin in this manner, the fact that they sin could not justify the same sin in others. All cannot break a law because some do. Nor do such Catholics think themselves justified. They know they are sinning just as men sin by breaking any other law of God. Protestants have admitted to me over and over again that their consciences have protested against such conduct, and that the Catholic law is undoubtedly right.

1316. The motive of your Church is to increase her numbers.

Her motive is to obey God. Temporal advantages certainly do follow from the observance of God's law, but those advantages are not the primary motive of the prohibition of birth-control. The Church cannot water down God's law to suit the passions of men; she must lift men to the observance of God's law. Whatever time-serving concessions other Churches may make, the Catholic Church stands for the law of God because it is the law of God.

1317. *Priests can be continent, but when they say that continence is easy in marriage they lack experience—an essential quality in a law-maker.*

No one dreams that it is an easy matter in marriage. It is difficult indeed. Prudent measures must be taken, and the definite help of Almighty God must be sought in prayer. But you cannot speak of lack of experience in the law-giver. God made the law, and we cannot accuse Him of not having foreseen all the future difficulties in each individual case. But the general good prevails over individual trials, even as the general good of a country may demand the very lives of some individual members in its defence. Continence is certainly possible, for it is absolutely necessary at times, as when the wife is ill, or during the weeks associated with actual child-birth. Is a man compelled to be unfaithful to her at such times?

1318. *The Catholic Church is inhuman and takes the joy out of life. How can one believe in her?*

The Church is not inhuman. She has never pretended that fallen human nature will find the service of God easy. She calls this world a valley of tears, and she has tears for the sufferings of her children. But she has to be true to God, and to tell us the law. What would be the good of the Church if she did not do so? The Church must tell us the right thing. Whether we do it or not is quite another matter which concerns our personal salvation. But to lose faith in the Catholic Church because she tells us the right thing is rather foolish. There would be some sense in rejecting her if we discovered that she was telling us the wrong thing. As for being deprived of joy, remember that there is no state of life which is one of unmitigated pleasure and self-indulgence. Every state has its irksome duties, even marriage. And no earthly pleasure or benefit is sufficient compensation for the loss of God's grace. Indeed, one who really and sincerely loves in a Christian way would rather endure a personal deprivation of pleasure than inflict the evil of serious sin upon the soul of the one loved.

1319. *It is impossible to live up to the standard set by the Catholic Church.*

The standard is not set up by the Catholic Church. She did not make the law and she cannot unmake it. And God does not ask the impossible. If a man takes the means he can live up to it, either practicing self-control, or accepting the children God sends. God offers sufficient help with every difficulty to the man of goodwill who meditates upon Christian truth and is earnest in prayer for the necessary grace.

1320. *One cannot keep on praying and denying oneself indefinitely.*

We must all keep on praying as indefinitely as this life lasts. Always to pray and not to faint is Our Lord's command. As for denying oneself indefinitely, many people do in this matter, and have to do so, when circumstances forbid anything else. Self-denial is burdensome. Children are burdensome. The choice allowed by God depends upon our idea as to which is the less burdensome. If self-denial is too difficult, God will give the grace to face the temporal trials associated with children, and the children themselves will prove a blessing and a consolation. If conditions render the prospect of children too burdensome, then husband and wife must ask of God the grace of mutual self-control.

1321. *I have tried prayer and self-denial and have found them wanting.*

Prayer may have been tried, but not fervently enough; self-denial, but half-heartedly. The goodwill to correspond with God's grace was wanting, and probably, too, ordinary prudence. Some measures must be taken to render the difficulty less, as by self-denying separation.

1322. *It tempts one to give up the Church.*

That is foolish, and will not better things. Will you neglect other obligations because you have failed in this, and give up religion on the principle that he who commits one sin might just as well commit a dozen sins? The only thing to do after failure is to repe as men do of other sins, and try again to be faithful.

1323. *You speak . laws adapted to the welfare of the race. But if married men are guilty in violating those laws, what of single men?*

The cases are not parallel. If a man enters that state which God ordains as the essential unit of society for the multiplication of the race, and if within that state he puts into operation those forces God intends to result in children, he is bound to accept the children in a spirit of service primarily to God, and secondarily to humanity.

1324. *The world cannot look after its present inhabitants. What is to happen when the earth is over-populated?*

Such considerations cannot affect the question. They are based upon the evil principle that the end can justify the means. You think you have a good purpose— let there be less of us to enjoy more. With this good end in view, you think to justify birth-control even though by immoral means! It cannot be done. The Church can never teach that it is lawful. Even did she teach that it was lawful, that would not make it lawful. God made the law. Meantime, if the world lived moderately and justly, it could easily provide for those already in the world and for millions more. The fault is not with the children to be born, but with the selfish men and women already in this world. The earth is producing more than sufficient for the people in it. Men are even complaining of over-production. And God is not to blame for men's failure to secure even distribution. Let men rectify their own fault. Finally, the Catholic Church is not opposed to the limitation of individual families where necessity and poverty justify it. If some families cannot afford to have further children, they are free not to have them. But the only way is by abstaining from the use of marital privileges, a continence possible by prudent separation, prayer, and the grace of God.

1325. *Birth-control may be necessary for the sake of the mother's health. What if the doctor says that she cannot have more children?*

Doctors are not infallible, and irreligious doctors are often only too ready to please women by telling them that they are unable to fulfill the duties of motherhood. And as a matter of fact contraception normally has a worse effect upon a woman's health than childbirth. She becomes a neurasthenic wreck in the end. But in any case, since contraception is evil of its very nature, no earthly consideration can justify it.

1326. *Then the pain and suffering and risk of death to the mother count for nothing!*

All childbirth involves some risk, and the merely possible danger would not oblige abstinence. Childbearing, too, is normally accompanied by pain. It is an inescapable penalty. "In sorrow she shall bring forth children." Christ Himself has said that a woman, when she is in labor, is in distress; but that her sorrow is turned to joy in her child. Every state in life has its difficulties, and marriage is no exception. But the danger of death is remote as a rule. Nature provides in a remarkable way for various contingencies. Even diseases such as cancer and consumption have been noticed to suspend their activities in the presence of this great physiological function of nature.

1327. *I know of one Catholic woman who defied the doctor. She said she would rather die keeping God's law than live breaking it. She died, leaving five little children to be looked after by strangers.*

She is greatly to be admired. "Die rather than offend God" is heroism. Far better die serving God than live offending Him. No one has greater love than to give one's life for God, and of such a woman St. Paul's words are surely true, "a woman shall be saved through childbearing, if she continue in faith, and love, and sanctification." 1 Tim. II., 15. The little children, deprived of their mother, may have difficulty and hardship for a time, but they will be grateful all their lives to the mother who gave them being, above all if they are brought up as fervent Catholics who realize the value of eternity rather than of time.

1328. *What if a doctor, a reliable doctor, says that death will result absolutely from any further conception?*

In such a case the moral theology of the Catholic Church says that a wife is justified in refusing marital privileges to her husband, and that he has an obligation to practice self-restraint and continence, thinking more of his wife than of himself. He must content himself with the other benefits of married life, mutual love, companionship, etc. But never can the Church permit contraceptive methods. The choice lies between offending God seriously with consequent risk to salvation, and continence. It may seem hard, but there is no other possible choice. And such continence is possible if a man is prepared to live a truly spiritual life and to avoid proximate occasions of temptation in the matter. If such difficulties drive a man to God, to more fervent prayer and a consequent deepening of faith and merit, he will bless God for the necessity of such Christian mortification.

1329. *Would it not be better for thousands of children of physically, mentally, morally, or financially unfit parents never to have been born?*

If there were no God; if there were no hope of any future life; and if I were not a Christian, I might be tempted to say yes. But there is a God who forbids contraception, and it is far better to accept what God's providence permits than to break any of His commandments. There is also a future life. A child does not consist of a body only. It has also a soul. If the child is baptized and attains salvation, far better be born no matter how physically deformed the body may be in this life. This life of so few years scarcely matters compared with eternity, where there will be no suffering and no deformity in heaven. Physical deformity often means pain, but pain is not an evil that really matters in the end. There was no real evil in Christ, yet He had much pain. Mental deficiency does not prevent the reception of Baptism, and diminishes responsibility. God knows how to make all allowances for factors diminishing such responsibility for one's conduct. Financial deficiency means poverty, but Christ too had much of that. The opportunity of attaining eternal salvation and happiness is worth any privation in this life. Many a cripple has been full of gratitude to God and to his parents for existence and the chance to love God and to suffer with Christ. God's ways are not our ways. With twisted and deformed bodies, it is better to be born if we do no wrong culpably. With a strong and healthy body, it is better not to be born if we sin like Judas and die without having repented.

1330. Which is the lesser of two evils—to bring undernourished children into the world for whom you cannot provide, or to practice contraception?

To bring children into the world and not to be able to provide for them is easily the lesser of the two evils. Better any temporal trials than sin by breaking God's law. But you have no certainty that you will be unable to provide for the children God sends, or that they will be undernourished. There is such a thing as Divine Providence, above all for those who are faithful to Him. In fact God has a special Providence for large families. At best you are but making a conjecture which may never be realized; yet you talk of violating a certain obligation by contraceptive practices because of merely possible contingencies; contingencies which, even did they eventuate, could not excuse such conduct. But there is another alternative, involving discomfort to self, I know, but less than either of the two you mention. It is self-denial. You speak as if one had to choose either of your two alternatives. He need not. Mutual self-restraint is lawful. Anyway, if people do use their privileges, God absolutely forbids contraception. Nor will He send a mouth He cannot fill. Even it it meant poverty; even if an orphanage had to take care of me, I would prefer to be born and have my chance of eternal happiness with God. And I certainly thank God that, when it was my turn to come, my own mother did not say, "No more."

1331. Do you say that all large families are sufficiently provided for?

If they were not, that would not justify birth-control. The end does not justify the means. However I do not deny that individual cases of extreme poverty occur where there happens to be large families. But they occur also where there are not large families. I deny however that parents cannot normally support the children which will result from their marriage if God's laws are observed. Because some large families suffer poverty, it does not follow that every man who has a large family can expect similar poverty. A lot of men's trials are those which never happen! I admit that many children mean difficulty, self-sacrifice, and real service of God. But as a rule the difficulties are confined to the early stages of married life, when youth is able to bear them. As the children grow up, begin to earn and bring in revenue, conditions are bettered, and the later years of husband and wife are doubly blest.

1332. A higher standard of life and education is demanded to-day than in mediaeval times, and one can't do it with a large family.

That could not justify birth-control by contraceptive methods. The choice to-day is between Christ and the modern pagan philosophy. If modern godless civilization is right, and this life is all, then let us measure everything by utility and pleasure. If Christ is right, and the beatitudes, directed against worldly wisdom, are the road to eternal happiness, then a small family cannot be had if it means sin and the re-crucifixion of Christ in the name of sensuality. And is not the higher standard of living based on discontent with the necessities of life, and upon the desire to possess as many superfluous and pleasurable goods as possible? A man who is not content with Christian simplicity of life will lack what he considers fitting means to support children. His preference is for temporal comfort. The idea of providing Christ with little children to redeem, who may share a happiness he himself hopes to enjoy for all eternity has little appeal for him. "The animal man," says St. Paul, "does not perceive the things which are of the spirit of God." And remember that many of the greatest geniuses in the world have come from large but poor families, whilst men whose parents spent vast sums on their education, have been failures. A child brought up without luxury is more energetic, more resourceful, and, if encouraged, can quite well make good in the world. Normally, it is good to give children a higher and a secondary, or even a university education, although they are not always the better for it. Character is the true education, and that is much better attained in a large family than in any other circumstances. The father and mother of a large family have more lovable qualities than those who restrict their families, and communicate their characteristics to a larger number of children who will glorify God and edify their fellow men.

1333. You seem blind to the practical reasons against the Catholic doctrine.

I am not. But you are blind to the innate immorality of contraceptive practices, and your reasons are based upon expediency only. And if what is expedient is going to be lawful, then goodbye to morality. Slanderers of the Catholic Church have accused her of teaching the frightful doctrine that the end justifies the means. The Church has always indignantly denied such a doctrine. She has ever taught that men are not free to do what is morally wrong because they think they have some good end in view. But where the world used to say, "Those evil Catholics teach that one may do any harm that good may come," it now cries, "Look at that tyrannical Church! She dares to tell us that the end does not justify the means, and that we are not free to do anything we like if we have a good end in view." Once again I must say that you cannot have it both ways!

1334. What help does the Church give a man to practice self-control?

She gives him right ideas of man's true dignity, of the law of God, of the rewards and punishments attached to the keeping or breaking of that law. A good Catholic has also the special graces dispensed through the Mass and the Sacraments, absolution for past sins in confession, and Holy Communion, or the reception of Christ's most holy Body and Blood, which directly attacks evil habits of the soul, and indirectly breaks the grip of passion upon the body. Let a man make good and fervent use of the means of grace, and take prudential measures even to the extent of a partial separation if necessary, and he will have the courage and receive the help from God to take up his cross, deny himself, and follow Christ even in the duties of the married state.

CHAPTER TWELVE

THE CHURCH IN HER WORSHIP

1335. On entering a Catholic Church I noticed people taking holy water. Why is this?

Holy water is placed at the doors of Catholic Churches to remind us of the waters of Baptism which once flowed over our foreheads, to signify that we are not worthy to enter into the Presence of Christ without purification, and to forgive us those venial sins for which we are sorry, as well as remitting the temporal punishment due to our sins according to the measure of our regret and contrition. I do not know how you feel, but I know that I am not worthy to enter into the Presence of God in a Catholic Church. When Moses approached the burning bush, God said to him, "Come not hither. Put off the shoes from thy feet, for the place whereon thou standest is holy ground." To Catholics it is a joy to be able to make straight for the holy water font on entering into the Presence of God in the Blessed Sacrament, and to make use of those waters of purification, asking God to make them a little more fit to appear before Him.

1336. What is holy water, and how does it differ from ordinary water?

Holy water is ordinary water sanctified by the blessing of the Church. It differs from ordinary water in so far as some salt has been added to it to signify preservation from corruption, and in so far as it conveys the blessing of the Church and of God where ordinary water does not do so.

1337. What can adulterated rain water do?

Adulteration supposes corruption. Salt preserves from corruption. Meantime, holy water confers a blessing upon those who use it with sincere dispositions.

1338. No Priest can make water holy.

God knows differently. In Numbers, V., 17, we read God's command, "The Priest shall take holy water." In Numbers, VIII., 7, God ordered Moses to purify the Levites as follows, "Take the Levites out of the midst of the children of Israel, and thou shalt purify them according to this rite; let them be sprinkled with the water of purification." God does nothing uselessly, and if you ridicule the practice, you ridicule God.

1339. How could water convey a blessing?

In the Gospel of St. John, V., 2-4, you will find that God used the waters of the pool of Probatica or Bethsaida at Jerusalem to heal the diseased. And as He gave temporal blessings to some through these waters, so He can certainly give spiritual blessings through holy water. In any case, if you are a Christian, you must admit that the waters of Baptism certainly convey spiritual graces to the soul.

1340. When did the Catholic Church invent holy water?

The Catholic Church did not invent it. Holy water is in accordance with God's ways in the Old Testament, and the Catholic Church has merely kept the Christian practice which has existed from the very beginning of Christianity, and which the Protestant reformers rejected as usual in the 16th century. St. Justin Martyr, who died in the year 163 A.D., tells us that the faithful at Mass were sprinkled with these cleansing waters. A document called the Apostolic Constitutions, which dates from the very earliest ages of the Church, gives us in Bk. VIII., sect. XXIX., the following significant prayer, "Let the Bishop bless the water, and if he be not there, the Priest. And let him say: O God, Creator of the waters, sanctify this water through Thy Christ, and grant it power to banish demons, and to disperse all snares through Christ our Hope, through whom be to Thee and to the Holy Ghost, glory forever. Amen."

1341. Why do Catholics genuflect before entering the seats?

They do so to Christ personally present in the Holy Eucharist. When Christ allowed St. Thomas the Apostle to touch the wounds in His hands and feet, St. Thomas said, "My Lord and my God." The same Christ left Himself present in the Eucharist when He said, "This is My Body," and when Catholics come into His presence they offer Him the tribute of their deep reverence and worship by genuflection. You, too, would kneel before Christ, if you believed as Catholics do.

1342. I was rather amused by noticing how Catholics superstitiously cross themselves before beginning their prayers.

A professing Christian laughing at fellow Christians for making the sign of the cross is an anomaly! It shows how far Protestantism has drifted from the spirit of true Christianity. Catholics at least say with St. Paul, "God forbid that I should glory save in the cross of our Lord Jesus Christ." Gal. VI., 14. The early Christians made very much of the sign of the cross, even as Catholics do to-day. Tertullian, who died about 240 A.D., wrote, "In all our travels, in our coming in and going out, in putting on our clothes and our shoes, at table, in going to rest, whatever employment occupies us, we mark our forehead with the sign of the cross." St. Ephrem, who died in 373 A.D., wrote, "My son, mark all your actions with the sign of the life-giving cross. Do not go out from the door of your house till you have signed yourself with the cross. Do not neglect that sign whether in eating or drinking or going to sleep, or in the home or going on a journey. There is no habit to be compared with it. Let it be a protecting wall round all your conduct, and teach it to your children that they may earnestly learn the custom." An early Christian would certainly be at home amongst Catholics, but like a fish out of water amongst Protestants.

1343. Why are Catholic Churches decorated with images and statues, in direct violation of the second commandment?

The second commandment is, "Thou shalt not take the name of the Lord thy God in vain." Protestants, of course, call that the third commandment. But they are wrong in doing so, having taken that part of the first commandment which refers to images as the second of God's commandments. But do those words forbid the making of images? They do not. God was forbidding idolatry, not the making of images. He said, "Thou shalt not make to thyself any graven image of anything in the heaven above, or in the earth beneath. Thou shalt not bow down to them nor worship them." God deliberately adds those last words, yet you ignore them. He forbids men to make images in order to adore them. But He does not forbid the making of images. You will find the commandments given in Exodus, XX. But in that same Book, XXV., 18, you will find God ordering the Jews to make images of Angels! Would you accuse God of not knowing the sense of His own law? He says, "Thou shalt make also two cherubims of beaten gold, on the two sides of the oracle." In other words, the Jews were to make images of things in the heaven above. And if your interpretation be true, why do you violate God's law by making images of things in the earth beneath? Why images of kings and politicians in our parks? Why photographs of friends and relatives? On your theory you could not even take a snapshot of a gum tree. You would be making an image of a thing in the earth beneath. You strain at a gnat and swallow a camel! This is the fruit of your private interpretation of Scripture. No. God does not forbid the making of images; He forbids the making of images in order to adore them.

1344. I have seen more idols in Catholic Churches than sincere Christians.

You have never seen an idol in a Catholic Church. An image is an idol only when it is the object of divine worship. You have seen images in Catholic Churches, but every Catholic knows that divine worship cannot be offered to such images. Would you call the Statue of Liberty, in New York harbor, an idol? As for your not seeing sincere Christians in a Catholic Church, you cannot expect to test the sincerity of a Christian by the color of his tie or the shape of his shoes.

1345. God forbade us to worship plaster statues as Catholics do; yet you send missionaries to convert heathens who do the same thing.

God absolutely forbids us to worship wooden and stone statues, and Catholics are not so foolish as to commit so serious a sin. But Catholics do honor representations of those who are in heaven, just as we all honor our dead soldiers by tributes of respect to the Cenotaph. If I lift my hat to the flag of my country as I pass the memorial to our dead soldiers, am I honoring the cloth or the stone, or what it stands for? If it be lawful in that case, it is certainly lawful to honor the memorials of the dead heroes of Christianity, the Saints. Our missionaries go to heathen tribes to save them from the idolatrous worship of man-made gods.

1346. I have seen Catholics on their knees adoring and praying to statues in their Churches.

You have not. You have seen Catholics kneeling at prayer, and perhaps kneeling before an image of Christ, or of Our Lady. But if you concluded that they were praying to the statues that was not the fault of the Catholics. It was your own fault in so far as you judged them according to your own preconceived ideas. Without bothering to ask for information, you guessed, and guessed wrongly. Before an image of Mary, Catholics may go on their knees and pray to God through the intercession of that Mother of Christ whom the statue represents. But you have no right to accuse them of praying to the statue. Were you to kneel down by your bedside at night for a last prayer, could you be regarded as adoring or praying to your mattress?

1347. But I have seen a Catholic kiss the feet of a statue of Christ.

If I kiss the photograph of my mother, am I honoring a piece of cardboard? Or is it a tribute of love and respect offered to my mother? A Catholic reverences images and statues only in so far as they remind him of God, of Christ, or of Our Lady and the Saints. Where a pagan adores and worships a thing of wood in itself, I kiss the cross not because it is a piece of wood, but because it stands for Christ and for His sufferings on my behalf. And I am sure that Our Lord looks down from heaven and says, "Bless the child; he at least appreciates my love for him." Your mistake is that you try to judge interior dispositions from exterior conduct—a dangerous policy always.

1348. Catholics raise their hats when passing a Church; why not when passing statues in a Catholic shop window?

The Catholic who raises his hat when passing a Catholic Church does so as an act of reverence for the Presence of Christ in the Holy Eucharist. But Christ is not thus present in shops selling Catholic articles of devotion. But of course you missed the point, and took it for granted that Catholic men lift their hats because statues are present in the Church. Then you concluded that they ought to do so when they see statues in a shop window.

1349. If the use of statues is all right, why did the Catholic Church cut out the second commandment?

You are asking an impossible question. You might as well ask me, "Why has Australia declared war on Afghanistan?" No man could answer that question, because there is no answer to it. He could only reply, "Tell me first, are you under the impression that Australia has declared war on Afghanistan?" And if you replied in the affirmative, he would proceed to correct your notions. Had you but asked me, "Did the Catholic Church cut out the second commandment?" a reply could have been given at once. She certainly did not do so.

1350. The Protestant Bible gives the second commandment as referring to images. But the Catholic Catechism gives it as referring to taking the name of God in vain, omitting the references to images.

Even the Protestant Bible does not give the second commandment as referring to images, though Protestants are usually taught that those words in the first commandment which refer to images constitute a second commandment.

1351. The Roman Church omits the second commandment, and then breaks up the tenth into two, in order to avoid having only nine.

The reverse is the case. Protestants make the first commandment into two, and then, to escape having eleven, turn the ninth and tenth into one! The first commandment, as given in the Bible, is as follows: "I am the Lord thy God, who brought thee out of the land of Egypt, out of the house of bondage. Thou shalt not have strange Gods before me. Thou shalt not make to thyself a graven thing, nor the likeness of anything that is in heaven above, or in the earth beneath, nor of those things that are in the waters under the earth. Thou shalt not adore them, nor serve them. I am the Lord thy God, etc." Exodus, XX., 1-6.

1352. You are deceiving us. That is not what Catholics are taught. I have a Catholic Catechism which gives the first commandment as, "I am the Lord thy God; thou shalt not have strange gods before me." You cut out the reference to images.

In the first place, if we wished to deceive our people, we would be very foolish to give them the full wording of the commandment in the Douay Version of the Bible, where they could detect the deliberate distortion! In the second place, in the Catechism we give the full substantial sense of the words I have quoted, but in a brief and summarized form which can be easily memorized.

1353. And you deny that you have changed the commandment?

I do. You notice words only, paying little or no attention to the legal substance of those words. To simplify the wording whilst retaining the full sense is certainly not to change the commandment. If you say, "He is under an obligation not to give expression to his thoughts at the present moment," I do not change the substance of what you say if I repeat to some small child, "He must not speak now." The first commandment contains within its involved Hebrew amplification two essential points: that we must acknowledge the true God, and that we must avoid false gods. Those two essential points are put briefly and simply in the Catechism for children who are more at home with short and easy sentences.

1354. *The commandments do not require such alteration.*

The commandments do not. But the hopeless tangle most Protestants get into where this first commandment is concerned shows clearly that it needs to be stated precisely, without any substantial alteration. It is not a question of words, but it is a question of law, and Catholic children at least know and can clearly state the law.

1355. *You are violating the text of Scripture. The reference to images is a separate verse.*

The numbering of the verses affords no argument. There was no numerical distinction of verses in the original Scriptures. Nor did God reveal such distinctions. All who are acquainted with the subject know that Scripture was divided into verses by men some centuries after Christ for greater convenience. The method of dividing the commandments, however, is not of very great importance. The complaints of Protestants against the Catholic division are rather like that of some modern daughter who would want to spell her name SMYTH, and who complains that her mother spells it SMITH. But the mother knows best how it should be written, and the mother Church knows best how the commandments should be numbered.

1356. *I am interested in Catholic worship. Christ was poor and humble. Yet Catholic ceremonial is full of pomp and display. Does your religion teach humility?*

Yes. We are taught to be humble. And Christian humility orders a man to be unassuming and gentle. But it does not forbid a man to worship God as befits God. In fact, the more humble a man is, the more he magnifies and glorifies God, and depreciates self. The Catholic Church says, "God certainly deserves the best we can give Him. Whatever else we may do, let us not be mean in anything where God is concerned. We personally deserve very little, and if by our gifts God's worship is magnificent and we the poorer, that is how it should be." Christ Himself commended the poor widow for giving all she had to the Temple. Yet He was the one who taught humility.

1357. *Is it not opposed to the simplicity of His principles?*

No. Christ was God, and in the Old Testament God dictated a ceremonial every bit as lavish as Catholic ceremonial. So that it cannot be against His principles. And Christ never condemned ceremonial. He instituted the ceremonial of Baptism with water. With ceremony He breathed upon the Apostles when giving them the power to forgive sins. He came to fulfill the law, not to destroy it. But above all, He founded His Church, giving into her care the guardianship of His religion, and conferring upon her the power to regulate its worship. Whatever the Church has sanctioned in this matter she has done in virtue of the commission given her by her Founder.

1358. *The ceremonial of the Church shows a great change since the time of Christ.*

You won't find the leaves of an oak tree wrapped up inside an acorn. Christ sowed the seed, and said that the small seed He planted would grow into a vast tree. Such growth supposes external changes without loss of identity. Because an acorn has no branches or foliage, will you deny its identity with the tree into which it grows?

1359. *The Last Supper had no elaborate ceremonial rites, yet look at the Mass to-day.*

The essential rites of the Mass are exactly the same as those of the Last Supper. Remember that before the simple Last Supper Christ had fulfilled the full ceremonial of the Jewish Feast. He ceremoniously washed the disciples' feet. And the growth of the surrounding rites in the Mass has been in accordance with principles dictated by God to the Jews, and by the actions of Christ throughout His public ministry, when He used so many ceremonies in the miracles He worked.

1360. Why do Priests vest so elaborately when going to say Mass?

In Exodus, XXVIII., 2-3, we read of God's prescriptions of the vestments befitting the dignity of His religion. "Thou shalt make a holy vesture for Aaron thy brother; for glory and for beauty. And thou shalt speak to all the wise of heart, whom I have filled with the spirit of wisdom: that they may make Aaron's vestments, in which he being consecrated may minister to me. And these shall be the vestments that they shall make." Throughout the rest of the chapter God deigns to give the most minute directions as to the various vestments Aaron was to use. Not for a moment would Christ have condemned the principle of vestments after such a sanction by the infinitely wise God. He would be contradicting Himself. There can be nothing wrong with vestments in principle.

1361. Christ dressed with the utmost simplicity and talked to God in the most humble places.

Priests also dress with simplicity. They are not always in vestments. As for Christ. He too went to the Temple, and took part in its worship, never condemning its ritual. With the establishment of His own Church in fulfillment of the Old Law, He ordained His own Priests after the Order of Melchisedech in place of the Levitical Priesthood, and left it to the Church to regulate the ceremonial surrounding the substantial form of worship He had prescribed. As I have said, He would have been the last to condemn a dignified ceremonial, and Anglican Protestants of the High Church group are rapidly trying to resume the vestments prescribed by the Catholic Church, vestments their forefathers so eagerly got rid of; mistakenly, now say the High Church Anglicans.

1362. Why the proud display of processions such as those of Eucharistic Congresses?

There is nothing wrong with processions. Christ entered Jerusalem with a procession of the populace crying hosanna, waving palms and strewing their garments on the roadway, making it as elaborate as they could. And He rebuked those who would have prevented it. Remember that Eucharistic Congresses are not in honor of ourselves, but of Christ, and love of Him suggests that nothing can be too good for Him.

1363. When I think of the expense, I think too of the poor, and ask why so much money should be wasted.

Such an objection recalls the words of Judas, "Why was it not sold and given to the poor?" Jn. XII., 5. In any case, the lavish generosity of the Catholic Church in the worship of God does not interfere with her work for the poor. She is the most active of all Churches in that work. No other Church has so many institutions, hospitals, homes, and orphanages; and in many parishes there is a weekly distribution of money and food to the poor through the St. Vincent de Paul or some other society.

1364. The ritual of the Roman Church is intricate, mysterious, and sensual, whilst the Gospel is simplicity itself.

The ritual of the Catholic Church is not intricate, save to those who are unfamiliar with it. It is certainly symbolical of many mysteries "hidden from the ages and generations, but now manifested." Col. I., 26. It also involves sensible and visible rites, but in no sense can it be called sensual.

1365. *Is it not blasphemy to use mingle mangle in baptizing children?*

It would be. But no mingle mangle occurs in the baptism of children. Mingle mangle means a meaningless jumble of formulas. But every least item in the baptismal rite is full of meaning and significance. And it is to God's honor and glory to use the holy ceremonies instituted by the Church of Christ with the authority of Christ. Was it mingle mangle when Christ touched the blind man's eyes with spittle before curing him?

1366. *I went to a Requiem Mass, and was highly amused at the antics of the Priest with his gabble and mumble.*

That you were highly amused at a Requiem Mass which you did not understand only proves that you are devoid of the power to sympathize with what is sacred to other people. Had you understood it, and then been amused, there might have been some excuse. You say that the whole ceremony was a gabble and a mumble to you. Were you to attend a session of the German parliament in Berlin, you would probably say the same. "But then," you will reply, "I am not a German. It was all right for them. I knew that well enough, and was not amused, because they were not talking my language, and because it is to be expected that their ways would differ from my ways." So I say in turn, "You are not a Catholic. Every Catholic understands a Requiem Mass. But you should have known that a Protestant would not be likely to understand a Catholic ceremony. That would have checked your amusement. I am a Catholic. But I have never felt like ridiculing the religious services of sincere Protestants.

1367. *Why does the Catholic Church surround death with gloom, offering the Mass in black vestments, and everything so sad and solemn?*

The Catholic Church does not surround death with gloom. But her liturgy is in keeping with man's nature as God intended it to be. Despite all spiritual joy and consolation, whilst hearts are human they break. Even God does not expect us to be hard and inhuman, unmoved when some dear one is taken from us. Our Lord wept with those who mourned the death of Lazarus. And He knew that He was going to bring him back to life again! It is natural to man to find relief in expressing his feelings. St. Paul says, "Be not sorrowful as those who have no hope." But he does not say, "Be not sorrowful." In fact he tells Christians to comfort one another. We do not go up to a man who has just lost his mother, and congratulate him, our faces beaming with joy. That would be inhuman, and the Catholic Church is never inhuman. Near relatives instinctively wear mourning and dress in black when a loved one dies. Very close friends do the same. And the Catholic Church is the dearest friend any Catholic has, a friend who identifies herself with his feelings in his great loss. It is all in keeping with what is best in man. Death is a solemn thing, and the Catholic Church treats it with solemnity. She does not ask us to sorrow as those who have no hope, but she will not turn a funeral into a wedding feast, and ignore genuine and deep sorrow as if we were so spiritual that we had ceased to be human. We are not in heaven yet.

1368. *Cathedrals costing thousands are nothing to God. He is a Spirit, and would love just as much without the earthly show.*

But man would not love so much! You fail to grasp a fundamental point. It takes two to make a religion, God and man. God is a pure Spirit, but man is not. Man is a composite of the spiritual and the material. And he must worship God according to his twofold nature. Man not only possesses spiritual thoughts; he gives them expression in speech, writing, music, art, and architecture. And, where God is concerned, he dedicates all these things to God's service in religion. God Himself ordered the Jews to do so, commanding the erection of the glorious Temple at Jerusalem. God wants the service, not of half our being, but of our complete being.

1369. In Europe I found glorious Cathedrals and pitiable poverty side by side.

The present-day poverty is not due to the Cathedrals which were built long ago by others, who gave their time and services as a voluntary offering to God. The poverty due to modern industrial conditions should not be attributed to buildings erected in other and happier ages. Meantime those beautiful Cathedrals do no harm to men. If the poor pulled them down stone by stone, they could not eat the stones. And even if they could sell them for thirty pieces of silver, the relief would be of a very temporary nature. Believe me, future generations would be just as poor temporally, and much poorer spiritually, with no inspiring Cathedrals.

1370. Should not the government at least confiscate all gifts and ornaments, and distribute their value to the poor?

No. They are gifts of the people, and if people wish to dedicate tokens of gratitude to the House of God, no one has any right to their possession. People are not free to distribute what is not their own to the poor. There were many poor in Israel when God demanded the dedication of a richly ornamented Temple to His worship.

1371. Does crawling up the Scala Santa at Rome on one's knees help save one's soul?

The Scala Santa, or Holy Staircase, consists of twenty-eight marble steps. They are said to have been brought to Rome from Jerusalem by St. Helena, the mother of Constantine, in 326 A.D. At Jerusalem they led up to the one-time court of Pilate, and the feet of Jesus had trodden them as He went down to be crucified by men. With no idea that such an act will of itself save his soul, the Catholic ascends them on his knees out of reverence for Christ, and you have not much reverence and love for Him if you ridicule such a tribute. We Catholics, after all, believe that He is God. We are quite prepared to kiss the very ground whereon He stood. The Pharisees once ridiculed a woman who went on her knees and washed His feet with her tears. But Christ justified her act of loving reverence. Cold Protestantism will never understand the warm-hearted love of Catholicism for the Person of Christ and of all connected with Him. I do not belong to the emotional and demonstrative Latin race. I do not live in the middle ages. I do not suppose I would be ranked as illiterate. Yet whilst in Rome I myself ascended those same stairs on my knees, and I experience no flush of shame as I say so. I have seen a Protestant kiss the pages of the Gospel. He kissed a printed sheet of paper. I admired him for it, and so would you, for we know what it meant to him. I certainly would not ridicule him and ask him sarcastically whether he thought that the smearing of his lips on a piece of paper would help to save his soul! Yet such a remark would be similar to that of a Protestant who suggests that Catholics believe they can be saved by crawling up a staircase on their knees. However you would not have asked such a question had you realized the nature of the subject and the motives prompting such reverence for Christ.

1372. Granted their belief that Christ once ascended that staircase, could they not show their love for Christ in some more practical way?

Other actions could certainly be more pleasing to God. But one has not only to go up a staircase sanctified by Christ. In fact, it is not necessary to do this. Life consists of a series of actions, not all of equal value. If I am in circumstances which give me an opportunity of showing my love and reverence for Christ, the question here and now is, "Is it better or not to offer *this* action?" No question arises as to whether this is the best possible action, or the only action, which can be performed for the love of God. It is the best *now*, although if afterwards I were to go and relieve some poor beggar in distress, that might have more value as a proof of my love for God.

1373. Do you believe that any good can result from the ceremonial blessing of a house built of bricks and mortar?

Yes, certainly. Every Christian believes in the value of grace before meals, asking God's blessing on both food and partakers. That bricks and mortar can contribute to man's welfare is already a blessing of God, and there is no reason why we should not ask God's additional blessing upon the use of the house. St. Paul speaks of "every creature" as being sanctified by the word of God and prayer. 1 Tim. IV., 5.

1374. Why the ceremonial kissing of the Pope's ring, risking infection?

Catholics kiss the Pope's ring out of reverence for the office which the Holy Father holds. No one has ever died from such a procedure, and a man who feared risk of infection from that might just as well give up eating, drinking, and breathing, for all the time he is taking in germs by the thousand. There is much more risk in kissing people of the opposite sex, yet people do not give up doing that! In any case, you are not called upon to kiss the Pope's ring, and have no reason to complain.

1375. The Pope is carried in solemn procession like some Eastern tyrant. Would Christ do that?

The Pope is not carried in procession like some Eastern tyrant. He is carried in procession according to the custom proper to Popes. Would Christ permit Himself to be treated in such a way? Christ never refused any tribute to His divinity. He let people worship Him; a woman anoint His feet; the people of Jerusalem enter Jerusalem with Him in solemn procession midst waving palms and cries of Hosanna. When some protested in this latter case He replied, "If you do not let them, the very stones will cry out." And because the Pope succeeds Christ, and is His Vicar, he allows those who regard it as a privilege to show their love for Christ in a similar way. The people honor Christ in His Vicar, and the Pope is not in the least unlike Christ when he permits it. No Pope is so foolish as to think that it is for himself. He knows that if he were not Pope those present would simply ignore him. It is a tribute to his office, not to himself. State honor given to a governor of a colony is a tribute to a king, not to the governor in person.

1376. In Acts X., 26, Peter refused to let a man kneel before him. Why does not the Pope behave as did St. Peter?

The passage you quote tells us that "When Peter was come in, Cornelius came to meet him, and falling at his feet, adored." Peter saw that Cornelius was giving him a worship more than could be permitted, and said, "Arise. I myself am also a man." If the Pope detected the same dispositions in those who came to honor him he would utter a similar warning. He would be the first to say, "I too am but a creature of God. You must not worship me like this." But kneeling is a sign of respect and reverence. When Sir Francis Drake knelt before Queen Elizabeth, he was not adoring her. In the good old days of chivalry, men proposed to the ladies of their choice on their knees, but that did not imply divine worship! Kneeling, therefore, can be a sign of ordinary respect, or of divine worship according to the intentions of the one offering such a tribute. As divine worship it cannot be offered to anyone less than God, and in this sense the Pope would forbid it as did St. Peter. But the same act can be offered as a sign of respect for the authority vested in the minister of Christ, and the utmost respect is due to Christ's Vicar, the Pope.

1377. *Why don't you include public healing services in your Catholic cere-monial?*

Because such services are not in the spirit of Christianity, nor included in the commission given to the Church by Christ.

1378. *If you are a Christian Priest, who told you to drop healing?*

No one ever told me to take it up.

1379. *Christ gave us the religion we need, and we need a religion of healing.*

We do not. We need the religion of Christ. The poor, whether by lack of health or wealth, have always existed, and always will exist, according to Christ. He healed some people to prove His mission. But by no means did He heal all whom He knew to be sick. Had he done so, there would not have been a single sick person left in the whole of the world. The same Christ in heaven now knows all the sickness on earth, and by one act of His will He could heal all. He does not do so. No sickness could occur unless God were to permit it. Yet God does permit it. If Christ healed the sick, it was not merely to get rid of the sickness, but to prove His revelation; and that having been proved sufficiently, the real need for miracles ceases.

1380. *How can you claim the same powers as the Apostles if you cannot heal?*

The spiritual powers given to the Apostles were to be permanent, and it is a greater miracle to restore the life of the soul by conferring grace than to heal the body from temporal illness. But the power of miraculous healing was given to various individuals in the early Church merely in order to secure the rapid growth of the Church, serving as a motive of credibility. Once the Church was solidly established the need of such extraordinary manifestations ceased. Men do not become Christians for temporal benefits, but for their eternal welfare. Those first miracles were merely signs, and if you want a sign to-day, the universal Church still existing in our midst after twenty centuries against such opposition is sign enough.

1381. *Should not Priests have the power to heal as well as to forgive sin?*

No. The chief thing in Christianity is the forgiveness of sin to secure salvation, not the healing of the body to put off a little longer the death which must come sooner or later. Christ gave the Apostles the power to forgive sin and to heal. The power to forgive sin was essential and necessary, and it has passed to all succeeding Priests of the New Law. The power of healing was not meant to be transmitted. God gave it to some in the early Church after the Apostles, but not to all. St. Paul says, "To one is given the word of knowledge; to another the grace of healing; to another, etc." 1 Cor. XII., 8-10. The Bible proves that the power of forgiving sin was to be handed on to the successors of the Apostles, and nowhere does it hint that this power was not to be given to all such successors. But St. Paul clearly shows that the gift of healing was not given to all. It is a secondary gift, not for the sake of restoring health, but to prove the mission of the Church. In I. Cor. XIV., 22, St. Paul says that the gift of tongues is "for a sign, not to believers, but to unbelievers."

1382. *Christ said that it is just as easy to say, "Get up and walk," as to forgive sin. Do this and we will believe in your power to forgive sin.*

It is just as easy to God to say, "Thy sins are forgiven thee," as to say, "Arise and walk." But it is not just as easy to a man unless God has given him the power. But I presume that you are a Christian, and believe in Baptism. What does Baptism do? It destroys sin. Prior to Baptism, the soul is without the life of grace and in a state of sin. But if, by the power of Christ a human being can destroy sin by the

Sacrament of Baptism, there is no difficulty in admitting that he could do it by another Sacrament such as Confession. And since you do not demand miracles before you will accept the Sacrament of Baptism, it is inconsistent to demand them for that of Confession. The only thing to prove is that Confession is a Sacrament to destroy later sins, as Baptism destroyed previous sins. That I have done.

1383. *Christ taught His followers to heal, and they in turn taught their followers.*

Christ did not teach His followers to heal. He bestowed upon some of them the divine gift of healing. And they in turn did not teach their followers. It is impossible to teach as an art that which is essentially a supernatural gift. Each one intended by God to have it had to receive it directly from God.

1384. *Do you deny that the early Christians practiced healing?*

I deny that it was anything like a universal practice. Some early Christians were specially endowed by God with the power of healing, in order that the Church might appeal to onlookers in a special way. But the Church has been built, and there is no need to show a stone from the quarry whence it was hewn in order to prove its existence and mission from God.

1385. *You keep speaking of miracles. Jesus never claimed that His so-called miracles were really such. He relied on mental healing by natural powers.*

That is really nonsense. Can you imagine the mental exertions of the dead body of Lazarus when invited by Christ to think itself alive again? Before raising Lazarus from the dead He lifted His eyes and said, "Father, I give thee thanks that thou hast heard me. And I knew that thou hearest me always; but because of the people who stand about have I said it, that they may believe that thou hast sent me." Jn. XI., 41-42. Those words prove His appeal to God's power, and not to natural created forces. And it proves His purpose in working miracles, not for the sake of the miracles, but that people might believe in Him. We do not need miracles before our eyes now to make us believe. Historical evidence is enough.

1386. *Medicine was in vogue before Christ came. But we Christian Scientists know that Christ ushered in a new dispensation.*

Christ ushered in a new dispensation, but not of medicine. He did not come to establish a medical clinic. He came to call sinners to repentance, that they might secure forgiveness for their past sins, overcome their moral faults, and serve Him in a life of virtue.

1387. *You have more faith in a doctor to heal you than you have in God.*

You have no evidence for that assertion. I know that God usually makes use of secondary causes which He Himself has established, and it is my faith that God will continue to grant them efficacy which takes me to a doctor who has studied their properties. But Christian Science is not faith in God at all. It is faith in self and self's own immense power of mental effort.

1388. *Jesus never advised anyone to see a doctor or pay attention to health laws.*

Jesus said, "They that are in health need not a physician, but they that are ill." Matt. IX., 12. And the same God whom we Christians worship gave most minute health laws to the Jews, laws which Jesus never declared to be false and useless.

1389. *The Church became corrupt and lost the power of healing.*

You do not know what you are saying. If you believe that Christ is God, you dare not say that a Church declared by Him to be indefectible ever failed; if you do not believe that Christ is God; it is little use your quoting Him at all.

1390. *But Jesus tells us to heal. You quote only one place from St. Paul suggesting that only a few could heal. Are we to believe Paul or Jesus?*

Nowhere did Jesus ever tell *us* to heal. As for your comparison of St. Paul with Jesus, remember that every word of the New Testament is the inspired word of God. We are to believe both St. Paul and Jesus, and their doctrines never conflict. If they did conflict the New Testament could not be God's word, and you could not use it at all to justify your notions. You must either accept the New Testament as a whole or reject it as a whole.

1391. *But Jesus said, "These signs will follow them that believe." He even said that His true followers would do greater things than He.*

The signs predicted by Christ did follow. But He never said that they would always follow, and that every single believer in Him throughout the ages would be able to do them. As a matter of fact they have not followed at the discretion of every follower of Christ, and if He had intended them to do so, then He has failed, *r*nd you are foolish to continue to believe in Him. All Priests of the Catholic Church, meantime, do greater things in the spiritual order than Christ wrought in th*c* temporal order; they forgive and destroy sin, raising the spiritually dead to life, a greater work than the raising of those who are bodily dead.

1392. *Why, in all ceremonies and sermons, do Priests speak in Latin?*

In the Epistle to the Hebrews, V., I., you will find these words, "Every Priest is ordained *for men* in the things that pertain to God, that he may offer up *gifts and sacrifices* for sins." A Priest has two chief duties: to offer sacrifice to God, and to sanctify men by his teaching and instruction. Now, when a Priest is speaking, not to men, but to God in the name of men, he speaks in the language of the Church—in Latin—a language God certainly understands, as does the Priest. When on the other hand he speaks to the people he speaks in their own language; in France, in French; in England, he uses English; in Germany, German. Sermons are always given in the vernacular, and not in Latin, because they are addressed to the people. Go into any Catholic Church, and you will never hear any sermons in Latin.

1393. *But the Priest says the Mass in Latin.*

That is a sacrificial action offered to God. Latin is the liturgical language of the Catholic Church, just as Hebrew is the official language still used in the Synagogue.

1394. *Do the worshippers understand all that the Priest says in the Latin Mass?*

Not all Catholics understand Latin, by any means. But they are all quite at home when assisting at Mass. They know what is being *done*, even though they cannot understand all that is being *said*. And it is not necessary that they should follow the sense of every word used during the sacrificial rite of the Mass. However, every Catholic *can* know what the Priest is saying, should he wish to do so. He has but to secure a prayer book containing the translation of the Latin into English. Most prayer books give the Latin and the English of the Mass side by side, in columns.

1395. *Why does the Church cling to Latin, a dead language?*

For one reason, precisely because it is dead! In modern and living languages, words are constantly changing their meaning whilst in a dead language, such as

Latin, they do not. The essential doctrine and significance of Christianity must not change, and the safest way to preserve it intact is to keep it in an unchangeable language. Again, a universal Church must have at least her chief form of worship in a universal language. Christ came to save all men, and wherever a member of the true Church may be in this world he should be able to find himself at home at the central act of Christian worship. The Mass, being said in Latin, is the same in all lands. If a Frenchman, who could not understand a word of English, were to enter a Catholic Church in London, he would be at home the moment the Mass began. An English service would be a mystery to him. I myself have said Mass with as many as fifteen different nationalities present, and not all could follow my discourse when I spoke to those present, though I spoke for a few minutes in English, in French, and in Italian. There were still many who could not understand any of these languages, but being all Catholics, they were quite at home the moment I turned to the Altar and went on with the Mass in Latin. It brings out the wisdom and the universality of the Catholic Church. The Priest ascends the Altar to intercede with God on behalf of the people. Those present kneel, and in their hearts pour out their prayers for their own necessities. They feel no more need to know just what the Priest is saying than the Jews who knelt at the foot of the mountain felt the need of knowing just what Moses was saying to God on their behalf at the top. And here once again let me say that if anyone should complain of the use of Latin, it should be those who have to endure it. And I have never yet heard a Catholic soul complain that it caused difficulty, or that he or she would like it changed.

1396. What good can result to the people if they cannot know what the Priest is asking in their name?

I have said that they can know if they wish, for they will find an English translation of the Mass in their prayer books. But even if they could not know, the Latin prayers could win for them the graces requested. If a German friend prayed for you in German, would that prayer be useless because you do not understand German?

1397. Is it not a short-sighted policy, since God hears hearts rather than words?

No. The Catholic Church is the greatest Church of all, and has preserved her unity despite her vast expansion. Those smaller Churches, on the other hand, which adopted national languages are divided one from the other; are national in character; and are splitting up into innumerable sects as their doctrines change with every change in the sense of modern words.

1398. God destroyed the unity of language at the Tower of Babel, yet you insist that all must worship Him in the one tongue!

We do not. Catholics may pray to God in any language they wish. It is only a question of the liturgical language in the official services of the Church, in which the Priest speaks, not to the people, but to God. In any case, at the Tower of Babel, men did not use their united language to worship God, but to rebel against Him, and it was that rebellion which God punished.

1399. At evening devotions in a Catholic Church I heard many prayers to Mary. I cannot find in Scripture where Mary is to be worshipped in the same way as Christ.

I am not surprised, for such a doctrine is nowhere taught in Scripture. Moreover, if any Catholic dared to worship Mary in the same way as he worships Christ, he would be guilty of a most serious sin, and no Catholic Priest could give him absolution unless he promised never to do so again. But that does not mean that one must deprive Mary of all honor.

1400. *St. Bonaventure said, "Into thy hands, O Lady, I commend my spirit." Thus he served the creature more than the Creator, to whom alone such words should be addressed.*

St. Bonaventure did not serve the creature more than the Creator. In commending his soul to Mary he was not commending it to anyone opposed to God. He did it because of God, who chose Mary as the second Eve. Eve brought us forth to misery and to death; Mary brought us forth to happiness and to life when she brought forth our Saviour. Like the kings from the East, St. Bonaventure knew that after the long journey through this life, he would also find the child Jesus with Mary His mother, and that if he commended his soul to the mother he would necessarily find himself in the presence of the child, even in eternity. Gladly on my own deathbed would I utter the words used by St. Bonaventure. As Jesus came to us through Mary, so we shall go to Him through her, whether we think of it or not.

1401. *Mary is no different from your own mother.*

As the street-arab replied to a similar objection, "But there's an immense difference between the sons. My mother is the mother of me. Mary is the mother of God."

1402. *You speak as if Jesus looks on His mother just as you look on your mother.*

As surely as my mother is my mother, He knows that His mother is His mother; and He treats her as such.

1403. *Jesus was a good son, but He recognized only one being, the Omnipotent God.*

Had He ignored Mary He would not have been a very good son, nor would He have had much respect for God who said, "Honor thy father and thy mother." Christ was a perfect example of virtue in all things. And if He did not recognize Mary, why did He go down to Nazareth and be subject to her? Why did He perform His first miracle at her request? And why did He make such special provision for her at the moment of His death?

1404. *When someone praised Mary, Christ paid no attention, but said that only those are blessed who keep the word of God. Lk. XI., 28.*

The Gospels are fragmentary accounts, and we do not know all that transpired on that occasion. But even so, the actual text is not opposed in any way to the honor we give to Mary. Someone praised Mary. Christ replied, "Yea rather, blessed are they who hear the word of God and keep it." Not for a moment did He intend to deny that Mary had done this. He practically says, "Yes. She is blest in being my mother. But it is a greater blessing to serve God." And, from one point of view, the fidelity with which Mary undoubtedly served God was a greater blessing to her than merely being the mother of Christ. Any idea that Christ, the best of sons, was trying to belittle His mother is absurd. And if you have such faith in Scripture, what do you do as regards the prophecy of Mary in Lk. I., 48? "From henceforth," she predicted, "all generations shall call me blessed." Yet blessed are they who hear the word of God and keep it! We Catholics call Mary blessed indeed, whilst many Protestants search Scripture in the fond hope of proving something to her discredit!

1405. *Christ called her, "Woman," when He said, "Woman, behold thy son."*

In the language Christ spoke, that word was a term of great respect however harshly it may sound in our modern English language. Our Lord would have been the last to slight His mother, a thing we despise in every man; and above all in His last and most tender words to her. Nor are we likely to please Him by seeking to dishonor her.

1406. Did He not say to her at the marriage feast of Cana, "Woman, what is that to thee and to me?"

He did. But most certainly He intended no reproach to Mary. Her action was one of pure charity to others. Foreseeing the possible distress of others, she asked Him to relieve them; and He would not rebuke so unselfish a thought. Nor would He speak to her with any trace of disrespect. Then, too, had Mary asked a wrong thing, Christ would not have done it, nor would He have sanctioned a request He had to rebuke. And Mary knew that she had not been reprehended, or she would not have told the waiters to do what her Son would tell them. She would have dropped the matter. Why, then, did Christ speak thus? It was His first miracle, the first public sign of His divinity wrought by Himself. And He wanted to bring out publicly the fact that He was doing it, not as the son of an earthly mother and according to His human nature, but calling upon His divine nature as the eternal Son of God. He did it because His mother requested it, but He did not do it by any power derived from His mother. He thus brought out both for the listeners and for us that this beginning of miracles was proof of His divinity, although in appearance He seemed but man.

1407. Why do you call Mary Queen of Heaven?

Because Mary is undoubtedly in heaven, and Jesus is King of heaven. Since Jesus is "King of kings and Lord of lords," it is certain that Mary His mother rejoices in queenly dignity.

1408. Why pray to Mary at all?

Because God wills that we should do so, and because such prayers to her are of the utmost value. God often wills to give certain favors only on condition that we go to some secondary agent. Sodom was to be spared through the intercession of Abraham; Naaman, the leper, was to be cured only through the waters of the Jordan. Now Mary is, and must ever remain, the mother of Christ. She still has a mother's rights and privileges, and is able to obtain for us many graces. But let us view things reasonably. If I desire to pray, I can certainly pray to God directly. Yet would you blame me if, at times, I were to ask my own earthly mother to pray for me also? Such a request is really a prayer to her that she may intercede for me with God. Certainly, if I met the mother of Christ on earth, I would ask her to pray for me, and she would do so. And in her more perfect state with Christ in heaven she is not less able to help me.

1409. But a prayer to God directly must be more efficacious than a prayer to Mary.

Not necessarily. It might well be that God intends to honor Our Lady by granting the favor I seek through her intercession in a particular way. In that case the grace is to be given through her provided I honor her by addressing myself to her. Again, every prayer to Mary is in reality the asking of a favor from God even as the mother of Christ is requested to ask the same favor also. It is often better to ask God for a favor and to have someone else praying to God with one for the same favor. Two prayers are better than one. And above all, when the other one praying is Christ's own mother.

1410. God loves you more than Mary loves you.

That is so. But He loves Mary more than He loves me. And as she is more pleasing to God than I am, He will be more ready to grant her requests.

1411. *It is unscriptural to attribute power to Mary.*

That is a very unscriptural statement. At His mother's request Jesus changed water into wine at Cana, though He had said, "My time is not yet come." St. James tells us that "the prayer of a just man availeth much." Ja. V., 16. How much more the prayer of Mary!

1412. *Does the Bible sanction such prayers to Mary?*

Yes. All through the Bible you will find God conferring favors through the prayers of others. In the Old Testament we read of the prayers of Abraham, Moses, and of the various prophets. In the New Testament, St. James tells us to "pray for one another," in the text I have just quoted. If we must always pray directly to God and may not ask the prayers of others, why did St. Paul write to the Thessalonians, "Pray for us that we may be delivered from importunate and evil men?" 2 Thess. III., 2. Why did he not ask that directly of God, instead of asking the prayers of the Thessalonians? Or would you be more scriptural than the New Testament itself?

1413. *There is but one mediator; there is no place for Mary.*

Christ is the principal mediator in His own right. Mary is a secondary mediatrix, through, with, and in Christ. Without Him she would have no power, and therefore He is the source of all mediation with God on behalf of men.

1414. *How can you blend the mediation of others with that of Christ?*

It follows from the doctrine of the Communion of Saints. Remember that, by Baptism, every Christian is incorporated with Christ. St. Paul says, "Christ is the head; ye are the members." So close is this union that Christ says, "Whoever gives you to drink a cup of water in my name, because you belong to me; amen, I say to you, he shall not lose his reward." Mk. IX., 40. Every Christian is Christ in a most intimate way. St. Paul tells us that if a baptized person sins, he takes the members of Christ and makes them the members of iniquity! When that same St. Paul was persecuting the Christians before his conversion, Christ appeared to him and said, "Saul, Saul, why persecutest Thou *Me?*" He did not say, "Why persecutest thou My disciples?" He could equally say, when we pray to Mary or to the saints, "What asketh thou of Me?" When we honor Our Lady or the Saints, we honor, not their own merely human and created nature, but we honor Christ in them according to the doctrine of Scripture. The Catholic Church is the only completely scriptural Church.

1415. *Do Catholics believe that Mary is omnipotent?*

No. God alone is omnipotent. But through Mary we have access to the omnipotence of God.

1416. *How do you know that Mary hears you?*

The Catholic Church guarantees that, and she is here to tell us the truth about such things in the name of Christ and with His authority. Reason also assures us that, as she could know our prayers in this life and pray for us in turn, so she can do so in the more perfect state in heaven. Finally experience proves it, for she has manifested her power in thousands of concrete instances in answer to prayer.

1417. *Attending a Catholic Church one evening I was disgusted by the rigmarole called the Rosary. What is that Rosary?*

The Rosary is a special form of devotion to Mary. One takes a set of beads, divided into five sections, each section consisting of one large bead and ten small ones. Holding the large bead, one says the Our Father, and on each of the small ones, the Hail Mary. Between each section or decade the Gloria is said. Whilst saying the prayers, one meditates or thinks of the joys, or sorrows, or glories of

Christ's life and of that of His Mother. It is a very beautiful form of prayer with which you were disgusted merely because you did not understand it.

1418. The Rosary is a relic of the superstitious middle ages, when it was meant for ignorant people.

The use of beads dates from the earliest centuries. The prayers embodied in the Rosary were composed by Christ Himself in the case of the Our Father, and by the Angel Gabriel, St. Elizabeth, and the Council of Ephesus in the 5th century, in the case of the Hail Mary. We are in very good company with those prayers. As a devotion, with its loving contemplation of the mysteries of the life, death and resurrection of Our Lord it appeals to rich and poor, to learned and ignorant alike, as Christianity itself was meant to do.

1419. When were beads invented, and what do they symbolize?

It is impossible to say when beads were first used. As an aid to memory, the early Christians used to put a number of pebbles in one pocket, transferring them to another as they said each prayer, so that they could be sure of completing such prayers each day as their devotion inspired. Later, berries or pebbles were strung together for the purpose. In the middle ages sections of these beads were adapted to the different meditations which compose the Rosary, the sections being a numerical help to meditate for a given period of time upon each allotted subject. The symbolism is expressed in the word Rosary. A Rosary is a garland of flowers. One rose does not make a Rosary. Prayers are the flowers of the spiritual life, and in offering that group of prayers, known as the Rosary, we lay a garland of spiritual flowers at the feet of God.

1420. Christ did not have a crucifix or Rosary beads.

He made the first crucifix. That He did not use Rosary beads does not affect the question. He never had a copy of the New Testament in His hands, yet you do not reject the New Testament because of that!

1421. Between each Our Father to God, it throws in ten prayers to Mary!

You've got it the wrong way round. Between each ten Hail Marys an Our Father is said. The Rosary is essentially a devotion to Mary, honoring her whom God Himself so honored. And it honors her particularly in her relation to Christ, whose life is the subject of the meditations. The Our Father abstracts from the incarnation of Christ; the Hail Mary is full of reverence to Our Lord's birth into this world for us.

1422. Would not the Rosary be just as efficient if said with one Our Father, one Hail Mary, and one Gloria?

It would not be the Rosary then, but some other type of devotion. Nor would such a devotion be as efficient, for meditation whilst saying ten Hail Marys is better than meditation whilst saying one. But your trouble seems to be based on the mere question of number. That is quite immaterial.

1423. It is not. Christ said, "Use not vain repetitions as do the heathen, who think in their much speaking to be heard."

Vain repetition in the manner of heathens is forbidden, but not useful repetition which is not in the manner of heathens. Vain repetition relies mechanically upon the mere number of prayers or formulas uttered. But Catholics do not rely on the mere repetition of prayers, nor upon their multiplication, but on the intrinsic worth of each prayer and upon the fervor and earnestness with which it is said. Two prayers said well, one immediately after the other, are as good as the same two prayers said well with twenty-four hours between them. Time is nothing to God, in whose sight 1000 years are but as a day. He does not mind whether there be two seconds between our prayers or two years; the prayers themselves are just as pleasing to Him. If you take the principle behind your objection, and push it to its full conclusion, you could say the Our Father but once in your life. If you said it once each year, it would be repetition. How often may you say it? Once a month? Once a week? Once a day? If daily, what would be wrong with saying it hourly? If you have just concluded one Our Father, why may you not begin it again at once? Does it suddenly become an evil prayer?

1424. If repetition adds to effectiveness, why stop at ten Hail Marys? Why not more?

It is the nature of this devotion that the Rosary should be composed of decades, or groups of ten. It would not be the Rosary otherwise. Repetition certainly adds to effectiveness, if the prayers are said well. Just before His passion, Christ prayed "the third time, saying the self-same prayer." Matt. XXVI., 44. He thought it good to say the same prayer three times in succession. Why did He limit it to three times? If good to say it three times, why not twenty times? He thought three sufficient for His purpose. So, too, we consider the period taken by the recital of ten Hail Marys sufficient time for the amount of reflection we desire to give to each mystery of the Rosary.

1425. Does not Scripture advise short prayer rather than long Rosaries?

No. Long hypocritical prayers are condemned. Prayer may be prolonged, but it must not be hypocritical, mechanical, or insincere. Christ said, "We ought always to pray, and not to faint." Lk. XVIII., 1. Again, "Watch ye therefore, praying at all times." Lk. XXI., 36. He himself "went out into a mountain to pray, and he passed the whole night in prayer to God." Lk. VI., 12. "We cease not to pray for you," wrote St. Paul to the Colossians I., 9. "Night and day we more abundantly pray for you," he wrote to the Thessalonians I., 3, 10.

1426. Anyway short mental prayers must be better than long distracted prayers.

Short fervent interior prayers are better than long distracted vocal prayers. But, given equally fervent prayers said with due attention, long ones are better than short ones. It is certainly better to give more time to prayer than less! And if distractions do present themselves, it is better to give up the distractions than to give up the prayers. Mental prayer is good, but vocal prayer is equally good if said well, and sometimes better. Thus Christ taught the Apostles a vocal prayer called the Our Father. So well did they learn it by heart that they were able to write it down years later word for word.

1427. Why do you omit from that Our Father the words "For thine is the kingdom, the power, and the glory forever and ever."

Because Our Lord did not add those words to the prayer as He taught it. There is nothing wrong with the words in themselves. In fact, they are very beautiful. But they are not Sacred Scripture. Some early Catholic copyists wrote those words in a margin; later copyists mistakenly transcribed them into the text; and the Protestant translators made use of a copy of the New Testament with the words thus included. All scholars to-day admit the words to be an interpolation. We Catholics do not use them.

1428. Why do Catholic Churches ring bells at daybreak, noon, and sunset.

The ringing of these bells is to remind Catholics to say the Angelus, a short devotion in honor of the incarnation of Christ. Three rings are given three times separately, and then nine rings, according to an ancient custom. The devotion is called the Angelus because the first words of the prayers to be said begin as follows, "The Angel of the Lord declared unto Mary." The Angelus, therefore, reminds us of the message of the Angel Gabriel who brought the good news of the birth of Jesus Christ. And Catholics are asked to begin the day by remembering this great benefit; to recollect it again at noon, and at sunset or the close of the day. An old English manuscript, written of course in England's Catholic days before the Reformation, says that the Angelus in the morning should remind us of Christ's resurrection at dawn; at noon of His death on the cross; and at eventide of His birth at midnight in the cave of Bethlehem. In any case, the Angelus is to remind Catholics of the fact that the Son of God came into this world for the redemption of mankind, and that they themselves should never forget it.

1429. What do the three threes, and the nine bells signify?

The origin of the number of bells to be tolled is uncertain. The triple ringing reminds us of the Most Holy Trinity. The final nine bells may have been arranged merely for the sake of harmony and symmetry, although some writers see in that number a reminder of the nine choirs of Angels who invite us to adore God with them.

1430. Why pray to Saints? Is it not better to pray to God direct?

Not always. The same answer applies here as in the case of prayers to the Virgin Mary, who after all is the greatest of the Saints. God may wish to give certain favors through the intercession of some given Saint. In such a case, it is better to seek the intercession of that Saint as God wishes. I can decide to give you a gift myself, or to do so through a friend. In the latter case you do me greater honor by accepting it from my friend than by refusing my way of giving it to you, and insolently demanding it directly from myself in person.

1431. I pray that you may see the futility of praying to Saints who can do nothing for you. Christ is the only mediator.

By your very prayer you are attempting to mediate between God and myself on my behalf. I do not criticize the principle of praying for others. I believe in that. But I do criticize your praying for me in violation of your own principles. If the Saints cannot be mediators by praying for me, nor can you. Your prayers would be futile; they could do nothing for me; and you would be wasting your time.

1432. The Lord's Prayer shows that God Himself hears our prayers.

Correct. And He hears the prayers we address to the Saints, and their prayers also on our behalf. And those prayers, added to our own, give us additional claims to be heard by God in a favorable way.

1433. When did God tell anyone to pray to human beings?

When the Catholic Church teaches us that prayer to the Saints is right and useful, it is God teaching us that truth through His Church. But the doctrine is clearly enough indicated in Scripture also. I have mentioned Abraham's prayer for Sodom. The Jews asked Moses to go to speak to God on their behalf. God Himself said to Eliphaz, the Themanite, "My wrath is kindled against thee . . . but my servant Job shall pray for you. His face I will accept, that folly be not

imputed to you." Job XLII., 8. Earlier in that same book we read, "Call now if
there will be any that will answer thee, and turn to some of the Saints." V., 1.
His enemies meant that Job was too wicked to be heard, but they knew that it was
lawful to invoke the Saints. Long after the death of Jeremiah, Onias said of that
prophet, "This is the lover of his brethren and of the people of Israel. This is
he that prayeth much for the people and for all the holy city; Jeremiah, the prophet
of God." 2 Mach. XV., 14. St. James says that "the prayer of a just man availeth
much." If his prayer is valuable, it is worth while to ask his prayers. If you say,
"Yes. That is all right whilst a man is still in this life and on earth," I ask whether
you think he has less power when in heaven with God? In Rev. VIII., 4, St. John
says that he saw "the prayers of the Saints ascending up before God from the hand
of an angel." If I can ask my own mother to pray for me whilst she is still in this
life, surely I can do so when she is with God! She does not know less when she
rejoices in the Vision of God; she has not less interest in me; and she is not less
charitably disposed towards me then. We Catholics believe in the Communion of
Saints, and are in communion with them. But for you the doctrine of the Apostles'
Creed, "I believe in the Communion of Saints," must be a meaningless formula.
Christ is not particularly honored by our ignoring those who loved and served Him
best, and whom He loves so much.

1434. By what authority does the Catholic Church make Saints?

The decree of canonization does not make a Saint. It simply declares infallibly that a given person has lived such a holy life with the help of God's grace that
he *is* a Saint. When someone like a Francis of Assisi lives such a holy life that all
people are compelled to admire it, the Church is often asked to say whether such
a person is worthy to be honored publicly as a Saint. The Church then carefully
collects all possible information, and, after due consideration, says yes or no. If
the Church says yes, the name of the person to be venerated is put into the Canon
or catalogue of those who have become Saints by their heroic lives of virtue. The
Church has the authority of Christ for these decisions, for He sent her with His
authority to teach all nations in matters of faith and morals, and she could not
tell us officially that a given person was a perfect model of Christian virtue if such
a person were not.

1435. Who has the final say as to whether a soul deserves canonization?

The Pope. Before he defines that a given soul is indeed a Saint, the advocates
of the cause must prove that the person in question exercised all Christian virtues
in a heroic degree—supreme faith, hope, and charity; perfect prudence, justice,
fortitude, and temperance. Also God's own testimony by proven miracles wrought
through the person's intercession is required. The infallibility of the Church in
such decisions is, as I have said, but an application of ordinary infallibility in
matters of faith and morals, in so far as the Church could not err in proposing a
given life as an exemplification of perfect Christian virtue.

1436. How does the Church know that those she calls Saints are in heaven?

With the assistance of the Holy Spirit, she can and does know. She knows
God, and knows what holiness is. She examines the life of a holy person, and says
that such a life certainly could not lead a soul to hell. The Church canonizes only
those whose heroic virtue has been proved. And perfect charity before death destroys all sin, and all punishment due to sin. There is no place where such a soul
could be save in heaven. Also miracles wrought by God in honor of such a one
are His guarantee.

1437. Why does the Church allot different duties to different Saints?

She does not. She asks the special protection and intercession of certain Saints in special circumstances; and this is based upon what we know of their particular interest whilst they were on earth, or upon favors obtained already through their intercession since their death.

1438. Why do Catholics worship relics of Saints?

They do not worship relics as they worship God, by adoration. If you mean worship in the sense of honor or veneration, then Catholics certainly venerate the relics of Saints. The law, "Honor thy father and thy mother" extends to their persons, body and soul; to their reputations, and to all connected with them. We reverence their remains even after death. And if we are not to venerate the remains and relics of the Saints who have been so entirely consecrated to God, are we to desecrate them? Or are we to be blandly indifferent to them as to the bleached bones of some dead animal lying in the fields? The Catholic doctrine, forbidding adoration, yet commanding respect and veneration, is the only possible Christian conduct.

1439. I don't object to that kind of veneration. I object to the expecting of favors through relics.

No real difficulty arises in this matter. No one holds that material relics of themselves possess any innate talismanic value. But God Himself can certainly grant favors even of a temporal nature through the relics of Saints, thus honoring His Saints, and rewarding the faith and piety of some given Catholic. St. Matthew tells us that the diseased came to Christ. "And they besought Him that they might touch but the hem of His garment. And as many as touched were made whole." Matt. XIV., 36. Again we read of a woman who touched the hem of Christ's garment and who was cured. "And Jesus, knowing in Himself the virtue that had proceeded from Him, said: 'Who has touched my garments.'" Mk. V., 30. You may reply that these incidents concerned Christ, and that, whilst he was still living in this world. But that does not affect the principle that God can grant temporal favors through inanimate things. And if you look up 2 Kings, XIII., 21, in your own Protestant version of the Bible, you will find that a dead man, who was being buried in the sepulchre of Elisha, was restored to life the moment his body came into contact with the bones of that great prophet of God. In the Acts of the Apostles, too, we read of a most Catholic, and most un-Protestant procedure. "God wrought by the hand of Paul more than common miracles. So that even there were brought from his body to the sick, handkerchiefs and aprons, and the diseases departed from them." Acts XIX., 11-12. But you will notice that it was God who wrought these miracles. And we Catholics say that God can quite easily do similar things even in our own days. As a matter of historical fact, He has wrought such things throughout the course of the ages within the Catholic Church.

1440. Are not relics received and venerated without a particle of proof that they are genuine?

No. The Catholic Church is very prudent in this matter, and her law declares that those relics alone may be publicly venerated which have authentic documents accompanying them, and proving them to be genuine. These documents can be given only by one authorized by the Holy See to grant them. If the documents be lost, no relic may be offered for public veneration by the faithful without a special decree from a Bishop who can guarantee the relic as genuine. But even should a Catholic venerate as a relic some object which is not authentic, such veneration is at least well meant, and directed towards the one whom the object is believed to represent.

CHAPTER THIRTEEN

THE CHURCH AND SOCIAL WELFARE

1441. *The Catholic Church is a blight on social welfare, asking the public to support too many religious institutions.*

The irreligious man perhaps thinks that there are too many. But the religious man will say that there are not really enough. God is not likely to complain that works of mercy are being multiplied in His name. And what public is called upon to support these Catholic institutions? Let those complain who do so. Catholic institutions are supported in the main by Catholics and by such generous non-Catholics who admire their charitable work. And the man who does not support them is not the one who should complain. If those who do support them had no wish to do so for the love of God and their fellow men, they would cease to give. But they must be allowed to do with their own property what they wish. If they wish to devote some of their earnings to charitable and religious works, those who selfishly reserve all for their own comfort or amusement should at least have the grace to keep silent.

1442. *How long will the country be able to stand this vast expenditure?*

The country is not asked to do so. Catholics give out of their private earnings, paying all public taxes required for the public finances. Catholic institutions are not a burden on the public. In fact they lessen the public burden, relieving the state of a great deal of financial responsibility. Public money is spent on state schools, and in them Catholic public money is spent to educate the children of non-Catholics, whilst Catholics have to pay privately over again for the education of their own children. Take my advice. Do not talk economics in reference to Catholic institutions. Just pocket Catholic money and be wisely silent!

1443. *Is not the money extracted from Catholics out of all proportion to their ability to give?*

Money is not extracted from Catholics. They delight to give what they can afford in support of their religion. They believe they can afford it, even if it does mean the sacrifice of some of the amusements those who don't give can enjoy. But they would rather give to God than spend all on superfluous self-entertainment. All Catholics know that they are not expected to give out of proportion to their real ability. Those who cannot afford it have no obligation to give.

1444. *The money is wrung from the people.*

It is not, and every Catholic would resent the charge that his offerings to God and to the Church are not prompted by supernatural motives, and are not voluntary, but given under compulsion. You have not the least idea of the Catholic spirit.

1445. *It is a wonderful way to get money; just tell people that they sin if they don't give!*

That would indeed be a wonderful way. It is surprising that the big business people have not thought of it. They have but to insert an advertisement in the newspapers, "It is sinful not to purchase at our establishment," and the first firm that does so will have all rival firms closed in no time. It is a wonder that the modern world has not yet thought of this.

1446. *All the same Catholicism keeps the people poor, for Father Martindale bewailed the fact that the Catholic religion is looked upon as the religion of the kitchen.*

That does not mean that it is the religion of the kitchen. Nor was Father Martindale alluding to the qualities of the religion. He was rebuking the dispositions of those who so regarded Catholicism. He was blaming men who are so blind to the real facts that, because many of the lower classes do happen to be Catholics, they look down upon Catholicism with prejudice and snobbishness. Such men would have despised Christianity in the first days of its existence because preached by a common fisherman, Peter.

1447. *Why are there so many Catholic employees, and so few Catholic employers?*

The duty of proving that Catholic employers are proportionately fewer than Protestant employers rests upon yourself, before I have any need to reply. And even if you could prove such to be the case, no question for or against the Catholic religion could arise from such considerations. Temporal prosperity is no index as to the truth of Christianity, for Christ did not promise that. He Himself knew no temporal prosperity, and predicted that His true followers would not be above their Master. In fact, from this point of view, lack of worldly prosperity on the part of Catholics would be, if anything, in their favor as disciples of a crucified Master.

1448. *If Catholicism is true, why are the most backward countries Catholic, and the most enlightened and progressive countries Protestant?*

Let me lay this ghost once and for all. The assertion implicit in such a question ignores the facts of history. A few centuries ago Spain was the dominant nation, and it rose to power as a Catholic nation. On your principles, pagan Romans could have argued that their paganism was true, pointing with scorn to Druid-ridden England, and its lack of culture. Italy, under Mussolini, is to-day leaping to the front and disturbing politicians of other countries; and its rapid advance has not demanded the relinquishing of Catholicity. As for enlightenment, Protestant artists and architects go to study the great masters and the architectural gems in Catholic countries, and are inspired by Catholic culture! Temporal progress is a fluctuating thing, dependent on political, geographical, racial, economic, and personal factors, and that quite independently of religion. I have mentioned that the assertion violates logic from the Christian point of view, since Christ did not promise temporal welfare. And it is absurd, on the face of it. For it is like arguing, "Jones is a millionaire; his religion must be true. Jones has become a bankrupt; the same religion must be false!" Finally, if Protestantism is justified by the present temporal prosperity of Protestant nations, it will be falsified by the future collapse of those nations. You can be quite sure that the present relative position of the nations of this world is not going to remain unchanged until the end of the world. That would be against all the laws of history and of the mutability of men. Alexander the Great longed for more worlds to conquer—his empire has crumbled and gone. The Roman Empire has crumbled and gone. The British Empire will crumble and go—yielding to further political changes and regimes, ever fluctuating and variable. Protestantism is changing daily, and will go even as the religions of the Greek and Roman Empires. The Catholic Church alone is changeless, and will last through all political and national upheavals, as she has done through all the changes of the last two thousand years. Talk about the relative temporal enlightenment and progress of various countries impresses no thinking man in the matter of religion. It is a phase which neither proves nor disproves the truth of a religion, but is simply irrelevant.

1449. Look at Catholic countries where Rome has power!

Yes, look at them, but with open eyes. The temporal administration of these countries is not in the hands of the Church. And, in any case, as I have said, Spain had the Catholic religion when she was the first power in Europe. Meantime, remember that the Catholic Church is the mother of civilization. She preserved literature, and but for the transcriptions of her monks, you would have scarcely a single classical author of ancient times. The Catholic faith has inspired the loftiest works of art, architecture, and music. The economic fluctuations are simply irrelevant.

1450. Catholic countries, burdened by Church institutions, cannot progress.

They have done so, and they do. And what do you mean by Catholic countries being thus burdened? The women of Jerusalem wept, in their health and strength, as they saw Jesus carrying His cross. But instead of accepting their compassion, He said, "Weep not over me, but over yourselves and your children." Catholics, too, say to you, "Weep not over us. Have your progress in worldly advantages, comforts, and pleasures. Christ promised happiness in self-renunciation and generosity. The comfort-lover does not know what these things mean." The Catholic Church is mainly interested in progress in holiness and virtue; and that is the only progress worth while in the end. The nations that have progressed in worldly goods have religiously progressed into indifference. As with individuals, the more these nations have, the less they want God. But this is not the fault of progress as such. It is the unhappy result of a Protestantism which came into being just as the swing towards scientific progress came upon the world. That swing would have come in any case. It did not come because of Protestantism; but Protestantism was unable to hold the religious allegiance of men in the midst of temporal prosperity. And in their luxuries, men are forgetting God.

1451. Why are Catholic countries always revolutionary?

They are not. Certain countries, whose inhabitants happen to be mainly Catholics, are characterized by frequent political upheavals, but that is a very different matter. Temperament accounts for this in some degree. Descendants of the Latin races have not the same calm self-possession of the colder and more phlegmatic northern Europeans. Again, economic prosperity in the northern peoples gave less cause for turbulence, though internal disputes are rapidly becoming a feature amongst these people also. But the Catholic religion as such is not involved in this question. Italy is at present advancing, whilst steadily restoring Catholicism after its disfavor since the revolution of 1870, a revolution produced not by Catholic but by anti-Catholic influences. Catholicism and progress are here going hand in hand. Another Catholic country could easily be on the decline. Holland has declined since it became Protestant, but no Catholic dreams of blaming Protestantism for this. We must look to natural factors to explain the natural swing of the pendulum in national and political matters. We can no more connect the rise and fall of nations with religion as such than we can judge an individual's religion by his material well-being. Catholicism, if accepted, will result even in the temporal well-being both of individuals and of nations. If Catholicism does not seem to do so, it is because it is not being put into practice sincerely by those professing it. But we are not justified in arguing back to religion from all types of temporal well-being and progress.

1452. Why, in Catholic countries, does the whole populace turn against the Church?

The whole populace does not. Political revolutionaries and anti-religious minorities take advantage of the lack of political organization of Catholics at times. In Russia, the attack on the Church is due to anti-religious forces, and to anti-Christian Communists. In Mexico, anti-religious forces are also responsible, even though some of the revolutionaries against the Church are nominally Catholic. In Spain, whilst the country was involved in political changes, an anti-religious minority, backed by foreigners and supplies from Russian and other Communists, attacked and looted religious institutions and churches. No well-informed Christians of any denomination rejoice over these anti-religious movements. They do not proceed from any desire of a purer religion, but work for the destruction of all religion.

1453. Protestants in Protestant countries do not rebel against the Protestant Churches, as Catholics against the Catholic Church in Catholic countries.

Atheists and bad Catholics may rebel against the Catholic Church, which condemns their vices. But why should anyone rebel against the Protestant Churches? Protestantism is most obliging as a rule, and instead of going against the grain, and ordering its adherents to renounce their evil inclinations, either remains discreetly silent, or breaks down Christian principles to suit the desires of men. How often we notice Protestant leaders first studying what men want, and then interpreting Christianity accordingly! The Catholic Church first asks what Christ wants, and then tells men that, even though it be uncomfortable, they must live up to it. Protestant Churches sanction divorce, birth-control, and almost any heretical doctrine about Christ and His teachings, impose no strict obligation of Sunday worship, and are so harmless generally that no one would think of being up in arms against them. If a man does not like them, he just ignores them. The Catholic Church, however, is known to be a really vital force, and men find that they cannot ignore her. Enemies of Christianity are not concerned much with Protestantism. It is in Catholicism that they recognize the deadly enemy of atheism, materialism, and Communism.

1454. Why is Southern Ireland so poor? Is it for want of ability, or is it because the Catholic Church has bled the people of all their money? What a contrast with the North of Ireland!

It is not from want of ability. Nor is it because the Church has robbed the people. It is because England drained the country dry, confiscating property from Irishmen and bestowing it upon Englishmen, and taxing the people to fill the English exchequer. This has been one of the chief causes of the dissatisfaction in Ireland through the centuries. On the other hand, money has been poured into Northern Ireland from England. Thus English policy has bought the love of the Protestant North, and driven the Catholic South to poverty and distress. I have not one drop of Irish blood in my veins, but I cannot shut my eyes to the facts of history. Any old stick will do, of course, with which to beat the Catholic Church. The Catholic Church is there to be the object of our contempt and hatred. And it is all the more inviting when it enables us to load the wretch with our own iniquities, and so divert attention from ourselves. But let us be honest. We Englishmen are dishonest when we suggest that the effects of our own injustice are really due to the blighting influence of the Catholic Church.

1455. Since the Reformation, Protestant countries have advanced in every way.

Many of them have not advanced from a worldly point of view, and none of them has advanced in Christian holiness and virtue. Those Protestant countries which have shown material progress do not owe it to their adoption of Protestantism. I admit, of course, that Protestantism has allowed men to divert their attention from spiritual to material interests. Undivided attention to worldly pursuits would make for additional progress in such affairs. But, in the main, scientific and temporal progress would have come in any case. The Reformation arrived almost simultaneously with an era of discoveries, which were the cumulative result of preceding Catholic genius. In the new industrial era, too, the northern European countries, which happened to be Protestant, had the necessary coal and iron. But the coal and iron would have been there just the same had they remained Catholic.

1456. Thanks to Luther, Germany became mighty.

Were that so, which I do not grant, Luther would have had the wrong influence from a Christian point of view. Christianity is to make people better, not to make them mightier. Catholicism tends to the material well-being of nations as of individuals by conferring peace and contentment, not by conferring might and luxury. And the fruit of German might was the Great War, in which Protestant Germany failed. Christianity, of course, was not responsible for that war. Abandonment of true Christianity by those who still nominally professed that religion, was the cause.

1457. Look at England's progress since she became Protestant!

England is not a Protestant country, except nominally. The irreligious easily outnumber the religious in England. Her material prosperity has been accompanied by frightful spiritual loss. Her subjects have drifted from God, and agnosticism, materialism, and atheism have swept through the masses. And that does not look much like a blessing of God. But, as I have said, you are on the wrong lines. Christ came to make men unworldly, holy, and spiritual. And His religion must be tested by these results. If prosperity and earthly might are to be the tests, then give up Christianity, as England, alas, is doing. For Christ died between two despised thieves, and predicted suffering for His followers. He said, "Blessed are the poor," not, "Blessed are the rich"; "Fear not little flock," not, "Fear not, ye mightiest of the land"; "He that exalts himself shall be humbled"; not, "He that exalts himself certainly has My true religion." His religion is not of this world, and He solemnly warns us that it is of little profit to gain the whole world at the expense of one's soul. If you base your religion on the political greatness of nations which profess it, the swing of the political pendulum will destroy your religion in no time.

1458. Anyway, we Protestants pray that America will never come under the domination of the Catholic Church.

You are wasting your prayers. The Catholic Church, even if our country became entirely Catholic, would not wish to assume purely civil government. Free and easy divorce laws would be repealed; the sale of birth-control requirements would be prohibited; and various other un-Christian liberties would be withdrawn. But where legislation did not conflict with God's laws, it would be unaffected by the predominance of the Catholic religion.

1459. Do Catholics regard state schools as monuments of blind bigotry, that they won't use them?

They are not monuments of blind bigotry. I believe that the state school system was evolved by men who honestly but mistakenly believed it to be the best system for our country. But they appealed to blind bigotry in order to secure their purpose. Sir Henry Parkes said publicly in support of the necessary legislation, "I hold in my hand a bill which will spell death to the calling of the Roman Catholic clergy." It did not. And in order to compel Catholic acceptance of the state school system, the government unjustly refused to allow Catholics to spend their share of the educational taxes on their own children. The government cannot have any objection to the standard of education in secular subjects given in Catholic schools, for they give an education fully equal to that given in state schools where these subjects are concerned.

1460. What is your attitude towards state schools? Do you think them Satanic and their founders devils?

I accuse the founders of no conscious error. But I say that the system, whilst not positively teaching Satanic doctrine, is truly an agent of the devil rather than of Christ in so far as it omits religious formation as an integral part of its program. The child may be taught to be outwardly respectable, but he finds no adequate interior motive for his private conduct. He is animal rather than spiritual. He is not conscious of being a child very dear to God. What religion he may have secured in other ways is not consolidated and it soon disappears. A very small proportion of children thus trained bother about religion after they have set out on the path of life. And all this is certainly not a matter of grief to Satan. An Anglican clergyman once said sadly to me, "We Anglicans played the part of Judas when we handed our children over to the tender mercies of the state by approving the state school system."

1461. The state offers the best schools in the world, irrespective of religion.

That is self-contradictory. Education which abstracts from religion, the very soul of true education, cannot be the best. That is not true education which fills the mind with facts and figures, but which does not form the whole man, intellectually, morally, and religiously. Every bit as much, if not more time, should be given to the child's moral and religious formation.

1462. State education is just as good as yours.

A system which does not teach the truths necessary for right living cannot be as good as one that does. All my own primary education was done in state schools. I did not become a Catholic until after I had left school and started out in business. I do not remember having had a teacher who was not a naturally good man, bent on teaching us to be naturally good and honest. But all the knowledge of religion I and my companions picked up in virtue of our state education would not fill a thimble. Religious motives were not taught. Religious duties were ignored, and man's greatest duty to God simply omitted. The result of such education is that the child is impressed with the idea that this life is all, and that an earthly career and one's relations with one's fellow men are the supreme duty. Motto cards on the walls advising boys to be brave and girls to be good are no sufficient substitute. The Catholic Church could not in conscience accept such a system. And Catholics made the very great sacrifice of building their own schools at the cost of double taxation. They are compelled to subscribe just as non-Catholics towards the support of state schools which they cannot in conscience use, and in addition they have to subscribe for the support of their own schools. But at least their children are taught that their first and greatest duty is to know, love, and serve God in this life, and that their true destiny is to be happy with Him in the next.

1463. My children go to state schools on week days, and get their religion at Sunday schools on Sundays. And they are a credit to me.

Whilst your children may be outwardly all that you wish them to be, can you read their souls? Christianity is essentially an interior and spiritual religion. Interior virtue is not regarded highly when religion and morality are excluded from week-day education. The mere fact that religion is excluded from the week-day curriculum and taught on one day whilst secular subjects are taught on several days tends to make religion seem a side-line of much less importance. And the logical consequence is that many regard religion, if they bother about it at all, as a matter for Sundays, and not as having any particular reference to week-days. Sunday-school training is not enough.

1464. Your Church fears that she will lose the whip hand over the children.

She fears lest the children should lose their education in Christian doctrine and in the necessity of religious devotedness to God, growing up deprived of their faith, of their zeal for virtue, and perhaps of their hope of eternal salvation.

1465. "Catch them young and hold them tight" is the worldly-wise motto of the Catholic Church.

That is simple prudence, and even God does not dispense from common sense. He Himself says that it is good for a man to have borne the yoke from his youth. The yoke of obedience and of virtue restraining children from ignorance and vice is good for them. And what utter folly it would be to begin to teach children the right thing only after they had learned the wrong thing; or do you think it right to speak of virtue only to people who have already contracted vice? The policy of catching children young for God and holding them tight for Him is the only sane policy. Is God the God only of adults, or is He the God of little children also, with a right to their love and gentle service? Would you teach the child anything? Or nothing? Or just to hate God rather than to love Him? I know which child would be the better off, were one trained on such theories as yours, and the other trained by the Catholic Church.

1466. Many of your religiously trained children go wrong.

They do. But it is not the fault of their religious training. It is their own fault. At least they know what is right. But to know what is right and to do it are different things. The Church can instill principles, but she cannot guarantee that a child will live up to them afterwards. Would you say that the religious training given by Christ to His Apostles was a failure because the high percentage of one in twelve went wrong? Or would you deprive all children of a knowledge of what they ought to do merely because some who have had that knowledge have not behaved as they should?

1467. Anyway, the Catholic religion does not turn out men of great learning.

Christ did not say, "Learn of Me to be a man of great learning," but to be "meek and humble of heart." His religion was not intended to turn out men of great learning, but to turn out men of Christian virtue. Men have been endowed by God with brains for the acquiring of ordinary learning, and that learning is the fruit of deep study and application. But if you mean that no man professing the Catholic faith has ever been a man of great learning you are sadly mistaken. Did you ever hear of a St. Augustine in the 4th century, or of a St. Thomas Aquinas in the 13th? Galvanized iron should remind you of Galvani, who died in 1796, an excellent Catholic. Volts in electricity should suggest Volta, a most devout Catholic, who died in 1827. Ampere, in the electrical world; Laennec, inventor of the stethoscope, in the medical world; Mendel, the great authority on heredity; De Lapparent in geology; Dwight, the anatomist; Pasteur, that great scientific observer; Foch, the military genius; all these were Catholics, and did not find their faith any hindrance in their acquiring of great learning. I could go on almost interminably, but time forbids more.

1468. *Instead of education we find illiteracy in countries where the Catholic religion prevails.*

Illiteracy does not prevail in Catholic countries. Nor does the idea of being illiterate exclude the notion of education. There are two kinds of education, verbal and real. You seem to think that if a man lacks book knowledge he must be uneducated. That is not so. Men who can construe Virgil believe themselves educated, yet often swell the ranks of the unemployed, whilst the practical tradesman, who has little literary knowledge, is enabled to support himself by his real education in practical things. Education is a relative matter, and only the fool thinks that no one is educated unless proficient according to his own standards. In remote country districts of old-world localities you may find men who have little verbal education, yet who have a real education in things, and who are expert agriculturists, miners, and vintagers. For that matter, a benighted Papuan would despise you for your ignorance of the habits of birds and animals, and for your inability to snare them as he does. If you would blame him for his contempt of your ignorance of his ways, you commit the same fault by despising his ignorance of your ways.

1469. *Mexico had the free scope of the Catholic Church, and her people are illiterate.*

The wonderful architecture and art in Mexico, dating from beyond 100 years ago, show a higher standard of general culture in that country when the Catholic Church did have a freer scope than she possesses now. Whatever faults may be attributed to the present generation, they cannot be ascribed to the educational influence of the Catholic Church. Political disturbances during the last hundred years have upset regular life, and put back the culture inspired by the Church. Moreover, seventy years ago, in 1859, legislation was introduced crippling the activity of the Church and suppressing her teaching Orders. The people were deprived of her full influence, and if the people are now characterized by illiteracy more than before, that but proves that the restriction of the activities of the Church was not a good measure.

1470. *It is no fault of the state that you have to have your own schools.*

It is. Catholic schools were once maintained out of the ordinary taxation derived from Catholics. In England Catholics receive back their own share of the taxes in the shape of government support for their schools. But in America the government uses Catholic taxes for its own state system, and forces the Catholics to pay over again for their own schools.

1471. *Why should Protestants have to pay for the education of Catholic children in Catholic schools?*

They should not have to do so. We do not want a single Protestant tax to be spent on Catholic education. But if Catholics educate their own children in their own schools, then they should be allowed to use for that purpose the taxes they themselves pay. We object to Catholic taxes being used to educate Protestant children in state schools, and ask merely that Catholic taxes be spent on the education of Catholic children.

1472. *If Catholics are so narrow-minded, they deserve to pay for their own schools.*

Even if the government returned Catholic taxes, Catholics would be paying for their own schools. The Catholic position is not unreasonable in this matter. If to have a conscience is to be narrow-minded, then Catholics are narrow-minded. They can never be broad-minded enough to say that education omitting religion and a knowledge of the truth taught by Christ is good enough. A one-time Anglican

Bishop of Melbourne, Dr. Moorhouse, said in reference to this matter, "I will not join in the howls against Rome. . . . Can I forget that Roman Catholics, with all their errors, love my Redeemer, and that, having such love, they are nearer to my heart than the most enlightened Secularist who reviles or disowns Him? Let others do as they please; I will never unite with the Secularists against Rome, to keep Christ out of the schools of this colony. I still advocate, therefore, the making in some form a grant to Roman Catholics for secular results. I seek this change, not as a Churchman, but as a Christian and a citizen."

1473. What becomes of the money paid by Catholic children in school-fees? Do not the Brothers and Nuns work for nothing?

The school-fees provide buildings and upkeep, together with food and clothing for the Brothers and Nuns. That is all the good Brothers and Nuns ask for themselves, and there is nothing left over after expenses are met. Oftentimes expenses are not met by school-fees, and other appeals have to be made. If it were not for the self-sacrifice of the Brothers and Nuns, a self-sacrifice inspired by God Himself, we could not continue. A government return of taxes would relieve the Catholic people of the necessity of school-fees, and remedy the present injustice.

1474. What is the use of educating children at all, when the Church does nothing to remedy the evil conditions of the society in which they must live?

No one can honestly accuse the Catholic Church of not endeavoring to do her part in this matter.

1475. Are not Catholics taught that the economic distress of the world is caused by supernatural influences, and that they must simply endure it?

No. Catholics have been urged over and over again by their Church to do their utmost towards the rehabilitation of the world. They do believe in God and in God's providence. They believe that all the miseries of this world have been permitted by God, or they would not exist. But they are due to man's own political and economic maladministration. Catholics also believe that, if men lead evil lives, they forfeit the right to God's blessings, both spiritual and temporal. They know that sin and corruption and irreligion are very wide-spread evils, and that there will be room for hope that God will spare men many of the afflictions they deserve if men will but remedy their lives and begin to serve God earnestly, loving their neighbors for the love of God.

1476. Are Catholic Priests forbidden to study economics?

No. In his Encyclical Letter, Quadragesimo Anno, of May, 1931, Pope Pius XI. says that "all candidates for the sacred priesthood must be adequately prepared by an intense study of social matters. It is particularly necessary that those specially devoted to this work should show themselves to be endowed with a keen sense of justice, ready to oppose with manly courage unjust claims and unjust actions, avoiding every extreme with consummate prudence and discretion." The Pope adds that "no stone must be left unturned to avert grave misfortunes from the human race"; that "much has been done in the social and economic field by various Catholics," but that now "let all strive to play their part in the Christian renewal of society." Far from being forbidden, then, Catholic Priests are urged to the study of economics and of social science.

1477. *Your Church will be useless until she preaches less individual salvation and more social salvation.*

The Church must preach that each individual soul will answer personally to God for its conduct during life, and also for its influence by good or bad conduct upon others. And each soul must answer to God for itself. No one else can answer for it. At the same time, any scheme of individual salvation which excludes all interest in the salvation of others is certainly wrong, and is forbidden by the Catholic Church. That Church is the greatest social institution in the world to-day, serving society both in temporal and spiritual needs.

1478. *Christ intended a Kingdom of Heaven in this world, but you despise it, arraying yourself and rejoicing whilst the world is still in despair and shackles.*

Christ never intended this world to be Heaven. He said, "My Kingdom is not of this world." The Church is His Kingdom on earth, but it is not a Kingdom of earth. And I esteem this Kingdom of Christ above all else. This does not forbid me to dress respectably. It does forbid me to rejoice in so far as humanity is in despair and shackles. But I do not rejoice in the sufferings of humanity. The miseries of men affect few people as they affect Catholic Priests, who, without telling you all about it, do their utmost to relieve the poor and their miseries.

1479. *I heard a Protestant clergyman say that the miseries of the world were an indictment of all Churches, including the Roman Catholic, for their lack of influence.*

I will not comment upon other Churches in this matter. But as regards the Catholic Church I must make some remarks. She certainly has the principles and teachings necessary to better the lot of men. But she cannot influence men much so long as they refuse to accept her principles. The only solution possible, and the solution which the Catholic Church proposes, is that all men, employers and workers, should become genuine Christians, and not allow their selfishness to interfere with strict justice and mutual charity. But the last thing the majority of employers and workers are prepared to renounce is just that selfishness which is the ultimate cause of most troubles. If all men were Catholics, and all lived up to the teachings of the Catholic Church, obeying the laws she has given for social affairs, it would be the end of strikes and friction with their consequent poverty and misery. The fact that these troubles exist, then, is not an indictment of the Catholic Church, but of men who cannot see the wood for the trees. For with the peace-giving Church in their midst, they either refuse to accept it, or refuse to live up to its teachings.

1480. *Why does the Catholic Church defend the capitalist and attack the worker?*

She does not do these things. The Catholic Church defends law and order, and human rights. She is ever ready to denounce injustice, whether of the government, or of any private individual. If a wealthy Catholic did not pay just wages, and were seriously defrauding his employees, the Catholic Church would be the first to condemn such conduct, and warn him that, if he continued in such conduct, he would risk eternal damnation. On the other hand, if an employee accepted good wages, and did not render equivalent service, he too, would be condemned by the Church. The Catholic Church neither denies nor approves present-day miseries. And since the world will not listen to her principles, she turns round and tries to relieve all the misery she can by every possible kind of charitable organization.

1481. *Why don't you condemn all rich men as criminals?*

Some may be, and then they sin, and are condemned by the Church. But not all rich men are criminals. A man can lawfully acquire property and wealth, and build up a legitimate state in life by his diligence and ability.

1482. *When did the Catholic Church first endorse the holding of private property?*

The right of private property is a natural right and has always been held by the Church. When God gave the commandment, "Thou shalt not steal," He acknowledged that men could acquire property to which others had no right.

1483. *St. Augustine says that the superfluities of the rich are the neces sities of the poor. Therefore those who possess superfluities possess the goods of the poor and are robbers.*

The Catholic Church agrees with St. Augustine in this matter, and declares that all who possess superfluities, that is, goods which are over and above that which is necessary for the upkeep of their state in life, are obliged under pain of sin to share their superfluities with their less fortunate fellow men. The hundreds of orphanages, hospitals, and other works of charity established by the Catholic Church are supported by contributions from such superfluities, as well as by contributions from Catholics who are sacrificing much that they could legitimately retain.

1484. *What do you say of rich men who derive an income which others have to provide, and who do not work?*

I hold no brief for the defence of rich men. But we must talk common sense. Income may be derived from honest sources or from dishonest sources. If from dishonest sources, the Catholic Church denounces it, and orders restitution to those from whom it is dishonestly derived. But a wealthy man's income may be derived from perfectly honest sources, and in that case you have no right to say that it has to be provided by others as if it were wrung from them against their will and their just obligations. If a man's business thrives, his income is honestly come by, provided each individual transaction is honest. And if, when he dies, he leaves his wealth to his son, that son honestly inherits his father's wealth.

1485. *Rich men who give no personal service to the community by real work are criminals.*

They may have given that service in the past. You overlook that service, and see only their present wealth. But what obligation does civic service involve? A man is obliged to preserve the individual life God gives him, and if work is necessary for that, he is obliged to work. But if he is already provided for by lawful means, he is not obliged to engage in lucrative or productive labor. For his own individual good, of course, he should avoid idleness, which is a source of many evils, and find some occupation. Where the social good is concerned, whilst he must practice the social virtue of charity, he is not obliged in justice to undertake personal labor. Personal work and productive activity are of great importance to the social good; but the obligation to render such service is a general obligation, and does not fall necessarily upon this or that individual. The majority of men will be compelled by individual necessity to contribute such labor as the common good requires. And do not forget that, even by living in the country, wealthy men render much social service by paying proportionate income taxes for the upkeep of public services, and by circulating money spent on personal requirements and in giving some measure of employment to others.

1486. Can you call a man a Christian who hoards up useless cash whilst another man starves?

No. And the Catholic Church says that a man who has superfluous goods, knows that some given man is starving, and lets him starve, commits a mortal sin in God's sight, the fruit of which will be hell for all eternity, unless he receives a singular grace of repentance for such evil conduct before he dies.

1487. If your Church won't denounce unscrupulous capitalism, how can you justify your faith in the Founder of your Church, who was a carpenter, a working man?

The Church certainly denounces unscrupulous capitalism. But not all capitalists are unscrupulous. No one has ever spoken more strongly and soundly on the abuses of capitalism than Pope Leo XIII. He upheld the rights of labor, denounced the injustice of many amongst the wealthy classes, and laid down rules which men can refuse to follow only so long as they refuse to follow the dictates of conscience itself. Meantime, the Church justifies her faith in her Founder by holding fast to all His teachings. She imitates His wisdom when the world tries to entangle her. You will remember how His enemies asked Him concerning the payment of taxes. If He said, "You must pay tribute," they hoped that the Jews would curse Him. If He said, "You must not pay tribute," they hoped that the Romans would arrest Him. Jesus therefore replied, "Give to Caesar the things that are Caesar's and to God the things that are God's." The Catholic Church says, "Give to the working man all that to which he has a right, and to owners all that is theirs." Every man has his conscience, whether employer or worker, and the Church tells men that they must be faithful to their conscience. If they will not, even God will not force them to obey His dictates. How then can you expect the Catholic Church to succeed in making them do so?

1488. Christ died to save men, not from the devil, but from earthly masters; and your Church claims to have His mission.

Christ did not die to save men from their earthly masters. The Jews rejected Him precisely because He did not offer to save them from Roman tyranny. If He had died to deliver men from earthly masters, be sure that the Jews would have been delivered from the Roman oppressors. Christ accomplished that for which He died. And He died to give all men the means of eternal salvation, if they have the goodwill to use those means.

1489. Considering that Christ preferred to die amongst thieves, what would He say of the rich to-day?

Although Christ was crucified between two thieves, He had friends amongst the rich, and often dined in the houses of the wealthy. If the rich to-day are unjust, and violate God's laws, Christ would condemn them according to the measure of their iniquity. He would not condemn them otherwise. He never condemned riches as such. When Job was a rich man, he was commended by God, and loved by Him. God does condemn the bad use of riches, and orders all men to be poor in spirit. Every man must be prepared to sacrifice all his earthly goods rather than commit sin to retain or increase them.

1490. Is it not the main function of your Church to support the ruling classes, and to keep the poor in their place?

No. The main function of the Catholic Church in relation to all classes of society has ever been to teach them that the main purpose of their existence is to know, love, and serve God in the duties of this life, and thus to attain their eternal destiny of happiness with the God who created them. As regards temporal affairs in the meantime, the Church says that all injustice and want of charity is opposed to the serving of God, and that those guilty of such injustice, whether peasants or princes, are in danger of losing their souls.

1491. You cannot deny that religion is a powerful tool in the hands of rulers to oppress the lower classes.

National religions have often been so abused. The Catholic Church as a Church has never been a party to such injustice, but has fought sedulously for the rights and dignity of the poor. That some Catholics individually have tried to use religious influences wrongly I admit; but that was their individual crime, not the fault of their religion which they abused.

1492. Is not this the reason why any religion will get thousands of dollars from the wealthy classes?

I am not speaking on behalf of any Church other than the Catholic Church. The Catholic Church is the one true Church, and the greatest of all the Churches in this world. But her position is not due to her possession of wealthy members, but to the vast number of those who belong to her, chiefly from the poorer classes, each member of which gives a little regularly towards the support of a religion which every Catholic regards as his greatest consolation. St. Paul could write to Catholics to-day even as he did to the Corinthians. "See your vocation, brethren, that there are not many among you wise according to the flesh; not many mighty; not many noble; but the foolish things of this world; the weak things of the world; the things that are contemptible in the eyes of the world hath God chosen."

1493. Has not the state always had the support of the Church in repressing workers?

Certainly not in the case of the Catholic Church. She has always condemned injustice, insisting that men should be brothers in Christ.

1494. Can you give me one case where the Church has actively assisted the lower orders against the oppression of higher powers?

Certainly. In Catholic times, when the Church had power, the people of England owed Magna Charta, or the great Charter of their liberties against the royal tyranny, to Stephen Langton, the Catholic Archbishop of Canterbury, and Primate of England. In 1929 Lord Strickland tried to trample upon the rights of the people in Malta. He was endowed with the "Divine right of Kings" theory. The Church fought him. The newspapers distorted the facts in favor of Strickland and against the Church. But England appointed a Commission which found against Strickland on almost every count. This was not given the same publicity as the earlier anti-Catholic cables.

Still later the Pope, notwithstanding all the concessions of Mussolini for the sake of the Concordat, fought him for the rights and liberties of the people, prepared to sacrifice the Concordat itself. Once more the newspapers tried to give the impression that the Pope was trying to interfere unjustly in political matters. But he was vindicating the elementary rights and privileges of the people.

1495. These things were in Catholic times and Catholic countries; but what is the Church doing for the down-trodden workers throughout the world?

The Church has always consistently used what power she has in the cause of the worker. With the very rise of the present industrialism Pope Leo XIII. insisted on the rights of labor in a series of almost revolutionary Encyclicals. He insisted that in justice the workers must receive wages that not only provide moderate comforts of life for themselves and their families, but enough to leave a surplus so that the thrifty may be able to save enough to provide for their future, and even to establish themselves in business and become employers also.   Each Pope since Leo has reiterated his protest against injustice, whilst defending, of course, fundamental rights to property.   Pope Pius XI., the present ruling Pontiff, says clearly, however, "If anything, the workers need the assistance of the Church in the obtaining of their rights, not the wealthy in the conservation of their rights."   And he gives as his reason the fact that the workers have less means of securing their rights because the wealthy have the control of the political machinery and of the press.

1496. *I admit that several Popes have expressed concern for the workers in vague and general terms, and that Leo XIII. gently admonished employers for their greed and brutality.*

The concern of the Church is deep where the wrongs of the workers are concerned, and it has been uttered in anything but vague and general terms.   Here are Pope Leo's words: "It has come to pass that working men have been given over, isolated and defenceless, to the callousness of employers and the greed of unrestrained competition so that a small number of very rich men have been able to lay a yoke little better than slavery itself upon the masses of the poor."

1497. *Mention one industrial dispute in which the workers have received the support of the Church in their struggle for decent conditions.*

In every industrial dispute, in so far as the obtaining of decent conditions is concerned, the Church has given strong support to the cause of the worker.   How? By her rigid denunciation of the absence of decent conditions, and her clear statements that social morality demands such decent conditions.   Having given this correct teaching to the world, she has done her part.   She has no means of forcing people to study her teachings, or to accept them and put them into practice when they have done so.   You do not seem to understand the mission of the Church.   Many men view her only in the light of their own troubles, and think that her chief duty is to remedy those.   The sick seem to think that she is a success only if she proves to be an efficacious medical clinic.   The starving man believes that she ought to be a universal soup-kitchen.   You seem to think that she was meant to be a Court of Industrial Disputes.   But Christ established His Church for the salvation of souls, and to tell men what they must believe and do if they would attain eternal salvation.   The Church condemns the unjust oppression of workers by capitalists and says to them, "If you go on like that, you will be damned."   She has done her part, and they must save their souls for themselves.   But you get a wrong notion into your head of what the Church ought to do, and then blame her for not doing what she was never supposed to do.

1498. *Why does the Church denounce the abuses of capitalism, instead of denouncing the whole existing system as evil, and as existing only for profit and not for use.   The Church ought to say, "Away with capitalized industry."*

You take too much for granted.   It is easy to say that modern industry under capitalism exists for profit and not for use.   But it is not true.   Industry produces things for the use of those who need them.   The public pays for the value of the thing, and something additional for the trouble of making it.   Portion of this something extra is distributed in wages, and portion is returned to those who have invested their savings in the enterprise.   If you think that the portion returned to investors is always excessive, just note the dividends paid by the average business to-day.   It is too sweeping to say that capitalized industry exists for profit and not for use.   This is but a catch-word which can impress only the unthinking, or those who want to believe it. I am not denying that abuses exist. Some wealthy owners are unwilling to let their dividends decrease, and would rather permit wages to decrease. They are wrong and eaten up with self-interest. But wholesale condemnation is nearly always exaggerated. The present system as a system is a mixture of advantages and disadvantages. It has its uses and abuses. And the Catholic Church does not support it with unqualified approval. Yet, whilst condemning the abuses, she does ask us to beware lest, in washing the dish, we break it.

1499. The Church commands the rich "religiously to refrain from cutting down wages." But the rich refuse to hear the Church.

The Church says that it is a crime to cut down wages in such a way that the worker is deprived of the ordinary necessities of life and of its moderate comforts. She has no objection to the reducing of wages if the cost of living be reduced proportionately. But these two reductions must be practically simultaneous. To reduce wages first inflicts hardship on the workers; to reduce prices first ruins many a business which cannot afford the unreduced wage. If the rich refuse the justice demanded by the Church, the Church says that the state has the obligation to force them to obey in these matters of social justice.

1500. What is the use of referring the workers to state authority? The state is merely an organized force to protect the interests of the wealthy.

By referring workers to state authority, the Church does not mean to any particular party which happens to be in power. But let workers unite, make use of lawful political influence, vote unjust governments out, and vote just governments in.

1501. So the Church, which says that "strikes are forbidden," offers us only that slow and uncertain remedy!

The Church does not say that strikes are forbidden. If the wrongs to be righted are serious and urgent, and ordinary means fail, then workers can have recourse to extraordinary means. A general strike is forbidden as morally wrong, because the evils it causes are nearly always greater than those to be remedied. But the workers in any given industry may go on strike, yet granted only that certain conditions are verified. They must be animated, not by a spirit of vindictiveness, but by a genuine desire to secure the justice due to them. They must not strike for trifling reasons, but for the remedying of a grave injustice. The evil to be remedied must be at least as great as the evil to the community and to the workers themselves which the strike will entail. All other just means, such as arbitration, must have been tried without success, so that the strike is the last resort. The strikers must rely on moral compulsion, and not resort to physical violence. Their demands must be such as not to destroy the business itself with resulting injury to themselves and their employers. And finally, the strike must have a probable hope of success, so that all the miseries and inconveniences are not caused for nothing.

1502. The Pope commands the poor to bear their poverty "in tranquil resignation."

That again is just untrue enough to give a perfectly false impression. The Pope says that the worker may and should do all that is lawful in order to secure the fair treatment due to him. But even after a man has done all that he can, there will always be some troubles, and the Pope rightly says to the worker as to every Christian soul, "Such trials as you cannot remedy by lawful means, bear with resignation to the Will of God rather than try to secure relief by unlawful means at the price of sin."

1503. *Why should the workers be such curs as to bear with tranquil resignation a poverty which is the cause of filth, drink, disease, insanity, suicide and war?*

You are over-stating your case. The workers are not expected to be curs in any sense of the word. They should be reasonable enough to view the case as it is, instead of working themselves up into a fanaticism based upon fictitious and exaggerated description. They should be men enough to unite and labor by all lawful means to remedy such injustice as does exist. They should be Christians enough to accept with resignation to God's Will such trials as human efforts cannot remove. And as long as we are in this life there will be inevitable trials and difficulties to endure. Meantime, poverty does not necessarily result in filth; I have been into very poor homes which are models of cleanliness; drink is more prevalent amongst those who can afford it than amongst those who cannot, even though "society" drinkers avoid publicity; disease and insanity are not the special prerogatives of the poor; suicides occur in all classes; war is more often due to wealth than to poverty.

1504. *You excuse the Church's lack of interest in these matters by saying that she exists to save souls.*

The Church does exist to save souls, even as Christ died for that purpose. But she does not lack interest in the social well-being of mankind. Moral law rules even man's social conduct, and since moral injustice can and does occur in the behavior of men towards each other in their social relations, it is the duty of the Church to give us correct moral principles covering such conduct. In addition to this, the Church makes very much of the corporal works of mercy, and the duty of Christians to benefit their neighbors even in the purely temporal order.

1505. *Christ came to give life more abundantly. How does the Church give life to the workers more abundantly?*

The text you have in mind does not refer to earthly life with its temporal comforts, but to eternal life—a far richer, fuller, and more satisfactory life than this world can possibly offer. He defined the life He offered when He said, "This is eternal life, that they may know Thee, the only true God, and Jesus Christ Whom Thou hast sent." He who secures the life of God's grace has life more abundantly than this world can give it. And to thousands of souls daily the Catholic Church gives this life. The workers who throng the Confessionals and the Altar Rails in the Catholic Church know that every absolution and every Holy Communion is giving them life more abundantly than this world ever could do.

1506. *I have heard you give the conditions which Catholic workers must observe before they go on strike. Your conditions render any strike sinful. But will you give us the conditions Catholic employers must observe before they decide on a lock-out?*

It is not impossible for the strike-conditions I gave to be fulfilled and for a strike to be without sin. Every one of the conditions I gave is sensible and moral. The end cannot justify the means, and the means must be within the limits of moral law. Meantime, an employer has by no means a free hand. If it is manifestly impossible for him to carry on his business, he is of course free to cease conducting it. But if he is able to carry on his business, and normally intends to do so, yet closes it up temporarily, dismissing or locking out his workers, he commits a very grave sin before God, unless he has serious reasons to justify such a procedure. What are those reasons? We can say that he sins if he does so for any reason which would justify his workers in striking. That is in general. In particular, if he locks out his workers in order to compel them to accept less than just wages, he sins. If he does so in order to make them work longer hours or harder than can be reasonably expected, he sins. An employer is obliged in conscience to pay a just and equitable wage; to treat his employees, not as slaves, but as fellow human beings with equal rights to human dignity and happiness in their own sphere as he in his; to help them even financially in sickness and trouble; to respect their union, and all the laws of the land in their favor. As long as the employees fulfill their duties strictly and justly, no employer is justified in a lock-out.

1507. Would a contractor fail in justice towards his employees if he secretly induced them to accept less than award wages on the score that many unemployed would accept the job?

Yes. Award wages are the legal price of the work to be done, and when a legal award is given, it binds in conscience. The Pope has condemned absolutely and most rigorously the conduct of those employers who exploit the evil of unemployment by inducing men to accept work at less than just wages. The legal award must be accepted as the measure of justice. Such conduct is unjust to the workers. Pope Leo XIII. says, "To defraud workers of a just wage is a great crime crying to Heaven for vengeance," and he quotes the strong words of St. James from the New Testament, "Ye rich men, ye shall weep and howl in the miseries that shall come upon you. You have stored up wrath against you in the last days. Behold the hire of the laborers, which by fraud has been kept back by you, crieth; and the cry of them hath come to the ears of the Lord of Hosts." Ja. V., 1-4. Nor is it any excuse to say that the men have agreed to work for less than award rates. The employer, in suggesting it, but trades on the idea that they will be compelled by scarcity of employment to accept. It is but trading unjustly on the suffering of the workers.

1508. Would one who employs such a contractor be guilty also if he knew that he resorted to such practices?

Yes. For such a person, knowing the fact, is endeavoring to secure his building at less than the just price, and is an accessory in the unjust exploitation of the workers. I would like to see all those who let contracts stipulate that award rates must be paid to the workers employed.

1509. A man might not be able to build if full rates were paid, yet might be able to do so, at the cheaper rate.

The principles of just price rule this matter as any other commercial transactions. If a man is too poor to afford a motor car, he has to do without it. If a man cannot afford the ruling price for a certain type of building, he must do without it rather than force workers to give him their labor at a valuation which inflicts injustice upon them. That is simply a form of unjust robbery. A less pretentious building could be erected, or the man should simply decide that he could not afford to build just yet.

1510. If all this be so, why does not the Church protest against that ingenious attack on wages, "work for the dole"?

If work for the dole were meant to be an ingenious attack on wages and decent conditions for the workers, the Church would undoubtedly declare it unlawful. But such is not necessarily the case. If, in a period of depression there be not enough work available to absorb all workers, the state cannot let her unemployed citizens starve. If individual employers are unable to engage them, the state has the social duty to provide them with at least the necessities of life, and this must be done from the general revenue. The choice lies between an unconditional granting of relief, or the creation of certain community works which would not otherwise be undertaken, and which are created solely in favor of the unemployed men. This latter alternative would be lawful if the motive be that some occupation is healthier and less degrading from the workers' point of view than idleness, or even that the contributions of the taxed community were resulting in some community advantage. But if it were intended as the thin end of the wedge to lower normal wages and conditions below just standards in ordinary enterprise, it would be unjust and morally wrong.

1511. You defend your Church against the charge of alliance with the capitalists. But I, as a socialist, still accuse her of disloyalty to the workers.

You would make some headway if you could prove that she has been disloyal to God. However, as a matter of fact, the Catholic Church is the best friend the workers have ever had, and the vast majority of her most loyal subjects are workers.

1512. Capitalists eat bread in the sweat of the workers' brows. What has your Church to say for the workers?

Most of those whom you would call capitalists have their own anxieties and labors. Do not make the mistake of measuring all labor in terms of muscular power. A man's intelligence is capable of true work, and financial administration is not free from the sweat of anxiety. Meantime the Church declares that the worker must be adequately rewarded for his services, and condemns the injustice and even virtual slavery too often present in the social system to-day. Pope after Pope has insisted that a bare living is not a just return for labor. Every worker has a right, not only to a living, but to a reasonable margin of comfort, with means to provide for his future and that of his children. And the economic situation must be so re-constructed that this is possible.

1513. Is it not a fact that the Catholic Church teaches the worker to submit to mammon?

It is not a fact. She stands for lawful authority, but urges all men not to be dominated by mammon.

1514. Workers are slaves held in bondage, their first and last thought the fear of losing their employment.

I suppose we are all slaves of life in some sense. The worker fears loss of employment; the employer, too, fears the loss of his business and the fruits of his anxious investments. We all fear to be deprived of food and the necessities of life, and God intends us to work to live. But in so far as injustice enters into the present social order, the Church condemns it, and demands that it be removed.

1515. Do not employers take advantage of this fear of the worker?

Not all do so. Many employers do not give a fair return for work done, and I have shown that the Catholic Church protests against such injustice. But the remedy is not to sweep the whole existing order away. Let us correct these abuses. In reality the world is suffering precisely because it refuses to live according to Catholic principles, both religious and social.

1516. Has not the Catholic Church withheld the light of knowledge from the worker?

She certainly tries to preserve her own children from the knowledge of evil. But she desires to hold from them no useful knowledge of all that is lawful.

1517. She teaches the workers to beg and to kiss the hand that smites them.

She does not. She insists upon the rights and the true dignity of every man. But she certainly does teach respect for property, for lawful authority, the obligation of rendering an honest day's work for an honest day's pay. She teaches the worker that he, like all others, must beg grace from God to enable him to fulfill the duties of his state in life, and that, whilst laboring to rectify wrong conditions, he must learn to forgive past injuries in a truly Christian spirit.

1518. *Your doctrines humble man and disfigure the soul.*

Men very much need humility. Few are overburdened with that virtue. But you would teach men a still more foolish pride. Christ said, "Learn of Me to be meek and humble of heart." Meekness demands manhood. It is much easier not to be meek, but to give way to the first impulse which surges upon one, and to pour out the first rush of words which comes to one's lips. Humility, too, is a virtue which greatly becomes a man who has offended God far more deeply than any of his fellow men have ever offended himself. As for the disfiguring of human souls, the only thing than can do that is sin, and the Catholic Church labors day and night in her efforts to destroy sin, teaching her children to hate it, and urging all men to avoid it. For sin is that breaking of God's laws which alone renders a man a criminal before God.

1519. *You sanction the great shame of almsgiving.*

It is inconsistent to demand that the rich share their superfluities with their less fortunate fellow men, and then to say that almsgiving is shameful. The Catholic Church teaches those who are endowed with this world's goods that they must redeem their sins by almsgiving, as God Himself commands. And there is certainly no shame in the giving of alms. You think that there is shame in the acceptance of alms. There is shame in merely human philanthropy, in which only too often money is thrown to the poor as a bone to a dog, the giver glorying in his superiority. But Christianity robs almsgiving of any element of shame. He who accepts alms given in a Christian spirit accepts what is really given to Christ and given by Him to His poor. Catholics are taught to see Christ in the poor and to give to Him in the persons of the poor. Such gifts are not thrown to the poor in any spirit of contempt, but are offered to Christ for the love of Christ, and are shared by Christ with his loved, though poverty-stricken friends.

1520. *Why does the Church sanction slavery by not paying its thousands of workers in the Religious Orders, who are scabbing on trade-unions?*

The thousands of members in the Religious Orders giving their services to God in the Catholic Church without wages do so cheerfully and freely. The Church has no obligation to pay those who refuse to be paid. And this self-sacrifice of so many Religious is really sparing millions of workers further expense. Nor are these Religious scabbing on unionists, for they are doing no unionist out of a job that he wants.

1521. *Why are all the clergy who preach social reform expelled from their churches?*

I omit any reference to other churches. Catholic Priests may and do preach social reform. But they must preach social reform on Christian lines. No Catholic Priest may preach social reform in the socialistic sense of the word, according to the anti-Christian principles of, say, a Karl Marx. Any Priest who would do so, and persist in doing so, would be expelled from the Catholic Church. Socialism, in the ordinary sense of that word, is theoretically self-contradictory; psychologically opposed to the very nature of human beings; practically impossible from the viewpoint of production and distribution; religiously evil, and ultimately ruinous to social and individual liberty. A socialistic system is never likely to become universal, and sectional experiments in socialism have always failed.

1522. Would you tell us the view your Church takes of socialism?

Socialism is a very broad term which men interpret in many different ways. Communistic socialism is, of course, condemned by the Catholic Church. Mitigated forms of socialism, which aim at social reform, but which ignore religion and rely upon purely materialistic methods, are also condemned. In these and similar senses of the word no Catholic can be a socialist. The Catholic program is social reform which demands true consideration of the workers by employers according to the demands of both justice and Christian charity, at the same time demanding of the workers a just quantity of work together with respect for other peoples' lawful possessions according to God's commandment, "Thou shalt not steal."

The Catholic program of reform is badly needed, and is the only way out. Economic reconstruction will not succeed unless it takes Catholic social principles into account. On the whole the sympathy of the Church is with the worker, who has less means of defence; and the capitalist is the one who should voluntarily begin to rectify the many abuses which undoubtedly exist. But no policy of socialism which aims at the destruction of all social inequalities can be tolerated. Social inequalities are essential to the general good of mankind; some men being employed on necessary manual works; others in intellectual pursuits; whilst various grades of ability or genius required in the work done demand various grades of remuneration. And this of course means social inequality. God Himself never condemned the employment of man-servants and maid-servants, but vindicated both their rights and the rights of their employers.

1523. I would like some further information on these matters. What does the word socialism mean?

Here is a dictionary definition with which I agree. Socialism is the name given to any one of various schemes for regenerating society chiefly by a more equal distribution of property possessed and regulated by state authority.

1524. Is socialism a religion, a form of government, or a state of society?

For some socialists it is all three. For others, it is a form of government leading to a state of society, either abstracting from religion altogether, or definitely hostile to it.

1525. Will you apply these same questions to capitalism?

Capitalism is the economic system in which industry, production, distribution, and exchange are controlled by individuals who possess property, and who devote some or all of it to enterprises of commercial value, subject to certain restrictive state legislation. It is not a religion; nor a political form of government, since it can function whether under a monarchy or under a republic. We can call it, however, an economic form of government, and it results in a certain state of society.

1526. Cardinal Gibbons says that your Church can function under any form of government. Is that correct?

It can function in any state, whatever its form of civil government, provided of course that the government in question at least leaves the Church to itself, and does not persecute or expel it.

1527. Then in that case, any form of government, even socialistic, is lawful as far as the Catholic Church is concerned.

That does not follow. A socialistic form of government may be quite wrong in itself, as violating the essential rights of man.

1528. *Was Christ a socialist when He said, "Our Father, give us our bread," instead of saying, "My Father, give Me My bread"?*

No. Those words have no reference to any particular civil or economic structure of society.

1529. *When He multiplied bread He did not sell the loaves and reap profit. He gave them away.*

His distribution of the bread has no reference to the matter under discussion. Firstly, it cost Him no effort so to multiply bread miraculously. If men could produce things miraculously, they would not mind giving them away. But ordinary human production costs the producer the employment of his own means of support, and he has a right to an equivalent return. Secondly, Christ's purpose in performing that miracle was to prove His claims to the religious convictions and adherence of the people. He blamed them for concentrating solely upon the provision of their temporal needs. "You seek Me," He said, "not because you have seen miracles, but because you did eat of the loaves and were filled. Labor not for the meat which perisheth, but for that which endureth unto life everlasting." Remember, too, that Christ paid for His necessities, Judas carrying the purse to buy those things which Christ and the Apostles needed.

1530. *God gave Manna to the Jews in the desert. Those who gathered little had sufficient; those who gathered much had but enough. Was not that socialism?*

No. It was the provision by God of a miraculous food for the Jews in crossing the desert, where their own efforts could not secure it. When they were able to provide for themselves, the Manna ceased. Socialism, in its wildest dreams, does not think of leading us all out into the desert, and relying upon God to rain down food miraculously.

1531. *God's providence gives enough for all. Why should there be such destitution?*

God's providence has not failed. He provides enough for all, but He does so in general, leaving it to men to use and administer earthly goods, commanding them to observe His moral laws of justice and charity. Destitution in the midst of plenty is due partly to human maladministration; partly to the inability and sloth of various individuals; partly to the injustice and dishonesty of others, as well as to their lack of fraternal charity.

1532. *You admit the failure of capitalism, yet deny the right to an earnest body of men to confiscate private property and usher in an era of happiness to mankind.*

I can see the evils of to-day, but they are not the result of the God-given right to private property. They are due to the abuse of that right, to the greed of people not satisfied with reasonable comfort, and to certain economic factors men have not been able to understand or entirely control. Men are forced to study deeply in order to find a solution of the difficulty precisely by the advent of the difficulty. And they must do so. I have never denied the right of men to try to usher in an era of happiness. The Church merely denies their right to attempt it by unlawful and unjust means.

1533. *The Catholic Church forbids a Catholic to be a communist!*

That is true. Communism is opposed to the law of God, is anti-Christian, and violates the fundamental rights of man. Apart from this, it will never remedy existing evils, and can only lead to the greater distress of those whom it pretends it will benefit.

1534. Your Church's solution of this terrible mess is faith!

It is not. Her solution is common-sense, strict justice all round, and Christian charity based upon faith.

1535. It matters little to me whether the Christian religion be right or wrong. I stand for communism which will rescue the workers from involuntary poverty and the rich from idleness.

You quote the usual promise which accompanies all new schemes of social reform conceived without reference to the principles of sound social morality, and the undiscerning are delighted with the rose without perceiving the thorns. Meantime the Catholic religion happens to be right, and being right, matters very much to all men who have been brought into contact with it. "He that believes shall be saved; he that believes not shall be condemned," are the words of Almighty God. And eternal issues are at stake.

1536. I have studied Christian doctrine and I find that it consists of a slave-complex, hypocrisy, pagan practice, mythology, deceit and avarice.

Whatever you studied, it certainly was not Christian doctrine!

1537. The Church stands four-square for a system which means poverty, unemployment, disease, and death for the worker, and idleness, vanity, comfort, and tyranny for the owners of the means of production—and you ask me to study Christian doctrine!

Since the Catholic Church stands four-square against all the abuses you mention I must reiterate my request. Please do study Christian doctrine.

1538. The Church worships the rulers as gods, and stands for their authority.

The Church does not worship rulers, but she gives those in lawful authority the respect due to them. St. Peter knew the law of God quite well, and wrote, "Be ye therefore subject for God's sake, whether it be to the king as excelling, or to governors as sent by him. Fear God. Honor the king." I. Peter, 11-13.

1539. You offer your brothers, "pie in the sky when you die."

That is a travesty and a caricature. The Catholic Church offers no pie (which would not be worth having) in any sky (which is not heaven). Alas for your knowledge of Christian doctrine! The Church does say that man was not made for this life only, and that he is a fool if he expects to find heaven on earth. He can look for a reasonable amount of comfort in this world, serving God meanwhile, and afterwards he can attain a happiness not to be described in terms of pies and skies.

1540. I prefer a little solid comfort on earth while I am alive.

If you prefer that to God, I ask with Christ, "What does it profit a man to gain the whole world, and suffer the loss of his soul?" God ought to know the relative values of material things and spiritual souls. He made both.

1541. The sufferings of the workers have made me a communist. I believe that we should destroy the Church, and work for universal freedom, brotherhood and peace.

I am afraid you are a communist only whilst other people have what you do not possess. Would you remain a communist if you had the goods and others had not? It is easy to remain a communist when you want others to give you their property;

but I know few who would remain communists when it is their turn to give away. And you seem to forget the communist objection to the shame of almsgiving when you demand that those who have more should give to those who have less. Or, instead of allowing them to practice charity, would you practice injustice by confiscating the possessions of others? And if you are out for universal freedom, why do you deny the freedom to men to better their positions by ability and diligence? If you want universal brotherhood and peace, why do you distort and ridicule the religion of Christians?

1542. *You do not preach virtue for the love of it, but because of the sweet profit.*

Then I do preach virtue! That is something. And you supply alternative motives—either for the love of virtue, or for the sweet profit. It is difficult to answer the personal charge. But at least I can say that were I out for sweet profit, it could be obtained better by other means. The man who becomes a Priest, and a member of a Religious Order involving the obligation of poverty, for the sake of a worldly income is a fool. The only profit in such a life is that of the friendship of Christ.

1543. *You have shown clearly that a Catholic cannot support communism, and have said that no Catholic can be a socialist. Can a Catholic, then, in conscience support the "Socialization Objective" of the Labor Party in Australia? That Objective is briefly, the socialization of industry, production, distribution, and exchange, by the constitutional use of Federal, State, and Municipal administrative machinery.*

Labor men are anything but agreed upon what that objective involves. They differ as to its interpretation and application. But taking it on its face value, I do not think any Catholic can in conscience support that objective as an objective; above all, if it be intended as a future permanent regime. Even if dispossessed owners were reasonably compensated, the system would violate moral and social justice. It would deprive men of their personal rights to their own property, and to their use of it to their own advantage, and to the saving up of the proceeds. Any man may voluntarily renounce his right to property, but he cannot impose that renunciation on others. If the expropriated individual be compensated, it would be difficult to admit that he could not use the compensating revenue in any form of personal industrial enterprise. The socialization of all industry, production, distribution and exchange is too sweeping, and cannot but violate the just rights of individuals. Without compensation, of course, the case would be far worse.

1544. *Many Catholics in the Labor Party have voted for this "Socialization Objective," and have seen nothing wrong with it.*

In the case of some Catholics, that is due to their lack of knowledge of the moral principles involved, and their lack of effort to find out those principles. In others, their careless support of the objective is due to a belief that it is but the dream of a few, and that it is never likely to become a practical issue. On the score that it is not worth fighting about, they vote for it, not really intending it, but intending other lawful measures in the Party platform. Others, again, interpret it in a much milder way than it stands, and intend only lawful applications of it.

1545. *Would you yourself say that a Catholic can in conscience support the Labor Party?*

I would say this. Without subscribing to the "Socialization Objective" as a theory, a Catholic could support the Labor Party in its present practical program, as being considered by him to be less oppressive than an opposing program. But within the Labor Party, he would be obliged to use his influence to secure a re-statement of the Objective on less drastic lines.

1546. *I believe that our Labor platform is the nearest approach to the principles of Christ of any form of present government in the world.*

Even if that were true, it would not necessarily mean that the policy of the Party is sufficiently conformed to Christ's teachings. The ideal of securing justice and fair-play for the worker must receive the approval of every honest Christian. But the sweeping "Socialization Objective" as worded, violates Christian principles. I hold no brief for the present system of what I would call "Unreformed Capitalism." It is neither reasonable nor just, and no Catholic is free in conscience to support its injustices. The Pope has so clearly condemned the economic evils prevailing in the existent system that at best a Catholic could support a modified capitalistic regime, purified of its present abuses.

1547. *All forms of production have socialistic importance, but the curse of usury steps in to mar the whole.*

All forms of production have socialistic importance in the sense that they are of social benefit in their results. But this does not mean that they must all be socialistically owned. Some undoubtedly may be so owned to public advantage, as the Pope himself would maintain. That usury is a curse to-day I admit. But whilst we denounce the injustice of the system we would rectify, we must take care that the remedy we propose does not equally or even more seriously injure social justice.

1548. *Would it be sufficient rectification of the "Socialization Objective" were it restricted to the socialization or nationalization of banking and of the major industries?*

The Labor Party's objective, of course, does not suggest that limitation. But with the limitation, I do not think that the nationalization of banking, with due compensation, would in itself be unjust, provided the country agrees that it is a necessary economic measure for the general good. The Pope himself advocates some form of public control of credit and banking. The question of major industries is more difficult. It is certain that the state can take over and control an essential enterprise if it be inadequately conducted by private owners. But the general proposition "Socialize major industries" is dangerous without any indication as to which will be declared to be major industries, and with no indication as to the reasons in each case. I think it is doubtful whether a Catholic could support even this modified proposition. To sum up:

The complete socialization of all means of production, distribution, etc., is unlawful as an objective from a moral point of view, and no Catholic could support it.

The nationalization of essential enterprises inefficiently conducted by private owners is certainly lawful.

The nationalization of banking is probably lawful as an economic measure, if the majority of the citizens believe it to be necessary. The socialization of major industries is a doubtful proposition because too general.

1549. *How do you justify Catholic support of the Labor Party at all, if all that you have said be true?*

When a man is confronted with two evils, he is free to choose the lesser in order to escape the greater. But though we choose the lesser evil, we are still bound to regard it as an evil, and to disapprove of it. Apply this to our present case. A Catholic worker finds that, on polling day, he has to choose between a socialist Labor candidate and one whose Party he believes to favor oppressive capitalism. If he believes that Labor is the lesser of the two evils, he is free to support the Labor candidate. Nevertheless, in doing so, he must not approve any complete "Socialization Objective." He must not, within the Labor Party, vote for or support so extreme an objective. Since it is an intrinsically wrong measure, he cannot assist in its maintenance or towards its realization. He cannot regard it as something good and desirable in itself.

We know that the Pope objects to "State Absolutism" on the one hand, and to excessive "Individualism" on the other. He objects to Fascism as a system because it savors too much of state tyranny. But on the principles I have given, he does not call upon all Catholics to desert it. So I say that Catholics are not bound to withdraw their support from the Labor Party, although they cannot in conscience support within that Party the particular plank known as the "Socialization Objective." That must be modified. Workers can be quite sure of the genuine sympathy of the Catholic Church. If that Church, whilst denouncing the oppressive financial system which is grinding the worker down, warns the worker against the other extreme of socialism, it is not only because of the moral principles involved, but also because the Church sees clearly that only a further increase of human misery can result from it.

1550. Have you ever heard of the Douglas Social Credit scheme?

Yes. It advocates the issue of free credit to consumers to enable them to purchase the goods they themselves make, but which in the present system so many of them cannot possibly buy. It is claimed that the scheme does not involve inflation because the amount of credit to be released is to be calculated only after the goods equivalent to it are actually in existence. The money-supply is to be strictly proportionate to the goods-supply.

1551. Does not this scheme conform with the principles given in the Pope's Encyclicals?

The Pope does not mention explicitly the particular system of social credit. But in theory the system does not seem to conflict with any of the Pope's principles. He has insisted that the goods of the earth must be made to minister to the needs of all; that the present financial system is preventing this, with consequent injustice to the worker, and that therefore the worker's lot must be improved by further means of income. But the Pope insists rather upon the just wage than upon the Social Credit "just price" plus a national dividend. However the national dividend idea does not seem to be opposed to ethical principles in itself.

1552. Douglas Credit does not involve confiscation or the destruction of existent society, but advocates a proper relationship between production and consumption. Why are you so hesitant in commending it?

In so far as it does not contemplate confiscation and revolution, it is in harmony with Catholic principles. But whether the plan is economically sound is much disputed, and if, as its opponents say, it would result in greater social distress and hardship for the workers, it would be opposed to social justice. The answer will no doubt emerge from the flood of arguments and counter-arguments.

1553. Does not the Pope advocate some form of state control of credit?

Yes, but not necessarily the control suggested by the Douglas Credit System.

1554. Is not the national dividend an essentially Christian idea?

It is not essentially Christian, for Christianity is essentially a religion of motives. An act is really Christian in so far as I do it for the love of Christ. A national dividend might be a purely philanthropic or humanitarian measure; or it might even be an attempt at natural social justice. And then it would not be specifically

Christian. But it would not thereby violate natural ethical principles, and if it could make the goods of the earth minister to the needs of all without leading to ultimate disaster, Catholics could certainly adopt and support it.

1555. Is it not the duty of the Church to endorse Douglas Credit, and wield her mighty influence in its favor?

No. It is a purely economic measure within the economic sphere. It may be as wholesome an idea as "Eat more fruit" for the health of the individual. But it is an economic plan. Christ did not establish the Church for the rectification of economic tangles, and she cannot use her God-given authority directly in such matters, behaving as if Christ had said, "Go, teach all nations the Douglas Credit Plan." The Church says that any lawful plan may claim the allegiance of Catholics in the temporal sphere. If a given plan obviously offends against justice and the law of God, the Church warns her children against it. If not, she leaves it a free matter. The Church is not called upon to advocate positively one economic system thought out by men rather than another.

1556. Why does not the Church give us a constructive plan?

She is not here for that. Christ did not say to her, "Go, teach all nations the best constructive economic plan." The Church has clearly laid down the moral principles which must be embodied in whatever plan is evolved by men. Temporal well-being is a natural good to be regulated by men according to the rules of natural prudence. The Church has but to watch lest their plans offend against the moral principles of justice and charity. She says that there is much injustice in the present state of affairs, injustice which must be speedily remedied.

1557. You speak of a Christian solution of social troubles, but did not the Great War show the utter failure of Christianity altogether?

No. Christianity did not fail. The nations failed to observe Christian principles, a totally different thing. When I say the nations, I mean those in political control of their destinies, and the general outlook of the peoples concerned. Many individuals who fought were excellent Christians, believing the cause of their own country to be just and defending the right as they conceived it with the highest motives. And this on both sides.

1558. What a contrast to the Western Christians was the peace amongst the pagan Orientals!

It may be that the Orientals were at peace when the Westerns happened to be at war. But a study of history shows that the West has been at peace when the East has been at war. If the Japanese are at war with China when Europe happens to be at peace, a Japanese could say with equal lack of logic, "Has not Shintoism failed when you see the Orientals at war whilst the Occidentals have peace?" These are the ups and downs of history. And in any case, as I have so often pointed out, temporal benefits are not the test of Christianity.

1559. Why did Christians fight, killing men they never knew and who never did them any harm?

Every war is a misery, and is due to injustice of some kind, or to misunderstanding. And whoever is really responsible for war is very guilty before God. But God alone can judge as to the guilt of the respective parties. As for the killing of men we never knew, remember that men can be considered as individuals or as units of another nation. If one nation is defending itself against the injustice of another nation, then the soldiers are considered not as individuals, but as national units. War is unchristian, but it is not unchristian for individuals to fight for their country.

1560. *I submit that no war is justified, and that it is wrong for individuals to kill each other in war time.*

You are confusing various aspects of the question. It is wrong for any nation or any group of politicians to give cause for war by unjust treatment of others, or by deliberate aggression. But if another nation wants to slaughter us unjustly, then, although the war as a war is unjustifiable, we are certainly justified in defending ourselves; and our soldiers are justified in killing the soldiers of the unjustly aggressive army.

1561. *God says, "Thou shalt not kill." How can my country send me forth to kill?*

"Thou shalt not kill" means without just cause. For example, if a thief is on the point of shooting me, I may kill him first if possible, provided I know that my merely wounding him is not likely to save my life. Therefore I am allowed to kill an unjust aggressor. And if my country is defending itself against an unjust attack, or defending its rights by just attack, it is not a crime to fight on her behalf. Loyalty to one's country is a virtue. As a rule, individual soldiers cannot decide whether the powers that be in a given country are right or wrong in their decision upon so extreme a measure as war. And with the good motive of defending what he conceives to be the rights of his country, the ordinary soldier is justified in his participation.

1562. *Christ said, "Love your enemies."*

He did. But He did not say, "Love their enmity." They do wrong in being my enemies, and the sooner I stop them from being my enemies the better for them.

1563. *Roman theology dispenses a man from the commandment, "Thou shalt not kill" in war time; it dispenses a man from the commandment "Thou shalt not steal" in times of grave necessity; why not from "Thou shalt not commit adultery" whilst the Church is at it?*

There is no parity between this last commandment and the two former ones under the circumstances of their application. We must be careful about the right interpretation of these laws. "Thou shalt not kill" does not prevent just and lawful killing. Legitimate public authority may condemn a man to death because the common good is more important than the individual good. Nor only is it lawful for the state to remove murderers completely from society by death. An individual may kill an unjust aggressor if it be necessary for the preservation of his own life. And in Scripture we notice how God Himself sanctioned war over and over again, when other means did not avail to secure justice.

"Thou shalt not steal" means that you can never take unjustly the goods of another against his reasonable will. But every word of this explanation must be noted. If a man is actually dying of starvation he may take food from those who have more than they need. But that is not stealing, for it is not unjust in extreme necessity to take food which is the product of the earth for the nutrition of the human race, nor is it against the reasonable will of the owner. It would be unreasonable to hold more food than you need and watch a fellow human being die of starvation.

But there can never be any exception from the commandment, "Thou shalt not commit adultery." That commandment is absolute, because it can never be necessary to dispense from it in the interests of justice or for the necessities of human life. Adultery is always a serious evil, and therefore always seriously forbidden.

1564. Because God ordained certain wars, it does not follow that wars not ordained by Him could be lawful.

From God's own actions in this matter it follows that, provided similar grave causes, and similar moral principles are verified, just and defensive wars are justified.

1565. I cannot conceive that the Catholic Church, if it be Christian, would say to the nations, "Well, since you cannot settle your difficulties by arbitration, fight it out in unrestrained butchery."

The Catholic Church would certainly never say that.

1566. Surely the Church should remain strictly neutral, and try to conciliate the wayward nations.

I agree. But the trouble is, what if the nations will not accept any of her efforts at conciliation? If one ambitious and aggressive nation unjustly invades another's territory, and insists on trampling down the people, the invaded nation must either fight for liberty or go out of existence. An unjustly attacked nation is not obliged to be simply trodden under foot. Its soldiers may lawfully fight back in defence.

1567. During the Great War in Europe, it is common knowledge that the Pope was not neutral, but sympathized with the Germans.

The Pope remained strictly neutral. When nations are angry, they are like angry individuals, who at once suspect that all are against them who do not side actively with them. Whilst many among the Allies accused the Pope of being pro-German, the Germans accused him of being against their nation. Count Ludendorf, in his book, "My War Memories," p. 514, says, "The Pope was in favor of a peace expecting us Germans to make considerable sacrifices, whilst the Allies got off very cheaply."

1568. The Pope rules 400 millions. Why did he not stop the last war?

He could not do so, or he certainly would have prevented it. He did his best, suggesting all means of peace, laboring for the welfare and exchange of prisoners, and giving utterly impartial advice. In 1914 Pius X. tried to prevent the outbreak of war, and urgently pointed out the terrible miseries which would ensue. In 1915 Benedict XV. made it his first duty to bring about peace if at all possible. But the Allies did not want peace then. They met in London, and drew up what is known as the "London Pact." In it we read, "France, Britain, and Russia undertake to support Italy in preventing the Holy See from taking any steps whatever for the conclusion of peace, or the settlement of questions bound up with the war." Under these circumstances you cannot blame the Pope for not having made peace. If the nations will not have peace, they won't have it.

1569. Had the Pope imposed peace he would have won millions of converts to the Catholic Church.

I do not think so. People become Catholics because God gives them the grace to see that the Catholic Church is the one true Church of Jesus Christ. This grace is usually the fruit of prayer, not the fruit of witnessing the Pope stop the nations from fighting. If the Pope cannot bring about peace, men say that he cannot be the representative of Christ. But had he succeeded in imposing peace, it is more than likely that men would have called him an interfering politician who should mind his own business.

1570. *Your talk about the Pope and peace is nonsense. Is he not trying to awaken a strong anti-communist feeling in order to launch a war against the Soviet?*

No. He is trying to preserve Christians from a very grave danger to their religion.

1571. *He conjures nations to unite together and to save themselves and mankind "even at the cost of heavy sacrifices." What do those last words mean but war?*

They have nothing to do with war. They demand that men be prepared for the sacrifice of their selfish commercial interests and their greed, in order that the inequalities and injustice prevailing in the present economic system be remedied. The wealthy capitalists must be prepared to forego some of their wealth, and make it available for employment and the bettering of the poor. Work must be made available to the unemployed, and those who are employed must be prepared to work for reasonable remuneration. If the nations would follow the advice of the Pope, war would become almost impossible. It is the absence of a spirit of self-sacrifice which is the very cause of war.

1572. *He urges the use of "all useful means" in his campaign. Does not that include war?*

No. The Pope is anxious to remedy the miseries of mankind. War is not a useful means to that end. It causes still more misery and abject poverty.

1573. *He speaks of the satanic hosts of militant atheism. That obviously indicates the Soviet Union.*

Many supporters of the Soviet Union will not thank you for your implicit admission. However, the Pope had not the Soviet Union in mind when he wrote those words. He was indicating forces actively working in the midst of almost every nation to-day.

1574. *Would the Pope approve of war against the Soviet to bring back Russian Catholics to the faith?*

No. The Catholic Church does not rely upon force of arms to propagate the Catholic faith or win back deserters.

1575. *Why does the Church maintain a criminal silence concerning the manufacture of munitions in order to have another war?*

They are not being manufactured in order to have another war. No one wants another war. But each nation has the right to possess adequate means of defence and self-protection, unless all nations agree simultaneously to disarm themselves. In November, 1932, Cardinal Bourne addressed a special disarmament conference in London, and said, "It is the manifest duty of Catholics to work and pray for disarmament; and the Holy See has often spoken in this sense." But he added, "This can only be, if the right of defence be safeguarded without such means of self-protection. We must not be led away by mere sentiment; and if we are apprehensive of future attack, we must rely on our own military protection, if other protection be not guaranteed."

1576. *Why does not the Church denounce absolutely the holocaust being prepared by capitalists for the people?*

Because the Catholic Church is eminently sane and Christian. Being sane, she realizes that the armament problem concerns self-defence and protection rather than aggressive tendencies. Being Christian, she grants to nations as well as to individuals the right to be prepared against possible unjust aggression.

1577. *Do you teach Catholics to be the disciples of the Prince of Peace on Sundays, and allow them to work in munition factories during the week?*

If self-defence is allowed, as it is, the preparation of means of self-defence is lawful. No individual nation can afford to disarm whilst others do not. General disarmament is good and to be attained if possible. But until that is secured, no individual nation is obliged to leave itself unprotected. The manufacture of war material is evil or not according to the intention prompting the manufacture of it. If for war of unjust aggression, it is unlawful; if for legitimate defence, it is lawful.

1578. *Is all this a temporal matter in which the Church does not see fit to interfere?*

It is a temporal matter in which spiritual and moral principles must be applied lest justice be violated. God has never forbidden war in all circumstances. In the Old Testament He sanctioned the vindication of justice by defensive and punitive wars. Christ forbade all injustice, but never forbade war. He praised the faith of the Centurion who had said, "I have under me soldiers," but added no command to give up a military career. So, too, He used an ordinary fact of experience saying, "What king about to make war against another doth not first think whether with 10,000 he can meet him who hath 20,000?" He takes the fact of wars as an accepted thing, and utters no word of condemnation.

1579. *You tell us, then, that killing is permissible in a just war, or by an agent of the state for the common good?*

That is so.

1580. *You have said also that motive makes morality.*

A good motive is a necessary condition of morality in the sense that an evil intention vitiates any action.

1581. *What would be the moral position of individual soldiers in an invading army?*

The invading nation could, of course, be justly aggressive in vindication of its rights had they been violated by the invaded nation. But if the invading nation has unjustly declared war, prompted to aggression by mere ambition, then no individual citizen of that invading nation who knows quite well that the war is unjust is free in any way to volunteer or assist. If he does so he is guilty of immoral and sinful conduct. Each individual invader therefore who is aware that the aggression is unjust, and who is voluntarily present in the army, is guilty of sin.

1582. *In the Great War some nation must have been guilty from a moral point of view in causing such suffering. Which nation was it?*

I have no idea. God alone can say.

1583. *Is every individual soldier bound to satisfy himself as to the justice of his side before participating in war?*

Catholic theologians say that volunteers must satisfy themselves that the cause is not unjust. Conscript soldiers are not obliged to solve the problem, but may obey orders, unless the war be clearly and obviously unjust. In this latter case they would be obliged in conscience to refuse service.

1584. *I am not satisfied yet that killing can be lawful. You say that the official hangman of the state is not guilty of sin. What of the one who authorizes his action?*

If the hangman be commissioned by lawful state authority, he is free from guilt. The lawfully appointed authority who sentences to death is free from guilt provided he rectifies his intention and has a good motive; provided the crime be a grave one; provided civil law has decreed death as a proportionate penalty; and finally, provided the judge, acting in his official capacity, has sufficient evidence to prove that the criminal was indeed guilty of the crime, having sufficient use of his faculties to be morally responsible for it.

1585. *You oppose sterilization of the mentally deficient for the common good, yet you justify the taking of the criminal's very life!*

There is all the difference in the world between these two things. Where sterilization of the unfit is in question, many other factors come into the case besides the common good. The state has no direct right over the life and members of its subjects. It has an indirect right to sentence to death as a punishment for grave crimes. But sterilization of the mentally deficient is a measure directed against those lacking moral responsibility, and who are guilty of no crime in being mentally deficient through no fault of their own. Nor could we support sterilization of those who have been guilty of sex crimes, and who are not mentally deficient, for sterilization is not proportionate as a punishment; and far from being a deterrent for the future, it leaves a man with all his passions and no fear of the consequences. Sterilization is useless both as a punitive measure and as a reformative measure; and it is not justifiable even where the death penalty is.

1586. *After all you have said about the lawfulness of killing and of war the crux seems to be as to who is to decide the justice of any particular war. What authority is entitled to declare a war just or unjust?*

The nations at present acknowledge no independent authority whose decision they would accept. The only suitable authority I know of in this world is the Pope, who is above all national considerations. The Pope has all the necessary qualifications, but the nations will not entitle him to decide. They make themselves judges in their own case, despite their experience of the consequences.

1587. *We do not have to appeal to the Pope. We have the League of Nations.*

That does not really escape the difficulty. In the League of Nations we have representatives of the very nations concerned. Both the cause and the power behind each individual representative is the cause and the power of the nation he represents. There are forty million people in the representative of a country with that population, and perhaps but five million in the representative of some smaller country. G. K. Chesterton has rightly pointed out that any international council is necessarily but a reduced model of the nations represented in it. "Suppose," he writes, "that in the international interchanges of the future some power, say Sweden, is felt to be disproportionate or problematical. If Sweden is powerful in Europe, she will be powerful in the Council of Europe. If Sweden is too powerful in Europe, she will be too powerful in the Council of Europe. And because she is the very thing that is irresistible, she is the very thing to be resisted; or at any rate to be restrained. I do not see how Europe can ever escape from that logical dilemma, except by discovering again an authority that is purely moral and is the recognized custodian of a morality." The Pope is the only one in this world who could possibly become such an accepted authority.

1588. Would you please tell me what steps I must take in order to join the Catholic Church?

By all means. Call at the nearest Catholic Rectory in your suburb or district, ask to see the Priest, and tell him that you would like to receive instruction in the Catholic Faith. He will arrange for your instruction, and if, after having had the Catholic religion fully explained to you, you still desire to become a Catholic, he will gladly receive you into the Church.

ALPHABETICAL INDEX

1st number refers to volume; 2nd to question.

327

338

341

342